FOUNDING FOLKS

AN ORAL HISTORY OF THE WINNIPEG FOLK FESTIVAL

BY KEVIN NIKKEL

UMP
University of Manitoba Press

Founding Folks: An Oral History of the Winnipeg Folk Festival

29 28 27 26 25 1 2 3 4 5

University of Manitoba Press
Winnipeg, Manitoba, Canada
Treaty 1 Territory
uofmpress.ca

For EU product safety concerns please contact Mare Nostrum Group B.V., Mauritskade 21D, 1091 GC Amsterdam, The Netherlands, gpsr@mare-nostrum.co.uk.

Cataloguing data available from Library and Archives Canada
ISBN 978-177284-110-7 (PAPER)
ISBN 978-177284-112-1 (PDF)
ISBN 978-177284-101-5 (EPUB)
ISBN 978-177284-111-4 (BOUND)

Front cover and page i–ii photograph by John Bachmann, Winnipeg Folk Festival workshop tent, 1974. Courtesy of Winnipeg Folk Festival. Back cover photograph by David Landy, Archives of Manitoba, Winnipeg Folk Festival 1975 Negatives, P5266/1, 75-4562. 5
Cover and interior design by Jess Koroscil

Printed in Canada

The University of Manitoba Press acknowledges the financial support for its publication program provided by the Government of Canada through the Canada Book Fund, the Canada Council for the Arts, the Manitoba Department of Sport, Culture, and Heritage, the Manitoba Arts Council, and the Manitoba Book Publishing Tax Credit.

Funded by the Government of Canada | Canada

FOR DALE

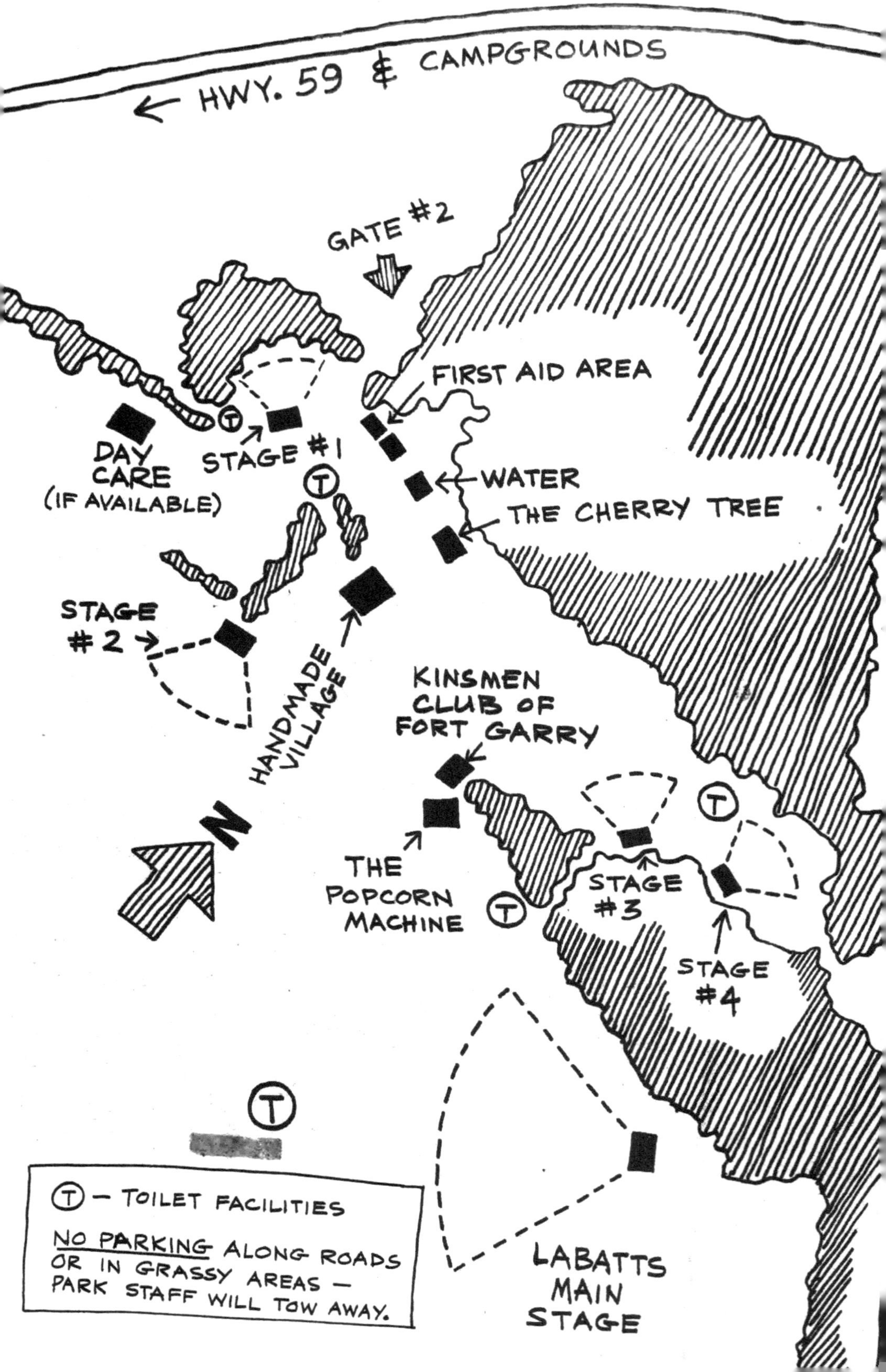
← HWY. 59 & CAMPGROUNDS
GATE #2
FIRST AID AREA
DAY CARE
(IF AVAILABLE)
STAGE #1
WATER
THE CHERRY TREE
STAGE #2
HANDMADE VILLAGE
KINSMEN CLUB OF FORT GARRY
N
THE POPCORN MACHINE
STAGE #3
STAGE #4
Ⓣ – TOILET FACILITIES
NO PARKING ALONG ROADS OR IN GRASSY AREAS – PARK STAFF WILL TOW AWAY.
LABATTS MAIN STAGE

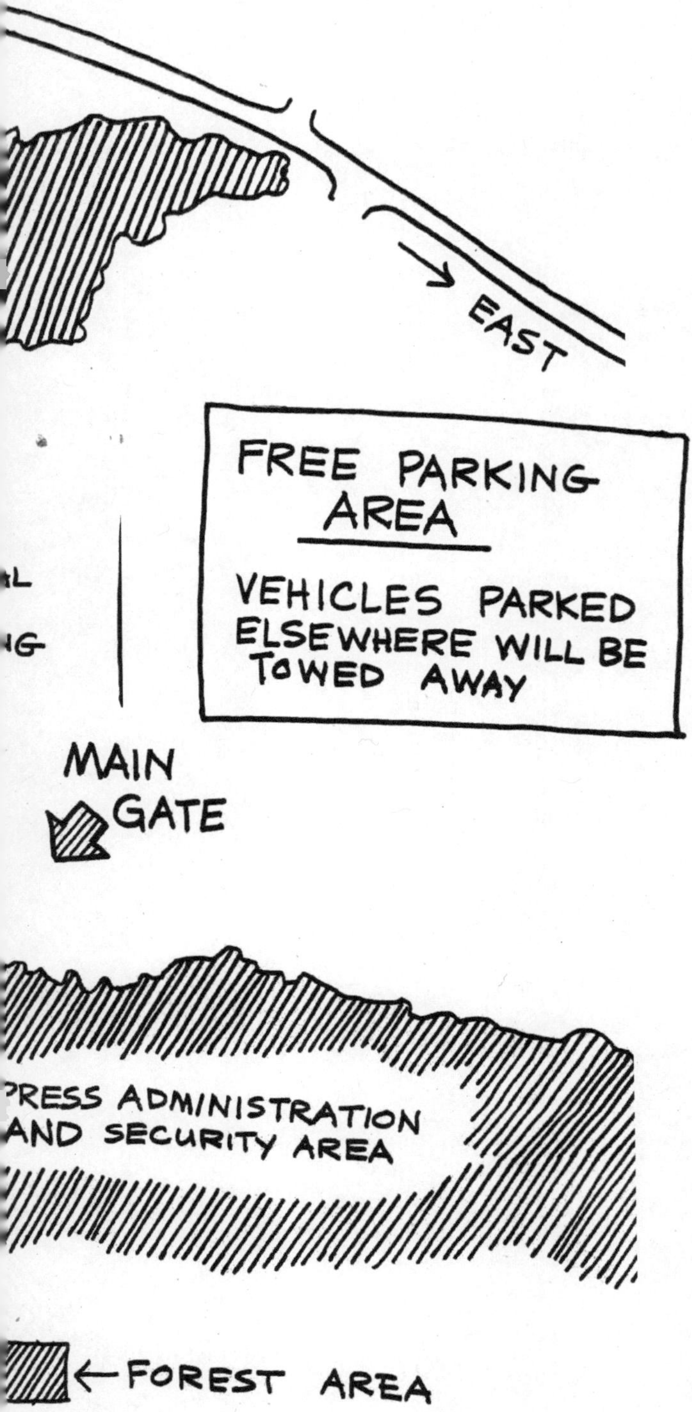

FIGURE 1. WINNIPEG FOLK FESTIVAL SITE INFORMATION, MAP, N.D. ARCHIVES OF MANITOBA, WINNIPEG FOLK FESTIVAL FONDS, PR1988-16, P-6-3-17.

Contents

THE WINNIPEG
FOLK FESTIVAL

THE 5TH ANNUAL
WINNIPEG
FOLK
FESTIVAL
78
KAREN BOUX
INFO

Preface

The idea for a project on the Winnipeg Folk Festival started while Dave Barber and I were finishing our documentary *Tales from the Winnipeg Film Group* (2017). Dave dragged a dusty box of Super 8-mm film over to my studio—four hours of footage shot during the 1975 Winnipeg Folk Festival. He insisted that it should comprise our next project. The cache of footage was from an abandoned documentary by members of the Winnipeg Film Group. It was a gem of a cinematic time capsule. We reached out to John Prentice, long-time Folk Festival volunteer and host of the folk radio program *Planet Mainstage* on UMFM. John had been the editor on the stalled documentary back in 1975 and he was keen to help. We agreed to start interviews for our own documentary on the beginnings of the Winnipeg Folk Festival. Mitch Podolak, the driving force behind the Festival, was at the top of the list, particularly because of his declining health. The interviews took place between 2018 and 2022.

As I had done with our previous documentary on the Winnipeg Film Group, and subsequent book *Establishing Shots: An Oral History of the Winnipeg Film Group*, I suggested we approach these interviews with a similar posture: using semi-structured/informal interviews as a means of gaining a sense of both the personal and the collective.[1] The method behind the process was purposeful and reflexive—we were admittedly "earnest documentarians" eagerly pursuing a new project, as Robert Coles jibes, but following procedures taken with "responsibility and accountability."[2] Interviews for the documentary were initially transcribed

FIGURE 2 (PREVIOUS PAGE). WINNIPEG FOLK FESTIVAL CROWD, 1970S. PHOTOGRAPH BY DAVID LANDY. ARCHIVES OF MANITOBA, WINNIPEG FOLK FESTIVAL 1983 NEGATIVES, P5267/4, 83/264. 24.

FIGURE 3. VOLUNTEER KAREN BOUX SELLS WINNIPEG FOLK FESTIVAL PROGRAMS. PHOTOGRAPH BY DAVID LANDY. ARCHIVES OF MANITOBA, WINNIPEG FOLK FESTIVAL 1978 NEGATIVES, P2566/7, 4/78. 16A.

FIGURE 4. WINNIPEG FOLK FESTIVAL MAIN STAGE, 1975. PHOTOGRAPH BY DAVID LANDY. ARCHIVES OF MANITOBA, WINNIPEG FOLK FESTIVAL 1975 NEGATIVES, P5266/1, 75-4554. 6.

MARGOT

FIGURE 5. WINNIPEG FOLK FESTIVAL WORKSHOP STAGE, DAVID ESSIG ON RIGHT, 1975. PHOTOGRAPH BY JOHN BACHMANN. COURTESY OF WINNIPEG FOLK FESTIVAL.

verbatim, edited for length, sent to the interviewee for approval, and then assembled into a manuscript—a structured process informed by the oral history literature.[3] The strategic list of interviewees was organic, not based on a master yearbook, but dependent on people that we could find, or people who were coming through Winnipeg—later it became who was available between waves of the COVID-19 pandemic. As the pandemic lockdowns eased, I was optimistic that we could resume our monthly interviews, only to be shocked by the sudden illness and passing of Dave Barber. John Prentice's deep connections with the Folk Festival and folk music community were essential to keeping this project alive. I could not have gotten this far without his generous support.

The purpose of this oral history project is both celebratory—coinciding with the fiftieth anniversary of the Festival—and exploratory; to contribute to the primary source knowledge of the Winnipeg Folk Festival and the broader understanding of culture on the prairies. In some ways this adds to the mythologizing of Winnipeg cultural icons like Mitch Podolak. In other ways it poses questions about the origin of the

Festival and the role Winnipeg played in creating the circumstances for the Festival's flourishing. For each in-depth interview I tried to allow part of the conversation to be about context, to hear from individuals placing themselves in the story of folk music, before they became associated with the Winnipeg Folk Festival.

While the book presents a collection of interviews, it is worth noting also that it is meant to depict the process and play of researcher, interviewee, and interviewers. Other oral historians mute evidence of this process as they disseminate their findings as prose. I've included myself as interviewer, and the other key collaborators involved in the process—Dave Barber and John Prentice—to present this as a lively exchange (or perhaps even a jam, like on a festival workshop stage) in pursuit of memories and history.

The introduction to the book provides the reader with a broad introduction to Mitch Podolak and the Winnipeg Folk Festival and suggests an approach to the collection of interviews. The first-person narrative interjections throughout the introduction provide a window into the process of research. Besides unearthing quotes from/about people like Mitch Podolak, the process provides an overlooked window into a diverse number of archival holdings (private and public) and re-engages material previously unavailable. It provides additional primary source material for future researchers and reminds us of the original nature of these forms.

Michael Frisch talks about the difference between "the raw and the cooked"[4] aspects of oral history collections, namely an untouched primary audio recording versus material that has gone through a preparation process for some sort of publication—something which the chapters that follow have gone through with participants.[5] Oral histories are certainly not free of weaknesses; interviewees have their biases and the stories told are dependent on the fallibilities of their memories. In the case of the Winnipeg Folk Festival, the near-universal affection for founder Mitch Podolak creates limitations due to the "selectivity of narrators" provided by the volunteers, staff, and musicians who are careful not to say anything derisive about their beloved founder, who was all too human.[6] This is likely a weakness of the book, that interviewees were overly cautious of their accounts of Mitch and the founding years of the

Festival—something that is difficult to prove, but apparent in the moment through a pause, or a qualification, or in subsequent edits to transcripts. Still, the interview genre has lots to offer in terms of entertainment and as a historical and academic reference. My inspirations for the project are the many curious historians and enthusiasts gathering stories and documenting history. I am fond of Studs Terkel in particular because of his penchant for talking with common people in everyday jobs—a motivation for including the volunteers interviewed in this volume on their experiences behind the scenes at the Folk Festival. Terkel suggests the need to fight against "a national Alzheimer's disease," and the recording of interviews is a prime way of combating this amnesia to "recreate history from the bottom up, not as seen by industrialists or by generals or by presidents, but by ordinary people and the work they did, especially those we call activists."[7] Mitch Podolak would appreciate this view as he considered everyone at the Folk Festival on the same level.

Art curator Hans Ulrich Obrist's two collections of interviews with artists act as a model for what I am attempting here, "neither a journalistic nor scholarly enterprise" but instead his collections of interviews appear more "encyclopedic," seeing the "conversation as a fruitful/successful exchange of ideas and exemplified in the form of the interview."[8] I hold to the value of volume—squeezing in as many interviews as possible into this collection from a range of voices. While I am not an academic and this is not a scholarly enterprise, I see it finding an audience both inside and outside academia. At minimum, the book contributes a host of primary source interviews from people too often left out of the historical record.

One of the traditions that is discussed in the interviews that follow is "fence-day" at the Folk Festival, when volunteers begin the process of encircling the grounds at Birds Hill Park as an act of demarcation. Inside this fence is the Folk Festival, and outside is not.[9] There is something satisfying to approach a topic, an organization, or an event like the Winnipeg Folk Festival and try to contain it, to understand it and say,

FIGURE 6. PERFORMER ON WORKSHOP STAGE AT WINNIPEG FOLK FESTIVAL, 1979. PHOTOGRAPH BY DAVID LANDY. ARCHIVES OF MANITOBA, WINNIPEG FOLK FESTIVAL 1979 NEGATIVES, P5266/9, 79/287.

"this, this is the thing we love." I'm conscious of the banging of drums around authenticity of what is folk, who should be included as the real thing, and who does not belong.[10] Personally, I fit in here somewhere, as a fan of folk music and as an appreciator of the Winnipeg Folk Festival and the grand vision enacted by Mitch Podolak.

As I found myself more deeply involved in the production of our documentary *When We Became Folk Fest*, I realized that I could bring my skills as an interviewer to document accounts of contributors to such a unique event evolving in the 1970s and early 1980s at Birds Hill Park. Regardless of whether they were still inside the fence or outside, the people we sat down to interview for this project were consistently friendly and welcoming at the thought of getting their memories down on record. For the folks who sat to answer questions, I thank them. For the many others who would have if we had found them, I hope they will enjoy this book. I readily admit that there are plenty more people—particularly the audience—who also have stories to tell. I hope this book inspires more sharing and enjoyment of their own Folk Fest memories. There are only so many pages allowed in a book like this. Regardless, this gets part of the story down, others can capture other aspects in greater clarity, or academic rigor. In the end, this is just a start; one contribution to a much larger oral history of the Winnipeg Folk Festival.

KEVIN NIKKEL
WINNIPEG, MANITOBA
MAY 2024

A Short Introduction to the Start of the Winnipeg Folk Festival

A PARK AND A MUSIC FESTIVAL

In the meadows and clearings of the boreal forest of Birds Hill Park, Manitoba, there is an established network of trails—well-worn paths across prairie ground that leave distinct scars. They could be mistaken for traditional Indigenous hunting trails, or the routes used by subsequent settlers to the land, and indeed may have been, but these trails are something more specific: they mark the home of the Winnipeg Folk Festival. With such a storied event that has lived for half a century and of such scale, where to begin? The Winnipeg Folk Festival is an annual weekend music festival started in 1974, held in Birds Hill Park, 24 kilometres north of Winnipeg, Manitoba. The Festival's land acknowledgement states "Winnipeg Folk Fest takes place at Birds Hill Provincial Park, Manitoba, Canada on Treaty 1 territory and the National Homeland of the Red River Métis."[1] The Festival runs in July every year, drawing an average of 70,000 people over a four-day weekend.[2] With an international reputation, its fans trek from across the continent on a regular basis to see their favourite performers and to hang out with friends who feel like family.

FIGURE 7. AUDIENCE MEMBERS WITH WINNIPEG FOLK FESTIVAL PROGRAM, 1977. PHOTOGRAPH BY DAVID LANDY. ARCHIVES OF MANITOBA, WINNIPEG FOLK FESTIVAL 1977 NEGATIVES, P2566/5, 77 /4. BETWEEN 7-9.

*I'm arriving at this Winnipeg Folk Festival project as a filmmaker, having researched archives and personal collections for photos, audio recordings, and film footage for the production of a documentary on the early years of the event—*When We Became Folk Fest (2025)*. Sitting in the reading room of the Provincial Archives of Manitoba with my co-director Dave Barber, we're looking through the textual records of the Festival. In this particular pile are site maps, festival timetables, and event posters. Rough handwritten copies of the Festival schedules, then the elegantly scripted versions created by graphic artists—with Mitch Podolak's signature at the bottom to approve the copy for print. Mitch's touches are all over this, as he was the main force behind the establishment of the Festival. We shuffle through posters for the summer festivals and the fundraising shows held throughout the year at the Winnipeg Art Gallery and the Sunday Night at the Norwood gigs—frequented by performers like the Red Clay Ramblers, Stan Rogers, Tom Paxton, and Sylvia Tyson. It is archival evidence of Winnipeg's folk scene from the 1970s and 1980s, lingering in carefully labelled boxes.*

THE FOLK WAVE REACHES THE PRAIRIES

There is a polished myth that says there is something in the water in Winnipeg that makes for exceptional creativity. Winnipeg rock and roll acts like The Guess Who, Neil Young, and Bachman-Turner Overdrive are favourite examples locals use to counter derision of critics hailing from more important cities. Winnipeg musicians were able to find gigs at coffeehouses, church basements, and halls around the city—fostering talent of surprising stature for a modest prairie city. Music historian John Einarson recounts, "A few years back, a CBC survey revealed that from a province of just slightly over a million people representing just over 3.8% percent of Canada's total population on a mere 3% of Canada's total landmass, we account for some 12% of Canadian singers and musicians who either come from here or got their start here."[3] In terms of folk music, Winnipeg's coffeehouse venues were important in giving emerging singer/songwriters access to audiences and building a following. It was a far cry from the Greenwich Village scene in New York City or Yorkville in Toronto, but it represented a beachhead for the urban folk revival that had crested in the 1960s, surging up from America—a movement that was "essentially a 'branch plant' of the American revival."[4]

The folk revival that swept across the continent had its limits. "By the early seventies, most of the folk coffeehouses of the sixties were dead, and the folk revival seemed to have come to an end."[5] Locally, "by the early 70's there were only two places to hear folk music in Winnipeg, The Ting and the University of Manitoba's Stillmore. Both were small coffeehouses with uncertain audiences."[6] "Clubs started, boomed, and died in every city in Canada. New clubs were founded, only to die in turn as the organizing individual or group moved on to other activities. . . The slow decline of this type of politics in society at large was reflected in the downturn in the clubs. As people moved forward in their careers, they left the clubs behind them, but younger people were no longer moving into them."[7] With the seeming decline of enthusiasm for folk music, the prospects for launching fresh new folk events did not look good. Yet hanging around the Toronto Bohemian Embassy folk club during the surge was an enthusiastic folk music fan, one Mitch Podolak. He planted

himself in Winnipeg, and we have him to thank for the growth of the Winnipeg Folk Festival.

> *I've got a box here of film and audio reels that was saved from the garbage by Dave Barber, Cinematheque programmer with the Winnipeg Film Group. A crew of filmmakers from the Winnipeg Film Group shooting footage at the 1975 Winnipeg Folk Festival left their audio tape rolling during one of the final stages of the weekend:*
>
> **PETER GZOWSKI:** We've got a second here . . . there's someone we can't find backstage. I have to tell you, the two key words heard mostly throughout this Festival are: Where's Mitch? We've just been saying it a couple times . . . Mitch is in the can? Never mind that. Mitch Podolak is the guy behind it all. I wanted to bring him out here so you could thank him. Put it on tape for *Touch the Earth*. Say thank you to Mitch. Let's hear it. He's not back there? Slim? He'll be around later. He's a great guy.
>
> **DON CULLEN:** Thanks, Peter, I'd like to add my thanks to old Mitch Podolak. He used to work for me at the old Bohemian Embassy in the early sixties and he used to serve coffee with dirty fingernails—that's Mitch, not the coffee. He was a great guy. A kind generous delightful guy.[8]

Mitch was a self-proclaimed Trotskyite, community organizer, and a banjo player. He came from Toronto to Winnipeg to support the anti-war movement and began working in radio at the CBC. "By the early 70's, folk music had become the ideal expression of Podolak's musical and social aspirations. An actual folk festival promised to be a massive demonstration of both."[9] Podolak had attended folk festivals at Mariposa, Newport, and Philadelphia and had a hunch that a festival could be launched in western Canada. It was partially a way to celebrate the traditional folk music that he loved, and also a way to engage in community activism. He used the Festival as a means to lift up the little guy and promote

FIGURE 8. PETER GZOWSKI AND MITCH PODOLAK, 1970S. *WINNIPEG TRIBUNE*, UNIVERSITY OF MANITOBA ARCHIVES AND SPECIAL COLLECTIONS.

equality—staff, musicians and volunteers were treated with equal respect and the stages were kept intimate, bringing the audiences up close to the performers. In many ways Podolak was an archetypical character, a man of vision and strongly held beliefs. He wanted to champion folk music and folk musicians.

We follow Irina Bissonnette down the staircase to the basement of 211 Bannatyne, a smartly gentrified turn-of-the-century building in Winnipeg's Exchange District. Irina is the person in charge of the Winnipeg Folk Festival archives. Mitch had mentioned in passing that he had recorded audio of all the performances of the first few Festivals and had given the audio reels to the Winnipeg Folk Festival for their records. We're hopeful that they're all here, ready to be rediscovered. The expansive basement room doubles as storage for essential Festival resources and their archive. There aren't as many audio reels as we thought—perhaps Mitch's recollection was greater than the actual recordings put to tape, or the rest of the reels have ended up somewhere else. Some is better than none. The following is from a stage recording at the start of a performance from the 1976 Winnipeg Folk Festival:

MIKE SEEGER: Don't bother about him, that's just our dog.

AUDIENCE MEMBER: What kind?

MIKE SEEGER: What kind of dog is he? He's a reactionary dog.

PEGGY SEEGER: Gandy, come.

MIKE SEEGER: Gandy, come over here by the microphone.

PEGGY SEEGER: Sit.

MIKE SEEGER: Gandy, what do you think of communists?

DOG: [BARK!]

CROWD: [Laughter and applause]

FIGURE 9. JOHN HAMMOND PERFORMS ON A WINNIPEG FOLK FESTIVAL WORKSHOP STAGE, 1974. PHOTOGRAPH BY JOHN BUCHANAN. COURTESY OF WINNIPEG FOLK FESTIVAL.

THE WINNIPEG CENTENNIAL FOLK FESTIVAL

BIRDS HILL PROVINCIAL PARK*AUG. 9, 10, 11/74
WINNIPEG, MANITOBA, CANADA

SPONSORED BY:
- THE CITY OF WINNIPEG CENTENNIAL ARTS COMMITTEE
- THE PROVINCE OF MANITOBA DEPT. OF TOURISM, RECREATION AND CULTURAL AFFAIRS
- THE CBC RADIO ARTS AND VARIETY DEPT's.
- CANADA COUNCIL: EXPLORATIONS PROGRAM
- COCA COLA CANADA LTD.

FIFTY CENTS PLEASE

> **MIKE SEEGER:** He's a reactionary dog. I don't mind him myself. Ever since we've had this dog, we've had no trouble with communists. Nearly tore into Mitch Podolak, but we won't talk about that.[10]

TO START A FOLK FESTIVAL

When the Winnipeg Folk Festival began in 1974, folk music festivals already had an extensive history in North America.[11] The Miramichi Folk Festival was started in 1958 in New Brunswick, the Newport Folk Festival in 1959, and southern Ontario's Mariposa Folk Festival had begun in 1961.[12] The most talked about music festivals were the larger events like the Isle of Wight in England and, in America, Woodstock and Altamont. The news coverage of these events built a myth of counter-culture gatherings filled with noisy music, shameless nudity, and casual substance use. Violence had erupted at Altamont in California, and the crowds pushing down fences at Woodstock created a certain reputation around festivals—different reactions depending whether you were a fan or a concerned civic administrator. How would the crowds respond if a large, free festival was held at Birds Hill Park in Manitoba? The 1970 documentaries *Woodstock* and *Gimme Shelter*, on the Altamont Festival, fuelled both the myth and notoriety of these events.[13]

> *The documentary* Woodstock *(1970) was a likely a motivation for a crew of filmmakers from the Winnipeg Film Group who thought they could recreate the experience documented in the Oscar-winning feature with their own local film about the second Winnipeg Folk Festival in 1975. The crew of seven headed out to Birds Hill Park with Super 8-mm cameras and reel-to-reel audio recorders—and the blessing of Mitch Podolak. As we look through the film reels now, it is evident that the filmmakers were certainly energetic about their passion for folk music and a bit naïve—the project had no director but was approached as a collective effort. Some of the workshop stage footage is strong, but the interviews lack depth—the collaborative*

FIGURE 10. WINNIPEG CENTENNIAL FOLK FESTIVAL PROGRAM GUIDE, 1974. COURTESY OF THE WINNIPEG FOLK FESTIVAL.

FIGURE 11. FILM CREW FROM THE WINNIPEG FILM GROUP AT THE WINNIPEG FOLK FESTIVAL, 1975. FROM LEFT: FENTON JORDAN, BOB LOWER, IAN ELKIN, CAL BAILEY, BRAD CASLOR, AND LOIS BROWNE. COURTESY OF BETSY THORSTEINSON.

documentary project was abandoned after the shoot in 1975 when there were issues with the sound and picture sync. Thanks to modern software—and the virtuoso skill of audio wizard Andy Rudolph—we were able to re-sync the footage and use it along with contemporary interviews for the documentary When We Became Folk Fest.

Despite the fears stoked by the media, other factors contributed to the right conditions for the Folk Festival's start. Following the excitement of the Canadian centennial celebrations of 1967, the bar was high for commemorative events, as the "afterglow" of patriotism lingered across the country with potential arts and culture funding accessible.[14] Podolak responded to a call for commemorative events in 1973 from Winnipeg's centennial committee looking to fill the calendar in 1974. Government funding and a broadcast licence from the CBC meant that the first festival could be put on free of charge to attendees. Bruce Cockburn was the headliner. After the dedicated folkniks that he knew Cockburn could attract, Podolak was optimistic that other potential converts would come

FIGURE 12. BRUCE COCKBURN AT THE WINNIPEG FOLK FESTIVAL, 1978. PHOTOGRAPH BY DAVID LANDY. ARCHIVES OF MANITOBA, WINNIPEG FOLK FESTIVAL 1978 NEGATIVES, P5266/7, 20/78. 2.

and be attracted to not just the concerts, but for the workshops and overall experience. The Winnipeg Centennial Folksong Festival was held 9–11 August 1974 with government funding: "Mitch used the money to create a structure that would celebrate folk music and progressive political ideals. As far as the government of the time was concerned the Winnipeg Folk Music festival celebrated the history of the city. Mitch was able to launch the Winnipeg Folk Music festival as a celebration of the people of the city and of the progressive concept of folk music he learned from Seeger."[15] Podolak was convinced that he could replicate what he had revelled in at Mariposa—a folk event wrapped in Estelle Klein's brilliant workshop structure—juxtaposing musicians on workshop stages playing to a particular theme, while paying a union rate no matter what the level of fame.[16]

> *One of the acclaimed guests of the Folk Festival in 1975 was David Amram—known for his keen ability to get the audience involved in his shows. An excerpt from a 1975 interview at the Winnipeg Folk Festival, recorded by the Winnipeg Film Group for their documentary, reveals the way the event was meant to have people feel part of the moment and the greater whole:*
>
> **VAL KLASSEN:** I'd like to talk to you about audience participation in your concerts. Can you tell me a little bit about how you handle that?
>
> **DAVID AMRAM:** Surely. I think that the idea of audience participation, basically, is a tool ultimately to show people that music first of all is a natural thing that we can all enjoy—we can all partake of. Secondly, it is a way, through rudimentary techniques of music, to show people by them being physically involved, that music is a natural thing and the construction of music is like cooking a meal, riding a bicycle, or doing anything else. So that when you show people the rhythm [plays a drum rhythm] that simple thing—the Arabic rhythm that has been

FIGURE 13. CROWDS DANCING AT THE WINNIPEG FOLK FESTIVAL, 1979. PHOTOGRAPH BY DAVID LANDY. ARCHIVES OF MANITOBA, WINNIPEG FOLK FESTIVAL 1979 NEGATIVES, P2566/9, 79/320.

> going on for thousands of years can be [plays rhythm]—you can have people clapping a rhythm that is not familiar to the western ear, and the concept, when I get everybody clapping and I play the flute melody on top of that [plays flute], and so forth. They are all physically able, by clapping, to be a part of that musical experience. When I make up the songs and get people to sing the lyrics back, some of it probably sounds a little outrageous, silly, or to some people crazy—hopefully fun. But through the fun, there is a deeper meaning and higher message, which is that spontaneity and the audience being part of it by suggesting the lyrics and most of all by singing and being part of the music, I hope brings a healthier picture of what music is about for many people in the world, including this mosquito. [Slap]

The first Winnipeg Folk Festival was a success, with an estimated 22,000 people coming out for the free event at Birds Hill Park.[17] While the crowd was enthusiastic, the reaction of the press was more guarded that such a local event could be repeated annually; journalist Chuck Grieve's article covering the event was titled "Folk Festival, Once Was Fine; Yearly Is Folly." He cautioned readers, "Winnipeg, a city with a sad track record for folk music. This city relegated folk music to church basements one or two nights a week when numerous coffeehouses turned belly-up or to rock music."[18] Despite this negative assessment, or perhaps emboldened by it, Podolak and his team began making plans for a second Winnipeg Folk Festival in 1975. It would have to be different because the same government funding was not available. CBC Radio was still interested in the broadcast rights, thanks to Paul Mills and his *Touch the Earth* program. The biggest change was that you had to buy a ticket to get in. The boreal forest's moat of poison ivy would have to be enhanced by a fence to keep attendees to the gate. It had been a problem elsewhere too, as festivals struggled to convince audiences that paying for access was only fair—likely too many people had seen the movie *Woodstock* with crowds overwhelming fences. Mariposa had had issues with people trying to hop the fence as well.[19]

From an interview with Mitch Podolak by Vonnie von Helmholt at the 1975 Winnipeg Folk Festival recorded by the Winnipeg Film Group for their unfinished documentary, Mitch reveals his assessment of how his fragile event is taking shape in its second year:

MITCH: The Festival is shaping up okay as a festival. I mean, I've never seen a more mellow audience than any festival I've ever been at. This is the most laid-back group of people. It's a real pleasure.

VONNIE: Like last year?

MITCH: Well, it's more laid back than last year. There is a lot less dope. There is a lot less . . . in fact the dope is infinitesimal. Alcohol is down to a tenth of what it was when we did a free festival. So, we're really pleased. People sort of responded to our requests.

VONNIE: Is that why the levels are lower? You think?

MITCH: That's one reason. The other reason is that the entertainers here—we only had a major problem yesterday was the weather—the entertainers are such a good group of people and they're so mellow. So mellowed out and tired. Everything is just really sweet. Really nice.

VONNIE: Have they been having a good time?

MITCH: Yeah, despite the weather they've been having a good time. A lot of performers have told me that this is a really fine festival. I'm really happy about that . . . I don't think the number is anyway about festivals comparing with each other. We're all different. It's what you create once the thing starts. What kind of dynamic gets going. In terms of our talent here, there's one fine dynamic going on. And I think that is really good.[20]

The Festival was organized deliberately by Podolak around willing volunteers—crews that became more dedicated as the years progressed. The organizational strategy that Mitch created gave particular attention to the volunteers, community, and the "devolution of authority." Through what ethnomusicologist Michael MacDonald has called a "Revolutionary

Establishment," Mitch managed to make a "community activity out of the folk festival which imagined itself more as a community picnic than a Hollywood blockbuster."[21] From the beginning, Folk Fest was about creating an intimate place to enjoy folk music. The relationship between the audience and the performer was preserved and nurtured—even the most celebrated musicians were human, and the smaller workshop stages were places where you could expect to get up close and share in the experience of folk music, creating a sense of unity behind the idea of "we are the folk" and that we are a part of something important.[22] Podolak was following Mariposa's artistic director Estelle Klein's approach of scheduling afternoon workshops, carefully juxtaposing musicians together on a small stage where everyone is on the same level and everyone is a star.[23] The goal was to create an atmosphere where each musician felt welcomed and lavished with great food and logistical support, building rapport with musicians who would in turn embrace the Festival. If they got big, they would still come back to play the Festival. Mitch explained: "What makes this festival work? First, you invite stars—not because they're stars, but because they're good. Then, you bring in acts people have never seen. But you don't have to bore people. You have to come up with a mix that will both educate and entertain."[24]

For Mitch, his politics and activism were a source of motivation for the type of work he did before founding the Festival and in the work he did after he left. He would certainly agree with scholars Eric Fillion and Ajay Heble that "curating a festival means bringing together an often unpredictable set of social engagements to hopefully foster an awareness of each other and a desire to care for the world around us. The act of curation can energize participation in the cultural public sphere."[25] The initial social gathering was much smaller in the early years, but the curation was purposeful.

FIGURE 14. ALANIS OBOMSAWIN AT THE WINNIPEG FOLK FESTIVAL, 1978. PHOTOGRAPH BY DAVID LANDY. ARCHIVES OF MANITOBA, WINNIPEG FOLK FESTIVAL 1978 NEGATIVES, P5266/7, 12/78. 25A.

FIGURE 15. PERFORMER AT THE WINNIPEG FOLK FESTIVAL, 1978. COURTESY OF WINNIPEG FOLK FESTIVAL.

The Festival took root and began to grow over the years. It quickly established a consistent reputation of a legitimate event through CBC broadcasts and by the talent attracted to the event, legitimizing it as a player in the music festival landscape. The Winnipeg Folk Festival's strength was in the mobilizing of the community and the depth of returning volunteers, something of which Podolak was proud because of how it mimicked the Bolshevik structure[26] and created a sense of belonging and shared vision.[27]

Still, one wonders how much of the activism and idealism of the 1960s and 1970s took root and persisted as the folkies grew up and found their way into responsibilities, mortgages, and pension plans. One audience member reflects on their impression of the Festival and this idealism:

> I always have such a bittersweet relationship with the Festival. It's lovely to see everyone bringing their kids and sometimes their parents, and it's a great place to meet people. So much better than a bank line-up or a shopping mall. The smell of happiness is there. In religious communities you'd call some

> of these people bliss bunnies. Here it's a temporary community with a lot of fond folkies. The hard part is looking at all of those people and recognizing how our generation had so many dreams and how few of them ever happened.[28]

There are gems that are left on the cutting room floor of a film edit. After our 2018 interview with Mitch for the documentary When We Became Folk Fest, *as the camera is still rolling we begin watching clips of the Super 8 footage from 1975. John Prentice asks Mitch what made him the unique person to start the Folk Festival. Mitch replies, "Nothing. I'm a trained revolutionary socialist. I got trained by Harry Paine, and a bunch of other people on how to do things when I was a kid.[29] And I was able to apply that knowledge. I just have a really strong love and knowledge of folk music. That's really what it is. I did it as a kid because I liked it. So, I learned about it. The more I learned about it, the more I knew. It was that simple. I just piled up information. When I started the Winnipeg Folk Festival at 25, I was relatively sophisticated in my approach to it. A lot of very loose ends, things that you don't know about, inexperience."[30]*

Mitch also appeared in a documentary called Harry Paine: Cooking the Revolution *(2013) by Dodie Graham McKay. In the extended interview rushes, Mitch talks about how Harry was integral to the launching of the Festival: "he helped build that whole idea of volunteerism and that idea . . . we brought from the Trotskyist movement to the Folk Festival was that basic social understanding of how you motivated people to do things for themselves. As I watched the guy one time in the Ottawa Folk Festival, meeting new volunteers, "we couldn't do this without you" instead of saying, "well, you're joining us, and now you're part of the* we."

SPACE, PLACE, AND PURPOSE

Rick Neufeld's song "Moody Manitoba Morning," a hit for the Manitoba singer/songwriter and well-loved by fans at the Winnipeg Folk Festival, is a reminder of how place is important. The story goes that when an American record promoter expressed interest in the song, he tried to convince Neufeld to change the song's lyrics to "Moody Minnesota

Morning" to attract the U.S. market and generate broader appeal.[31] To his credit, Neufeld refused—the song was about here, not there.

> *I'm in audio engineer Andy Rudolph's basement studio in St Boniface with a coffee. We're listening to audio reels from the 1975 Folk Festival. Andy has had to work magic to make the audio sync with the old Super 8 film footage—solving the creeping sync issue that had caused the Winnipeg Film Group to abandon their project in the 1970s. We'd reached out to the NFB in Montréal to see if they had the technology to make a fresh transfer of the audio reels, which were on an odd format—magnetic tape but with an edge of sprocket holes, like Super 8 film uses for projecting. Andy had to jimmy rig his Nagra reel-to-reel audio player to accommodate the peculiar sound reels, then painstakingly adjust the sync with software to match the picture. The audio reels are resurrected—workshop performances of Tom Jackson, Curtis Jonnie, and Floyd Westerman play on the speakers, magnetic strips sharing their secrets of the stages at Birds Hill Park half a century ago.*

There is something special about the Winnipeg Folk Festival site, which has consistently been at Birds Hill Park, only shifting slightly from the first year's placement in the park grounds. Author Lucy Lippard writes about how what is "seen from the inside" is inherent to a place, "the resonance of a specific location that is known and familiar . . . what happened there, what will happen there."[32] The repeated use of the same terrain has allowed the Festival to hone its use of the location—making deeper impressions across fields and meadows—and thereby permitting attendees to become acquainted and endeared with the place year after year. Contrast that with the Mariposa Folk Festival, which has moved locations several times over the years, leading one journalist to remark, "Generally, the strength of a folk festival lies in its links in the community. Mariposa's enduring problem has been its inability to put down geographic roots."[33]

> *Roots are deep here though, if you base it on the number of folders on file. Back to the Provincial Archives of Manitoba on Vaughan Street. I'm looking through folder after folder of contact sheets and negatives taken by David Landy—the government photographer who took thousands of photographs at the Winnipeg Folk Festival over the first decade. Year after year*

FIGURE 16. PHOTOGRAPHER DAVID LANDY, 1970S. COURTESY OF WINNIPEG FOLK FESTIVAL.

Landy's eye gathered faces, crowds, and the community—capturing People and Music, as the Festival slogan would later declare. The photographs are celebrated by Steve Johnson and Sheldon Oberman in The Folk Festival Book, *released in 1984 for the Festival's tenth anniversary. Landy's photo archive is a gold mine for cultural workers like me, searching for images to include in a film or book.*

Dedicated fans and volunteers were drawn back to the Festival site year after year. Community organizer Joseph Wasylycia-Leis explains how "one social function of festivals is that they strengthen the identity of cultural groups and their attachment to particular values and meanings."[34] The intersection of place and folk music contributes to a growing sense of local identity. Scholar Sarah Moore suggests, "The folk and folk-rock music of the late 60s and early 70s was a natural genre for the expression of Canadian nationalism and Canadian identity, because of the common association with rural space, wilderness, and country life. The folk music genre, like the country music genre, spoke to an identity of vastness and simplicity."[35]

From another rare look at the Winnipeg Folk Festival, this time on early video tape from 1976 shot by John Prentice on a Sony Portapak borrowed from the local office of Canada's Secretary of State—video cameras weren't as plentiful back then, so this footage is unique. It is The Ceilidh *stage, and we see performers take their turn offering a tune: Archie Fisher, Friends of Fiddler's Green, Margaret Christl, and Tommy Makem and The Clancy Brothers singing "Rosin the Beau." The stage is set in a meadow, the performers are under a tent roof with the stage a foot off the ground—there is no back to the tent, so behind the performers there is boreal forest. The video's degradation—generational loss from dubbing—is evident in the form of noise added to the audio, and the horizontal jitter at the bottom of the frame is a reminder of the fragility of the medium. Watching it, I'm captivated by the performances and conscious of the importance of media preservation. Just as the songs drift from the stages on summer afternoons at the Folk Festival and fade, the recordings of these songs are ephemeral too—kept for now on* DVD *in John's collection. There are likely other surreptitious recordings out there of folk stages captured by the dedicated Folk Festival audience over the last half century. Are these recordings stored in closets remembered? Can the format still be played? Where will they end up?*

FIGURE 17. FAMILY WALKING THE PARKING LOT AT THE WINNIPEG FOLK FESTIVAL, 1981. PHOTOGRAPH BY DAVID LANDY. ARCHIVES OF MANITOBA, WINNIPEG FOLK FESTIVAL 1981 NEGATIVES, P5266/13, 81/196.

One wonders how deep is the sense of local community at the Winnipeg Folk Festival? Is it only superficial, or perhaps it is greater amongst volunteers who are working together on a common cause they feel is important? Michael MacDonald has written extensively on Mitch Podolak's work at the Winnipeg Folk Festival. He distills Mitch's thoughts on what happens when people work together: "Nationalism, regionalism, ethnicity, tradition are all parts of why people do things but ultimately it is 'that thing' that happens when people do things together that allows all of these other concepts to exist."[36] But how deep is "that thing" and the connections between these friends that are made at the Festival?

As Dave Barber and I were trying to find a way of framing our contemporary documentary, we headed to Birds Hill Park with a camera and microphone in 2019 to see if our story should be about the Festival then and now. Maybe we could gather interviews with musicians and audience members like the

Winnipeg Film Group had tried in 1975. By the second day, I was overwhelmed by the thought of thousands of people, each person in the audience having their own perspective on what the Festival was to them. It was a transitional moment that confirmed we would focus our project on the early founding of the event and seek out folks from the first years. While the Super 8 film rushes from 1975 had sat in a dusty box, our new abandoned rushes from 2019 now remain backed up on identical hard drives in my studio—where this footage will end up is unclear.

From an impromptu interview at the Winnipeg Folk Festival in 2019 with a woman in the audience at one of the smaller stages, sitting in the shade with a toddler and a sleeping baby in a stroller, we see how the community and relationships so celebrated at the Festival do have limits to how deep the connections might actually be:

DAVE BARBER: How long have you been coming to Folk Fest?

WOMAN: This is my twelfth year.

DAVE: What do you look forward to?

WOMAN: I look forward to watching . . . now I look forward to watching my kids play. And the community that's here, even though you don't know people. They act. . . they act like they know you. Old friends.

DAVE: Do you run in to the same people over the years?

WOMAN: Yeah. I see the same people every year. Old friends, new friends.

DAVE: Any groups you're looking forward to?

WOMAN: To be honest, with two kids under two, I don't plan what I'm going to see. I just park somewhere in the shade and I always hear something amazing.[37]

Wasylycia-Leis explains, the Winnipeg Folk Festival "is a part of the cultural psyche of Winnipeg" and what this means is that the "event can help foster social capital in the community and strengthen the local economy. However, there are limits to these assertions. Those who make up the festival community represent only a small portion of Winnipeg's population and certain groups are excluded from the festival and the community created through the event."[38] As much as it would be assumed that there is a rabid collection of folkniks in Winnipeg—whether in greater numbers than elsewhere is hard to determine. Podolak conducted a survey of who was attending the festival: three percent of those surveyed identified themselves as dedicated folk fans, and 97 percent were what Podolak called an "Eventer." He summarized, "This is the extraordinarily loyal audience of the folk festival and they didn't listen to folk music during most of the year, but they were loyal to the event."[39] At the end of the day, as much as Winnipeggers want to cultivate the idea that there really is something different in Winnipeg—and that it is passionate about folk music—there might not be something so special about the place. It does not matter that the Festival is not particularly unique to Winnipeg. It matters that Mitch Podolak was a strong personality who decided to stick his neck out and create an event that has enjoyed success for half a century.

From the Super 8 footage and audio captured by the Winnipeg Film Group in 1975, a recording from backstage at the Folk Festival following a workshop with Sam Chatmon, Mitch Podolak sits to one side as the camera moves on to record a conversation with Don Hill and Sam Chatmon, we see a young fifteen-year-old Colin Linden is compelled to record the moment on film for posterity. His enthusiasm is a reminder that what might seem like just another encounter with a performer after a gig is actually an historic event that ought to be recognized:

COLIN LINDEN: You can quote me on this, Sam Chatmon is the finest living delta blues singer. He comes from a large family of musicians, among the most popular of the twenties and thirties. I think it's an honour for him to be here in Winnipeg right now. He's going to be around for another seventy-five years.

DON HILL: Colin, you're Sam's pupil. Have long have you know him?

COLIN: Well, Mariposa in '74.

DON: What is he teaching you?

COLIN: A lot more than just music. When you talk to a person who knows that much, you learn a lot about your attitudes towards other people and your relationships. I've learned a whole lot of guitar from him. He knows all the different positions.

[. . . TALKING ABOUT GUITAR PICKING STYLES]

SAM CHATMON: . . . use my fingers and my thumb.

DON: So, you pop them?

SAM: Yeah, go up on them.

DON: Right underneath? Like a frailing on a banjo sort of idea?

SAM: Uh huh. When I'm frailing. When I'm picking—see I frail with this thumb, and pick with my fingers. I be as confident as if I was hitting with a pick . . . you pick up on your finger you're not going to sound right, you got to go down on it.

DON: Right.

SAM: That's the way, three of them were made to pick up and three of them were made to pick down.

DON: Thanks, Sam.

[. . .]

DON: Well, Sam, maybe we'll be able to see you at the hotel tonight?

SAM: Oh yeah. Come on down to the hotel, if you want to come down there.

COLIN: I want to get a picture of me with Sam. Anybody who's watching this film, you can tell that I met Sam Chatmon. July 20th, 1975. Birds Hill Park. Winnipeg, Manitoba, Canada. Okay?

FIGURE 18. SAM CHATMON AT THE WINNIPEG FOLK FESTIVAL, 1975. PHOTOGRAPH BY DAVID LANDY. ARCHIVES OF MANITOBA, WINNIPEG FOLK FESTIVAL 1975 NEGATIVES, P5266/1, 75-4789. 16A.

In most artistic genres the centres of cultural power gravitate to the major cities. In Canada, in the music industry, that is Toronto. But there is a contrarian point of view that suggests that what is happening on the edges of other regions of the country is not relegated and dismissed as provincial and insignificant—rather, as Lippard points out, "regionalism is not a limitation but an advantage."[40] MacDonald makes a connection to what Podolak was doing, and how he approached it in Winnipeg by starting a folk festival: "Perhaps it was possible to develop this approach in a place that is far from the ever-watchful eyes of both government and industry. In the west where there is so much space, so few people, and so little infrastructure, maybe here it was possible, or required, to experiment with contemporary culture."[41] The flourishing of arts and culture in more remote and regional locales presents an immense opportunity for trying something new and interesting without the pressure of conforming to the expectations of the centre.

> *During the 1975 Festival, Allan Kroeker—filmmaker from the Winnipeg Film Group—snuck up close to a stage with his Super 8 camera to film the workshop "Working Class Heroes and Enemies" with Perry Friedman, Ian Robb, Jack Nissesson, and Rambling Jack Elliott. During Rambling Jack's singing of the song "Pretty Boy Floyd," Kroeker got a little bit too close. Rambling Jack stopped between choruses to offer a rebuke, "How about use a long lens and get back where it doesn't bug me so much." The film footage changes from the hand of a steady operator, to a nervous amateur as he sheepishly backs away from the unwanted spotlight. Kroeker's instincts were right though, it's in the close-ups where we find resonance. Legendary cinéma vérité filmmaker Bob Drew told his colleague Abbot Mills, "Look, for God's sakes, stay on their faces! I don't care if they're hitting a hammer or they're putting something in a bag. Show me what their emotions are like while they're hitting the hammer."[42] The filmmaking process—even projects that rely primarily on archival materials—is driven by the search for close-ups, intimacy, to see the real motivations and effect a character has on*

FIGURE 19. COUPLE WALKS THROUGH MEADOWS OF BIRDS HILL PARK AT THE WINNIPEG FOLK FESTIVAL, 1974. PHOTOGRAPH BY JOHN BACHMANN. COURTESY WINNIPEG FOLK FESTIVAL.

their environment. I'm looking for close-ups of Mitch, the musicians, and the volunteers in the archival footage and still photography.

RIPPLES IN A GREAT SEA

Like the reaction of dropping a pebble into a still body of water, Mitch Podolak has left a significant legacy in the cultural events that showcase folk music. The measure of that success will be different depending on who you ask. Is success measured by size and budget? That sort of metric quickly prompts comparisons with other festivals. Should success instead be measured by meaningfulness and usefulness? Arts educator Doris Sommer suggests we "would do well to consider art's ripple effects, from producing pleasure to triggering innovation."[43]

Where do the ripples of the Winnipeg Folk Festival extend after a half-century of annual events? Locally, the Winnipeg Folk Festival has extended its reach to folk events throughout the year at various urban venues. One could point to the establishment of the West End Cultural Centre and Mitch's subsequent work with Home Routes—a non-profit that supports house concerts for independent musical acts touring across the country. The Winnipeg Crankie Festival, reviving and celebrating an old storytelling art form, is a logical extension of the first ripples started in 1974 at Birds Hill Park.[44] Besides the founding of the festival in Winnipeg, Podolak contributed to the founding of folk festivals in Vancouver, Edmonton, Calgary, Owen Sound, and Canso.[45]

Over the years the Festival grew and matured, and other folk festivals across western Canada sprouted—often thanks to Mitch sharing his blueprint. The chemistry was working, people latched on, and these festivals found a following. In some ways, festivals fell into the trap of trying to one-up themselves each year to be a greater spectacular event. Winnipeg's festival was gradually eclipsed in size by other festivals, like the Edmonton Folk Festival. Responding to the question "why are we letting Edmonton beat us at our own game?" journalist Morley Walker recognized our city's virtue of "stability and maturity" rather than a quest for the biggest and best.[46]

In the Super 8 footage from 1975, the Winnipeg Film Group, Vonnie von Helmolt stops Mitch Podolak for a quick interview on the last day of the Folk Festival that reveals both his optimism and the fragility of the event in the earliest years:

VONNIE: What is happening, tell us the state of affairs?

MITCH: Well, the way I see it now, we're just about there.

VONNIE: You're just about there? Where is there?

MITCH: Same place we were this time last year, about $5,000 in the hole.

VONNIE: Are you serious?

MITCH: Yes. Absolutely.

VONNIE: How do you feel about that?

MITCH: Well, that's okay. That's not a bad place to start from. I mean, every major organization in the world uses deficit financing.

VONNIE: Damn rights.

MITCH: We're no different.

VONNIE: That's probably the sign of a truly great talent as a matter of fact.

MITCH: That's right. To be able to con and lie and cheat and bullshit my way through. It'll be fine.

VONNIE: That's right.

MITCH: But very seriously, this festival is going to survive.

As folk festivals across Canada—including Winnipeg—grew larger, there were consequences to the intimacy that was once a key aspect of the experience. As performers, educators, and festival organizers Jon Bartlett and Rika Ruebsaat explain, "we see the total attendance more and more divided into 'performers' and 'audience,' and so too does the distance increase between them. It becomes increasingly more difficult for a member of the audience to talk to a performer."[47] Wasylycia-Leis suggests that large contemporary festivals "appear more as spectacle than ritual. In contrast to the recipe for intimacy foundational to Podolak, spectacles are elaborate "cultural productions" designed to entertain by creating a sense of wonderment and awe.[48] When asked about the prospects for more folk festivals in North America emerging in the future, Mitch Podolak responded:

> I don't know. I hope there are a lot more small ones! Personally, I'm really interested in ones like Hiawatha because the quality of the experience is way higher even though there is a lot less there. Because the relationship to music is a lot closer. Absolutely everybody . . . I mean when you have that many players in the audience. When you have 3000 people at the festival and there is only one primary stage and there is a 1000 [people] there at any given time and when you're walking through the rest of it there is a lot of people playing music all day. Then you have to ask yourself what is the relationship here? And you will say that it is more to music than to almost anything and that's way better . . . it's a better experience. It's different. I think we'd be way better off with a couple of hundred more like that in North America.[49]

CONVERSATIONS WITH THE FOUNDING FOLKS

The folks interviewed for this book are the ones who can best tell us about how it was founded, and their interviews help us address some key questions: What was the impetus for making a festival? Why and how did they get involved in this Festival? Why did this happen here in Winnipeg? The answers are found in the opinions and memories of people who filled a range of roles and responsibilities during the early years of the gathering at Birds Hill Park. The first group of interviews, in the section titled "Kicking off the Day," take us back to the genesis of the event. Mitch Podolak and Ava Kobrinsky each discuss what the early conversations were like, with the call for proposals for Winnipeg's centennial and the difficulties convincing funders to support the Festival.

Co-founder Colin Gorrie talks about how he played the straight man to Mitch's brash hippie persona. Harry Paine and Lorna Hiebert both knew Mitch well and their reflections help build our understanding of Mitch behind the scenes of the Festival.

In the next section, "Sittin' on Stage a Singin,'" we hear from a range of musicians who played the Festival, performers well remembered who valued their chance to collaborate with Mitch: Bruce Cockburn, who was used as bait to attract the audience the first year; Paul Mills, who brought funding along with his connections at CBC; Tom Jackson, David Amram, and Len Udow each share how important the Festival was for the friendships and collaborations made on and off stage as their tour stopped in at the Festival.

In "Tunes from the Far Out East," we hear from another group of performers who played the Festival in the early years. Cathy Fink notes how hungry she was to learn from veteran banjo players she met at various folk festivals. Mary Faith Rhoads explains how coming to Winnipeg was her chance to play in the big pond. Ken Whiteley and Grit Laskin bring a perspective of Toronto musicians and how the Festival compared to Mariposa. American David Essig talks about how he found his home amongst the community of folk musicians up in Canada.

The next section, "The Lure of Local," provides accounts from Manitoba musicians. Artists Rick Neufeld and Curtis Jonnie talk about their lasting friendship with Mitch outside the Festival. Al Simmons, Peter Paul Van Camp, and Winston Wuttunee offer stories of their experiences on stage. Big Dave McLean and Dan Donahue get into the uniqueness of Winnipeg—a recurring theme of the book—and how the underdog attitude results in the remarkable community spirit and creative talent that have been central to the Festival's thriving for all these years.

What Mitch embodied in his approach to the Festival was a sense of equality and comradery—most notably in the gathering of the volunteers. In the section titled "The Strong and the Mighty," we dig into what it means to be a volunteer in interviews with veterans like Jane Graham, Candice Masters, and Karen Dana. Marsha Wineman talks about what it was like to work with Harry Paine in the kitchen. Jon Singleton provides a unique perspective from his work supporting Mitch with the financials.

FIGURE 20. CROWDS AT A WORKSHOP STAGE AT THE WINNIPEG FOLK FESTIVAL, 1975. PHOTOGRAPH BY DAVID LANDY. ARCHIVES OF MANITOBA, WINNIPEG FOLK FESTIVAL 1975 NEGATIVES, P5266/1, 75-4641. 19A.

FIGURE 21. MITCH PODOLAK AT FOOT OF A STAGE AT THE WINNIPEG FOLK FESTIVAL, N.D. PHOTOGRAPH BY MARSHA WINEMAN.

Martin Landy talks about his father, David Landy, long-time photographer for the Folk Festival, and what it was like, as a volunteer, setting and tearing down Main Stage.

The final section of the book, "Setting the Stage," explores the broader evolution of the Festival from its early years with voices such as John Prentice, host of the local folk radio program *Planet Mainstage*, and Pierre Guérin, former artistic director of the Festival. We look also to where the Festival is heading, in conversations with Mitch's son Leonard Podolak and former Winnipeg Folk Festival Executive Director Lynne Skromeda.

DO YOU LIKE YOURS RAW OR COOKED?

Beyond the chronicling of the beginnings of the Folk Festival, juxtaposing the history with first-hand accounts of sorting through shelves, boxes, and folders of various archives for audio/visual memories allows us to gain a sense of perspective about the event's past and its ongoing legacy. The purpose of this structure is to ground the narrative in that process—and to keep these sources from disappearing from awareness. The shorter moments captured on tape are more than fleeting comments, they offer fascinating glimpses of our cast of characters on and off the stage.[50] Even when recordings are uncovered, too often they are not given much attention. As I mentioned in the book's preface, Michael Frisch compares original oral history recordings and distilled prose to the raw versus the cooked, and we too often prefer processed and truncated audio and video to save the time and effort of sifting through extended and aged media formats. Frisch goes on to say, "The Deep Dark Secret of oral history is that nobody spends much time listening to or watching recorded and collected interview documents. There has simply been little serious interest in the primary audio or video interviews that literally define the field."[51] This is part of my motivation for including short narrative accounts of finding these elements—a laying out of bread crumbs for others to find where collections of raw audio and visual material can be found. Perhaps at some point in the future advanced technology and archival access will converge to allow for anyone cooking in their kitchen to stream their choice of an uncut recording from one of the stages from the Winnipeg Folk Festival in the 1970s. Hearing a musician doing a sound check and asking for more guitar in the monitor contributes to a greater sense of presence and place.

This book acts as a companion to Steve Johnson and Sheldon Oberman's great 1984 *The Folk Festival Book*—a volume that is structured as a narrative introduction, but primarily constitutes a collage of quotes by a chorus of Folk Festival people accompanied with the excellent photos by David Landy. As opposed to Johnson and Oberman's book, *Founding Folks* allows for a deeper dive into the memories and opinions of each individual through extended interviews. Both approaches contribute to our understanding of the Festival and its founding. Perhaps what is most valuable to me are the voices documented here that are too often overlooked but that play an important role in the creation and evolution of artistic endeavours of all sorts. My other intent for the book is to bring increased attention to the surviving motion picture, audio, image, and textual elements too often overlooked in archives—collections preserved by vigilant archivists, but sometimes held more precariously in shoeboxes and personal photo albums. My filmmaker's narrative in this introduction shares insights gleaned in the process of my archival digging and captures additional moments of conversation missing from accounts of the Festival. They are unvarnished, verité glimpses from a stage, or outtakes from documentary rushes, but they too contribute to our understanding of the establishment of the Folk Festival. We need to remember that these collections and archives exist, are available, and need preserving.

> *I'm listening to the tapes from the Winnipeg Folk Festival's internal archive—recordings that Mitch had made of most of the stages in 1976. This tape is the Working People's Songs workshop from 1976. Hedy West is hosting the workshop, along with Enoch Kent, Saul Broudy, and Vera Johnson. I'm sure Mitch would have been at this workshop stage in the crowd to hear the performance—he was a fan of the banjo, for one, but also this topic matched his politics and drove much of the work he would do in his life. West is describing the origin of a song, "Palms of Victory," from the American*

south about a farmer in the 1890s in Georgia "who never departed from the straight and narrow. And he cared nothing at all about his life on earth, about worldly goods, he was simply fixed on heaven . . ."

I saw an honest farmer

His back was bending low

He's picking out his cotton

As hard as he could go

He piled it in the rail pen

Until the merchant came

That he might attach his cotton

That he should pay his claim

It's pans of biscuits and bowls of gravy

It's pans of biscuits and bowls of gravy we shall have

I imagine Mitch as the farmer. Maybe the Folk Festival's backstage kitchen once served up biscuits and gravy. The Folk Fest seems a bit like heaven.

FIGURE 22. TED BOGAN ON A WORKSHOP STAGE, 1976. PHOTOGRAPH BY DAVID LANDY. ARCHIVES OF MANITOBA, WINNIPEG FOLK FESTIVAL 1976 NEGATIVES, P5266/3, 76/2. 31.

FIGURE 23. HEDY WEST AT THE WINNIPEG FOLK FESTIVAL, 1977. PHOTOGRAPH BY GERRY KOPELOW. COURTESY OF THE WINNIPEG FOLK FESTIVAL.

FIGURE 24. STEVE GOODMAN PERFORMS AT THE WINNIPEG FOLK FESTIVAL, 1976. PHOTOGRAPH BY DAVID LANDY. ARCHIVES OF MANITOBA, WINNIPEG FOLK FESTIVAL 1976 NEGATIVES, P2566/3, 76/15. 31A.

Oral History Interviews with

Winnipeg FOLK FESTIVAL folks

PART ONE

KICKING OFF THE DAY: How it all began

Mitch PODOLAK

Podolak grew up in Toronto where he began hanging around the Bohemian Embassy Coffee House—working his way from cleaning tables to booking performers. Besides his keen interest in folk music—he played the banjo—Mitch was a frequent organizer and social activist, involved in the movement to stop the war in Vietnam. With his move to Winnipeg in the 1970s, he became a freelance CBC radio documentary maker for such shows as Five Nights, CBC Radio Tuesday Night, Between Ourselves, *and* This Country in the Morning. *He hosted the program* Simply Folk *from 1987 to 1991. Mitch founded the Winnipeg Folk Festival in 1974 with Ava Kobrinsky and Colin Gorrie. He used the successful template for the Festival to help start folk festivals in Vancouver, Edmonton, and Calgary—and was a major contributor to the establishment of many others. The Winnipeg Children's Festival, the West End Cultural Centre music venue, and Home Routes—the house concert support organization—all owe their start to Mitch and the collaborators he brought together.*

FIGURE 25. MITCH PODOLAK DURING THE SETUP OF WINNIPEG FOLK FESTIVAL STAGE, 1975. *WINNIPEG TRIBUNE*, UNIVERSITY OF MANITOBA ARCHIVES.

EDMONTON MUSICIANS' ASSOCIATION

MITCH PODOLAK

19 DECEMBER 2018, WINNIPEG

MITCH PODOLAK: Do you want to do any kind of sound test?

KEVIN NIKKEL: Yes, thanks.

MP: This is the Canadian broad corpsing castration coming to you directly from my living room.

KN: Sounds good.

MP: I won't do my CBC voice, it's not fun anymore to do. When I had that show I used to fuck with that a bit.

KN: Let's start from the beginning. How did you end up in Winnipeg from Toronto?

MP: I came through here on a speaking tour for the Vietnam mobilization committee, back I think it was 1968. I'd been here before. I had a girlfriend in Winnipeg, so I'd spent a bit of time here. But I came here formally as a speaker for the Vietnam mobe.[1] I made my best friend there . . . at that particular gathering. Lifetime pal there that day. I picked up on the fact that there was a real radicalization in the left in Winnipeg. So, I went back to Toronto and reported to my comrades in the Trotskyist movement that Winnipeg was the perfect place for us to colonize, and they said, "Great. You go colonize!" So, I got sent out here with a $100 a month. I think it was in September of 1968. The first thing I did was register at the university as a mature student because then I had some legitimacy, and wasn't just an outside agitator, though in reality that's exactly what I was. Then I helped form the Vietnam committee, a committee against the war. And that thing attracted all kinds of people from all kinds of leftist ideas, and liberal ideas, and it created a milieu for me to work in and be part of. I made lifetime friends there. It was a real good beginning for me in Winnipeg. I always carried a banjo with me. Wherever I went the banjo went. Since I was fourteen.

FIGURE 26. MITCH PODOLAK AT THE WINNIPEG FOLK FESTIVAL OFFICES, 1980. *WINNIPEG TRIBUNE*, UNIVERSITY OF MANITOBA ARCHIVES.

FIGURE 27. BUKKA WHITE ON A WORKSHOP STAGE AT THE WINNIPEG FOLK FESTIVAL, 1974. PHOTOGRAPH BY JOHN BACHMAN. COURTESY OF WINNIPEG FOLK FESTIVAL.

DAVE BARBER: Who taught you the banjo?

MP: Well, I got inspired by Pete Seeger to play the banjo. There is no doubt. I went to see a concert that my sister took me to. She had a date, who stood her up. I got the other ticket. It changed my life, that sure did. I'd never seen a banjo played before that night. I had loved the clarinet, but I took a very good $300 clarinet down to a pawn shop and traded for a really shitty banjo which I learned on with Pete Seeger's book on how to play the five string banjo. I was putting on my first shows in Toronto at the Bohemian Embassy Coffee House when I was sixteen and I started to work with Mike Seeger. The truth of the matter is that Mike really refined my playing an awful lot. He really was a brilliant player and a brilliant teacher. I'm one of Mike Seeger's many victims, to fall in love with American folk music. I learned from Mike.

KN: When you came to Winnipeg, you clearly had an agenda and a purpose. Talk about the origins of the Folk Festival in relation to that other reason for coming here.

MP: Well, the purpose was, I came here to form a revolutionary organization. I came at a time when that was a very active purpose for a lot of young people. You start listening to those songs and you start believing in them. The right songs. The good songs. It gave me politics and gave me music at the same time. I got interested in folk music because of politics. Because I got interested in folk music, I started listening to the banjo. Then I got fascinated by the banjo itself, never mind the politics. As I learned how to play the banjo, I started learning how to play traditional music on the banjo because of the logical way for it to go. Even today when I pick up the banjo and play—which I don't really do much because my hands are screwed up—I play some political music. I play a lot of old-time Appalachian music, because that's where my heart is musically. The question?

STARTING THE WINNIPEG FOLK FESTIVAL

KN: I want to bring that over to the Folk Festival. What brought things together?

MP: So here I am, this folkie in Winnipeg, trying to earn a living. Trying to be revolutionary in the great Canadian communist conspiracy—the CBC intervened and hired me to do freelance radio stuff. I started doing commentary about various things, which was good because I was a left-wing commentator, everybody else was a right-wing commentator. I had my place in radio here in town and I made friends in the Corporation. I made friends at the CBC. I start talking about music with people and about life. Then I saw an ad on television that said, "Winnipeg is having a centennial," and instantly the idea of a folk festival popped into my brain. I said it to Ava and she said, "You're crazy. That will never, ever, ever happen."

Well, I went and talked to a producer and he hooked me up with Colin Gorrie. Colin Gorrie is my partner in starting up the Winnipeg Folk Festival. He was a professor of architecture. He's the guy who created all the children's festivals in Canada. Colin is a brilliant guy. He was a landscape architect, so he knew things about sites and management and had been involved in children's theatre. He was a British guy who wore an ascot, and I was a dirty old hippie—the two of us were an interesting combination. We'd go to these committee meetings and they didn't know what to make of us.

KN: What is the landscape of Folk Festivals like in Canada at this time when you came up with this idea?

MP: At the time of the Winnipeg Folk Festival there was the Miramichi Folk Festival, which was 105 years old at the time, something like that. It was one day, and no performer or member of the audience was more than fifty miles away. There was the Mariposa Folk Festival, which was the granddaddy of folk festivals in Canada, and it was still going full bloody blast—it was a wonderful festival. There was the Philadelphia Folk Festival. Newport had died some years earlier, which was too bad. I was at the 1963 and 1964 Newport. I was there when Dylan went electric. I was shocked along with everybody else. I didn't boo, because I had too much respect for him, but I did not like it. I think he should've said something instead of just doing that, and then people would have accepted it.

Winnipeg was the first time anybody besides people in Toronto tried to do it. The fact that it was an immediate success, and the performers took the word and spread it, all of a sudden by year two we were a player in the game in a real serious way. It surprised me. I was happy because we'd seen our fantasies come true and it was shocking us, but we just kept going. We were really committed.

KN: Before the first festival was launched, what was your idea of what festivals should be?

MP: Mariposa.

KN: Tell me about what that meant.

MP: Clearly, the breakdown between doing individual concerts and artist workshops. We were trying to create a situation where people interact with each other, and artists interact. There was a woman at Mariposa named Estelle Klein, she'd been doing it for about five or six years when I started Winnipeg. I have to say if there was ever a smart programmer in the world it was Estelle Klein. There is not a better, cleverer person in the world for reaching into people's brains and picking things out that only she saw that were sitting there. When I got down to the business of daytime programming, I would just start reading her stuff over and over and over again and try not to steal directly, but I stole a million good ideas. I remember thanking her before she passed on. She absolutely had a sense very few other people had. Her vision of what a festival was, that mixture between contemporary and traditional and the idea of bringing these things to intermarry on the stage, that was her vision. I am a follower of Estelle, I would say. No one was smarter, ever, ever, ever. And I've read every program that has ever existed in North America that artistic directors have done. I can't touch Estelle.

I tried to reach some basic ideas in the first year of the Festival. For instance, what exactly is a banjo? What exactly is a guitar? And how do they work with folk music? What is folk music? What is harmony singing? What is Irish music? I wanted to do a bit of everything. I wasn't very good at it that first year. I was okay. Mike Seeger at Mariposa a few months earlier had a look at the program. He said, "Not bad. You could use a bit more traditional music here." Then I gave it to a singer-songwriter and they said, "Not bad. You could use a bit more singer-songwriters." So, I figured I was getting it right and getting the balance.

From that first-year experience, the one thing I began to do about programming generally was to try to think of it in balance. Since folk music is 90 percent of the world's music, and has influenced the other 10 percent pretty fundamentally, then really when you program a folk festival your reach is extraordinary. But how do you make those things come together? How do you take a band from Peru and put it together with a bunch of French Canadians on the stage together and make really beautiful music and get everybody excited and crazy? Partly luck. You want to create a situation backstage when the artists gravitate to each other. So that's one of the things I understood that a folk festival better be a good internal party. If you want to create good music, you got to let that natural thing come out.

DAVE BARBER: You once told me you'd tried to get Bob Dylan because you had his grandmother's phone number.

MP: I got his mother's phone number.

KN: Do you want to tell that story?

MP: No. [Laughs]

KN: This is a Herculean feat that you're pulling off. How did you survive in the first couple years?

MP: Well, the first year, the Festival really was an eighteen-month year. It really wasn't a twelve-month year. The task is to organize as many volunteers as you can. To create some kind of structure and to program this thing. Then to advertise and convince people to come because they've never heard of a folk festival before. No one here knew what a folk festival was. But when I think about it and what we did and how we approached it, we just approached it like this was the most natural thing in the world. We're going to do this and of course people are going to come. We just did it totally naïvely and totally straight ahead as we possibly could, because that was all we were thinking about.

At seven o'clock there were 150 people there on the first Friday night. At eight o'clock there were about 14,000 there. But the guy that gave us our money was having a shit out in the field when there was only 150 people there. "You're a con man and a thief," he said, that first night of the Festival. When he walked up to try to apologize an hour later, I told him to fuck off and die. Some jerk with white patent shoes and grey flannel pants and a blue blazer and a lot of fucking money—he was the chair of the committee that gave us the money. He went through a brief moment of, "I've been fucked." May he rot in his grave, the lousy bastard.

THE VOLUNTEERS

KN: Tell me more about the volunteers that helped make the Festival happen.

MP: The answer to my understanding of things was right in front of me and I didn't see it the first year. I knew we needed volunteers and I got volunteers to agree to do various things. I didn't really have enough, so it was real hard. People were running the stages and running the barbecue in the middle of the night for the performers' party. We didn't have enough. But between year one and year two, a woman named Judy McGuire was a volunteer at the Festival and she said, "Look, let me do some of this." I said, "Sure." Because I didn't know any better.

Judy didn't have the theoretical understanding, but she had the practical understanding. She did a brilliant thing. She created the structure—she left after that. I looked at the structure that she created and understood it in a completely different context. I understood something about structure because I came through the far Left.

I looked at it organizationally and I put up a chart of the Folk Festival, based on Judy's ideas, and there was the Bolshevik party. There was a group of units out of which every unit had to be self-active: the hospitality committee, the environment committee, box office. Whatever task there was, every section of it had to be self-active, without me having to stand there with a stick. So basically, I adapted Judy's ideas and fused them with Bolshevism. The best way I can describe the Bolshevik structure is independent units that are self-managed—that's what the Folk Festival is.

KN: Had you seen this elsewhere?

MP: I'd never seen it, only read about it in history.

KN: Have you since seen it used elsewhere?

MP: Every festival in the country uses that system. Whether they understand it in those sociological terms or not, doesn't matter. Every single festival has adopted it, and we adapted Mariposa's idea. Mariposa's idea did not involve inviting volunteers to the parties. A friend of mine was volunteering at Mariposa the year I was there and I said, "I'll see you at the party." And he said, "I can't come, they didn't invite us." "What?" I said, "You work all day for nothing and they don't invite you to the party? What a bunch of assholes." So, I got that after year one—year two invite the volunteers to the party. Feed them with the performers. Treat them the same as everybody else, and treat the performers the same as every volunteer. What a unique idea, treat everybody like a human being and maybe they'll come across for you. Where did that come from? I think it was Lenin, myself. Some people may say it was Jesus, but I don't believe that.

KN: I want to know if you think this happened uniquely here in Winnipeg because it was Winnipeg? Did that matter?

MP: No. I don't think it happened here uniquely. I think it happened here first, after Mariposa. That is, we took the Mariposa system—Judy did—and she improved upon it, and I improved upon it. By making a more social thing, and then we repeated it in Vancouver two years later, and Edmonton a year later.

BEING FROM WINNIPEG, THE UNDERDOGS

KN: I'm curious about the ways in which being from Winnipeg is considered a liability—did it ever cause an issue when someone might say, "You want me to come to where? Winnipeg?"

MP: [Laughs] The first couple years. My line was, "north of North Dakota." I used to have to say that a lot. Not anymore. Not ever.

KN: It wasn't a problem.

MP: No. Shit. Being in the middle of the continent was an advantage. All kinds of ways.

KN: Was the Folk Fest an underdog?

MP: Well, you see, that's a really interesting question. It depends on how you look at it. We were $17,000 in debt, an enormous amount of money after the third year. That was a hardship because $17,000 was a lot of dough in those days. I got to be really good at keeping creditors at bay. You'd be nice, you'd be polite, you constantly phone them to make sure they never felt left out. But if they phoned you up to tell you something, you'd tell them to fuck off. You had to be hard because it's a business, and a business needs toughness. The truth is, running a nonprofit society needs more toughness than most businesses. People wanted to do benefits for us. They thought we're the underdog. They liked us, but I refused to have anybody do a benefit. I didn't want anybody to do a benefit for us. I wanted to do benefits for other people. It was a headspace not allowing us to be the bottom of the pile.

We had a hard time. And then 1977 came along. And Buffy Sainte-Marie came along and there was 15,000 people on a Saturday night, and that was the end of our problems in lots of ways. That was Buffy, thank you very much. It's never been that busy again. Never. Not by my hand, not by anybody else's hand.

KN: Would you say the Folk Fest was an underdog, but you just didn't call it an underdog?

MP: Yes. It was financially. First of all, the funders didn't think of folk music as an art form. I don't know what the fuck they thought of it, but they sure didn't think of it on the same level as Brahms. I remember telling one of those idiots, wasn't Brahms something they dropped on Vietnam? I remembered fighting and fighting and fighting

FIGURE 28. WINNIPEG FOLK FESTIVAL STAFF; FROM LEFT: KATE CAREY, LINDA CUBBIDGE, TASIA GERAS, BILL MERRIT, MITCH PODOLAK, ROSALIE GOLDSTEIN, AND MARY JOHNSTON, 1993. PHOTOGRAPH BY ROBERT TINKER. COURTESY WINNIPEG FOLK FESTIVAL.

with those pricks. Those classically trained unaccomplished bureaucrats, which is what the arts councils are full of in this country—on the whole, not all. Folk music was just an anathema to them. We made an application to the Canada Council on behalf of the Winnipeg Folk Festival for an operating grant in the amount of one dollar. We forced a discussion with those pricks. It didn't help. Just about the time I left the Festival along came the Department of Heritage, with lots of money and no criteria other than that the people show up. They started funding the folk festivals, which is the very essence of shitty funding. It began to lower the level of the art of the folk festival. The Canadian government is pretty much responsible for fucking up the folk festivals.

KN: Why?

MP: Because they provided money without criteria. Without cultural criteria. Without a cultural agenda. What is the cultural agenda of the Winnipeg Folk Festival today? To make money.

KN: What was it back then?

MP: It was to promote folk music. That's what it was started to do. And now it's a different thing.

DB: What is folk music to you?

MP: That is the worst question anybody ever asked.

JOHN PRENTICE: But you can answer it.

MP: Pete Seeger said, "A folk song is only a folksong when it's been passed down from one generation to another without being written down." Big Bill Broonzy said, "All songs is folksongs, I never heard a horse sing 'em." I think that's full of shit too. As director of the Winnipeg Folk Festival, my definition of folk music became, if I say it's folk music, it's folk music. That was a real practical application, but I think that folk music is music that is not written for the marketplace. Not written with the, "I'm going to make a hit and make a million bucks." It's written for whatever good reason it is written. I think that's what defines it from a literary point of view. Musically there is a lot of different points.

KN: So, it's a lot like independent film. It'd be great to make money, but you probably won't. But make it anyway.

MP: The average—last time I had a look, we did a quick study—it was $11,000 a year in gross average for a Canadian folk artist. We did that a few years before we started Home Routes.

KN: How important were emerging and unknown artists to what you were doing in the early years?

MP: I never thought of it, but really important. Stringband. Bob Bossin Trio. Leon Redbone—[who] no one had ever heard of—did a stunning performance. So, it was a whole bunch of things that came together, including some absolutely mind fucking brilliant shows that happened on the stage of the first Winnipeg Folk Festival. Leon Redbone got a twenty-two-minute standing ovation! We timed it afterward. There were some brilliant things that happened.

We passed the rumour; [Bruce] Cockburn is doing a free concert in the Park. That's what we had to do to get people to come out to the Folk Festival. Eight acts including Cockburn. So, it was a real basic experience. Year two, in 1975, was the first year people got in for twelve dollars for the whole weekend.

KN: One of the things that was important for those early years would be the Indigenous talent that you brought.

MP: There wasn't a lot.

KN: Talk about that.

MP: There was some. There was Tom Jackson to start with. I'm trying to remember who. It wasn't until another year or two that we got really serious about people like Alanis Obomsawin.

DB: Floyd Westerman.

KN: Shingoose.

JP: I think there is Floyd on the video we'll show you.

MP: Goose was, yeah. Floyd Westerman was there in 1975.

KN: And this was a conscious thing?

MP: No. Aboriginal artists . . . I was watching other festivals, and what they were doing and a lot of them were over-killing it. They're doing it because they felt like they had to. I thought we should just do it the same as we do anything else that we liked. We should put the same amount on the Main Stage and the same amount on the daytime stages and it is based on whether somebody was good, not because they were Aboriginal. We didn't bring somebody because they were women. We brought them because they were good artists. And it's the same on every issue. What had to be is the quality. That became difficult at times. I remember a long discussion I had about hiring a bunch of Aboriginal artists with an Aboriginal agent and me saying, "Well, this one sucks. This one is brilliant, I want him." I wouldn't take people because they were Aboriginal. I wouldn't take people because they were women. I wouldn't take them because they're Canadians. No national chauvinism. No sexism. Just what was good. What was good, was a really good criteria.

FIGURE 29. MITCH PODOLAK AND CREW AT THE WINNIPEG FOLK FESTIVAL, 1980. PHOTOGRAPH BY DAVID LANDY. ARCHIVES OF MANITOBA, WINNIPEG FOLK FESTIVAL 1980 NEGATIVES, P2566/11, 80/509. 2A.

THE SECOND WINNIPEG FOLK FESTIVAL

KN: What are some other things you did differently for the second year of the Festival?

MP: We put up a fence. [Laughs] And we didn't know how to do that, and we learned how to do that. The third year was more interesting because the third year we had a wrestling club running the fence. We just had a rule, first time someone comes over, pitch them. Second time, punch them in the face and pitch them. Third time, beat them up and pitch them. That's what I told those guys.

KN: They should learn by then.

MP: Yeah. There was a number of people that got punched in the face. You know Lorna Hiebert? My favourite memory of 1975 is watching Lorna watch a guy jump the fence and go over and get the money from him. Guilt him into paying. It was great.

DB: Did you have to battle any weather issues?

MP: Weather was weather. Man plans, God laughs. You've got to learn how to perform in the weather. You've got to not be afraid of that tornado coming, and [that it] is likely to go through the Main Stage of the Festival, and everybody is saying, "Cancel, cancel, quick, quick!" I never did, not once. Now it was done after I left a few times. But I never pulled the stage, not once. Better we should die together.

KN: I'm going to play you some film footage from 1975.

[Watching Super 8 film footage from the 1975 Winnipeg Folk Festival shot by a crew from the Winnipeg Film Group]

DB: I went to those first few festivals. I have great memories.

MP: Have you been lately, Dave?

DB: Not recently. I used to volunteer quite a bit. What do you remember about Duck Donald?

MP: Whenever I'd finish a workshop schedule in the middle of the night, I'd phone him up and he'd come over and I'd go to sleep and he'd make sure I didn't have people beside themselves. Duck was one of my partners in doing the Festival in a real way. I loved working with Duck. He was just another pair of good eyes. Duck was important to

FIGURE 30. AUDIENCE IN THE RAIN, 1975. PHOTOGRAPH BY DAVID LANDY. ARCHIVES OF MANITOBA, WINNIPEG FOLK FESTIVAL 1975 NEGATIVES, P5266/1, 75-4776. 19A.

me as a person, he actually taught me an awful lot about bluegrass. I knew more about old-time music.

KN: How does it feel, watching this footage?

MP: It's good. I'm happy we did it. I think we accomplished a lot. I don't think it is accomplishing much more, unfortunately. And it could be.

The work that we're doing with Home Routes, the organization I've created now, is a folk music organization, right to the core of its being. We set up a lending library for instruments. We're going to make them available for people who can't afford it. We'll give free lessons. We're going to be doing what we're supposed to be doing. Everybody plays banjo that works there.

Colin GORRIE

Originally from Bristol, England, Colin Gorrie came to Winnipeg to study architecture at the University of Manitoba. He connected with Mitch Podolak to help organize the first Winnipeg Folk Festival in 1974 and was actively involved the first two years of the Festival before moving to the West Coast. He also assisted in founding the Vancouver Folk Festival with Mitch. Besides his specialty as an architect, he helped run a theatre company and supported many other arts festivals. He eventually returned to England where he was the co-founder of the Bristol International Jazz and Blues Festival.

FIGURE 31. COLIN GORRIE AT THE WINNIPEG FOLK FESTIVAL, 1975. COURTESY OF WINNIPEG FILM GROUP.

COLIN GORRIE

10 DECEMBER 2019, BRISTOL, ENGLAND

CHRIS NIKKEL: Who are you and what are your connections to the Winnipeg Folk Fest?

COLIN GORRIE: My name is Colin Gorrie. I had the pleasure of creating a partnership with Mitch Podolak. The two of us basically started the Winnipeg Folk Festival back in 1974. It was a centennial event and therefore Mitch and I had to sell it to the Centennial organization.

CN: Do you remember the first time you met Mitch?

CG: Yes, I do. He had been doing broadcasts on folk music with the CBC in Winnipeg and his producer was a guy called Walt Unger. They were friends because Walt was a follower of folk music. I knew Walt because we played bridge—he and his wife and my wife too. That's how we knew each other. What happened was Mitch had broached this idea for a centennial event to Walt and said, "I really need somebody to work with. I need somebody who can pick out a site and figure out how we are going to lay this whole thing out for a summer music festival." Because of Walt's friendship with me, he said, "Why don't you to talk to Colin 'cause he's a young architect. He'll know what to do." And that's how it happened. This friend of both of us basically put us together.

CN: If I were in that room for that first initial conversation, give me a flavour of how awe-inspiring or underwhelming it would have been?

MITCH PODOLAK

CG: Well, Mitch was certainly an overwhelming type of person. I was quite surprised. I was looking at some journalist's reports on the start of the Folk Festival and the sentence that really caught my eye was the reporter had said, "If you think about two people walking into a room to sell an idea, one was basically a bearded hippie, and the other was a cravat-wearing English aristocrat." The image was really very strange. What is interesting, of course, is Mitch and I played on that theme. He was the bad guy and I was the good guy. I was the respectable one and

FIGURE 32. AUDIENCE AT A WORKSHOP STAGE AT THE WINNIPEG FOLK FESTIVAL, 1978. PHOTOGRAPH BY DAVID LANDY. ARCHIVES OF MANITOBA, WINNIPEG FOLK FESTIVAL 1978 NEGATIVES, P5266/7, 16/78. 3.

Mitch, of course, was not respectable. But the reason I say not respectable, it's because folk back in the seventies, particularly to Winnipeg, was some unfortunate type of music—from the government's point of view. So, we had to convince the people that, no, folk is a genre of music by itself. It's not rock. And of course, back in the late 1960s and early 1970s, there were some major rock festivals, and interesting things would happen with those festivals. We had to convince these people that we were seeking money from to run this opening festival. We had to convince them, no, we won't have riots and people undressing and doing all these sorts of funny things that the rock festivals do. That's not what we're at all.

CN: It sounds like you and Mitch had a good relationship. You took care of things and compensated for each other. Talk about your relationship?

CG: It was an excellent working relationship. On the surface you would think, who the hell are these two people working together? They seem an unlikely couple, but we both basically respected each other. It sort of worked, and we were very careful to accept the other's viewpoint in terms of criticism or whatever. We were very fond of each other and I have an enormous respect for him because I think he was the type of music expert that knew the product. He did play banjo, although he didn't normally ever perform. He knew the music industry and I had a huge amount of respect for that.

CN: What were the challenges?

CG: Because it was a centennial event, we had to find the full funds to do it, there wasn't going to be a charge, so the challenge was to raise the money. I guess the bad boy / good boy roles that we played—I had done a bit of acting, actually—together with Mitch, I was quite good at that sort of stuff. We were successful, but it was a challenge.

CN: Was there a difference in vision?

CG: No. Mitch was the visionary, and it was his idea. He knew what a folk festival would be like. For me, it was a new experience and I was coming in more as a sort of technological sort of help. I very quickly found out about what a folk festival was, and got to know the music, and loved some of it. But I wasn't the one that was contributing in an artistic way to the program. I was looking after how we were going to do it. How many stages are we going to have? How are we going to set this up?

The first challenge basically was to find somewhere to do it. We visited every single park in Winnipeg—of which there were lots—and tried to figure out what would be the best place. We didn't really find any of the parks very satisfactory. I can't remember how but Birds Hill Park had recently opened up, and we went out there. When they said, "A festival? A music festival? Of course, you must come here." That was that. Like having a big door opened, and that's why we ended up there, and continued to run it out of Birds Hill Park which is of course very beautiful and very suitable. That first year, because it was a free event, we didn't have to worry about fencing it off, that came in the second year, and that was much more of a problem.

CN: Before that first year, what was the best-case scenario and what was the worst-case scenario?

CG: Well, Mitch being a musician, and familiar with music festivals, he was concerned about the fact that some of the audience would consider this to be, well basically, a folk festival is the same thing as a rock festival. He was very concerned that it would be misinterpreted. Because the city publicized it across the country as part of Manitoba's centennial celebrations, it would draw crowds from other areas that would probably be more akin to rock festivals. He was much more worried about that than I was. Anyway, it didn't happen. That first festival came off very well.

I do have one really lasting image of Mitch at that first festival. Because it was a new experience for a lot of the audience, particularly when there was a big crowd of people, towards the back of the crowd, they would be talking and chatting and eating. As far as Mitch was concerned, that's not acceptable. You can't do that. And I said, "Mitch, you can't do anything about that. If people want to talk during a performance, you're not going to. . . ." He said, "You wait and see!" He grabbed a baseball bat and started at the back of the audience and walked straight through the middle saying, "Shut up. You listen to the music, alright. You don't talk, alright." People accepted that. I thought he was going to have a riot on his hands, but then Mitch was the type of guy that could get away with that type of behaviour.

PLANNING FOR THE FIRST WINNIPEG FOLK FESTIVAL

CN: Bring me in to those first planning stages.

CG: The key plan was obviously the programming of what artists were going to come. The Festival was held in mid-August, I think the weather was great. We had a really nice lineup of artists. But then, how many stages are we going to have? Are we going to have workshops? Those were the sort of more technical decisions that had to be made. For that first festival we had one Main Stage and one small stage. It's changed quite a bit, obviously, because the festival has been very successful over the years and has grown hugely since. That first year we had good crowds, better-than-expected, particularly coming out to Birds Hill Park. Birds Hill being whatever it is, five miles out of, out of the city, but that didn't seem to bother people. I think for a lot of people, they were hitchhiking because there was a lot of young people who wanted to come. They didn't necessarily have cars, but that was okay. That didn't stop them from coming.

CN: Can you give me a picture of what the Festival was like on that first day? Was it a fly-by-the-seat-of-your-pants type thing? Was there a relief? This was going to work?

CG: Well, I think we were all concerned about the public's lack of distinction between a rock festival and a folk festival. I think that was our concern because we didn't quite know how the audience were going to respond. It was fine, there was no problem, but certainly at the time it was a concern. The other thing was, it's completely open because there was no charge so anyone who was already in the park could just wander in.

There was no control and that was not as comfortable because you were initiating a music festival, yet there was no way of controlling who was going to come and what they were going to do. I was only there really for the first two years because then I moved away from Winnipeg to the West Coast. In the second year that was a bigger problem, because the first one was so successful, we decided that, okay, we'll do this again. But then of course we didn't have government support because it was no longer a centennial event, so we had to raise the money by charging. That meant we had to fence effectively a portion of Birds Hill Park, that was a problem. We had to have fencing that went through a wood and how are you going to control this? People are going to be jumping the fence, which of course they did. So, we had a small contingent patrolling the fence. It was important that we got that paid response from everyone who was attending. It did well because the first festival had really been so successful. Getting an audience was not a problem.

ADMINISTRATION AND VOLUNTEERS

CN: Was there a vision in terms of how the staff or volunteers would interact with the musicians? What kind of atmosphere was built behind the crowd?

CG: We had a lot of volunteers, obviously. As anyone who is running that type of an event, you make damn certain that you treat your volunteers well, which we did. We supplied food on-site for the artists, and for the staff, and for the volunteers. That was always very important. There was a really nice cooperative feel and most of the volunteers, of course, were folkies. They loved the music, that's why they did it, and we encouraged that very much.

The other thing that I think is interesting about the Winnipeg Folk Festival—although the Toronto festival preceded the Winnipeg festival—it was more confined in its musical agenda. [The Toronto festival] had developed a strong audience and because they operated on one of the Toronto islands, it was more expensive and so it appealed more to a pocket that could afford the prices that they gave. We were in a different situation. Birds Hill never charged us for the use of their park.

My job was the administrator, if you like. That was sort of my role—negotiating fees and services that we would offer and developing a body of volunteers that would successfully run it. I currently run a big jazz festival here now with another partner who is a well-recognized jazz guitarist and we've been doing this since we did our first festival in Bristol in 2013.[2] So we're coming up next March to our eighth festival in the city and it's again been very successful.

CN: I assume that the Winnipeg Folk Festival was your first go at organizing a festival. How do those early experiences come into your work now with the Bristol Jazz Festival?

CG: I've done some other music festivals as well on the West Coast. I was running a theatre company. Because of the success of the Winnipeg Folk Festival, the next year Mitch and I were invited to Vancouver because they wanted to start one. Basically, we set it up for them and I arranged for the site to be in Stanley Park. Mitch helped with their staff in terms of developing a program. That was a nice opportunity for us to take our experience and set it up elsewhere.

After being with the Festival for two years, I moved to the West Coast, but Mitch would always invite me back to look at the site problems. And I think it was more to do with the fact of Mitch, who he was. He felt that he wanted to include me. So, I kept flying back for a week or two and helped set up the final arrangements in Birds Hill and do whatever else I could do to help.

CN: You mentioned you often were the one negotiating with the musicians. Were there any fish that got away?

CG: Well, you wouldn't get the really international huge names, just because of their agents. An agent is obviously most interested in his client making the most money, both through selling his product, and also in performing it. A festival is really not the right venue for an international star because he or she is just one of many. You have to go after people who are sympathetic to a music festival's situation. And they don't have an agent behind them who is going, "What do you mean, offering me that amount money? You can double that and I might think about it."

CN: How did that play out in terms of what musicians a festival would go after?

CG: Mitch had a stronger background, he knew the industry in terms of its music, who the artists were and therefore he was able to choose people that he felt we would be able to persuade, rather than going after a musician and knowing damn well that his agent wouldn't allow it, there was no point. It's the same thing with this jazz festival, my partner does the programming, he plays with a lot of well-known artists both national and international, so he knows them and they know him, and that makes it much easier.

CN: In those first two years, how did you prepare for things like rain and weather?

CG: Yeah, you can say that again. I'll give you an example of a situation which we just went through in 2018 with the Jazz Festival that I do here in Bristol. Usually towards the end of March, the festival dates you set months ahead. You have to book your program, but also to sell the tickets, and we were obviously doing that in Winnipeg. The Jazz Festival that I did in 2018, the weekend coincided with a snow and ice weekend. We are talking late March here in Bristol, very unusual. It decimated the response. There was a lot of ice on the streets, driving was difficult, and it nearly put us out of business. It's an indoor festival, a little different with the Folk Festival, an outdoor festival. If it rains, it rains and people just sit under their umbrellas, or hoods, or whatever, and listen to the music. Nothing you can do about it. You just hope that the weather is not going to impact too greatly. Particularly walk-ups. I assume it's like most music festivals, if the conditions are right, the walk-up trade is good. Obviously

FIGURE 33. AUDIENCE AT WINNIPEG FOLK FESTIVAL, 1979. PHOTOGRAPH BY DAVID LANDY. ARCHIVES OF MANITOBA, WINNIPEG FOLK FESTIVAL 1979 NEGATIVES, P5266/9, 79/307.

FIGURE 34. MITCH PODOLAK AND COLIN GORRIE, 1975. COURTESY OF WINNIPEG FILM GROUP.

if you have a rainy weekend then your walk-up trade is not going to be that good. Nothing you can do about it.

CN: I assume there was a togetherness with the volunteers, especially for the first years; it's like being a part of something?

CG: Yeah, Mitch and I, after that first Festival, decided to open a store.[3] Partly to keep that feeling. The connection that you had made with the general public but also particularly with the volunteers because yes, that's a camaraderie and a friendship that stays. Because you are sharing something with people you might know, or not know. But you're sharing something that is very meaningful and brings you together in a very close way.

CN: Are you surprised that the Folk Fest has continued as long as it has?

CG: No, I don't think I'm surprised. I'm more surprised because there are now other folk festivals across the country, and we generated that. I know they didn't come from Toronto's festival; they basically came from ours, starting with the Vancouver Folk Festival.

I gather that the Festival now is pretty big. One of the reasons that it has continued—it's not just because of a supportive audience—but the advantage of Birds Hill Park is that people started coming to the festival in their campers and trailers. Because Birds Hill Park is huge and they were encouraging that type of trade—people coming to the park in effect for a holiday. I know that the financial strength of the Winnipeg Folk Festival has switched to an event encouraging that sort of camper-type of tourist trade. That's a huge support factor in the continuation of the Festival. More power to them.

CN: What is the lasting legacy for a guy like Mitch?

CG: Oh well, establishing folk festivals in Canada. No question. I think that it was his idea and I helped to make it successful. When I first met Mitch, I used to bug him about it because he would bug me about being a bloody English aristocrat. In those days my English accent was much stronger than it is now, having lived in Canada for most of my life, but I remember he would bug me and I would bug him about his hippie beard.

CN: What is the importance of the city of Winnipeg in all of that you've mentioned? There is this Toronto versus the rest of Canada thing, but did it play a part?

CG: Yeah, a very unlikely part in a sense. I suppose it's partly the fact that it was unlikely. This thing wouldn't have happened if it wasn't a 1974 centennial. Yeah, it was an unlikely place, but it just so happened that Mitch had moved and was successful in his love and knowledge of folk music and doing programs for the CBC in Winnipeg. I happened to be there because I had very recently graduated from the school of architecture, which was one of the top schools in Canada at the time. We both happened to be there.

Mitch came up with the idea, well, let's have a folk festival. In a sense, under the circumstances, I guess part of his success is also the fact that it is Winnipeg. I think if you read one of the journalists' reports about the start of the Festival and his comments: "Why Winnipeg, when it's about 500 miles from the nearest major city? What on earth is this thing?" You know? I would ask the same question, but it was a set of circumstances that just happened and Winnipeg happened to be the place where it came about.

Ava KOBRINSKY PODOLAK

Ava Kobrinsky Podolak grew up in Winnipeg, attended University of Manitoba and later moved to Toronto for further schooling. While in Toronto she met Mitch Podolak and the two returned to Winnipeg to start a life together. Ava was a key collaborator and co-founder of many of the projects that Mitch began—initially the Winnipeg Folk Festival, and also the West End Cultural Centre, and Home Routes / Chemin Chez Nous. Her involvement on the Board and as administrator of these organizations are key reasons they were able to flourish. She has also played a pivotal role in the operations of Prairie Theatre Exchange, Winnipeg Jewish Theatre, and Winnipeg Contemporary Dancers. She has had a long and distinguished career contributing to Canadian culture.

FIGURE 35. MITCH PODOLAK AND AVA KOBRINSKY, 1977. PHOTOGRAPH COURTESY OF AVA KOBRINSKY.

AVA KOBRINSKY PODOLAK

28 JULY 2021, WINNIPEG

KEVIN NIKKEL: Where are you from and how did you eventually get connected with Mitch Podolak?

AVA KOBRINSKY PODOLAK: My name's Ava Kobrinsky Podolak. I'm from Winnipeg, I've lived here my whole life, except for about three years when I was going to school and working in Toronto, which is where I met Mitch. I studied at University of Manitoba and United College. I was fortunate to be able to study theatre, Shakespeare, poetry, and all of those things. I ended up doing arts administration, bookkeeping, and grant writing. I was fortunate.

I met Podolak when I was working for, believe it or not, the Ontario Department of Transport as a temporary job before I got teaching. I met a fellow who was involved with the Young Socialists and the League for Socialist Action. I was kind of thrilled to hear about them because he told me that they wanted to change the world, and I wanted to do that also. There were things that could be done to make things better for folks. His name was Frank, and poor Frank, he took me to a party at the League for Socialist Action at their headquarters on Queen Street and I ended up with Podolak. And that was a good thing. The rest is history, fifty years later.

THE START OF THE WINNIPEG FOLK FESTIVAL

KN: How long after you met Mitch did you decide to come to Winnipeg?

AKP: I had a job teaching in Ontario. Mitch loved Winnipeg and we decided to get married, so we came to Winnipeg and got married in July. He was working for CBC doing radio documentaries, working with Peter Gzowski and the folks in Winnipeg doing national radio with the show *Touch the Earth*. Then we were watching our little black-and-white TV and an ad came on about the Winnipeg centennial, which was 1974. Mitch looked at me and he said, "We should make a folk festival." I knew what a folk festival was, but I looked at him anyway and I said, "Well yeah, what's a folk festival?" I'd been to outdoor festivals in Toronto, and we watched *Woodstock* and *Monterey Pop*.

When he said we could do a folk festival, I thought okay great. I said to him, "Well, hire Sylvia Tyson." And he did. Every now and then I'd make a little bit of artistic input. Not too much, but a little. And that's what happened. The way that it got funded really was with the support of Paul Mills and CBC behind him. He had the wherewithal to say that somebody else thinks this is a good idea. In fact, I understand that it was the only project that came forward with other funding. And that was a good lesson to learn in terms of future grant applications. And we got to be good at that.

There was a lot of trepidation in terms of funders, shall I say the word Altamont, people were afraid of that festival with the Rolling Stones and there'd been violence and whatnot. But somehow Podolak, with the CBC behind him, convinced folks that it would be a good thing to do. Then of course the folks at Birds Hill Park and the park police and everybody, they were so supportive and so happy. I heard later that Winnipeg Folk Festival actually helped to put Birds Hill Park on the map and bring people's attention to it. It was a brand-new park in those days.

I have a funny story I can tell you. So, after the Centennial Committee approved the money that was to come from the city and the province, Mitch went to meet with the fellow from the city—I'm really sorry I don't remember these folks' names. We made the Festival happen, but it was kind of dicey at first, and this is the reason why. Mitch could see the cheque on the desk, but the fellow said, "We'll release the cheque once the province releases their cheque." Both departments had agreed they were going to fund it. So, Mitch went to meet with the person at the province who had graciously found a way to support the Festival, but he said to Mitch, "We'll release the cheque after you get the cheque from the city." So, Mitch thought, okay fine. He left and went to meet with the person at the city—another reason why we have the Festival, with their support. They said the same thing, "We can't release the cheque until the province releases their cheque." I can just imagine Mitch scratching his head. He said, "Okay, fine."

As he is walking out the door, he sees on the table a stack of City of Winnipeg letterhead. He snatched the paper and wrote himself a letter. He takes a copy of the letter to the province and gets another letter from the province and the cheque. Takes it to the city and the city guy gives him the cheque. That's what happened.

KN: That's a great story.

AKP: Isn't that fantastic? Talk about chutzpah.

KN: It just seems like the only way, or they could have met in the middle of a bridge somewhere, halfway.

AKP: Or something. Maybe they left the letterhead there on purpose.

JOHN PRENTICE: It's all beyond the statute of limitations now.

AKP: Yeah, what are they going to do? Cancel the Festival?

KN: Any memories of the first festival? How was Mitch on that first night?

AKP: This is what happened at the very, very first Folk Festival. Mitch and I were standing around there at seven or eight o'clock and nobody was there. And Mitch is looking at me, "I've got all these people involved and what the hell are we going to do now?" I just said, "Look Mitch, people don't know from folk festivals yet. They came home from work. It's a hot Friday night. They're going to have dinner. They'll take it easy for a minute. They'll drive out here. They'll be here." I made it all up. Well, it came true. They came in droves. They packed out the place and they bought tickets next year. So here we are.

At the very first Folk Festival my mother came out there with my father. I was totally impressed that they showed up there. But she was so impressed she looked around and saw all these thousands of people. She thought I did okay after all. He played the banjo, he worked for CBC. What can I say? They were happy.

OVERCOMING OBSTACLES

KN: I'm curious about the transition from the first Folk Festival to the second. Any lessons learned? Or was there a chance it might not happen again?

FIGURE 36. MITCH PODOLAK AND AVA KOBRINSKY, 2017. PHOTOGRAPH COURTESY OF AVA KOBRINSKY.

AKP: Well, the first festival had a deficit, $1,200. Oh my. That worried Mitch. We were naïve about those things. Our legal advisor Nate Nurgitz encouraged Mitch to go forward and see that it is nothing relative to the whole budget of the thing. So, we went ahead. The other curious thing after the first Folk Festival, the article from the *Tribune* said, "Yeah, this was a great event but it'll never become an annual event."[4] So that was one reason probably why Mitch said, "Never mind, we're going to go forward." And of course, we did. History speaks for itself in that regard.

But another person who really made the thing happen is my friend Karen Dana. She's one of the people instrumental to the place. She started the apprenticeship program to keep young people as volunteers. She told me that she came to the first Folk Festival because Bruce Cockburn was going to be there. I also heard through the grapevine that Bruce felt very supported in his career by his gigs at the Folk Festival the first couple years. So that's nice. He came in for one of the anniversaries and the fundraisers and everybody was impressed to see him.

Here is another story. We took donations after the first year, with baskets all around, because Peter Gzowski had said, "This is a great event. This can be a world event. Make sure it happens." Then people started waving money. I guess they planned on it ahead of time so they had baskets. We were at Colin and Liz Gorrie's house with me and Mitch separating out quarters and dimes and pennies and rolling them up. Oh my God. We also did bottle drives because there were months and years where the staff paycheques weren't regular. Luckily, I had a job with the federal government so that worked out okay, we could still keep going.

The other thing for 1975, the second year, it was the first year the people had actually paid to get in and that was one of the struggles that Podolak and everybody faced. There were quite a few fence jumpers. There's a woman, Lorna Hiebert, who is still a true friend of the Folk Festival, and she just shamed people. She would go patrol up and down the fence, Mitch told me this. She'd put her hands out like this and say, "Shame on you! You better pay for this." And she'd take money from them. So, people got the idea. She is one of the instrumental people getting the Festival going in those days.

WHAT'S BEHIND THE WINNIPEG FOLK FESTIVAL

KN: I'm interested in this idea that everyone got paid the same. Was there a philosophy behind it?

AKP: The reason behind it was the idea to share equally. If you had a band of four people, it would be four hundred dollars per person plus their expenses, plus all their food. That was the whole idea, it was goodwill for everybody. That was our philosophy of sharing.

KN: It seems that this is really a core value of Mitch, and the Festival?

AKP: I would say so, yeah.

KN: What were other ways that we could see goodwill and sharing present at the Festival?

AKP: Just the whole idea of the way performers and artists and volunteers and everybody involved were supposed to be treated. And the idea of the volunteers was to make the artist as happy as possible. And if you have happy artists, they will do a terrific show. Then the audience is happy and then things are going back-and-forth and they'll come next year. The artists tell their friends and want to come to the Folk Festival and play. So, it's just a whole circular thing.

The first year we had a professional company feed everybody and it was really good but it wasn't homey. Mitch and Harry Paine had a falling out after the first festival. I just went to him and said, "You're crazy. You got a terrific friend here who can make everybody so happy, just do it." He listened to me that time, too. So that was good. Harry was happy to show up and he was there for years and years and years. He had to do different kinds of food for everybody and he did.

Then the other thing about the volunteers, Podolak would have crew meetings the week before the Folk Festival. He gathered all the stage crew, or all the kitchen crew, all of this or that. Finally, he realized he needed a bunch of volunteers, thousands of people to make this mini city out at Birds Hill Park work. He told every crew that they were the most important crew. He said, "Without you we don't have this, and that." It's absolutely true, because if we didn't need that crew, we wouldn't have it. It all worked together as a major team. He's a charismatic guy and was able to gather a lot of people to make his vision come true. He actually used to say, "First you tell the lie, and then you have to make it happen." And reports tell the truth.

KN: That's a great line. I might borrow that.

AKP: I found a bunch of programs, just today. The first two programs, they don't even mention my name! [Laughs] That's where the pride part comes in, but it was me, Colin Gorrie, and Mitch Podolak who were the founding Board of Directors.

KN: Tell me more about your role?

AKP: In the lead up, it was just being there, I guess. And I didn't cast any doubt on the fact that it would be a perfectly wonderful thing to do. My job with the federal government was a good thing because it was steady and it covered things for family illness when Leonard got pneumonia and Mitch could keep on working and doing this thing. It made it possible for me to do all this other Folk Festival work.

They had a tiny little office on Hugo. The person who was selling ads for the program book went away and I just picked it up and then I sold ads for that program book for quite a few years. There was a little contracts table from the year before, I phoned up the CBC and I said, "We're going to print next week, can I come and pick up your ad copy?" And they said, "Sure." I went to the ones first who I knew were going to work. And then from there the Art Gallery came to me, and MTC, and the Royal Winnipeg Ballet. I had a whole business.

Then later on I was just on the board. I forgot I managed a stage every festival. I was really fortunate because Podolak always organized that Jimi Kinsman, somebody really technically good, would be there on my stage because I didn't have a clue. I could get people on and off the stage, but don't make me touch any technical stuff. Then I became coordinator of the whole stage crew. I gathered all the coordinators. That was a lot of fun, gathering everybody and getting to talk to everybody. I quit doing that when we moved away to BC.

KN: You were talking about the stages you were part of, I wonder if you have any fond memories about the Festival site? Especially the earliest years?

AKP: I remember the second year quite a lot, I was pregnant that year. In fact, I had Leonard I think ten days or so after the Festival. I was so grateful it didn't happen at the same time because I didn't want to do it by myself. I got a lot of attention, I must say. Then the next year I remember watching from the side of the stage and little Leonard was there on the ground. Then whenever everyone would stand up, "Be careful of my baby!" Everybody had their babies lying around on the ground.

KN: That makes me think, what is happening in the 1970s amongst the crowd? What are some things you remember about attitudes of the people at the time?

AKP: A lot of people found out about folk music because of coming together to be at the event. I think those people just like to be together. What people are wanting to do, and what they were actually doing is . . . I know that a lot of people were conceived at the folk festivals. I also know that people got married at the Folk Festival. Some of the musicians became the bands for the weddings. Mitch was really proud of both of those things.

KN: Any other fond memories of the Festival?

AKP: It was so fun first arriving at the site when it was starting and to do the tour around. I had a couple friends that I always did that with. One was Karen Dana and one was Marie Grehan, who is gone now. Everybody did that. Mitch had a few guys that he used to go around with every year. He'd checked it out already, but he liked to show folks around. David Asper and Marv Terhoch were regulars for that, and whoever else was around. He was in a golf cart and Mark Peikoff was honoured to drive him around. So that was good. A terrific volunteer, there.

I just love to see all the people. I miss all those people. That's what it is. I remember the year I was pregnant, walking around before the Festival. I think Barb McKell was there. We used to wear tents in those days. I remembering wearing this big flowing outfit and we were walking around and suddenly I couldn't walk anymore. I just got too tired and sat down at a picnic table where the kids' area used to be. Mitch brought the car. You don't drive cars on the site.

THE LEGACY OF MITCH PODOLAK

KN: I'm interested that your son is born the year after the Festival and he is growing up basically at the same pace as the festival.

AKP: That's exactly right. He's a year younger than the Folk Festival.

KN: In a sense the Folk Festival is maturing and your son is too. Did you see a parallel with the growth, and your son growing up?

AKP: Not really. I just love seeing my son wanting to do more and more and more and more stuff, which reminds me of his father. He's Co-Artistic Director at Home Routes / Chemin Chez Nous. He's absolutely continuing the legacy of Mitch. He learned the work ethic. We're still going and we still have staff, I'm really proud of his ingenuity and what he's learned from his father. What is inherited I think is that charisma and the ability to build a team to make stuff happen because you can't make a Folk Festival with 100 artists and 35,000 people and 1,600 volunteers by yourself. Maybe you can think it, but he knew it. It is really a true people kind of thing. I think that brings people together and why they want to volunteer. I think it is the same thing with all the arts organizations. Without volunteers, they don't happen.

KN: I'm wondering about the first couple years at the Festival, you're seeing Mitch as the public face of the Festival. But was there a quieter Mitch that people didn't get to see?

AKP: I don't think so. He said what he thought all the time. I guess he found a way. He was on good behavior in public, I'd say. A lot of times he stood up for whatever. People got annoyed from that, but oh well.

KN: Any examples of where he had to push back and stand his ground?

AKP: No. I just think he just kept persevering. People would say no to him and he would just keep on going. One of the reasons we have the Folk Festival among other things is he didn't think he couldn't do it; he knew he could.

KN: Did the vision of what the Folk Festival meant evolve or grow over time?

AKP: I guess it was always, we're going to be big. Then in 1986 from the point of view Mitch, he felt like he couldn't grow anymore doing that. And he just moved on and then all of a sudden, we were doing all sorts of other things.

JP: The West End.[5]

AKP: Right. So, he said to me, "you're going to work harder than you've ever worked in your life." We talked to Judy Wasylycia-Leis[6] and she's the woman behind the West End Cultural Centre. She just thought that was the greatest idea. So that's good that we did that.

Then we went to BC again and then we came back again and did The World Next Door.[7] We don't want to get into that. I forget when that was. I don't know how he did that. Then Dan Frechette came along and we started promoting Dan Frechette. Then we learned that it's a lot easier to start your own volunteer gigs than to get other professional profit-making promoters to hire your acts [through Home Routes]. We got the idea from Paul Robeson and Pete Seeger who were blacklisted during McCarthyism. Instead of doing one-off house concerts he got a bunch of volunteers starting with the help of the CBC and lo and behold we had forty-eight volunteers across the country in four different regions. Volunteers in twelve communities, each hosting concerts. We're doing the same thing that the Folk Festival is meant to do, which is lift up folk musicians, bring them to audiences, and get them some money. And it's a lot more than $400 these days, so that's a good thing. So, the legacy of Podolak is still going on.

THE WINNIPEG FOLK FESTIVAL 77
OUR MASTER CHEF HARRY PAINE

Harry
PAINE

Harry Paine (born Henry Joseph Paine) moved from England to Canada in his twenties where he worked as a plumber, an activist, and community organizer in Toronto. He gained experience cooking for the anti-war movement—it was in these circles that he met Mitch Podolak. When Mitch set out to start the Winnipeg Folk Festival, Harry was invited to organize a backstage kitchen to feed musicians and volunteers. He was a key member of the Folk Festival kitchen for forty years. The success of Winnipeg led Harry to help Mitch start up festivals in Edmonton, Vancouver, and Owen Sound. Harry's collaboration with Mitch eventually meant a move to Winnipeg, where he helped found the West End Cultural Centre. In 1998, he was awarded the Winnipeg Folk Festival's Glass Banjo award for outstanding contributions to the Festival.

FIGURE 37. HARRY PAINE AT THE WINNIPEG FOLK FESTIVAL, 1977. PHOTOGRAPH BY GERRY KOPELOW. COURTESY OF WINNIPEG FOLK FESTIVAL.

HARRY PAINE

2013, WINNIPEG

INTERVIEW RECORDED DURING THE PRODUCTION OF THE DOCUMENTARY *COOKING THE REVOLUTION* (2013), DIRECTED BY DODIE GRAHAM MCKAY.

DODIE GRAHAM MCKAY: Fill us in on what year it was that you moved to Winnipeg?

HARRY PAINE: In 1974 Mitch Podolak called me at home. He was organizing a folk festival in Winnipeg and asked me if I was interested in getting involved. Mitch and I had been friends since he was fourteen years old. We had got together for anti-war work. The personal aspects of that are not that important, there were some problems between Mitch and I, but eventually I joined. I said, "Fine. I'll come and talk about it." So, I flew to Winnipeg—I was living in Toronto at the time—and to cut a long story short, got involved in organizing the Folk Festival.

I moved to Winnipeg in 1987 because Mitch and I had always had this dream of having a folk festival that would be ongoing, and that wouldn't be inhibited by snow and rain and sleet and so on. And we would've liked to have some kind of a museum, almost of folk music. A place where people could come and learn to play instruments, where working people with very little money could come and enjoy good music and develop their own kind of music. We'd always had that dream. We talked about it on and off over the years. Then in 1987 it became a reality when I moved here and we opened the West End Cultural Centre.

I think that at that particular time, in 1987, there wasn't very much going on, politically. It was during one of those periods of a few years when the working class were not in a state of rebellion. So, our dream, I guess, when we opened the West End Cultural Centre was, this will be a place where we could make the revolution. We would make the revolution through music. We would be able to concentrate on musicians who expressed the ability of the working class to organize itself and do its own thing.

FIGURE 38. HARRY PAINE COOKING AT WINNIPEG FOLK FEST, N.D. PHOTOGRAPH BY MARSHA WINEMAN.

The important thing about Marxism is that really what it does is, it imbues the working class with the idea that they themselves can make their own revolution. Marxism enables the working class. It arms them with the ability to be able to do things for themselves. I think that that's what is happening big time now.[8] It's part of the historical development of working-class consciousness. Communities are organizing around issues that affect them strongly, simply because they can't rely on capitalism or governments to do it for them anymore. I think that when we opened the West End Cultural Centre, we saw music as being part of that process. We saw music as expressing that part which has the most integrity. It expresses love, hate, and the feelings that people feel as a result of their life's experiences. The hardships that they suffer are expressed in that music. That's what folk music is all about and it's what a lot of classical music originally was about, too. I think that it's the model of troubadours who used to go around the country singing minstrels. Who would sing about great battles that'd taken place, or the hardships of people in this part of the world, or that part of the world? They were the original news broadcasts and newspapers. So those singing minstrels, we saw on the stage of the West End Cultural Centre.

THE FIRST WINNIPEG FOLK FESTIVAL

DGM: Can you talk about what you did with the Folk Festival?

HP: I guess it was 1974. When Mitch decided to make the Folk Festival an ongoing thing, as a result of the success of the centennial year. Mitch decided that. He conned a number of organizations into putting up the money for it. I think Mitch did a wonderful thing for this part of Canada. He called upon the people who he had had experience with in his political and his musical lifetime, who he knew had certain skills. He got those people together and he brought people from Vancouver, and me from Toronto, and others together in order to organize the first Folk Festival. What he wanted from me was my experience as a hospitality person to organize a backstage kitchen. We had no idea how to do that, except that I had experience cooking for the anti-war movement. Cooking for the masses, cooking for hundreds of people. I had that kind of experience.

At the first Folk Festival we had a big tent backstage and it was the whole hospitality area. In one corner of the tent, we had set up this kind of table and counter and refrigerator. Most of the stuff we cooked off site and we served mostly, I remember, roast beef, some salad, and sandwiches. I was not happy with that. I felt that we could do much better.

We got through that year okay, and then I sat down with Mitch and the people and said what I would really like to do is, I would like to set up a backstage kitchen and cook real food for the performers and treat them really well. We had this notion that if you treated the performers really well, they would play their hearts out for you. They would be happy and that would reflect itself in their performances. So, the next year I came to Winnipeg early. I was living in Toronto, and I came here in March, and we started to plan. Luckily, I had a group of people, mostly women actually, who had some experience in organizing. They couldn't cook. Hardly any of them could cook. [Laughs] It was really funny, actually. But we found used kitchen equipment and we put together a couple of old stoves which we then changed so they could use propane. We had some kind of flat barbecues and we really fudged it. But that next year we put together food that was really quite acceptable, and we served breakfast and lunch and dinner.

The Festival then was just Friday night, Saturday, and Sunday. And we partied a lot too. I think that we set a kind of standard. Then it gradually grew. We went to Edmonton for instance and we got a trailer. The Festival bought a trailer which had a couple stoves in it that was used up north for logging. We brought that down and set it up. It was just gradually year by year we added new things.

We put on meals which were outrageous, absolutely outrageous. We had huge big slabs of beef, which we did on the rotisseries. I remember one year we had whole shoulders of lamb, and we put them on these barbecues and just let them cook slowly. I can't remember what year that was but it would be 1977 or 1978, something like that. The Festival then was enclosed by these stake fences. The fence used to come right down behind the kitchen area. I looked around and there were what I thought were dogs, but they were actually wolves who were on the other side of the fence, and they were pacing up and down with their noses in the air because they could smell this cooking lamb. So, we had to call the security in and get them to chase them off. At that time, we were using off-duty RCMP and police officers for security and so they were able to chase the wolves off.

We began to develop a reputation for having the best food in the whole festival circuit throughout North America. We set a standard for food and the other festivals had to follow. Then I guess in 1981, Mitch and myself and another small crew went and set up the Edmonton Folk Festival and the Vancouver Folk Festival. We helped to pull together the Owen Sound Folk Festival. We developed a style of feeding performers which I think other festivals had to follow pretty well. If you go to Vancouver even today, I look at the menu and I think to myself, this looks very familiar.

Probably Edmonton is one of the most sophisticated, they really got it down. Probably because they have really good community involvement. The whole business community and everything else comes together to produce that festival and get behind it. We've always had a little bit of trouble here in Winnipeg. It tends to cost a lot because we have to pay for all the stuff that in Edmonton and other places they are able to get for free. Some festivals they have festival gardens in which the volunteers set up gardens where they grow all the vegetables the festival uses and then they harvest them just before the festival and use them to feed the performers, which is really a great idea. For the first early years it was a struggle. But a number of the people who were around who were on the crew in those years are still on the crew.

"HARRY'S EATS" AND "LA CUISINE"

DGM: What was the crew called?

HP: For many years it was known as "Harry's Eats." Not sure whether I should tell you this story. [Laughs] We had these yellow T-shirts. I remember somebody took this photograph of four women who were on the crew, and myself. We were walking to one of the stages and they took a photograph of us from behind. Here you have four women who had "Harry's Eats" on their T-shirts and then you have me in the middle which just said "Harry." The crew was still dominated by women. A lot of the women who were involved in organizing the thing lived here in Winnipeg, and I was living in Toronto still. I would come in and I would design the menu, sometimes on the plane coming to Winnipeg, and often they wouldn't even know what they had to do until I got here. Eventually they got fed up with this and they decided they wanted to have more say in the production and what we did. Mitch was horrified. Mitch believed that the reason that our kitchen was so successful was because we had a reputation built on my name and there is a certain truth to that. We actually had performers who when asked if they would like to play at the Folk Festival, when they went to sign the contract, they would have written into the contract that I was going to be there cooking. There was a certain truth to it.

But we had developed a whole new system of designing the menu. I would come to Winnipeg, and we would sit down and I would make suggestions and the other women on the crew would say, but you can't put this in the oven at the same time as that. I suddenly realized that you could do the thing by committee and that a committee was much easier to do than for me to agonize over designing the menu by myself and making those decisions by myself. We would get a group of people together and we would make assignments. One would look after the volunteers. One would look after the buying of the food and planning. Suddenly I found the whole process so much easier. So, we decided then to change the name and we changed it from "Harry's Eats" to "La Cuisine" and it's been that way ever since. And it's very much a collective.

At the moment, I don't do any of that stuff anymore, because Danielle and Alex [Carignan Svenne] do most of it. But they're professionals. We didn't have any professionals. I was the closest thing to a professional, but I was a plumber. What the hell. [Laughs] But now Danielle and Alex are professionals and they have a staff of people who are able to help them, and we have five or six crews of people and the leaders of those crews are all people with a lot of experience. It's a real professional organization, it's certainly true of the backstage kitchen, but it's also true of the rest of the Festival, too. People who are plumbers, lawyers, doctors, or candlestick makers, are now stage managers. They come once a year to the Festival and they take on a whole new persona that makes the Festival what it is. There are some 1,200 volunteers or something like that, I think. A huge number. Whereas the first festival we fed 375 people and we thought that was huge numbers, now we feed 6,900 or something at the last [Festival].

I am still involved. I've never missed a festival. The closest I ever came was one year I broke my hip three days before the Folk Festival and I had to come to the full festival in a wheelchair. But I still came and still did my shift.

THE PHILOSOPHY BEHIND THE WINNIPEG FOLK FESTIVAL

But I guess, like a lot of other people, you count the days down to the Festival and their year revolves around the Folk Festival. And I'm not sure whether people really understand the importance. I guess one has to say what Mitch did in organizing that Folk Festival. He established a style of organizing folk festivals that he learned from a woman named [Estelle] Klein in Toronto who ran the Mariposa Folk Festival. He developed on her methodology. He made her methodology better. He developed the whole workshop structure. I remember the first workshop I ever went to at a folk festival, Joni Mitchell was the performer and we were sitting under a tree near Orillia, Ontario in this field. There was a bunch of us, maybe thirty or forty people who were still sitting around on the grass and there was a tree there, and she was leaning up against the tree and we were discussing folk music and she would sing a couple songs to illustrate what she was talking about. But they were real workshops in which we talked about folk music. People learned from the nature of folk music. That was what workshops were like. It was Mitch that developed the style of workshop that exists now.

Lenin said that trade unions are the cradle of the revolution, but in some ways the folk festival is also the cradle of a revolution, too. Even though they have a Board of Directors, which is very corporate in the way it's structured, but when it comes down to it, on the day that the Folk Festival gets rolling, on the Monday beforehand when the volunteers take over the site, the whole thing is run by volunteers who are not professionals. Well, they are professional in the way they conduct themselves and the way they do their job, but they are not people who do this 365 days a year, they just do it for that week and they do it in a way which is important because it teaches self-reliance, and it makes them feel confident in themselves. It has taught people a lot of things about themselves—philosophical, psychological—all kinds of things.

And the point of view of people who come to the Festival and think, "Hey I could do that. I would really like to learn to play that instrument." Then go on to become really famous and really important contributors to Canada's cultural heritage. I think that Winnipeg plays a unique role, in a sense, because we are sort of like the centre of Canada and in some ways maybe it's got something to do with that. The coming together of two rivers. Whatever other kind of ideas that are in our heritage, in the tradition of the people who have inhabited this area for thousands of years. We carry on that kind of tradition of the coming together. The Aboriginal populations from all over the prairies would come to the Forks and it didn't matter whether they were Blackfeet, Cree, or Iroquois, they would come in peace and they would fish and they would hunt from there and then they would move on without warring with one another. So, in a certain sense the Folk Festival kind of embodies that concept again. People come from all over the world to attend that Folk Festival. They come and they create a certain kind of atmosphere. I remember we used to talk about how if you lost your wallet in the Folk Festival for instance, don't worry about it, just go to lost and found. It will be there. And it will be intact, the money will still be in it. Whether that's still true, given the economic conditions?

It didn't matter whether you were royalty or whether you were from an inner-city area. Whether you were poor or rich, whether you were talented or not talented. It didn't matter what you were. When you came in that Folk Festival gate, everybody's equal. That's one of the reasons we started the Folk Festival and I think that tradition continues. And will continue as long as the Folk Festival's around.

DGM: Are there any performers that really stand out in your memory?

HP: Yes. There are some performers who, I find, have always stood out in my memory. I guess David Amram was one. David is still performing in New York City, where he lives. David Amram used to come to the Festival a lot in the early days. I can remember one time he was performing on the stage and there was a huge storm. The RCMP came and jumped up on the stage and said everybody should clear the area because it's dangerous. So, people just said, "No, no. We won't do that." They just shared tarps, they covered themselves and everybody sort of huddled together in the rain. Then David Amram just kept playing and that kind of thing would happen frequently. But David was a person who travelled around quite a bit all over the world and he used to have these instruments he used to wear around his neck. He had this little thong that had this tiny small flute, it was more like an ocarina. He could take it and get his fingers on it and blow in it and make a tune with it. He would always carry around with him a whole sack full of these different kinds of instruments that you could bang, blow, or ring. He would go into a workshop, or even a room at a party, and he would gather a whole bunch of people—especially kids. He would just love to work with kids. He would pass out this sack and out would fall all these instruments and he would pass them out to people in the room. He would say, "Okay, now let's write music," and he would start off, and then someone else would, and they would write a piece of music in the room using their instruments. People who never played an instrument before could pick up these little instruments and play them. It was people like him who I really admired because I thought he really embodied the ideas of folk festivals.

Peggy Seeger, of course was always my favourite. I fell in love with Peggy the first I heard her and saw her because she was a communist, a feminist. She was a working-class singer. She was, of course, the sister of Pete Seeger. I can't help but be oriented towards left-wing kinds of singers and so she was one of those people. And she wrote a song about me which is in her song book, which I considered to be a real honour.

Stan Rogers was probably the most important Folk Festival person in my life. In my opinion, he was probably the best singer-songwriter this country has ever produced, within the framework of what he does. He was not the most likable guy, but you can't be a really good performer, often, unless you're a bit of an egomaniac, and I suppose he was. He was justified because he was such an incredible talent. I worked with him not just in Winnipeg but I worked with him in Toronto. We started a couple of festivals in Toronto at one point.

Stan and myself and a few other people got together and formed a Board of Directors and we set up the Northwind Folk Festival board and we organized the Folk Festival which ran for a couple years when Mariposa decided not to have folk festivals. I remember we were totally disorganized for the first Folk Festival. I was running the site crew. Actually, I was waiting for the site crew from Winnipeg, they were going to come help us and I had no real idea how. He just came in like gangbusters and demanded that Mitch Podolak get his ass to Toronto right away. Mitch knew how to do all these things, though he was really overwhelmed and had a lot of stuff to do. Trying to do it is always very difficult. So, Stan was an important person. I think he was an important person in folk music generally, not just as a performer, but as a person who knew what he was doing, was dynamic in getting there, and got things done.

Here in Winnipeg the kitchen crew liked Stan because he was the first person who would come every Sunday afternoon when we were working our butts off to try to get the last dinner on the table and everybody was really tired and he would come and stand in the middle of the kitchen and start playing and singing to us and would make sure that everybody knew that the kitchen crew was a really important part of the Festival. That happens a lot now, but he was the first person that did that and he did it year after year after year. Nathan Rogers does it now, actually.

WHY COOK FOR PEOPLE?

DGM: All these different causes that you've been standing in the kitchen: "Harry's Eats," "Chili at the Snow Ball," "Turkeys at the NDP" suppers, why is it important to cook food for people?

HP: I can remember the first big things that I took on, I probably was involved in the sort of left-wing radical movement and I think I had cooked for small gatherings. We used to get the comrades together at Christmas time and we would cook for ten, fifteen to twenty people or so. I learned to cook from my mother and for my father when I was six or seven years old. I enjoyed cooking. I got a bunch of people together who were interested in volunteering and helping and we cooked a whole lot of food and we had enough food for everybody and people were really happy. I think that was probably one of the first times that I saw radical politics and food coming together because people who were interested in our ideas, if you feed them good first, then they are much more willing to listen. I suppose that's the basic tenet of people who have dinners and speakers. If you feed them good, they're more likely to come back again and listen to the speaker.

The clearest and most obvious example of that was the Folk Festival, actually. When we first started to cook for the Folk Festival, there weren't very many folk festivals throughout North America in 1974. I think there was the Philadelphia Folk Festival, Newport Folk Festival, some places like that. I heard these horror stories about how performers would go there and hospitality was at a minimum. They would have to find their own way from the airport to the hotel and from the hotel to the Festival grounds. When they got there, they were

FIGURE 39. HARRY PAINE TAKES A BREAK FROM THE FESTIVAL KITCHEN. PHOTOGRAPH BY MARSHA WINEMAN.

famous for their bologna sandwiches, which was what they were fed when they got there. How exaggerated that was, I don't really know. What we decided was to bring in a backstage hospitality area.

At the first Folk Festival, we didn't really make a big deal out of it, we just fed them. We had some roast turkey sandwiches, or roast beef sandwiches or something like that. We relied on their being able to eat when we got them back to the hotel. But on the last day of the Festival, I kept thinking to myself, you know these people deserve more. They spent a lot of time travelling around and they spend a lot of time away from home. What we really needed to do was give them decent meals. Besides, for me as a creative person, I just felt making sandwiches was not very creative, or not very satisfactory to me. That's what we did. We set up a backstage kitchen. I think the performers really appreciated it and my impression was that they really loved to come to Winnipeg. I think it placed Winnipeg on the map as being the place to come. I think that that's probably a sort of further indication of what the role of food can play in that particular setting.

So, I think those things are tied up in that sense. My creative skills in some ways are, that's what I do. And I guess if we are talking about what it is that you can contribute to making the world a better place to live [in], then one of the first things that comes to mind for me is to cook good food. Find a way to make that part of my thinking, of my ideas. I don't know whether that's unique or not. I didn't read anything about it in Marx's work. He talked a lot about art and the relationship between art and politics but somebody sometime should write another book about the relationship of food to politics. That might be a bestseller.

DGM: You should write that book!

HP: Well, I've got a lot of books in mind now. But that's not a bad idea. Maybe I'll put that on my bucket list.

DGM: You could have *Harry's Common Cook Book*?

HP: We did have an idea at one time of putting together a *Folk Festival Cookbook* which would have on one page a recipe for six and on the other page would be the same recipe for 600. Nowadays the Folk Festival is more in the realm of 6,000 that we cook for. I don't design the menu, or am not in charge of it anymore. We have professionals who do that. But I do like to participate. This is my fortieth anniversary this year of being in the same backstage kitchen and the same crew. I've never missed. It's something that I really enjoy. There are people still on the crew now who were on the crew the first couple years and they're still around, looking forward to coming to the Folk Festival every year. I think that's an accomplishment too.

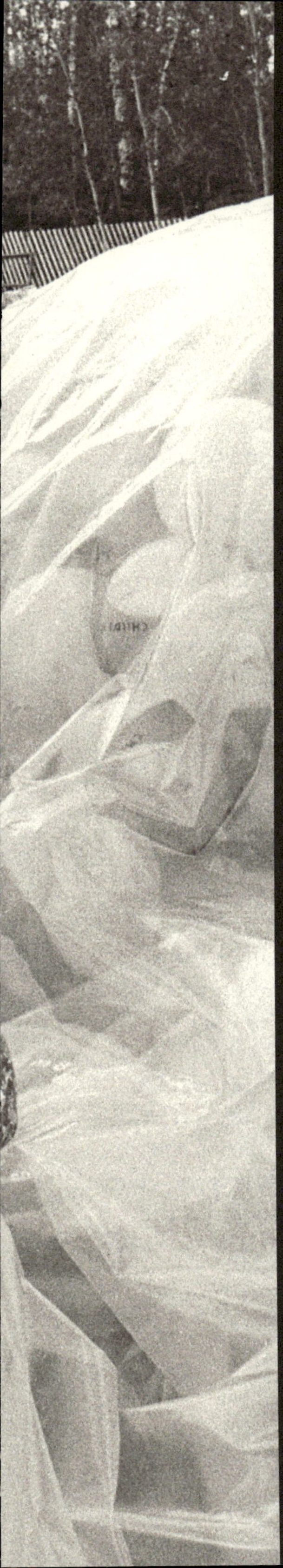

Lorna HIEBERT

Lorna Hiebert is a fabric artist based in Winnipeg. She grew up on a farm in southern Manitoba and her attraction to the arts and culture scene was expedited by her family connection to Rick and Rosie Neufeld, hosts of many musicians on their property—Mitch Podolak was one of the frequent guests. When Mitch started the Folk Festival in 1974, Lorna and Rosie helped start the Handmade Village, the arts and crafts area on the Folk Festival site. Lorna worked as the office manager of the Folk Festival from 1975 to 1979 and was a long-time volunteer—manager of the Main Stage being one of her key positions.

FIGURE 40. LORNA HIEBERT, 1977. PHOTOGRAPH BY DAVID LANDY. ARCHIVES OF MANITOBA, WINNIPEG FOLK FESTIVAL 1977 NEGATIVES, P2566/5, 77 /14. 11.

LORNA HIEBERT

9 FEBRUARY 2020, WINNIPEG

KEVIN NIKKEL: Tell me about your background. How did you get involved in the arts scene?

LORNA HIEBERT: I came from a zero background in terms of culture and arts. I was born and raised on a farm. A Mennonite community. When I was sixteen years old, my parents sold the farm and moved to Niverville. Shortly after that I met my brother's wife's cousin and we became immediate friends. Her name is Rosie Neufeld. She was married to Rick Neufeld at the time. They had this big farm, just outside of the city of Winnipeg. And Rick being the person that he was, and Rosie also being very vibrant and entertaining, they had a lot of parties at their place. It didn't take long before I was required to go and live on their farm and help manage the parties and direct traffic across a railway track over to the back thirty [yards]. All these big tour buses would come by. It was just that kind of place where there are parties all the time. Like a mini festival. One of the people that I met out there was Mitch Podolak.

It was just sort of a coincidence really. If it hadn't been for my brother marrying the cousin of Rosie, I don't know if I would've ever gotten involved. I'm generally just a shy person, especially coming from that background. I'd never met anybody outside of my cousins. This was a much more interesting way to live. So that was the beginning.

1974 was approaching and there's all this potential for getting funding for different kinds of activities. And here I am just sort of a floating around on the edges. It was Rosie and I that started the Handmade Village, it was called that at the time: a little arts and crafts area at the first Folk Festival. We'd been doing these arts and crafts ventures. That Handmade Village is still a highlight for a lot of people every year.

Lorna Hiebert

THE VISION BEHIND THE FIRST WINNIPEG FOLK FESTIVAL

KN: What would you say was the original vision for the Festival?

LH: The vision was to promote folk music, certainly. We had a lot of Manitoba artists there, which was always a high focus for Mitch. Mitch had been at Mariposa many times and he knew Estelle Klein, who was their general manager and artistic director. He had a kind of a love-hate relationship with her, but I think that she must've really respected him because she gave him a lot of information and a lot of help in getting going. He also had good friends at CBC. Walt Unger was one of them. And at Travel Manitoba, he'd been around. He did have some radio programs; I think with the CBC. He did have this group of people in the higher levels who had access to funding, who knew how to get it. Marv Terhoch was one of those very important to the Festival for many years.

Mitch was really good [at] talking to the government. He had a lot to do with that. He had a really good set of connections and was able to convince the right people that it was worth their investing. I'm talking about government sponsors. When you think of this thing and you can see it twenty years later, maybe you don't have a particular plan, but you've got vision. I think that is the word: vision.

Having all these great authentic blues and folk musicians from all over North America coming here. You'd never heard of Sam Chatmon before, but somehow Mitch got him to get on a bus to get to the airport and get on a plane for the first time in his life to come to Winnipeg and play in front of a crowd. He had no clue what he was coming into. Elizabeth Cotten was another one. That was a similar story where she had never travelled that long a distance before.

KN: What if we backed up a bit and talked about the attitudes of the folks during these years?

LH: Well, I think it was a peace and love experience. It was our version of the 1960s. The people in the audience—the artists and everybody—were in such a mellow state of mind. It was maybe after the Vietnam War where all these people were doing demonstrations and working together for a better tomorrow. I think the whole idea of what you need to do with your life was starting to change. Instead of making a path right from when you're young and people telling you, "You should do this, you should do that." People were getting open. They're opening themselves up to a community, a temporary community that weekend.

There were enough of them that were dedicated enough that this [festival] is going to stay. It's going to live. It's its own entity now. It's not just something that you did on the weekend and some people showed up. It's got its own soul. You can still see it today. People don't even know each other and then at the evening concert they'll say, "oh, we're going to get some Whales Tails, you guys want us to bring you some?" You get that kind of cooperation. It was just one of those things that attracted the kind of people that were looking for a beautiful world and finding it there. Or were at least finding that it was possible to have it.

I don't know if it was something to do with Winnipeg. I'd been to the Mariposa Folk Festival. It was beautiful music and on an island and everything was great—but I never saw that kind of interaction and people helping each other out. I'm not putting it down, but there's something about this Winnipeg group. I don't know what to call it.

KN: Were those values embedded in the atmosphere at the Festival office?

LH: When I started working for the Folk Festival, I was one of those people that was in that basement. I climbed down the ladder and there's us. There literally is a light bulb hanging from a cord. There is damp on the ground and the room wasn't any bigger than this space. You're constantly thinking: *well, at least we're safe from any kind of explosion because we're underground.* No tornado is going to get us here. It was kind of dismal, but we had a space. We had no money. When I got involved in the staff—everybody bailed and it was just Mitch down in the basement of the Folklore Centre. I thought, well I could come and help out. I'm not doing anything. I can do stuff on the weekends or evenings.

So, the role that I played was basically office manager. We had to develop the volunteer organization. I say we because it was mostly Mitch and I, Hal wasn't always there. He found the tension was high sometimes. We would have to find a way to keep on coming out of that basement and say, "yeah this is a great thing." In the meantime, I'm not getting my paycheque because we don't have any money. I was young and innocent, or a bit naïve. I was just there because somebody needed to be there. That's the way I felt about it at the time. I thought this was difficult, but I moved into my sister's basement. It was hard times, really.

OVERCOMING ADVERSITY

DAVE BARBER: What were the issues?

LH: When the only people that phone you are people that want money. They're mad. You're trying to figure out how to get that money and you're wondering, are we crazy? You think about that a lot. Where is this going, really? Am I insane to be investing my energy in this?

We always lost money for those first few years. We owed money to everybody and then you had to go and visit them. Mitch would always say, "Oh yeah, we're going to give you a cheque." Then I said, "Well, we don't have the money to back the cheque. But we gotta have a good plan here." So, we made kind of a good-guy, bad-guy routine.

All you really wanted to do was to keep this event going, that's all you wanted to do. You don't want to stiff the company because you want to give them their money. But at the same time, Coca-Cola was getting really angry. "We're going to send the courts after you." I said, "Well, you're lucky that we've got you as a sponsor because this is going to continue on for a long time. One day, you're going to be asking us if you can sell your product. There's a lot like you. Just back off a little bit and relax." I don't know where that came from, but to me you don't just walk away from somebody because they don't have any money. I know with Mitch, that was one of the first things that impressed him about me is that I could talk to a company like Coca-Cola and tell them something like that. And it's true, today companies are trying to get in and be sponsors and be involved in a visible way.

In the beginning it was hard to get sponsorship from companies that we owed money to because they were just seeing the short term. They wanted the accountant to make sure that that account was flush. So, it was hard to get the infrastructure sometimes. But we also had good support from the local sound company and they said, "We're in with this and we got the equipment, we know where you are." That was one of the great things about Winnipeg, too, is that there was a lot of interest and infrastructure like that. This company, for instance, were supporting artists—were doing big tours and so they had the equipment.[9]

KN: What is your impression looking back on those difficult times now?

LH: Well now obviously, that's the thing in my life that I'm the most proud of. I'm just so excited that I was able to be there in the beginning. I didn't see it that way in the beginning. I was happy to be there because I really found that it was worthwhile and interesting, but it was very difficult, too. But we weren't just trying to pay the bills, we were also looking ahead and saying, "this is going to keep on going." We had a lot of volunteers already. There were a lot of good people that were involved with the Festival and in those days, they couldn't always bring us money, but they'd bring us food, which is as basic as it can get.

You realize a lot of scheduling needs to be done. This is you just sitting in your office in the basement and you're thinking about all these things before the third festival is happening. People are interested. There were a lot of people that had a lot of competence and were willing to get involved and didn't want to be paid because they had their job. We were really lucky we got some really experienced, intelligent, wise people. And because they were from Winnipeg, they all got along with each other. They knew the same people. They knew who would be able to sponsor the vans for the weekend. We got a lot of help from people. They'd come in and say hi, and the next thing you know they're right there doing something really important for you. It just kept growing and growing. That was another testimony to Mitch's way of just being able to stay present with everybody. Everybody was Mitch's best friend and that's how people treated the Festival.

JOHN PRENTICE: There is also the story of security.

KN: Tell that story.

LH: Mitch liked to tell that story. It was a one-time incident. I was a very innocent person.

KN: What happened?

LH: This will show you a little bit of my personality. We were walking along from one Folk Festival stage to another in the rain. We've got all this fencing up to delineate the perimeter of the event. If you're on this side of the fence, you should have a ticket and if you're on the other side of the fence, you're going to catch poison ivy, because it's infested in there. So don't do that. Don't jump over. Don't try to get through there to jump over the fence to come in without a ticket. Number one: we need the money. The way that it happened was, we were walking along from one place to another with our plastic sheets over us and discussing that kind of incident that we're going to deal with. Through the bush stomp these guys with ponchos and stuff on and they're intending to jump over the fence. And I go, "You should be ashamed of yourselves! You shouldn't be coming over the fence! Go and buy a ticket like everybody else. This is a great event. We can't afford to have people . . . if everybody did this . . . you just don't do that!" It was a one-time incident. It was sort of a hidden side of me. I don't show that side of me very often. But I am very, very vocal when I want to be. I wasn't meaning to hurt those guys or anything. I'm just astounded that they would want to steal five bucks from us. Why don't they just go in and buy a ticket and support us? But he used that as an example of how tough I was, I guess. I really am not tough, but I'm capable of being tough.

KN: That's a wonderful story because that gets back to values—Winnipeg values that you are trying to defend. But it also shows how things had to stay organized.

LH: In the years that I was working there, I left in 1979, we didn't have the big monster acts. One of the reasons was because for many years CBC did a live broadcast on Sunday night. A live radio broadcast and so you couldn't just give the band another encore, you had to stick with the schedule. I say we because by that time I wasn't living in Winnipeg anymore, I was living in Montréal, but Mitch would fly me back to manage the Main Stage. I was lucky, I had a teammate, Peter Gzowski,[10] and he was incredible. He was really interested in all the music, and he would do his own research. It was after Peter left that they decided that they had to write up little bios for everybody because Peter was just so good about knowing these things. He was interested in it himself. He did so much for the Folk Festival even through the

rest of the year. He knew that it was a live broadcast, too, because he was working with CBC. Even after the crowd is roaring for an encore, you know that you have to get the next group on. In those years we had smaller groups and we had maybe two mics or three mics at the most. Sometimes we had to put a stool on the stage, then we would do those two-minute changeovers. We didn't have tweeners in those days. But those changeovers had to happen exactly at that time because that's what the radio broadcast required. We had a lot of funding from the CBC because of that radio broadcast.

That's another part of my involvement with the Folk Festival that I take so much comfort in, because every year for about eight years, I spent three days and nights with Peter Gzowski. Who else would you want to spend time with? The crew that we had was very small but extremely dedicated.

KN: Any other stories about people coming to the Festival?

LH: I can brag about Pete Seeger wearing a Winnipeg Folk Festival T-shirt. The reason he wore it because the T-shirts said, "Environment Crew" and back in the early years we decided we needed someone to pick up the garbage. That was important to all of us, behind the scenes. Even though you go to any festival and there's garbage all over the place, but we just didn't want to be like that. Mitch said, "We'll have a garbage crew." My idea was, you don't call it the garbage crew, call it the "Environment Crew." That was before the environment was such a catchy catchphrase. Now it's like *the* word, but in those days, they were cleaning up the environment. We're not picking up garbage, we're cleaning up the environment. And because the environment crew has a big environment crew T-shirt, Pete Seeger wore the T-shirt all over the place and did some promotion for the Folk Festival because we had an environment crew. That was my doing.

FIGURE 41. PETER GZOWSKI AS EMCEE ON MAIN STAGE, 1975. PHOTOGRAPH BY DAVID LANDY. ARCHIVES OF MANITOBA, WINNIPEG FOLK FESTIVAL 1975 NEGATIVES, P5266/1, 75-4836. 6.

THE LEGACY OF THE WINNIPEG FOLK FESTIVAL

KN: Has the Festival met the goal that Mitch was setting for it? Not just Mitch, but what you had in mind as well?

LH: Yeah. What we wanted it to be was to be alive. I never gave birth to a child, but to me the Festival is one of the things that I did. Even though I was only there for a few years in the beginning. But it was so touch-and-go all the time. All the time. Every day was a life-and-death kind of scenario. So, just the fact that it is surviving is amazing. That was the plan, but plans don't always work.

You had a certain demographic of people that would come every year. More or less the same people. These people were having kids and were bringing their kids and the kids were having fun. And now those kids are our volunteers, and they're bringing their kids. We dreamt about that kind of thing in the beginning, that it would be that kind of an event. Mitch knew that it could be like that because Toronto had that kind of longevity, the Mariposa Folk Festival, they lasted for years and years and years. But it didn't have nearly the scope that this event does. It didn't have nearly the challenges we had. We were out in the middle of the park, and we had mosquitoes and rain.

Just the improvements to the infrastructure off the ground was a dream in those days because we had so much rain in the beginning and everything was just muddy. In the mud up to your knees, in those days, and now you can get a pouring rain fall one night and the next day because of all the swales that have been built and all the roads and all the trees that have been brought in—the infrastructure is so amazing. Now all the running water all over the place, and electricity. You can charge your cell phone. You get Internet out there. I mean those are things that you didn't think about in those early years. You were thinking, *how are we going to keep this thing going financially from one year to the next?*

You'd just think, wow, *it's happening. It's incredible.* And now I don't know why that event would ever stop. I don't think I ever imagined a festival like what is there today. But I think that this Festival is alive and it's its own entity. It's not something that you made, it is something that is. You can count on it.

FIGURE 42. WORKSHOP STAGE WITH (FROM RIGHT) DAVID AMRAM, LEON REDBONE, MICHAEL COONEY, AND JOHN ALLAN CAMERON, 1975. PHOTOGRAPH BY DAVID LANDY. COURTESY OF WINNIPEG FOLK FESTIVAL.

PART TWO

SITTIN' ON STAGE A SINGIN': Performers from the Early Workshops

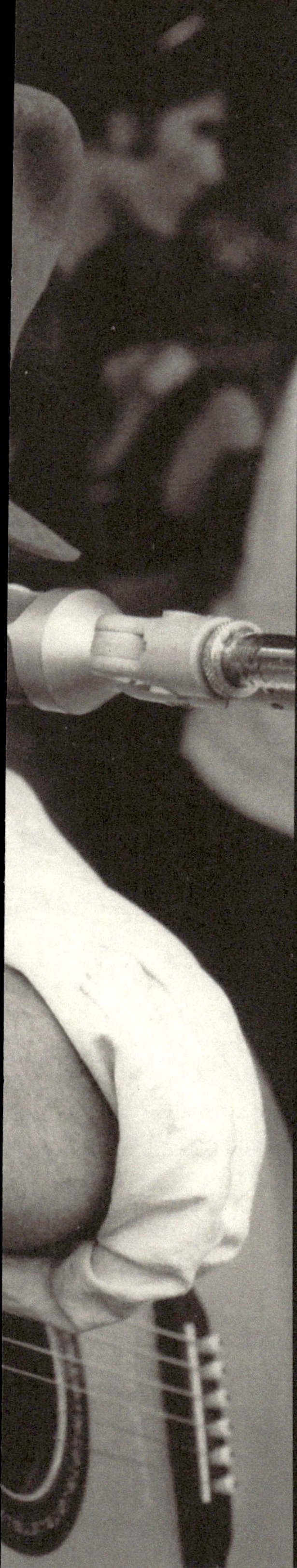

Bruce COCKBURN

Bruce Cockburn has enjoyed a phenomenal musical career that has seen him embrace folk, jazz, rock, and worldbeat styles, while travelling to such far-flung places as Guatemala, Mali, Mozambique, and Nepal. His guitar playing, both acoustic and electric, has placed him in the company of the world's top instrumentalists. He headlined the first Winnipeg Folk Festival and returned to play a total of seven times. He remains deeply respected for his activism on issues from Indigenous rights and land mines to the environment and Third World debt. For his many achievements, the Ottawa-born artist has been honoured with thirteen Juno Awards, an induction into both the Canadian Music Hall of Fame and the Canadian Songwriters Hall of Fame, as well as the Governor General's Performing Arts Award, and has been made an Officer of the Order of Canada.

FIGURE 43. BRUCE COCKBURN. PHOTOGRAPH BY DAVID LANDY. COURTESY OF DAVE BARBER.

BRUCE COCKBURN

2017, SAN FRANCISCO, CALIFORNIA

[FROM A PHONE INTERVIEW BY JOHN PRENTICE FOR THE UMFM RADIO SHOW *PLANET MAINSTAGE*.]

JOHN PRENTICE: An opening sentence on his website says, "One of Canada's finest artists, Bruce Cockburn has enjoyed an illustrious career shaped by politics, spirituality and musical diversity." We in Winnipeg are lucky to have him coming back for the forty-fourth Winnipeg Folk Festival this year, and right now we have him online from his home near San Francisco. Hello, Bruce. How are you?

BRUCE COCKBURN: I'm doing alright. Thank you.

JP: It looks like you're about to embark on another extensive tour and the launch of a new album in the fall?

BC: Yeah. I'm actually quite impatient about that. I wish we didn't have to wait that long to get it out, but that's just how the machinery works. It's not that I haven't been touring. I do quite a bit of touring solo. But this will be—as it generally is the case with the release of an album—it's occasion for a band tour. I'm quite looking forward to that.

JP: And when you start the tour, it will be with the band, but then at the Folk Festival you'll be solo, is that right?

BC: Yes.

JP: What are some of your early memories of the Winnipeg Folk Festival?

BC: I remember making a lot of friends and meeting a lot of really great people. I think I was at the first one, if I'm not mistaken.

JP: Yes.

BC: The first few, perhaps. Then there was a bit of a hiatus. But there are good memories of travelling west and connecting with all kinds of people and audiences in nice settings.

JP: Just before we came on the air, I thought I'd give a quick call to the founder of the Winnipeg Folk Festival, Mitch Podolak, and ask him if he had any Bruce Cockburn stories that I could relate or ask you to talk about. He was very flattering I think because he said the Winnipeg Folk Festival wouldn't have gotten off the ground if it wasn't for you.

BC: I am not certain I can fully take credit for that. [Laughs] Also, I'm not quite sure what he means by that. But it's nice that he thinks that I had an important part to play. I don't know. To me it was—if that's true—it's kind of a mutual thing, too, because it was a big shot for me in the west to be able to play for such a large audience and get out past the edge of Ontario.

JP: What he said was that it was a free festival the first year in 1974, sponsored because of Winnipeg's 100th anniversary. They would go about the city saying, "it's a free Bruce Cockburn concert, plus more." And that's what attracted people to it.

BC: We hooked them good.

THE EVOLUTION OF FOLK FESTIVALS

JP: Yeah. So, they came out and got to see the likes of Leon Redbone and many more. So, Mitch passes on his good wishes. Staying on festivals in general, what do you think of the way they've evolved these days? Do you have any opinions on that?

BC: It varies and it's always in flux. And I've come and gone. There's been quite a few years where I didn't really do any festivals. I don't really remember that there was a particular reason for that, it just worked out that way. But certainly, the festivals have become more eclectic, musically. Most of them have. If you go to the Montréal Jazz Festival, you'll hear many things that don't really fit the definition of jazz. If you go to any given folk festival there will be things . . . that's a little harder . . . because I was going to say, that don't fit the definition of folk music, but there is no definition of folk music, really. So, I suppose that doesn't hold up.

Back in the day, when people used to argue over whether something was folk music or something else, I remember Bill Broonzy saying, "It's all folk music, man. I never heard a horse sing a song." So, people were very hung up on—some people were—whether it was blues or folk music or something else. That was his response. But certainly, the big western festivals, in Canada especially, have really taken off. And I think have formed a kind of really important cultural element in Canada, from beginnings that were for the most part fairly humble and speculative, in a way. I think things have gone in a good direction.

JP: The smaller the festival, or the smaller the stage you are playing on, do you think it's good if you can still achieve that sort of intimacy with the audience? And with other performers?

BC: Intimacy with an audience is great. And it's true that the bigger you get, the less of that there is. Although, that's partly the combination of what everybody brings to it. You can have a big audience feel pretty close if they come in the right state of mind, let's say. But yes, smaller stages. For me, if I'm playing on a small stage, I'd rather be indoors though, somehow. It doesn't feel . . . there's something about the absence of walls that makes a setting feel less intimate. Unless you're just sitting around a campfire with four or five people, then it's like frighteningly intimate.

JP: You can get a feel, I guess, with the walls, of who's out there.

BC: Yeah, it's just a vibe thing. I've never really analyzed why it feels that way. But basically, any setting in which people want to listen to you is a good one.

JP: So, as an activist, do you ever come to a festival with a specific plan that you try to open the eyes to the needs of that geographical area, like for example, in Manitoba you might say, the needs of our Aboriginal communities would be a good one. Does that happen with you?

BC: No. I don't think like that. If I have things to say about given issues, they're generally in the songs, or maybe I'll just get mouthy one night on stage and say things. But that's not planned. It's just really—what I hope happens, doesn't always—but the ideal is to show up and be in the moment. And so, I don't really have much of an agenda, beforehand. I definitely will work out what I'm going to play a couple of hours before the show. But that's as far as I go that way. Unless . . . I mean occasionally something very specific comes up that requires that kind of attention, but most of the time it's best left to the songs.

FIGURE 44. BRUCE COCKBURN. PHOTOGRAPH BY DAVID LANDY. COURTESY OF WINNIPEG FOLK FESTIVAL.

JP: Will we be hearing new songs from you at the Winnipeg Folk Festival?

BC: Yeah, very likely. I think in the festival setting, it's not really appropriate to fill up a set with new stuff that most of the people are not familiar with, but it's very likely there'll be some. I haven't given any thought at all to what I'm going to play in Winnipeg yet, but I want to be doing the new songs. They're the ones that are the most fun for me to do.

Paul MILLS

Paul Mills is a distinguished musician and record producer based in London, Ontario. He completed a master's degree in chemical engineering but left that to pursue his passion for folk music, first as a music producer for CBC Radio starting in 1972, and later as an independent record producer. Paul was instrumental in assisting Mitch Podolak with the first years of the Winnipeg Folk Festival by arranging for the CBC to buy the broadcast rights for live Main Stage performances for his radio show, Touch the Earth. *Paul was coerced by Mitch to participate in workshops at the Folk Fest under the performer name Curly Boy Stubbs for many years. His recording studio, The Millstream, has produced close to 200 albums. His involvement in the Canadian folk music scene is extensive, including serving as past president of Folk Music Ontario, on the boards of Folk Music Canada and the Canadian Folk Music Awards, and he was past Chair of the Board of the Home County Music and Art Festival in London, Ontario.*

FIGURE 45. CURLY BOY STUBBS (AKA PAUL MILLS) PERFORMS AT WINNIPEG FOLK FEST, N.D. PHOTOGRAPH COURTESY OF PAUL MILLS.

PAUL MILLS

26 NOVEMBER 2021, LONDON, ONTARIO

KEVIN NIKKEL: Why don't we start off with you introducing yourself—how would you say you fit into the folk music scene?

PAUL MILLS: I'm Paul Mills. I've been involved in folk music ever since the sixties, actually ever since the late fifties. I think it was 1958 when I was listening to the radio at home. This was when it was Elvis Presley and Buddy Holly, the Everly Brothers and all that. A song came up on the radio that started with a banjo and somebody talking about a guy named Tom Dooley, and then they sing a song about this guy. Tom Dooley is hanging in the morning. It was The Kingston Trio. That was folk music in its purest form, but it was a hit on the radio. I thought to myself, *that is so cool.*

It was around the same time that I was starting to play guitar. Initially, I wanted to be like Elvis until I started hearing this folk music and I wanted to be like The Kingston Trio. All through high school I was in folk music groups. Even through university, I was involved in the folk music scene here in London, Ontario. It was alive and kicking in the late 1960s, early 1970s. There was a coffeehouse named Smale's Pace and one at the university called The Hub. It was a very active scene and I was heavily involved. I was actually going to university to become a chemical engineer and I ended up graduating with a master's degree in chemical engineering but it was during the postgrad years that the music scene here in London was really exploding. I decided then and there that I didn't want to be an engineer, I wanted to be a record producer. Fortunately, it was during a recording session at the CBC Radio studios in Toronto that I overheard the producer and engineer talking about a producer's job that was coming up, so I applied for it. I didn't get the first one but a couple months later, another position came up and I got that. I ended up being a music producer for CBC Radio.

KN: The London connection is fascinating to me. I've been doing some research about small centres and regionalist art movements. London just keeps popping up because of Greg Curnoe and all that. Were you associated with what was going on in those years?

PM: Well, on the music side of things, I was. There was a very lively music scene here in London in the early 1970s. Folk was very much a part of that. It's interesting because London was just named a UNESCO world music city.

KN: Really?

PM: The first one in Canada.

KN: There was a local London group, the Spasm Band?

PM: Oh yeah, the Nihilist Spasm Band. Ha. Yeah, crazy bunch of guys.

KN: There would've been those guys, and then the folk side was a different kind of pool?

PM: Different venues and different participants. But Smale's Pace coffeehouse actually became a kind of a hub for that music and artists like Willie P. Bennett, Stan Rogers, David Essig, David Bradstreet. They all came through and performed at Smale's Pace. Actually, Stan Rogers lived here in London for a couple of years, and that's how we became friends. It was interesting, actually. One night he was at my place and we were enjoying a few Glenlivets, it was shortly after I had decided to become a record producer and I announced to Stan, "Stan, I'm going to be a record producer."

And he said, "Well, when you're a record producer, you can produce my records." And we drank to that. It ended up coming true.

MEETING MITCH PODOLAK

KN: So eventually you're going to connect with Mitch Podolak. You're in Toronto and Winnipeg is a long way away. Fill in some of those gaps.

PM: One day I got a Telex, do you remember those? I got a Telex from a fellow producer in Winnipeg whose name was Walter Unger. Walter said that there is this guy in Winnipeg who is starting a folk festival. Now the reason he Telexed me was that I was in the throes of beginning to put together a folk music program for the CBC Radio network. We were just starting to work on the concept and flesh out some of the ideas and artists. I was so hungry for material and Walter

FIGURE 46. PAUL MILLS AND SYLVIA TYSON FROM THEIR CBC RADIO PROGRAM *TOUCH THE EARTH*, N.D. PHOTOGRAPH COURTESY OF PAUL MILLS.

knew that. He sent me a list of the artists this guy was thinking of having at the festival. The guy's name was Mitch Podolak.

The list of artists was very impressive. I did note, however, that there were a couple names on the list of people who had passed away, but I didn't hold that against Mitch. I liked the idea that he was presenting. So, I ended up going to Winnipeg because I wanted to meet this guy and find out more about what he had in mind for the festival.

I went to Winnipeg and I met with Mitch. The festival he was putting together was to coincide with the centenary of Winnipeg. I think he hit on that as a way of getting some funding because he wanted to put on this festival and he wanted it to be a free access festival. We started talking and I really liked the way he was presenting his ideas. I really liked him as a person. I liked his taste in music. It felt perfectly in line with what I was putting together for this folk music program for CBC Radio. I said to Mitch, "My show *Touch the Earth* would like to come to Winnipeg and record your festival and put it on the air as a special."

He said, "Brilliant."

I said, "We'll pay you broadcast rates for that." We negotiated a figure. I think it was around $15,000, something in that range and he was delighted.

It turned out with that $15,000 promise from CBC, which I wrote to him in a letter, he took that to the city, and the province, and was able to secure matching funds with CBC's support behind him. He told me afterwards, had it not been for CBC's support in those early days, it wouldn't have happened. I was thrilled. It came to be and the festival was put together for 1974. I flew to Winnipeg and the Winnipeg CBC crew and I recorded the Festival over the three days. I ended up getting two ninety-minute specials from it. It was great content for my show and was well received. He had a great lineup of artists. It was a terrific venture, for sure.

CURLY BOY STUBBS

KN: There's another story that I've heard about. Mitch actually drafted you to play at the Festival?

PM: I'll tell you the story. I met with Mitch, we negotiated the broadcast rights. Once the business was over, he picked up his banjo. He said, "I hear you play guitar?"

And I said, "Yeah, let's have some tunes." He started to play, and I was playing along and played a few things of my own.

Then he said, "You're a pretty good guitar player. You will have to do a workshop at the Festival."

I said, "Mitch, no. I'm there for CBC. CBC is paying you all this money. It would not look right."

He said, "Oh, whatever." So, we continue having a few tunes. It was a lovely evening. I end up going home. A couple weeks later I got a phone call from Mitch. He says, "Okay listen. You're going to do a guitar workshop with John Hammond Jr. and Michael Cooney, and we're going to call you Curly Boy Stubbs. Okay?"

I said, "Mitch!"

He said, "Nobody will know it's Paul Mills, it's Curly Boy Stubbs!" I ended up doing a workshop with John Hammond Jr., one of my idols, and Michael Cooney, a great Canadian folk musician. It was a lot of fun. I didn't get paid anything, but it was just great.

It was interesting because a few months later, I was in the studio with Stan Rogers and we were working on his first album and he caught wind of this Curly Boy story. He said, "Okay here's the deal.

When this record is done, Paul Mills will get credit as the producer, but the guitar player is going to be Curly Boy Stubbs, okay?" And from that point forward, just about every record that I played guitar on I was billed as Curly Boy Stubbs on guitar. So, thanks, Mitch.

KN: Tell me a bit more about Mitch. How would you frame his character?

PM: Interesting character. Headstrong. He knew what he wanted, and he put his head down and went for it all the time. But he was also extremely conscious of all the people that worked with him. He put a lot of emphasis and care on the volunteers that did the Festival. He considered the volunteers to be as important as the musical artists at the Festival. He showed that, in terms of how everyone was treated. The food was amazing. The accommodations for both artists and volunteers—all together, by the way—was just first rate, all the way. I really admired Mitch for not only his organizational skills and his ability to get things done, but also his caring attitude for the people who worked with him. He was a communist and that sort of ethic, that we're all in this together, I think really showed through in the way he operated. He was a lovely man. Headstrong, and we got into the odd argument, but nevertheless, he remained a very close friend of mine for all those years.

KN: It's the essence of Mitch, that you're describing. But if we wanted to describe the essence of the Winnipeg Folk Festival, how would you describe the organization of that?

PM: Mitch actually took a cue from Estelle Klein, who was the artistic director of the Mariposa Folk Festival in Ontario here. She operated the Festival with a series of workshops during the day. She was very careful how those workshops were put together and Mitch took that model to the Winnipeg Folk Festival and applied it. Artists were put together in workshop settings who often had never met before. Mitch knew that, musically, there would be some kind of magic happening on that stage. He designed the subject matter of the workshop to feed that. The artists would be working with a common theme and it would be something that each one would, perhaps, have a little different take on. It would end up often in magic.

KN: And you were in these workshops, year after year?

PM: No, I'm not. Curly Boy Stubbs is.

KN: Pardon me.

PM: [Laughs].

KN: When you got the program, what went through your mind?

PM: A lot of times we found out ahead of time, which was good because I would look at the topic of the workshop and think, *I better learn a couple of tunes.* But often we wouldn't find out until we actually got there. So, there is a bit of rushing around and ad libbing. But it all contributed to the magic.

KN: Dan Donahue mentioned the anxiety and mindset of, "I better be on my game for this workshop."

PM: There was one workshop that Mitch put me in, and it was a guitar workshop because I was a finger-picking guitar player. There I was, on the stage with Don Ross, the incredible Canadian finger-style guitar player, and Leo Kottke, who I've admired for years and years. He was like a god to me, and here I was in a workshop with the guy. It got a little nerve-wracking but we got through it. I played a couple tunes and Leo smiled and applauded. I thought, *I've gone to heaven.* There were a few surprises like that, where I find I'm in a workshop with some of these people, and the pressure is on.

FOLK FESTIVALS IN WESTERN CANADA

KN: It makes me wonder. The Festival is a great show and the audience loves it, but there's more of importance to this event. I'm hearing you describe this chemistry. This leads to something else.

PM: Absolutely. And the Winnipeg Folk Festival actually led to other festivals in western Canada, because it was after Winnipeg had such a success that other centres started to get the idea and Mitch had a hand in getting those other festivals going, as well. Calgary, Edmonton, Vancouver, all of these festivals are still going on. Edmonton is one of the largest music festivals there is and I think they were all spawned, in part, by Winnipeg, and Mitch actually said in an interview once that because of the CBC's support, they were able to get the Festival going and if it had not been for the CBC support, all these other western festivals probably wouldn't have happened either. So, it's pretty significant. Quite a thrill.

KN: What was the folk scene like in the years before the Festival started in the 1960s? What was happening with folk music in Canada?

PM: Folk music really hit the major leagues in the early 1960s. That's when festivals like Mariposa were formed. Folk at that time was mainstream music. It continued to be that through the 1960s and into the 1970s, but it was waning a little bit. Groups like The Beatles came along and drew the attention away. However, I have to say, groups like The Beatles took a lot of cues from folk music in that they started putting out songs that had something to say. Unlike the "Oh my baby left me" songs of the 1950s, the songs of The Beatles did actually have some poetry to them and things to say, which is the hallmark of folk music. I think there was folk influence on all that. It continued along and once we got into the 1970s, there was really a growth of the singer-songwriter. Whereas before that, a lot of the folk music had been traditional folk music, the singer-songwriter started to really emerge in the late 1960s and into the 1970s. Led by songwriters like Phil Ochs, and Bob Dylan, and so on. The singer-songwriter became the core of the folk genre in the 1960s and on our CBC program, *Touch the Earth,* we featured a lot of singer-songwriters. I think that exposure on the public broadcaster helped to make the genre grow in Canada during the 1970s.

KN: Was the spreading of folk festivals really taking advantage of the singer-songwriter movement that was happening?

PM: Primarily, yes. I mean, festivals also had a traditional music element to them, of course. But the singer-songwriters thing became a kind of building block for a lot of these festivals. Some festivals emerged that were entirely traditional music, and that's fine. Most of them were based on singer-songwriters.

THE LIFE OF THE SINGER-SONGWRITER

KN: I want to talk about the issue of trying to live as a folk musician in Canada. Was it easier in the 1960s, 1970s, or 1980s, to be a working singer-songwriter? Did festivals help in any way?

PM: Yes, the festivals helped a great deal. But back in those early days, in the 1960s and 1970s, it was an entirely different scene for the working musician. The musician's union was so much stronger back then.

People were paid union scale. Quite often gigs would be a week long, as opposed to one night, and you would get union scale for each night of that week. So, it was completely different. Then in the 1970s that started to change. Prior to that, musicians, when they wanted to put out a record, they had to get a record deal with a major label and had to negotiate all that. But in the 1970s, artists—folk artists, in particular—started to produce their own records and form their own labels. David Essig comes to mind. He was one of the first folkies in the early 1970s to do that. He formed a record label and he ended up bringing other artists on to his label,[11] like William P. Bennett. Stan Rogers formed his own label in the mid-1970s.[12] So that was a factor in the equations as well. But in the 1970s and 1980s, artists were actually able to tour and get paid proper wages for their work and they were able to sell records at their gigs. Record sales often became a major part of their income on a tour. Nowadays, that's no longer the case because people aren't buying records and they get their music from streaming services, or for nothing through YouTube or what have you, so it's completely changed.

KN: Talk a little bit about the Festival in the 1970s when you were there, and some of the attitudes that people were exuding in those years. The 1960s have a reputation with the civil rights movement, and the whole sex drugs rock 'n' roll culture. Is there something that is measurable in the attitudes and opinions of people that were around the Festival site in the 1970s?

PM: That's a tough question. A lot of the music that emerged through the 1960s had to do with peace and love and anti-war. Those were the themes of that decade and then some of it continued through into the 1970s. There was definitely a feeling of: *we're all in this together.* There is a kind of a unifying feeling between the audience and the stage at all times. The audience would be participants in the music. You have audience members singing along. You have a lot of them dancing, often around the edges of the crowd, things like that. There was that communal kind of togetherness that we all felt, the audience and the artists together. Then backstage and afterwards back at the hotel, there would always be an after-party and there was that same communal feeling among the artists and volunteers because Mitch insisted that the volunteers be at the party. As equal at the party as the performers and no rank or anything. No favouritism. We were all there at this big hotel ballroom together having a good time. There'd be jam sessions going on in the corners. People enjoying a beer and having a good time together. It was a feeling of community and was a common element in all the festivals, and to a large degree it still feels that way today.

KN: You've got a unique perspective because you were so involved with the CBC, through various festivals, and as a musician. Now that you are an elder in this community, what kind of thoughts do you have about the legacy—not just yours—but of the culture that you helped as a shepherd of sorts?

CANADIAN FOLK MUSIC SCENE

PM: I think what we established—I'm thinking particularly of the Canadian folk-song-writing community—has a certain kind of a feel about it that you don't find south of the border. Maybe it's the fact that we're living in this huge open space or that we're living in a country that has more liberal values in many ways than south of the border. It's a combination of a lot of factors that lead to the kinds of songs that are written and performed in this country. I felt that forming during the 1960s and 1970s and growing through the 1980s and 1990s, and it is still with us. And it just makes me smile. There's a radio program that comes out of Ottawa called *Canadian Spaces*[13] which celebrates that and features Canadian folk-artist singer-songwriters. When you listen to that program you can hear what I'm talking about. If you switch to an American folk show, it's completely different. It's got a completely different feel about it. I can't describe it very accurately but I just say it feels different. Maybe it's because, as a Canadian, I grew up through this but I just find it more welcoming and more interesting and it touches my heart.

KN: It's interesting when you say that. It reminds me of how David Essig described his experience coming up from the United States to Canada. He described his first efforts of playing down in the U.S. as this cold, businesslike environment. He came up here and he said, "I found my family." Night and day difference.

PM: It's a totally different scene. In Nashville, I visited friends who are songwriters and what they do in Nashville is to try to get appointments with well-known songwriters so they can co-write and create something that will make them money. It's more about the money than it is about fellowship, or humanity, or community, or any of those things. Up here, at least in my experience, it's been more about community. More about just creating wonderfulness together. We get together and have jam sessions. I belong to a musical gathering group here in London. We meet every month, sometimes more often. A dozen, or twenty people, or whatever. We sit in a room together to make music. We go around the circle in which we share songs. It's about sharing, it's about learning.

KN: That's great, but the devil's advocate in me would say, "Yeah, the fellowship and the community is good, but it doesn't put food on the table."

PM: No, it doesn't, but it does lead to the creation of some pretty nice music, which can put food on the table. But you know what they say, folk music is an industry in which you can make tens of dollars. [Laughs] Be that as it may, we're still doing it. Why? Because we love it.

KN: I wonder how, as the Festival grew to the size it is now and became much more of a business—and necessarily so—was it able to maintain that attitude and Canadian-ness, or community-mindedness?

PM: I think to a lesser degree. I haven't been to it for quite a while, so I can't really attest to what it is like. I've heard from some people who bemoan the fact that there's not enough folk music at the Festival anymore. I think that's true of a lot of the festivals. Here in London, the Home County Festival has tried to maintain its folk centre, but it wants to attract more than just the old fogies, or the old folkies. So some more contemporaries are brought in to the mix. Some festivals are going further in that direction than others, but that's to be expected; that there will be less of that folky idealism that we all loved in the 1970s now than there was then. It's evolution.

Tom JACKSON

Tom Jackson has had a distinguished career as an actor, musician, and activist. Originally from the One Arrow First Nation in Saskatchewan, he had a guitar in his hands at age ten. Eventually settling in Winnipeg at the age of fourteen, he began playing coffeehouses at seventeen. His performing took him across the country, including on stage at Mariposa in the 1970s. During the early 1970s, Tom became the CBC Radio host of The Tom Jackson Show *in Winnipeg—it was here he met Mitch Podolak, who invited him to help contribute to the Winnipeg Folk Festival and perform on stage. He would play the Festival seven times by himself over the years, as well as an additional visit with Kansas City Dave Cramer. He has recorded sixteen albums. Tom's busy career has included an impressive list of acting roles for television. His activism and philanthropic work are equally notable—his annual Huron Carole Benefit Concert Series in support of food banks and other causes sets an example for the rest of us to follow.*

FIGURE 47. TOM JACKSON PERFORMS AT WINNIPEG FOLK FEST, 1970S. PHOTOGRAPH BY J. WYNE. COURTESY OF WINNIPEG FOLK FESTIVAL.

TOM JACKSON

25 AUGUST 2021, WINNIPEG

KEVIN NIKKEL: Tell me about how you got connected with the Winnipeg Folk Fest and Mitch Podolak?

TOM JACKSON: I was doing a weekly radio show for CBC. I came on in the afternoon saying, "My name is Tom Jackson, you're listening to 94.3 on your FM dial." Down the hall was an office for freelancers. Mitch Podolak was in that office. In 1972 or 1973, he came down the hall and said, "Tom, if I ever started a folk festival, would you be interested in playing?"

I said, "Sure."

He said, "Okay, you're the first act." He asked me if I would participate as a co-assistant director for Indigenous programming. And I did. So, I was part of the Festival staff for a couple years. It was fun.

KN: Let's go back into those years. Before that, you were doing work for CBC. Were you touring a lot as well?

TJ: I was, but I was just getting my wings, so to speak. I was playing pool with my brother at the Westminster Hotel. A guy comes over to me—burly, with a beard, wearing a black T-shirt—and said, "You Tom Jackson?"

I said, "Yeah."

He said, "Well, I think we have some things in common."

I said, "Like what?"

He said, "Well, you're a singer-songwriter and I'm a singer and songwriter. You like the land, and I like the land. My name is Rick Neufeld." Now Rick Neufeld, for those who are not familiar with that name, was probably one of the most prolific writers that ever came out of Manitoba. And he said, "If you ever want to come out and visit, here is my address. Give me a quick call." I called one day and he said, "Well, pick up a bottle of CC [Canadian Club Whisky] and come on out to the farm." It was out and around Île-des-Chênes.[14] I did and we got into this groove of writing. We didn't write with each other, but he'd write a song and say come on over. Then I'd write a song, and head over. Each morning. Starting the whole idea of writing songs.

Then in 1973 I was invited to the Mariposa Festival. I went to Montréal to do a gig at a place called the Rainbow Bar and Grill. Great. So, I'm playing at the bar and there's a guy in the shadows at the back. Two guys, actually. One of them got up and came over and said, "I've got a friend at the back who'd like to make your acquaintance." He was very formal. I remember it specifically. I walked over and he said, "This is Mr. Leonard Cohen." That was his territory, in Montréal. I was also there because there was a movement to raise money for an injunction against the James Bay hydroelectric project. Prior to getting there, Rick Neufeld said, "You gotta learn this song." It was this song written by Ian Tyson and it was called "The Renegade." I learned it and sang it like it was mine. I went to this festival at the Place des Arts in Montréal, very prestigious place to be. And Ian Tyson was there.

I went up to Ian and said, "Are you going to sing 'The Renegade?'" Because I wanted to sing it.

He was always great and gracious and said, "Go ahead." So, I did, and that changed my world. That moment. I decided I didn't want to have to ask someone if I could sing their songs. So, I started writing. Rick Neufeld and I became very close. But yes, Rick was a big part of those years. Mitch, Rick Neufeld, Marv Terhoch; there was a group of people that were artistically connected, and I was on the far edge of it. But nevertheless, they were grand years. Bruce Cockburn, Kitty Macaulay, lots of long-term relationships made.

PLAYING THE WINNIPEG FOLK FESTIVAL

In 1975 I met this guy who lives just up the street here. His name is Dave Cramer. I was working with Bill Merritt—Red River Merritt—and everybody had to have a name in the band. My name was Timber Tom. So, we had to figure out what to call Dave Cramer, so Bill said, "Let's call him Kansas City. He'll be called Kansas City Cramer."

David said, "I'm not from Kansas City, I'm from Milwaukee." Yeah, well, Milwaukee Dave doesn't really have a ring to it. So, we settled in on Kansas City Cramer. There were other players in and around at that time from Winnipeg. Good players. And we had a band that had eleven people in it. Graham Shaw was around in those days.

Graham Shaw and the Sincere Serenaders, if you don't recall that. He was great.

One day at the Festival, Dave was working the lock-up, where you secure instruments. This was the kind of guy he was. He was a teacher by trade and in 1975 there was a bus breakdown or some such thing. The band was booked. It was an eleven-piece band, booked for the Winnipeg Festival. Which didn't mean to say we got more money, it just got divided up eleven ways. But the band doesn't get there. And we got this gig. Our schedule is up. And I said to Dave, "Do you want to do this, just me and you?"

And he said, "Sure." So, we did.

I'd say halfway through the first song I went, "Who are you?" I'd never heard his harmonica because we had two guitars, the keyboard, drums, three vocalists. I'd never actually heard him play. So that was the last time we played as a band. He decided to go crazy and he quit teaching, and we went on the road. Tom Jackson and Kansas City Dave Cramer. That was from the 1975 Festival.

KN: What were the conversations with Mitch like, about his vision for the Festival?

TJ: Having an Indian artistic director was really following the suit of Mariposa. They had one, so we had to have one. But really, I was in over my head. I had no idea how to book anybody. I got to know some folks and made some phone calls, but really, to say "co-artistic director," that's a bit overstated. I was just helping out, hanging around the office because it was great and there was a folk music store and I could go play instruments I couldn't afford. All sorts of wonderful things came about as a result of the focus of the Festival.

I'm not really part of the community per se, but I remember the community. I remember Dave McLean, Gord Kidder, Brent Parkin at the Royal Albert. Downstairs at the Zoo. I walked by there recently and the whole hotel is gone, half the Village is gone.[15] But I remember clearly what the community was like. Although there wasn't a huge folk community here, it was a strong community.

Winnipeg is a breeding ground for great musicians. One of the reasons, I guess, is that you can still get a job in this town, even today, playing music six nights a week. In the same place. You don't have to necessarily circle around. I think that that's a big thing. I don't know what's happened recently. I don't know what happened with the cycle. I don't know if there's been a lot since the Crash Test Dummies came out of Winnipeg. Like Chantal [Kreviazuk]. But for the music community, those were really serious vintage years, the mid-seventies. Bachman, Cummings, Bachman-Turner [Overdrive or BTO] in 1975.

There was another festival. I ventured off to Edmonton for work and I got a call from a guy who said, "We're going to create a festival here on the Sandy Bay Indian Reserve[16] and it's going to be called the International 75." There was a rumour and a movement to reunite The Beatles. BTO was booked. Elton John was booked, and there was a guy by the name of Billy Graham who was a promoter out of California backing that event.

So, when they called me in Edmonton they said, "We're going to run some workshops. We're on the Sandy Bay Indian Reserve and we need somebody to run workshops." This was because they had heard I did something for the Folk Festival. So, I came back from Edmonton to work on the International 75, which didn't happen, because it turns out that there was a little bit of politics going on out there. One of the promoters leaked a six-word two-line thing in *Billboard* magazine that there was going to be a festival on an Indian reserve in Manitoba. That hit the press, and CJOB in particular made a phone call up to the reserve and somebody picked up the phone on the other end and started yelling rape and pillage. So that little line in *Billboard* canned the festival. It never happened, but it almost happened.

But if it weren't for Mitch Podolak and the Winnipeg Folk Festival, I don't think it would ever have come up as a possibility. That they could actually run a festival of that magnitude here. I won't say that the Edmonton Folk Festival was modelled to suit, but it kind of [was]. And there were others that we travelled around to—the Northern Lights Festival in Sudbury, that was a cool festival. But a lot of them took a snapshot of what Mitch had created and tried to cut-and-paste it.

KN: In the years where you were helping to do some programming at the Festival—who were some of the names that got on the bill?

TJ: It was pretty obscure. In those years there weren't a lot of Indian singers. There was Buffy,[17] but she wasn't really accessible. She wouldn't have played it, but she was "up there." And I don't know if the Festival at that time could pick artists that were "up there," maybe just for financial reasons. I think I relied on a phone call to Mariposa and said, "Who did you book last year?"

You might say Shingoose, but I don't know whether that would be true. Shingoose and I worked together with Dave Cramer and that was probably the best unit that I ever worked with musically: Dave and Shingoose. But I don't recall others that were brought into the fold. It wasn't really me signing the cheque.

KN: What do you remember about the Folk Fest crowd? Is it any different than other festivals you played?

TJ: I'm hesitating because I'm just recalling semblances of other places. The one thing that Winnipeg did, simply by sheer volume, was create a community that appreciated folk music, more than it had prior to that, and to this day remains enthusiastic. I think that the Festival has grown, as things should and would, in terms of the kind of music. What is folk music these days? I don't know. It's really defined by the artistic direction. But to say that we didn't have AAA acts would be crazy. I remember when k.d. lang showed up. A very young teenager wearing funky clothes, laying down on the stage, and doing stuff like singing like a bird. Colin James, another great example. When he was thirteen, he showed up at this festival and blew the doors off any guitar player that was around. And I'll say that to any guitar player that is around. He did. There were others. Colin Linden. Jimmy Rankin. Greg McIntosh. But the crowd would really lap up anything you put in front of them. The folk music days really had sort of petered off by then. It was more the late 1960s. But Simon and Garfunkel I think changed that. John Prine and Johnny Cash, those guys, they changed what we were used to listening to. Kris Kristofferson. I believe that music is one of the most powerful instruments of change in the history of human beings. That was very evident at that time. Singer-songwriters became very important, around the world, as they are today. There's a void between that time and this time; there is a big difference. Guys like Kristofferson, and guys I've mentioned, they were great. Rick Neufeld—I acknowledge and recognize his talent, because I was a fan of music and poetry. I think Rick personified that.

KN: Any thoughts on the way Mitch was setting things up with the workshops?

MUSIC COMING OUT OF WINNIPEG

TJ: I didn't find it any different than Mariposa, as an example. Mariposa was really the model to follow. And then Winnipeg became the model that enhanced that model and carried on. That said, it was always fun, it was always intimidating. There were always great harmonies that came out of the middle of nowhere. Winnipeg is an interesting place and Winnipeg doesn't necessarily create music that everybody else understands. If you go to a disciplined and numbered musical community, numbers being 12345678, do re mi fa so—like that—if you go to a numbered community, it's much more rigid. In Winnipeg you go to that community and they say, "You can't do that." It doesn't fall in this category. It doesn't . . . where is the click? What are the beats per minute? They'll go, "It doesn't go like that, it goes like this." It's all different. It breaks out of meter. Drops bars. But it's wonderful. It's its own manifestation of creation. For those who are musically inclined, it's a freedom to create as you will.

KN: So, spontaneity. Improvisation?

TJ: Yeah, collaboration more. Yet I don't create an image that it's so avant garde, so that it's not accessible. To us, it's really good. It's more a collaborative community when you sit down and you don't negotiate. You collaborate. Okay, what would you do? How do you think this works? At the end of the day, collaboration is an interesting thing. If you get together to collaborate on something, I can guarantee you that it's not going to be perfect. But I guarantee this: it will be better. It won't be perfect, but it'll be better. And what if you go and collaborate more than once? What if the same group gets together and you do it again and you do it again? What do you think can happen then? Not going to be perfect, but it's going to be better.

KN: Do you have any stories of some of the workshops where you were put together with any characters?

JOHN PRENTICE: We're testing your memory.

TJ: Shingoose. The Goose. He was always present there. There was a guy named Floyd Westerman who came up from the South. I got to know some of them just by name because of the radio show that I did. I'd research and find various artists. I couldn't rattle off the artists, but I do remember being there with Floyd and one other person.

JP: Winston?

TJ: Winston Wuttunee. Duke Redbird. Laura Vinson. A lot of those guys are still around, too. Shingoose is gone.

KN: So, in the first few years of the Festival, what might have been your set list? Songs you were singing?

TJ: "The Renegade" would have been one of them. I can't recall. I'd started to write, as I mentioned, but I don't remember a lot of songs I would've written back then. I should. There is actually an album out there somewhere that I recorded at Wayne Finucan's, right around that time.

ATTITUDES OF THE 1960S AND 1970S

JP: Did you have any sense of Mitch's broader politics? And the way he wanted the world to be?

TJ: I think that the only real conversations Mitch and I had about his vision for the Folk Festival was probably before the Folk Festival actually took place. He felt that it was a dying breed and he wanted to make sure that that didn't happen. He was going to do something about that. And he was clearly aligned with others who felt the same.

It was really his passion and I don't know where that came from. I'm guessing he had a history with festivals. And certainly, was born to lead it. But really his vision was—be true. Be true to the roots of it all. Having singer-songwriters, then digging into the past. Bringing people to the show to play.

FIGURE 48. TOM JACKSON, 1980. PHOTOGRAPH BY DAVID LANDY. ARCHIVES OF MANITOBA, WINNIPEG FOLK FESTIVAL 1980 NEGATIVES, P2566/11, 80/292. 35A.

KN: I was thinking about your career, which includes so many areas, including activism. Did that connect already back in the 1970s and at the Festival?

TJ: Not necessarily related to the Folk Festival, but not disengaged either. When we go back to think about and talk about the overall movement of change that had been created by music, it was very evident in and around that period of time, and driven in part by the Festival, but it was also a very radical and turbulent time. In particular for Indian people, Indian folks. I remember my brother Bernie and I sitting in a Main Street diner. The question came up. Because there was a lot happening in that period of time—I told you about what happened in Montréal. Well, there were a lot of other things that went on at that time. There was this thing called the American Indian Movement, there was the Native movement and this was coming out of the civil rights movement, which was the Black movement. And if you were any kind of a renegade, pardon the use of the word again, then there was something to hang onto. Bernie and I were sitting at the diner and I asked the question, "Would you be willing to die for being Indian? Would you be willing to kill?" I don't know. But in 1973, there was a militant movement that occupied Pine Ridge, South Dakota. Wounded Knee. Bernie and I went. We stationed ourselves in Rosebud, which came up in the news just the other day. There was someone who died. I came back and I decided that ballads, not bullets, were a better choice. That, too, drove me into writing songs. Meaningful things that I wanted to say and talk about.

KN: What was the attitude like at the time? Was there a genuine attempt at understanding other people, and Indigenous people at the time, or was it more of a token thing? How mature was the Indian Movement in the 1970s, with all the other protest events in Vietnam and so much else going on?

TJ: As the society that we live in, my opinion is that evolution never happens without revolution. It has its place. But at times like this, today, times like the early 1970s, there was a lot of frustration, and I think it's happened once since then. There was a lot of frustration amongst younger people not having a voice. When they found their voice, they used it. And it was very critical to define the path of change. A lot of frustration with the generation, two generations, three generations away that said, "You have to be patient." Not me. I can't be patient. I can be patient if I try, I suppose. But the reality is whether you're fifteen, twenty-five, or seventy-five, you've got a runway. How long is that runway, is the question. If you want me to do something, like this interview, better get to it. Because I've got a runway. And every day my runway gets shorter. So, what are you going to do? Do you want it to be meaningful? You want to wait and be patient? I say you need to shout, and shout loudly.

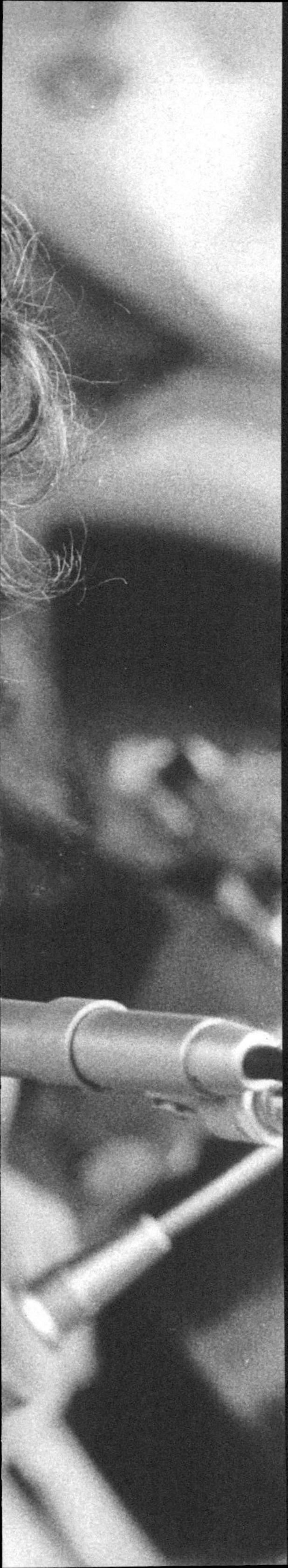

David AMRAM

David Amram is a multi-talented musician, composer, and conductor. He grew up in Pennsylvania and studied music at Oberlin Conservatory of Music. Among other instruments, he plays the piano, French horn, guitar, and various whistles and flutes—all of which he is famous for using to perform on stages small and large the world over. The roster of his collaborations with A-list writers, directors, and performers is as distinguished as it is long, from Jack Kerouac to Charles Mingus to Dizzy Gillespie. His music scores for Hollywood features, stage plays, and symphony performances are extensive. David's inspired performance at a Mariposa workshop stage with Steve Goodman caught the eye of Mitch Podolak—leading to an invitation to the Winnipeg Folk Festival in 1975 and on seven other occasions. His performances at the Festival were much lauded, as was the friendship he offered to musicians and volunteers alike.

FIGURE 49. DAVID AMRAM ON A WORKSHOP STAGE, 1976. PHOTOGRAPH BY DAVID LANDY, ARCHIVES OF MANITOBA, WINNIPEG FOLK FESTIVA 1976 NEGATIVES, P2566/3, 76/15. 30.

DAVID AMRAM

3 MAY 2021, NEW YORK CITY

KEVIN NIKKEL: Why don't we start off with you introducing yourself and how you fit in with the story of folk music?

DAVID AMRAM: I'm David Amram. I first came to the Winnipeg Folk Festival in 1975. I'm delighted to send a big hello—a big thank you—to everyone at the Festival, all these years later. It's a wonderful festival. The whole city of Winnipeg—with the Ballet Company, with the Symphony I was blessed to work with as well—certainly must be proud of having one of the best folk music festivals in the world. There's no place like it. Birds Hill Park will always be in my memory. It was my chance to play with the great Steve Goodman and Floyd Red Crow Westerman, and all the wonderful Indigenous musicians. And the traditional musicians, and the great singer-songwriters who came from there.

I started off playing folkloric music. Listening to it without even knowing that's what it was. Being brought up on a farm in Feasterville, Pennsylvania, population 200, and hearing Polish kazatsky music played by the Polish folks next door. And country music, and jazz, and all of the musics which we now appreciate as world musics. I got the inkling that there was some place beyond Feasterville. My uncle, who was a merchant seaman having been all around the world, told me I should listen to the music of the Indigenous peoples who have been here for 50,000 years. So, by the time I finally got older, I was already thinking in terms of all music that touches your heart being of value. And then of course the great Odetta told me, "Whatever genre you work, folk is the root of the tree."

KN: When did you first hear about the Winnipeg Folk Festival? What had you heard?

MEETING MITCH PODOLAK

DA: I was at the Mariposa Folk Festival in 1974. Steve Goodman and I did a whole program, we'd just met. Mitch Podolak was there and he said, "You blew me away making up all those rhymes and also being a

FIGURE 50. DAVID AMRAM PLAYS PIANO AT WINNIPEG FOLK FESTIVAL, 1978. PHOTOGRAPH BY DAVID LANDY. ARCHIVES OF MANITOBA, WINNIPEG FOLK FESTIVAL 1978 NEGATIVES, P5266/8, 78/4.9.

backup player with Steve Goodman, and being able to do all the stuff you do. I wish you could come to the Festival but we're already booked. Could you come in 1975?"

I said, "Man, I'll be there." And that's when I first came. And of course, I was so happy that Mitch had invited me because all the musicians said that's the one to go to. If you liked Mariposa, you've got to come here. We've got something different and beautiful.

KN: What were your impressions of Mitch?

DA: I was amazed that he even asked me to be in the Festival. In 1975, I'd played with Jack Elliott and with all the different folk players before there was a folk scene. So, I knew about that and I enjoyed doing that. But I figured I wasn't exactly into the folklore circuit in any way. I was never part of any circuit, I was just part of whatever happened each day in music. Then I realized he didn't look at the music that way either. He had a strong political basis, being a Trotskyite when he was a young fellow. He hung in there as it was something that wasn't that popular because he believed that was the right thing to do. He also respected anybody and everybody else, whether they agreed with him or not, if he felt that they had a good heart and they had something to offer. He had such a broad appreciation of all musics.

When I was doing my first program guest conducting the Winnipeg Symphony in 1975, I said, "Man, I want to have Mitch come and join the other folk musicians from Winnipeg that I'd invited for a piece I was doing." Mitch finally came in at the last minute, since he was somewhere else at some big conference. He had to catch a later train. He just walked in and played up a storm.

But he was so much fun to be with. He loved the music so much that when you were with him you felt there was a guy whipping up enthusiasm among the people who were supposed to be whipping up enthusiasm themselves. He made you feel like you were a wonderful person and had something to contribute. He made you feel good. He had the ability to make people feel worthy and feel appreciated. And it wasn't an act, it was the way he was. That was part of his way. Like Dizzy Gillespie told me on his seventieth birthday, "It's time to put something back in the pot." Mitch was a believer in always putting something back in the pot. I think all the people who worked with him appreciated that. He really, really cared. And he also didn't believe in snubbing people. If people were disrespectful to others, that they considered to be lesser, he would call them on that immediately. He really wanted people that were with him to do their best, but also to be decent and respectful to one another. That's a very, very important thing and that's what you call a real leader.

PLAYING WINNIPEG FOLK FESTIVAL

KN: What do you remember about the Folk Festival?

DA: Well, I remember going out to Birds Hill Park, driving out with Steve Goodman. He said, "Man I always get lost, but being with you, that'll be fun. We'll get an early start." I remember going through all the countryside—and getting lost—and seeing how beautiful it was.

And just as we thought we were about to hit the Bering Strait, sure enough, instead of landing in Yellowknife, we got to Birds Hill Park. And it was just so magnificent. And so much fun.

When I was with Richie Havens, we spent four hours walking slowly from one end of the park to the other. He spoke to everybody. Playing there with Odetta. Playing with Floyd Red Crow Westerman, among the Indigenous musicians. All the wonderful singer-songwriters, many of whom are not with us anymore. I just remember the good feeling and how much fun it was. And how wonderful it was to play, and listen, and hear so much good music. And then to spend time with the musicians after the concert, just jamming with them, and learning from them. It was like a wonderful crash course. A university of world music, before it was even called that.

So many of the extraordinary people that Mitch got to come were just so wonderful. Every one of them that I ever saw always appreciated the Festival, wherever they were. It was a place where people could get together and play music. That's the magnificent thing about those festivals.

KN: Tell me more about your experience with Steve Goodman. I heard something about Moby Dick?

DA: That was the very first time I'd played at the Mariposa Folk Festival in 1974. I had never met Steve. I'd heard of him, of course. In New York, all the musicians said, "You've got to hear this guy from Chicago, the man is fantastic." So, there he was.

And he said, "Hey, we were put on the workshop tomorrow, what do you want to do?"

I said, "Well, I'll play the flutes and the French horns, and then I'll get the audience to suggest four topics and I'll make up the song."

He said, "Really?"

And I said, "Man, we'll just do it." So that was our rehearsal. Then we just jammed till about four o'clock in the morning. We had so much fun playing together.

He said, "Well, I don't know what we're going to do, but I know it's going to be fun."

And I said, "Well, that's the whole idea."

One of the four topics suggested by the audience was Moby Dick. I can't remember what the other three were. I made up some dumb song about the harpoon of truth, and the whale of destiny, Moby Dick or some stupid summer camp type stuff, free association. Like I used to do with Jack Kerouac. Now they call it freestyling, with skat rapping, with rhymes—which I have been doing all my life, way before I had ever heard of a folk festival. And Steve was sitting there, he had a look of amazement on his face while I did this whole ridiculous thing. He said, "How am I going to follow that?"

And I said, "Come on Steve man, everybody is here to see you, including me." And he gave one of his magnificent songs where in three minutes he could say it all, where it took me half an hour. Then to my amazement, a few months later, he made a song called "Moby Book" and credited me as a writer. I said, "Good Lord, Steve, if I could write one sentence equivalent to one of your songs."

He said, "No, no. You gave me the idea."

I said, "Well, just having your energy gave me the chance to dare and go out and do all that stuff with all those people who were coming to hear you, basically."

I did so many different things with him. He was so amazing and he had such a broad knowledge and appreciation of jazz and symphony music. When the Philadelphia orchestra played my piece, he came. And he was an usher at my wedding. We were just so close, as everyone was, I think, that knew him. He was such a warm, delightful, and creative person, and very serious. He's the one that said to me years later, "That song that I made into 'Moby Book,' that was fun." But he said, "You know, when you do your jazz programs, and you do the symphony music, you're concise. You have a beginning, a middle, and an end. A structure. You don't go on too long. You should do that when you're doing folkloric music, too. Keep that structure. Keep it simple. Have the spontaneity as the root of the feeling, but be a craftsman. This is an art, songwriting is art, just as much as writing a string quartet, or an opera, or a symphony." And Steve is the one who made me aware that less is more. Organization and an appreciation of the classic forms are worthwhile and important in whatever you do. But he didn't tell me that for years. I think he figured perhaps I would appreciate that.

KN: I wonder if there was something different about the Winnipeg Folk Festival?

FIGURE 51. DAVID AMRAM ON A WORKSHOP STAGE, 1975. PHOTOGRAPH BY DAVID LANDY. ARCHIVES OF MANITOBA, WINNIPEG FOLK FESTIVAL 1975 NEGATIVES, P5266/1, 75-4684. 5.

DA: Well, what I found when I went to Birds Hill Park, and when I was in the city of Winnipeg, even in the wintertime when it was cold, I didn't feel like I was nowhere, I felt like I was somewhere. And that good community feeling was what I always searched for, and somehow was lucky enough to find. Even in the most dreadful, crowded, urban, nasty places, you could always find a little centre of warmth. Even if it was just a friend's old apartment, or a loft somewhere, or some little coffeehouse that you went to—there was always that sense.

Then being brought up on the farm, you always see the animals hanging out with one another. There is some communal sense that we all have, and fortunately the festivals were not the holier than though, New Age freak-atisimo, blasphemy of ancient religions, trying to make some kind of formula, and charging thousands of dollars to be groovy or spiritual. Just a natural, simple, familial, human, tribal scene. We're all here, the two-legged, that's us. And the four-leggeds, and the wingeds, as the Indigenous folks would say. Every single breathing species that we have, more or less, has an essential need, and an essential naturalness of being together. Share that with other people, and you can be with any bunch of people and be familial. And feel like you're on the planet Earth with brother and sister human beings. Without having to go in all that rhetoric. And you don't have to have sides. You know that song "Which Side Are You On," Pete Seeger told me that was true when the West Virginia miners were getting killed, but when you're hanging out, you're on everybody's side. You're the human side. And for the bird to fly successfully, somehow the left and the right wing must find a way to work together in harmony. That's what the folk festivals represented. A reminder that we're all here for a while as human beings and we should celebrate that.

LESSONS LEARNED ABOUT HOW TO LIVE

DAVE BARBER: Can you speak about the importance of Floyd Westerman and Indigenous music?

DA: I met so many Indigenous folks later on when I was in the Army during the Korean War. Afterwards, especially in New York City, they had an American Indian community house and I would meet different Indigenous folks. I met Floyd Westerman there way before we did the Winnipeg Festival, and so many other artists. With my interest in the music, Floyd said, "Well, you can play with me." I was able to be his backup player. Just plain and simple to accompany him. I was able to go with him, so that I was not trying to be *Mr. Anthropologist* or, *Mr. I am slumming with you inferior people in order to raise my self-esteem*, or any of that stuff. Just that I was trying to be of some help and have some respect. They'd say, "We'd like to show you something." And they would show me a song. Gradually the more music I learned, the more I realized I could try to interest other people in that and enrich myself and through the music. I learned a whole bunch of other stuff and am still learning, and realize how much there is to learn that I will never know.

KN: I want to bring this back to folk festivals and how important the folk festival circuit was when musicians were starting to build their careers. How important was it for you?

DA: Well, to be perfectly candid, I never thought—even at ninety—I still don't think about building a career. I think about building a life. And if your music, which is part of your life, is going to have a life of its own, it has to be good. It has to be well done. And it has to be saying something. It has to tell a story and, if it does, you'll touch other people's hearts. And if not, it will be eminently forgettable. And that's nothing you can control. What you can control is trying to eliminate the swinish instincts of stomping, trampling, disrespecting, and violating everything that you're brought up to think is the right thing to do to make you successful.

So, the best thing is for each person to find the path they feel they were put on [Earth] to do and then just to try to do that the best they can. Just keep on trucking. Following your heart and trying to be the kind of person you hoped you might possibly become. And if not, as Shakespeare said, "Assume a virtue if you have not." Or as they say in the jazz world, "Just fake it because you feel better if you do."

I think the folk festivals remind us of how we would like to be. And how we would like life to be, and then we try to continue doing that. Now with the complete collapse of the music and entertainment industry, there is room for almost everybody and anybody to get a little bit of something out there.

Charles Mingus told me, when I was playing with him in 1955, he said, "Man, no matter how ratty the joint, every night with me is Carnegie Hall. Look, if there is only eleven people out there and ten of them are stoned out of their heads and passing out, or want to get some money from the band, or have a romance, or score some dope. That's okay. If you could find one person that's actually listening, that's all you need. Just play for that one person." And he said, "I know you're trying to write symphonies like me, and nobody's interested. Just find one person to write a symphony for. That's all you need in life." He was great back then. He said, "The reason I'm working in all these dumps with untuned pianos and no sound systems, is because

I don't think I'm worthless. This is the only place where we can get to do what we love to do." And sure enough, playing with him was like being at Carnegie Hall. Even at the old Cafe Bohemia, with that out of tune piano and the manager who would beat up the customers if he didn't like their attitude. And if you couldn't threaten to beat [the manager] up, you might not get paid. It was not ideal, but it was the

best the people could do. But boy, when you went to hear them, or you went to play with them, it was serious. And it was beautiful, and it was sounding good.

FIGURE 52. STEVE GOODMAN AND DAVID AMRAM ON A WORKSHOP STAGE, 1976. PHOTOGRAPH BY DAVID LANDY. ARCHIVES OF MANITOBA, WINNIPEG FOLK FESTIVAL 1976 NEGATIVES, P2566/3, 76/16. 15.

Len UDOW

Len Udow is a singer, songwriter, musician, teacher, and music producer based in Winnipeg who has enjoyed a six-decade-long performing career by travelling to a wide range of stages—from clubs and festivals, concert stages and universities, to radio and television. Len played the Winnipeg Folk Festival the first year and returned for a total of seven more visits. He lived and worked in Toronto where, for many years, he pursued his music along with a calling to teach. Len moved back to his hometown on the prairies and, like his mother before him, he began to teach and create music for and with children—he was particularly active with the Manitoba Arts Council's Artists in Schools Program. He became associated with musician Fred Penner, both in the television studio and touring for many years. In recent years, he has followed his voice and returned to his childhood roots as the Cantorial soloist at Temple Shalom in Winnipeg. He has also recently recorded three albums under the Appellation Music label.

FIGURE 53. LEN UDOW ON A WORKSHOP STAGE, 1977. PHOTOGRAPH BY DAVID LANDY. ARCHIVES OF MANITOBA, WINNIPEG FOLK FESTIVAL 1977 NEGATIVES, P2566/5, 77/15. 2A.

LEN UDOW

8 DECEMBER 2021, WINNIPEG

KEVIN NIKKEL: How were you drawn to folk music?

LEN UDOW: That's a good question that takes me back a few years. How does one start on a lifelong journey being musical by inheritance? This is going to be a long and winding answer to your question. Making music was just what we did in my family; my parents, my aunts and uncles, my cousins in every school I attended. There was a wonderful choir tradition in Winnipeg, and I was very much a part of that. I entered festivals. Sang my heart out, like most children then. Perhaps more than that, we were all taken with the melodies and stories in the *Manitoba School Song Book*, basically British "folk" music. This was one of many sources where folk music appeared in my young life. In junior high I dallied with acting and singing in a Gilbert and Sullivan production of *Trial by Jury*. As well, I grew up in a very insular Jewish community, where Yiddish and Hebrew folk and liturgical music played a central part in all community gatherings.

My first recollections of performing folk music in a wider context was in a club in Winnipeg named The Fourth Dimension [The 4D]. Audiences were charged by the hour, so you clocked in and out with a ticket. This venue was a gift really. For twenty-five cents an hour you could listen to touring folks from all over Canada and the U.S. share their chops. The 4D was a "black box" club, with no decor but just light and sound and a little stage. Even the chairs, tables, floors, walls, and ceiling were painted matte black.

Sometimes other instruments would appear but usually guitars were the norm and, from time to time, songwriters would come through. I remember one writer who wrote for the Smothers Brothers show, Gene Farmer. There was Phil Ochs, and Joni Mitchell. During open mic on Sunday nights, people were welcome to perform. I took my guitar and my nerve and went on. At some point, the owner of the club, Mickey Cooperband, asked if I would be the master of ceremonies for their Sunday "hootenanny" night. I met many of Winnipeg's finest talents, all of whom were coming from different parts of our city to play on the stage, including Neil Young, Jim Donahue, and Daisy DeBolt.

I befriended Chick Roberts of The Dirty Shames and their excellent guitar player, Amos Garrett. I was fortunate to see different expressions of unadorned music and performers who were developing their skills playing on the coffeehouse circuit throughout this country and beyond. I recall being asked if I would come to Toronto and try to make a go of it there, as well. At one point I met a fellow named Sid Dolgay, who was in a Canadian folk group called The Travellers. I think he played mandolin. Sid was starting up a talent agency and offered to act as an agent/manager. Off I went to Toronto.

That's where I lived for almost fifteen years, through part of the 1960s and up through the 1970s. During that time, I played just about everything that was available. Coffeehouses for sure; however, I avoided playing the bars. I didn't want to sing cover songs and was not a drinker looking for a good time. I was more into following my creative yearnings and began to write on a personal, esoteric level. That's when I first started to record in the early 1970s, which culminated in my album *Through Curved Glass* in 1976.

WINNIPEG MUSIC SCENE

KN: Tell me about the attitudes of the youth culture back then.

LU: That's the question that only the future could ask of the past. You might remember the 1960s—if you were there. There were many of us fledgling young musicians. We started up bands gravitating to the hit parade; Gene Vincent, Buddy Holly, and the British sounds trickling in. I was in high school with Randy Bachman and Garry Peterson. In my class was the piano jazz genius Bernie Senensky. We had some amazing guitarists like Lenny Breau and Ray Moga, who were jazz masters playing the downtown clubs. I was singing in a "folk" quartet we formed called The Wayward Four, with Marvin Shane and the Zippursky twins.

Possibly the prevailing attitude back then was that the previous generation was handing us an opportunity to develop our talents and carry on what they had started. For example, this was a time to salute the last remnants of the beatnik era. I had a little taste of it, playing the bongos back then, and joining up with a hip poet and a swinging lady singer. Simplicity was the code in dress and manner and the stress was on urban life and, ultimately, anti-establishment. I played a club called The Establishment on Kennedy and met the poetic character of Bill Jewel. The age of the big band was over, the Rancho Don Carlos and the Copa were mostly gone and this was a minimalist time to challenge the material values of the middle class.

Exciting times awaited at a club called The Cellar across from the [Winnipeg] *Free Press* where Lenny Breau would play, or the City Centre Motor Hotel, where you could hear Mike Lewis and Bob Erlandson explore their congenial jazz sounds. Then, there was a jazz-folk-rock fusion that was going on. All genres were getting melded together along with the last of the "beat" perspective. We said goodbye to the fifties and looked to the coming sixties.

There was an abundance of recordings and television series that were coming out of the States and England. All the folk and rock recordings were readily available and helped coalesce a culture for a whole generation of baby boomers. Our town, like cities all over the world, was full of young people who wanted to congregate, no matter where.

I joined a theatrical troupe called Interfaith Musical Harmony Theatre, where kids from all over the city came to sing, dance, and act in an original production based on a true historical event: *The Republic of Manitoba*.

In the meantime, there were also those who played the community centres and then eventually went on to booking agents and the smoky dim-lit bars, taverns, and legions. The community centre was a place where we played minor league hockey and baseball, but occasionally they would have a "dance" in the social hall. You needed a band that would just pound away the volume and play the familiar sounds we were all listening to. I stayed clear of those dances. I heard that they could be violent, with fights that would break out and probably some substance use at that point as well. More to myself, I took my case of 45s to basement dance parties with my friends instead. Unlike the bars and social dances, folk music was about coffee and some thoughtful fun. My quartet entered the *Amateur Hour* contest on CKY TV, and, to our surprise we won that year! We just barely beat out a young fellow on trumpet whose name was Burton Cummings. Our prize was identical curling sweaters made here in Winnipeg.

So, by process of elimination, I found myself increasingly more into what I thought of as folk music. The folk expression that Pete Seeger tried to show us. This bringing people together and having them find their voices, share stories, and explore other cultures from a world that was now opening to discovery.

On the other hand, the whole basis of rock was the blues, and I was definitely into the blues with the likes of Big Bill Broonzy, and Sonny Terry, and Brownie McGhee: "The blues got my generation making bad, feel so good." It was a very soul-searching time, musically, morally, and philosophically. I remember the revelation on first hearing the radio station out of Chicago where on a clear night we could listen in the car to Dick Biondi. Hearing rhythm and blues, Jimmy Breedlove, Jackie Wilson, Booker T. and the M.G.'s. Quite a contrast with our CBC, which featured Alan Mills, *Don Messer's Jubilee*, *Hymn Sing*, and "Our Pet" Juliette (Juliette Augustina Cavazzi).

To go on, I discovered the Alan Lomax Library of Congress recordings made in the fields of Virginia and the Carolinas. Then, hearing the luminous voices of Odetta, Dave Van Ronk, and the Welsh poet Dylan Thomas. These were sparse but dynamic recordings with simple guitar, bass, and voice. Along with lots of record outlets both in the stores and on the main media. So, the culture proliferated everywhere and I guess the culmination of all those folks at coffeehouses and universities prompted the "new," more massive gatherings at summer festivals that started up and ideally celebrated our sense of multiculturalism.

KN: Regarding the activism of the 1960s, Seeger was very much about purpose, and this was part of the folk movement as well. An effort to be intentional. How would you describe the attitudes of musicians in those years?

LU: I guess you're right. I think there was a sense of social justice, but not necessarily interpreted into political activism, but awareness of injustice or lack of fairness. Just listen to Woody Guthrie and Huddie Ledbetter, or read Mahatma Gandhi who lived in the 1930s through the Depression and war years and had to deal with some very drastic historical inequities. Eventually in the fifties there emerged new ideas, despite the attempts to silence. What better way [to speak] non-violently [than] with song and story? I think that was evident to us all as kids in the 1950s and early sixties. We got that communique. The Great War ended, maybe the bad guys were gone, and we could pursue our dreams of democracy. Can you imagine hearing "Last Night I Had the Strangest Dream" for the first time?

KN: The Folk Festival audience and people going to the coffeehouses, were they more likely to be socially active and interested in changing the world than the crowd going to the rock shows? With the crowds of Woodstock of the 1960s, you could detect that interest in protest and trying to stop the war in Vietnam.

LU: To me, the gatherings here were purely social gatherings. Winnipeg was made up of different towns which were just beginning to evolve into one. I was not looking to affiliate or align myself or associate with any political intent to organize. Yes, we were all quite alarmed about what was going on in Vietnam, but so was living with the A-bomb threat of extinction years earlier. We heard the air raid siren tests from the West Kildonan City Hall on Main Street. The idea that there was a fate waiting for us was well established. The challenge was, could we somehow learn to understand what we could achieve, beyond that fate? That question seemed to be always present. That was a quest for a lot of us; to live our lives despite knowing that the tides of history seemed determined to end us meaninglessly. From this perspective, I began to write and look more intently at my surroundings.

I remember when I lived in Toronto there was a big county fair in Pickering, Ontario where they were going to build a nuclear power plant. Eventually, they did, as we know. I wrote a song called "It's Just a County Fair." I found it the other day, when I was going through some old journals, and I realized that I was very much aware of the risks in forsaking the simple, good things in life in the name of progress. Who, in fact, were we accommodating? I think a lot of that questioning comes from the previous generation, who came to understand our new affluence made us accumulate much more. Why do we need all the hoopla to enjoy fulfilling lives? I think Bob Dylan, much like Allen

Ginsberg and Jack Kerouac, had that beatnik sensibility, to remain steadfast when there was less humanity to be found.

KN: I love how you described this as a fate. It makes me wonder what that could mean for the generation now. There is a lot going on now, too, and for the next generation. When did you meet up with Mitch Podolak?

MEETING MITCH PODOLAK

LU: I used to play in Yorkville when I lived in Toronto. I gravitated toward the village with fellow musicians, artists, poets, and activists. I remember playing in a club there and I could've been auditioning at an open mic. When I finished a set, I stepped off and this familiar, bearded fellow with a lisp came up to me and said, "Hi, my name is Mitch, who are you?" After a while he asked, "What brought you to Toronto?" You know that he already knew—my story was not unique. He said, "Are you looking to do music elsewhere, other than here in Toronto?" So, we walked out of that club, went to his home, which was not far from where I was staying in the Annex area. He introduced me to his mother and insisted I stay for dinner, and so while sharing a steak we talked of future plans. That was our initial meeting, and he booked me into several clubs with his connections from his former management of the club called Bohemian Embassy. After that, we met several more times and, to my surprise Mitch ended up in Winnipeg, married Ava, a wonderful Winnipeg girl, and settled down to carry on and do what he loved the most, which was to organize and bring people together over a meal and a song. So, one day I got an invitation to come back to Winnipeg because he and Colin Jackson—

KN: Colin Gorrie?

LU: Yes, Gorrie, but also Jackson—were involved in organizing government support of this first "freebie" festival out at Birds Hill Park. One evening I remember, after arriving back in Winnipeg, I drove out to the field with friends. Mitch said we should come out for a preview, the night before the opening. They had just completed setting up the stage and sound. What I remember, which may not be accurate, was coming over a hill to where the Main Stage is today. In the dark of night, we had walked in from the road toward a banjo playing somewhere off in the distance. As we got closer it became apparent that Mitch was on a stage playing. That was my first and foremost memory of the very beginning of what was to become the essential International Winnipeg Folk Festival.

I also remember that Mitch kept sharing his concern and hope that this festival would not become just another example for politicians to claim that young people only wanted to take drugs and act out. I don't remember him saying what he wanted it to become, other than, this festival was going to be a larger-than-life musical event with the kind of intimacy and exchange of ideas developed in the coffeehouses and concert halls, throughout those formative years of the folk boom. Mitch envisioned a success, based on the strength of the combined efforts of volunteers and performers.

Don't forget, there were a lot of us postwar babies. And to draw a connecting thread through us and wrangle us together was quite ambitious. I think Mitch probably saw that we all should have a place and a voice on the doings on this planet. After all, he was the "Ambassador of Bohemian Embassy."

Like Seeger and The Weavers, who brought that same sensibility that we were all a welcome part of something meaningful. We all had a purpose; to meet our higher ideals and to help each other. We were all validated in some way. In contrast to those ideals, Mitch's big concern that first night was that a bunch of guys were going to show up with their coolers of beer and their garden furniture and guffaw and ruin the whole thing. Aware of the RCMP presence who were going to come and shut it all down. It didn't happen, although there were a few characters with coolers but they mellowed and enjoyed that first evening alongside the folk devotees.

For most of us, we all showed up with the question, "what could this be?" That first night captured us. So beautiful, out there under the stars. It just seemed to be something that represented our combined aspirations, I guess. In every sense of the word, we felt lucky to be at the start line.

KN: It sounds so delightful, but also idealistic.

LU: I think there had to be some idealism. I think you're right. Mitch didn't really speak, to me anyway, as a visionary. He was a stubborn, hard-nosed functionary. I think he needed everyone to join in, and especially the Colins, to front the endeavour—very practical of him—with their talents of persuasion and strong community ties.

KN: Tell me more about your designation of Mitch as a functionary and what that would look like at the Festival. How did he act and how did people see him?

LU: Mitch was an unabashed enthusiast. I think he knew his place was to somehow bring us all together to have a good time and, from that, something extraordinary could happen. The music, the food, the outdoors, and the sky. The only stars at the Festival were in the night sky. I remember Stan Rogers's voice sounding into the woods from the Main Stage and then careening up into a chorus of many voices. In this, Mitch's enthusiasm, and the Festival, has no bounds.

JOHN PRENTICE: You were one of the last ones playing on stage that first weekend Festival, with Fraser and DeBolt? Do you remember what the last song at the finale would have been?

LU: Yes, that set ended with a combination of two songs. My friend Daisy DeBolt joined me, singing the black spiritual "Let Me Fly" combined with a new song, "Glorious Night," written by our friend Patrick Godfrey.

JP: Was that the finale for the whole festival? Or did they do "Goodnight, Irene"?

LU: I don't remember that part. I think "Glorious Night" was the finale the first festival. Or did I read that somewhere?

KN: I love the description of that last evening of the first weekend. There was a lot of excitement that this weekend was good, but Mitch had a lot more planned. What is the conversation that comes after?

LU: I can't speak for everyone, obviously. My sense of that, if we're capturing the memory from that last evening—is this ever going to happen again? That's why it fell upon Mitch to go out and get some long-term support from funding organizations. Especially from the provincial government of the day, and possibly the Feds. That was the big question, how was this going to work? How is this going to pay for itself? It was a successful, modest start. Now, would the stars align for it to ever happen again?

You could feel the challenge in those beginning years, thinking back on how Bill Merritt and Gord Osland, along with Mitch and many others, tried everything to keep this festival alive. I remember when they did a bottle drive and the office on Lilac was filled with empties, waiting to be cashed in. This drive to survive, despite what some might consider to be a very successful cultural phenom here on the Canadian prairie. The best folk festival in Canada, and the office was desperate, was run on pennies and nickels.

WORKSHOPS AT THE FOLK FESTIVAL

KN: Let's talk about the Festival workshops.

LU: [Laughs].

KN: I want to know why you're laughing.

LU: Because it was so puzzling and fun. Mitch would spend weekends sequestered away to think of all the clever titles and themes of the workshops. The performers, whom he chose carefully, were then expected to take the theme so deliberately conceived and relate to it with story and song. We could pull out any tune from our repertoire and somehow fulfill the thematic mandate he'd set for the workshop. These workshops always felt unrehearsed and spontaneous.

The gospel workshop on Sunday morning was easy. All you needed was a good night's sleep the night before. I think Mitch really enjoyed that. The fact that we came out on the early bus on a Sunday morning and sang our hearts out on the prairie. What great voices, remembering Claudia Schmidt, and Sweet Honey in the Rock, Leon Bibb, Odetta, and Ken Whiteley starting off the day with intimations of spirit. I was honoured to be invited.

The last Festival I was invited to, I sat in on a "banjo" workshop. We were a half dozen banjoists, including Leonard Podolak (who was born during the second Festival). What fun. It was so great, seeing how we all approached the instrument so differently. I admit, being a guitarist caught playing banjo to accompany my friend Fred Penner in the family entertainment business. Adults and children really enjoyed the bright cheerfulness of the sound of the banjo. One of my favourite memories for me was of this particular crowd, who were there to enjoy the fun. I took Bob King's song, "Sandwiches are Beautiful," and rewrote it as;

Banjos are beautiful
banjos are fine
I like banjos
I play them all the time
I play them for my supper
I'd play them for my lunch
If I had 100 banjos
I'd play them all at once.

Another memory that strikes home is having a hard time with Mitch because he didn't think pianos were a folk instrument. I'm not opening a can of worms here. I think Mitch had a very definite idea of what folk music should be, and that it remain within a traditional instrumentation. However, I was already playing with a piano player. I was also writing with piano, and occasionally playing with a sax and full set of traps. Much to his credit and the developing musical inclusivity of the Festival, Mitch's wall eventually came down.

I remember in year one or two, it being a rainy and cold day. The workshop stage was under a little tarp and it was starting to rain. I'm thinking this festival was like a musical Olympics—challenging audience and performer to make it to the finish. A question of endurance. Some kind people in the crew or audience sent up a jacket to help brace me against the wind. A little girl sitting right below came on stage and sat on my lap, and I gave her a kazoo. We shivered together. David Landy, the official Festival photographer, caught that moment in a photo. I think, to me, that's the essence of the Folk Festival, brushing shoulders with other people. That musicians were just good folks with stories to tell and sensitivities to portray with their talents. The Festival was not just an art form, it was a unique experience, a people procession. I think that's maybe where the Winnipeg Folk Festival found its niche, in this otherwise isolating and alienating society. To me, the culmination is putting my arms around this child and, together, we were warmed by the music and the company.

KN: Great image.

FIGURE 54. LEN UDOW WITH A YOUNG FAN ON A WORKSHOP STAGE, 1977. PHOTOGRAPH BY DAVID LANDY. ARCHIVES OF MANITOBA, WINNIPEG FOLK FESTIVAL 1977 NEGATIVES, P5266/5, 77/19. 19A.

LU: It was a special occasion, but there are many like that for me. I remember Mitch finally got Pete Seeger to come and play and put him in what was called then "The Kids Tent." Pete, his long neck banjo and all us kids. I swear, there wasn't a dry eye when he sang "Kisses Sweeter than Wine."

KN: I like how you describe the audience and performers, not as separated, but as intimate.

UNIQUENESS OF WINNIPEG

KN: I want to explore the idea that this is happening here on the prairies. Why here? Why did this thing grow so healthy and strong? Could it have just as easily grown in Regina?

LU: Yeah, I would think so. Mariposa was already fading into a school program. I remember playing Mariposa in the 1960s and at one of the last Mariposa Festivals on Ward's Island, but it wasn't a people spectacle. Well, Toronto Harbour didn't have our sky, nor the evergreen forest. Maybe it missed having that sense of going back to the earth. I think the prairie earth, after a long winter, won out.

I've been to many Folk Festivals over the years, but today I'm reluctant to go. I prefer the workshops. They're captivating, quite ingenious, especially when musicians and songwriters come out and share their creative insights and their varied, human imaginations. The Main Stage is a different matter. It's the last stop of the day. People throw their blankets down early. My brother and his family have made it a tradition. It's a family affair, an essential summer event, to feel the sunset with your loved ones. The light, wafting sounds from the distant stage is hard to make out, but that doesn't matter. The place has all the presence and charisma you need.

JP: The "Why Winnipeg" thing, the history of the city, the people that are from here. Is there more tolerance here? Because we have that multicultural background?

LU: I think it's a nice idea, John. The fact that there are so many intact cultures here in Winnipeg and how often they like to celebrate in their own districts. That might play an important role in the effort to make the Folk Festival so magnanimous. I think what does play so well is the

magic of a starry night, a sun-packed day in a shady grove, and being given a unique opportunity in our modern lives to touch the earth. Maybe this is an opportunity for us to see what can be, for a whole generation. What is surprising is that the Festival started with a seed on the prairie, growing more and more each year, until the wonder of it can fill the eye and soul.

KN: I wonder if you could discuss a bit about the 1960s and the passion that was present amongst the audiences at that time. What has been the legacy of the Folk Festival and how it might translate to the next generation and the optimism we need now?

LU: For myself, the gauntlet was set by those songsters who are all still in our lives, one way or another. One knows that life can be pretty unfair, and the universe is somewhat chaotic and cold. However, if given a chance to watch and listen carefully, you will find in others the hopes and skills to survive and fundamentally help us to make the most of our existence.

Maybe you can find some answers in taking in many performances and expressions of your fellow humans. What better way than a folk festival, where there are not only the arts and crafts for living now, but new ways to find an entrance into the next era, the next great idea. Folk artists and musicians do inspire us to keep working on the building and, besides, enjoy the ride. The hope is that we can learn from others to create a better life with a folk wisdom, tinged with compassion and dignity. The Festival points to a cycle that is a worthwhile, a memorable, marker to have on your life journey. To set a time, and then wander on again to the next orbit around the sun, and returning yet again for another Sundance.

KN: I like the idea of the cycle and beginning again. For each generation.

LU: It's that way when there is success, but it's also the same when there's failure, you know, when you have another chance at it. Nature is showing us that these cycles can be very understanding and forgiving.

FIGURE 55. LEN UDOW ON A WORKSHOP STAGE, 1977. PHOTOGRAPH BY DAVID LANDY. ARCHIVES OF MANITOBA, WINNIPEG FOLK FESTIVAL 1977 NEGATIVES, P2566/5, 77/11. AFTER 36.

So, our traditions grow, year after year. We go back and check out how far we've come.

KN: When you played the early folk festivals, you played with more senior players, because Mitch was scheduling some of these old-timers.

JP: Like Roosevelt Sykes.

KN: So there was this idea of passing on knowledge.

LU: Right on. Yeah. But it was already there in my collection. It was already there in the travels of my youth. Of course, I understood that in my Judaism as well, from the ancient psalms were the songs, passed on to the generations. Now today, in this last part of my life, I'm taking those poems and composing melodies, hopefully to pass on. During the pandemic, I wrote a series of songs concerning growing up in Winnipeg, i.e. "Riding the Salter Bus," "A House by Two Rivers," "Saturday Deluxe." The messages have been sent and, if we are open to receive, maybe we should pass them on as best we can. Could that be the signalling heartbeat of the Folk Festival? Maybe that's just me cogitating something that can't be understood?

FIGURE 56. LIAM CLANCY ON A WORKSHOP STAGE, 1974. PHOTOGRAPH BY JOHN BACHMANN. COURTESY OF WINNIPEG FOLK FESTIVAL.

PART THREE

TUNES FROM THE FAR OUT EAST:

Musicians Attracted into Our Orbit

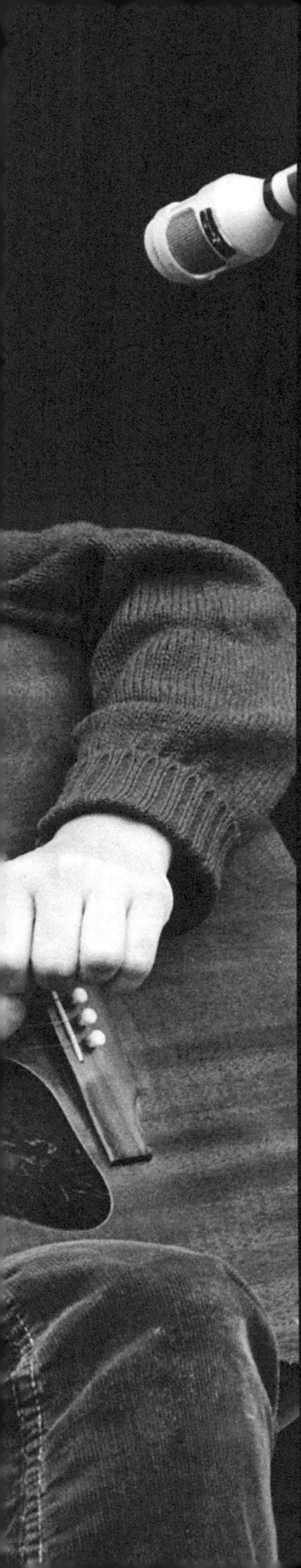

Cathy FINK

Cathy Fink is a distinguished musician and singer-songwriter, and a master of the guitar, banjo, and ukulele. She was born in Maryland but moved to Montréal to study in the 1970s, where she began her career in folk music while busking and playing coffeehouses. She started her career performing solo in 1973 and, in 1974, formed a duo with Duck Donald, touring with him for five years. During this time, she came to Winnipeg and played the Folk Festival—a venue she would return to often, three times by herself, four times with Duck, and five times with her partner, Marcy Marxer. It was while playing the Toronto Folk Festival in 1980 that she met Marcy—digging into traditional Appalachian music, contemporary folk music, and music for children and family audiences. This collaboration would prove extensive and fruitful. Their career together spans forty-three years, with performances at hundreds of festivals, concerts, and music camps, and fifty recordings for which they have numerous nominations, and have won two Grammys.

FIGURE 57. CATHY FINK ON A WORKSHOP STAGE, 1975. PHOTOGRAPH BY DAVID LANDY, ARCHIVES OF MANITOBA, WINNIPEG FOLK FESTIVAL 1975 NEGATIVES, P5266/1, 75-4660. 17.

CATHY FINK

31 MARCH 2022, SILVER SPRING, MARYLAND

KEVIN NIKKEL: How did you find your way into music and the creative life?

CF: I found my way into music as a kid. Or it found its way into me and I followed it. I was always a singer, played a little bit of piano, took up the guitar when my next-door-neighbour-best-friend got her guitar at the age of twelve. Had a few lessons, she quit because she really had no talent, and I just kept on playing.

When I moved to Montréal in 1972 to go to McGill University there was an extremely fabulous, active, folk music and coffeehouse scene. I literally moved from Baltimore, Maryland, where that music was right down the street from me—but not in my neighbourhood, no exposure whatsoever—to Montréal and to where it was all around me. I lived about half a block from the Yellow Door Coffeehouse. I went to every open mic. I visited all the coffeehouses and really had my ears open to all kinds of wonderful music. Took up Appalachian dulcimer, up there in Montréal, and that led me into more traditional music. And there were so many great players around.

Everybody was in what I'm going to call the "earn while you learn" mode and the best time to learn something from somebody is when they've just learned it and they're so excited about it, and they want to show somebody. I'm like, "Oh that's how you play 'Freight Train' by Elizabeth Cotten. Will you slow that down and show me how you do that?" A lot of that kind of stuff. It's really become my whole life, for my creative life, as you said.

KN: You arrived in Montréal. At that point, how aware were you of the trajectory you wanted for yourself, or the type of music you wanted to play?

CF: I really didn't know at that time exactly what I wanted to do. I was in school for a year, going to coffeehouses, listening to music, hearing music, hanging out, imbibing it. Eventually at the end of the school year going, "hmm, I wonder." I got one of those, what we like to call, "only in Canada" grants. That grant was to take a troop of musicians around Montréal for the whole summer. Then I just started hustling to book concerts and workshops.

I practised a couple hours a day, but I also knew that there were only officially five or six folk club gigs in the area and that's not going to sustain anybody. I realized that if I started playing community centres and seniors groups, and a little of this and a little of that, and clubs that might want a performance, that could sustain me. And it would be really fun. So, I just literally went through the phone book and started making calls, and handwriting letters to places, and filling up my calendar. While in school at McGill I had worked very part-time as a substitute teacher at day care centres and I'd always take my guitar. Word got around. People said, "Oh, you need a substitute? Get that girl that plays guitar and sings with the kids." That launched the other side of my career of playing a lot of music with kids and families. So those two things, the folk music world and my kids' music worlds, converged. They did that for a long time.

KN: At what point did you start travelling beyond Montréal?

PLAYING WITH DUCK DONALD

CF: What happened is that I became very good friends with Duck Donald and, in that process, he taught me an enormous amount of music. He was really encyclopedic about bluegrass and the history of bluegrass. And the history of what I would call old-time music, pre-bluegrass music. He was a quirky, left-handed guitar player and mandolin player with a high tenor voice, which suited bluegrass just great. We started playing music together. We started busking, particularly in the metro stations. I'll never forget, there was one phenomenal busking session where people just gave us so much money, but we realized that it was the night of Bob Dylan's Rolling Thunder Revue and half the people passing us in the subway were on their way to that show, assuming that we were trying to make enough money to go to the show.

But the two of us started making music together a lot. Formed a duo. Actually, became a couple. We took the advice of another Canadian folksinger that we totally loved, Vera Johnson. We had decided we were going to get out of Montréal. We didn't know what we were going to do, but we were going to make our way across the country, somehow, doing shows. Vera said, "Oh well, call these friends of mine and ask them if you could set up a house concert." One was in Winnipeg, one was in Calgary, one was in Vancouver. I didn't even know what a house concert was. I didn't ask her. So, at the age of twenty, I just boldly made these phone calls—long distance phone calls were a big deal back then, if you recall—you waited until after six when the rates went down. I made these phone calls and I'd say, "Vera Johnson suggested I call to see if you would host a house concert."

And the next thing they'd say would be, "What's a house concert?"

I'd make it up. "Oh well, I think you invite people over and we do a concert in your living room and they throw some money in the hat, everybody's happy." We played Fiddler's Green in Toronto. We lined up a house concert in Winnipeg, with Paul and Donna Phillips, who were friends of Mitch's. Calgary with Barry and Lyn Luft. In Vancouver, nobody wanted to do a house concert there.

It's 1974. Winnipeg centennial. Paul and Donna said, "There's going to be a big folk festival. This guy Mitch Podolak got a huge grant to put on a free folk festival, blah blah blah. Maybe I can get you an audition." He managed to get us an audition. Meantime, Paul and Duck had gotten into Paul's homebrew that day. By the time we got to Mitch's house, Duck was drunk as could be. I wasn't convinced that he could play two notes, let alone pull off an audition. I moved my chair a foot in front of his, and Mitch is sitting back like this in his reclining chair, and I'm sitting in front of Duck and I'm playing dulcimer and guitar and we're singing. Mitch looks at us and he goes, "Tell you what, if you join the union, I'll book you at the Festival." Because it was a CBC thing, that you had to join. Next day, we booked it down to the union.

WHY WINNIPEG?

So, we did Calgary, then we went on to Vancouver. We miraculously got hired through some friends to play for three weeks at the World's Fair in Spokane, Washington. Then we were like, "Okay, now we don't know what we're doing." We just said, "Well, let's move to Winnipeg. That's our union local." And also, we felt like Winnipeg was sort of the new frontier, in terms of a fresh new community of people interested in folk music. We knew we didn't want to live in Toronto. The Mariposa Folk Festival did eventually hire us, but one person who worked at that Festival prior to that actually said, "Well, the main reason people move out west is because they can't make it in the east." I'm like, that's not even an attitude I want to be around. We just felt like there's a new vibe here. We had the opportunity to be part of a new community, and that was a really exciting thing. It was a really, really exciting thing.

We played the first [Winnipeg] Festival. We were involved in all kinds of different musical events around town. We had started touring across Canada and down to the U.S. That's when I met Daniel Koulack, because I think after the first or second Festival, Mitch started the Winnipeg Folklore Centre. It was really modelled after the Toronto Folklore Centre, which was modelled after other folklore centres that had been around. We would go down there sometimes at lunchtime and hang out and do lunch with whoever was there, play some music with whoever was there. One day, this kid walks in, he was about twelve years old. It was Koulack, and he played some banjo already. He was pretty darn good. I said, "Have you thought about taking lessons?"

He said, "Well, I don't think my parents would let me do that."

And I said, "How about if I teach you for free? Will they let you come if I teach you for free?" He's an amazing musician. We're still good friends and it's fifty years later. That was the vibe at the time. It was exciting. It felt new. It felt like something was going to open up.

KN: Let's pick up on this idea of Winnipeg as a new frontier. As a Winnipegger, I'm constantly fascinated by the question of, "Why Winnipeg?" Why not Regina or Saskatoon?

CF: The centrepiece of why the folk scene sort of landed in Winnipeg as opposed to Saskatoon, as opposed to Regina, as opposed to Edmonton, any place, was really Mitch got the grant. Mitch seized the day. He saw the opportunity to celebrate the hundredth anniversary of Winnipeg with this big, free, musical thing at Birds Hill Park. He saw an opportunity that was a combo of self-serving and community serving. He had a personal love for a certain style of music, and now somebody was giving him money to throw a party

Blue

with that style of music. I say that style; it is really so many different styles of music.

He had a budget to fly people in. He had a budget to give them good hospitality. He had a budget to treat them well. He had the inspiration of the Newport Folk Festivals, the Philadelphia Folk Festivals, the Mariposa Folk Festival, but nothing like that had happened out west. So, it was really his baby. It was a combo—luck and a brilliant moment. Mitch was always very good at getting grant money. Also, very good at spending it. But I think that's why Winnipeg, at that time.

Two years later, he did something similar and started the Vancouver Folk Festival. His tenure there was only two years long and then it was taken over by Gary Cristall and a bunch of other people. Mitch and Gary went back a long ways. I don't feel that, festival-wise, any of the other things that Mitch really tried to do had the same legs. The year that Mariposa decided they weren't going to have a festival that year, he swooped in for the Toronto Folk Festival (1980). It was not well organized. It was a huge financial disaster. The joke in my life is that the partnership of Cathy Fink and Marcy Marxer is one of the few good things that came out of the Toronto Folk Festival because that's where we met. She was playing in a group called the Bosom Buddies from Michigan—an all-girl string band. I was in my first foray of festivals as a solo artist after leaving Winnipeg, after going out on my own. That's where we met and forty-three years later, we're still here. Which is fabulous. I think the Festival has its own legacy. And it's not to say that Mitch didn't do other things, but I think the Festival is the big part of the legacy.

FIGURE 58. CATHY FINK AND DUCK DONALD AT WINNIPEG FOLK FESTIVAL, 1977. PHOTOGRAPH BY GERRY KOPELOW. COURTESY OF WINNIPEG FOLK FESTIVAL.

BACKSTAGE AT THE WINNIPEG FOLK FESTIVAL

KN: You were at the first Winnipeg Folk Festival?

CF: I turned twenty-one at the first Winnipeg Folk Festival. Big deal. It was literally smack in the middle of my birthday.

KN: What was it like? What sort of expectations did you have?

CF: I don't remember how we got to town, but what I do remember is everybody stayed in the same hotel, and they piled us into buses in the morning and we'd drive out to Birds Hill Park. Four or five stages and a Main Stage. The model was very Mariposa-like, except there was an evening concert. Mariposa had dropped their evening concerts at that point.

There were so many magic things about it. Backstage was magic. I can't tell you how many lifelong friends I made backstage at that Festival, and many other festivals. Now when you go to the Festival, everybody comes in, they do their thing, they leave, they move on to the next gig. It's rare that there will be an hour-long or two-hour-long slot, where at least fifty percent of the performers are all mulling around in the same place. The jam sessions backstage were terrific. The friend-making was terrific. In fact, at the first Winnipeg Folk Festival, we're playing backstage and Shirley Eikhard heard me play Appalachian dulcimer and she said, "Will you join me on stage for a song?" I mean that kind of magic happened.

And the hospitality was fantastic. Mitch, as a foodie, believed that the way to people's hearts was through their stomachs. He made sure that there were great backstage meals. I mean, that was a primo thing and not enough festivals have taken note of that. As a performer, when you're travelling around, looking for decent food takes up your time, it takes time away from preparation for the gig. It takes time away from this, it takes time away from that. It's not always easy. Even now, I don't think the Festival does much backstage hospitality. They give you vouchers and you go get your food at various food booths, etc. But what they've lost in that process is the community that was built backstage.

That community continued late at night at the hotel for the parties and it wasn't just partying, it was playing music until two o'clock, or three o'clock, or four o'clock in the morning. Those are the friends that you kept. You couldn't wait to see them at the next festival, or the next time they came through town. Or you went through their town, you were going to get together, you were going to play music again. I can't tell you how much I learned, sitting in the front row of concerts and workshops at Winnipeg and other festivals. I mean, I was a brand-new banjo player, I was going to sit in front of every banjo player and watch everything they did. I followed Hedy West around. I followed Peggy Seeger. I followed Mike Seeger around. Some of these people became very dear friends of ours. Those connections are what happened at these festivals and that's the biggest part of them.

KN: I want to hear more about playing the workshops.

CF: People would say, "Okay what kind of workshops do you want to do?" In those days, workshops were workshops. They weren't mini performances, which is what you see now. You'd actually go to a workshop and learn something. You might even learn the technique, or at least understand it. We would connect with the festival presenters. They'd say, "What workshops do you want to do?"

And I'd say, "Tell me who else is performing," because then I can visualize how we can lead certain workshops with groups of people. That's a lot of how it worked.

The workshops were really amazing back then and the Festival was much more intimate. That's before the age where anybody plugged in. We didn't have electronic tuners. You actually knew how to tune your instruments by ear and be in tune with the other person by ear. I feel like, what a magic time. The other thing about it was, what an incredible honour. What an honour, to be on a workshop stage with someone like Mike Seeger. To be on a workshop stage with a group like the Red Clay Ramblers. To be on a workshop stage with any number of people. Paul Mills and Bill Garrett.

The other thing is that we were young. We were the newbies, so every one of these was an opportunity to reach further. We practised a lot. We never missed a day of two to three hours a day of practice together, and then some time practising separately on instrumental stuff. We were hungry for every piece of music that we wanted to learn.

MITCH PODOLAK'S APPROACH TO PROGRAMMING

KN: Tell me about your interactions with Mitch.

CF: Mitch was a character. He had a vision. He had multiple great visions. He played a little bit of music. Mitch played the same three old-time banjo tunes as long as I knew him. He was very good at those tunes, and he owned a banjo, the neck of which was made by Jean Larrivée. A nice little banjo. I hope that Leonard owns it. Mitch always had a new, big idea. He was a dreamer. He wasn't always a realist when it came to making those dreams come true, and then you try and surround yourself with people who know how to do that. Sometimes it worked, sometimes it didn't. I think what he gets credit for is that magic moment of attaching the centennial to grant money to the beginning—I'm going to give him credit for what he did.

And he also raised a great kid. Leonard Podolak is sweet and smart and passionate about music and organized. I think Ava did a lot of the biz work behind Mitch's dreams, and I think Leonard got a little bit of both. I think that's one of the most wonderful things for Mitch. And also, I know that Mitch and Ava took in some kids who needed help. I think that's a big deal. Those kids absolutely became part of the family. They became Leonard's siblings.

KN: I wanted to come back to what you were saying about the workshops and how they were like a seminar. People sharing their knowledge about their instrument. What was Mitch's approach to workshops?

CF: Mitch's method in the workshop world was really modelled after Newport, Philly, and Mariposa. In the beginning there was a lot of attention paid to workshops that really imparted information. When there was a banjo workshop, for instance, there'd be four or five banjo players who specialized in different styles, and they'd talk about those styles, and they'd talk about where those styles came from, and they'd demonstrate those styles. To me, that's the kind of event where you don't know who's in the audience saying, "Oh I've got to learn to play that," or "I've got a banjo and I've never picked it up, and now I'm going to do that." It might be guitar. It might be a harmonica. There were all these instrumental workshops with specialists of different styles. They were always awesome. There were musical style workshops, and then there was also musical topic workshops.

In the later years of Mariposa on the island, they started having more topical kinds of workshops. There might be a workshop on English ballad singing. There might be a workshop on traditional French-Canadian songs. There might be a fiddle workshop where you'd have Jean Carignan, Gilles Losier, an American old-time fiddler and maybe a Swedish fiddler. Then you have this beautiful compare / contrast, and let's also see where what we do is similar. Those were great moments.

I think one of the interesting things about Winnipeg, I think it's also true with Philly, is that the infrastructure community also becomes very tight. Right? There are people who work at the Festival who barely ever hear any music. They're on crew. They're guarding a fence. They're doing this. They're running around. They're doing transportation. They're doing all these other things. They built their own community around supporting the music, but also someplace in there they made friends that they don't want to lose, so they keep coming back to the community.

KN: You and Duck playing together. Any memories of what that collaboration was like at the Festivals?

CF: The first year of the Winnipeg Folk Festival, we were not Main Stage performers. I can't remember if we had our own little concert on stage ten miles away or not. There weren't that many stages, but we were in a couple of workshops. I can't remember what year we were on the Main Stage. It might've been the second year. The third year, I think we brought a bluegrass band. We called it the Duck Mountain Bluegrass Band with John Weier, and I'm not sure who on bass. A four-piece band. We hung out at the Festival a lot. I came back and played it solo. I emceed it one year with Bill Garrett. That was after Mitch had left and I believe Rosalie Goldstein was in charge that year.

What I feel badly about is that the way so many festivals are run now, people who forty years ago would've run into each other backstage and become friends or jammed or co-written a song, they just won't even be on the premises at the same time. So, I think what happened in those early years, there was a community being built amongst performers, amongst performers and the audience, amongst the audience, amongst the crew, that was the centrepiece of the whole thing. What do you do this for? Community or something, because you certainly don't do it to see how much money you can make.

Another thing that was important about the early years of the Festival, in line with festivals like Mariposa, and Newport, everyone was paid equally. Even if you were more famous than other people, you weren't getting more money. You had to want to be there. Clearly the connection with CBC was a bonus. But I think the dynamics of the Festival began to change quite a bit as the financial dynamics changed. As the concept that we have to have bigger names and, therefore, we have to pay them more. Then some of those bigger names never did a workshop, they were only on the Main Stage. All of that changes the vibe in the community. I'm not saying that it's all for the worse, but I will say that it changes things.

KN: Anything else you want to add?

CF: Playing the first Winnipeg Folk Festival at the age of twenty-one, even though we didn't have a big slot and we weren't all over the place, it was a step up in our career. It was a prestigious event. It allowed us to contact other festivals and say, "We just performed the first Winnipeg Folk Festival." I mean, two years later Duck Donald and I performed at the Philly Folk Festival. They had very few Canadians, and they certainly had no completely unknown Canadians playing at that festival, and we had a dang-good evening concert set. The person who was booking the Festival got our LP in the mail and actually listened to it and loved it, and of course in our press materials—which if I looked at them now, I'd laugh—it included the fact that we had that experience under our belts. It gave us some prestige that we might not have otherwise had. I think that worked for a lot of performers.

While Mitch is well-remembered, I also want to say that I'm really glad that Ava Kobrinsky got an award for her part. I think very much like Pete and Toshi Seeger, Pete had these big ideas, Toshi implemented them, and they had a wonderful, interesting partnership. I think that few people knew how much Ava was involved, right down to the part where the Festival really didn't provide a livelihood for the family; she was working a government day job. That's its own kind of support and that's a love of the person, and a love of the project. I'm glad that she got recognized for that.

FIGURE 59. WORKSHOP STAGE AT WINNIPEG FOLK FESTIVAL, 1976. PHOTOGRAPH BY DAVID LANDY. ARCHIVES OF MANITOBA, WINNIPEG FOLK FESTIVAL 1976 NEGATIVES, P5266/3, 76/15. 9A.

What Leonard is doing with Home Routes is the logical extension of the community side of what a festival can do. And, of course, Home Routes is not really related to the Winnipeg Folk Festival, other than the fact that it's all cut from the same cloth. I think that the Winnipeg Folk Festival scored an important place in history and I'm glad to have been part of it.

Ken WHITELEY

Ken Whiteley is a Toronto-based singer-songwriter. He began his career in folk music collaborating at fourteen with his brother Chris and the group The Original Sloth Band. Ken was a regular at Toronto coffeehouses and folk festivals—volunteering at Mariposa Folk Festival at a young age and mentored by festival programmer Estelle Klein. Ken's musical collaborations over the years have been many: playing guitar and mandolin in the style of jug band, folk, swing, blues, gospel, and children's music. He has to his credit seven Juno and sixteen Maple Blues Award nominations. He's been awarded a Canadian Folk Music Award, a Genie Award for Best Original Song in a Canadian film, and Lifetime Achievement recognition from Folk Music Ontario, Maple Blues Awards, and from the Mariposa Folk Festival. As a record producer, Ken has worked on over 180 recording projects and won ten Canadian Gold and Platinum records and four American Gold records, received twenty-four Juno and two Grammy nominations, and sold over 8 million copies.

FIGURE 60. PERFORMERS WITH KEN WHITELEY (THIRD FROM LEFT) ON A WORKSHOP STAGE, 1974. PHOTOGRAPH BY JOHN BACHMANN. COURTESY OF WINNIPEG FOLK FESTIVAL.

KEN WHITELEY

27 NOVEMBER 2021, TORONTO, ONTARIO

KEVIN NIKKEL: Introduce yourself. How did you find your way into the creative path you took in your life?

KEN WHITELEY: My name is Ken Whiteley. I'm a musician, and have been for a long time. I actually joined the musicians' union when I was fourteen. My brother Chris is three years older and he and I started a jug band, back when we were in high school. Originally called Tubby Fats Original All-Star Downtown Syncopated Big Rock Jug Band and gradually, over time, it morphed into this group called The Original Sloth Band.

I attended my first folk festival in 1964 when I was thirteen, and it was a life-changing experience. My brother and I were already into folk music, and going to Mariposa in 1964 was so important, for many reasons. It was held at Maple Leaf Stadium at the foot of Bathurst Street in Toronto because at the last minute the town council in Orillia passed a bylaw forbidding them to have it up in Orillia. My mind was blown: an unknown Gord Lightfoot, Jean Carignan, Mississippi John Hurt, Rev. Gary Davis, Buffy Sainte-Marie, and more.

Then later that summer we talked my parents into letting us go to the Philadelphia Folk Festival. It was like a side-trip from a family vacation. So, there I saw Son House for the first time. Son House is, of course, the man who taught Robert Johnson and Muddy Waters, and he was so intense and playing slide guitars. For me it was like, "That's it, I just have to get a slide guitar. I have to play resophonic guitar and do that." That was huge for me. I was like a sponge and I was just so ready to absorb this all. By the next summer we were playing music and we did our first gig in the summer of 1965. Went to Mariposa in 1966 to volunteer. Estelle Klein, who ran Mariposa for many years, was the artistic director. She really mentored us and took us under her wing.

TORONTO FOLK MUSIC SCENE OF THE 1960S AND 1970S

KN: What was the folk music climate like in the 1960s and 1970s? Was it in tandem with rock music?

KW: Toronto was a really exciting place to be in those days. There were a lot of things going on and a lot of change happening all the time. One of the things was a lot of progressive Americans, both directly as draft dodgers, but also, they weren't necessarily evading the draft, but like "I gotta get out of here," and coming to Canada. That was one thing that was changing the scene in Toronto. Estelle Klein and people around her, Lee Cline (no relation) and other people that worked with her. They had the Guild of Canadian Folk Artists. Bram Morrison, from much later Sharon, Lois, and Bram, Klaas van Graf, and different people. There was this scene at the Riverboat Coffeehouse, where every Monday night there were hootenannies and there would be one artist hired and paid and then other people coming down and singing.

There were so many good musicians and good players and people who would share things. Lonnie Johnson, the great bluesman, was originally from New Orleans and played with Louis Armstrong, he really invented lead guitar. He had moved to Toronto in 1965. Amos Garrett was so nice to us and showing us things. I'd say, "What is that that Lonnie Johnson played?"

He would reply, "Oh, he's playing a 13th chord. You can get the different number. . . ." And he would explain all those kinds of chord substitutions and different things like that to me.

Later in the 1960s, the Toronto Folklore Centre opened up. Eric Nagler, who was an American folkie frailing banjo player, and Paul Hornbeck—a frailing banjo player—they move up and they're running this Toronto Folklore Centre. All of a sudden, there's this place you could go to six days a week and hang out, play instruments, and talk about folk music with people. You'd see all kinds of people always coming and going through there. This whole scene evolves and there is this steady stream of the best of the young American folk artists.

There used to be a little coffeehouse in Scarborough we would go to, The Seven of Clubs. The first time I ever saw Arlo Guthrie was there, playing in a room the size of this room, to about fifteen or eighteen people on a Friday night. There was all of this incubation going on. And Mariposa was huge. It was kind of like the big celebration at the end of June every year. When they moved it in 1968 to the Toronto Islands, that really kind of cemented its role within the Southern Ontario folk music scene. All these people would come up from the States for Mariposa, not just as performers but as audience members.

It was actually a lot more porous, really, in a lot of ways between the folk scene and the blues and the rock scene. So, you had people like Adam Mitchell, or Zal Yanovsky was another who went on to be part of the Lovin' Spoonful, he was another guitar student of Amos Garret's—unofficial. So, there's all this kind of back-and-forth. The Festival Express—which was in 1971—which was this rock tour with The Band, but Eric Andersen, singer-songwriter, was on it. Ian and Sylvia, with Amos as the bandleader, all of these kinds of things. There is this kind of back-and-forth.

Then you get the early 1970s Mariposas with Bob Dylan, Neil Young, and Graham Nash just coming to be there. Graham Nash came to the 1971 Festival when Joni Mitchell was playing there. At the 1971 Festival, there were people trying to break down the gates saying "Free festival, free festival." That same summer, there was the Toronto rock 'n' roll revival where John Lennon played with Yoko Ono and Eric Clapton on guitar. People were breaking in and scaling the back wall of Varsity Stadium and getting in free.

It was the revolutionary times. The times were full of this kind of foment of social change and some of it really was rooted in progressive causes. Some people were really committed. Certain socialist groups would not agree with each other about, whatever. There was this kind of spillover, if you will, of people just sort of saying, "Fuck the System." That kind of attitude, a lot of people were along for the ride. A lot of people along for the drugs, or the sex and the rock 'n' roll. And a lot of people were deeply committed to it and coming from a very sincere and rooted place.

Buffy Sainte-Marie talking about Indigenous issues in the 1960s, and she was one of my favourite songwriters when she sang "Now that the Buffalo's Gone," and any of those songs that she was singing back in the 1960s on Indigenous issues. The same with the civil rights movement and how that spilled over. Then of course, the anti-war movement was huge. The first demonstration I went to was during the March on Selma down at the American Consulate, the first of what were to be many times I would go to the American Consulate to demonstrate because there were also Vietnam demonstrations there. Eventually they put up big barriers so you couldn't be on the sidewalk in front of the American Consulate. So, there was this real foment of political activism that ran a gamut, from people who were very sincere and very committed to try to make the world a better place, and then some people were just kind of in it for the party.

KN: And that was welcome amongst the folkies?

KW: A lot of that was nurtured in the folk community. The people who are writing songs and the civil-rights singers, the Freedom Singers, Bernice Reagon, who later started Sweet Honey in the Rock, was in the original Freedom Singers, which were a group affiliated with the Student Nonviolent Coordinating Committee (SNCC). A whole bunch of singers who were doing that kind of work. The whole political unit of people writing political songs like Tom Paxton, Malvina Reynolds, and Phil Ochs and many others. A lot of the real people who were bringing together music and political action. Pete Seeger, Joan Baez, of course, Bob Dylan, of course. By 1967, Dylan really was not making explicitly political music, right, he came out with *Bringing It All Back Home.*

In the late 1960s there was this convergence. Dylan is playing with the group that would become known as The Band and in 1966 they played at Massey Hall. At the time the marquee outside said Bob Dylan with Levon and the Hawks, because there they were, just around the corner from Yonge Street, where they had spent a lot of time playing music. I was at that concert and it was one of the best concerts I'd ever seen. Mind blowing.

But a lot of the really influential rock music was rooted in what was folk music. The way that the guys in The Band backed up Sonny Boy Williamson and different blues singers. The way that they knew the Appalachian music and those kinds of harmonies and the bluegrass and all that kind of stuff. Bob Dylan is of course heavily rooted in it. And that spills over into so many other people. In Toronto people like Adam Mitchell or other people who form rock bands but had their roots in folk music.

FIGURE 61. KEN WHITELEY, DAVID ESSIG, AND JOHN HAMMOND ON A WORKSHOP STAGE, 1974. PHOTOGRAPH BY JOHN BACHMANN. COURTESY OF WINNIPEG FOLK FESTIVAL.

MITCH PODOLAK

KN: Connects a lot of dots. So, you're attending these shows and festivals and eventually you bump into Mitch Podolak, probably at some of these same events?

KW: Absolutely. And he's in one of those socialist groups.

KN: Exactly. And eventually he comes to Winnipeg, but there was a seed planted.

KW: Absolutely. I didn't really know Mitch when he was living in Toronto. Although we were at many of the same events, from demonstrations at the U.S. Consulate to festivals and so on. I didn't really know him until I began hanging out in Winnipeg. I was very good friends with a singer named Len Udow. Len and I used to play together and I went to Winnipeg and played with Len. Daniel Berrigan came and taught for a term at the University Manitoba and I had friends who went out specifically to study with him. So, I went out and did some gigs with Len. Played a benefit for the farm workers, met Daniel Berrigan and all this kind of stuff. I was starting to get to know Winnipeg and then I began hearing about this guy, Mitch Podolak, and he had this idea to start a folk festival. He hired my friend Raffi, who was at that point still a singer-songwriter. And he hired us, The Original Sloth Band.

That first year it was a free festival. He had friends in the NDP Manitoba Government and he got them to foot the bill. He put on this great folk festival and, because it was free, got a huge crowd. Then the following year they do it again, this time start charging admission, and by then the word's gotten out.

At that point, as we're heading into the mid-1970s, there starts to be this movement all across Canada of new festivals. Within a year of Winnipeg, the Owen Sound Summerfolk, the London Home County Festival, and Hamilton Festival of Friends, and Blue Skies Festival out in the middle of Eastern Ontario, and all these other festivals start forming and there is this whole circuit. I'm a musician in my early twenties and I'm going to a festival every weekend pretty soon. By the mid-1970s, this has become my life. And that creates an audience. In each of these towns, there were coffeehouses to play. Things like that. You'd go and play for two or three nights. It wasn't like just a one-nighter here and there. So, you develop friendships in the towns.

And a whole scene began to develop between the Canadian performers who knew each other, but also Americans who were coming up and doing the same circuit, there becomes this unique kind of community amongst all the musicians.

KN: I heard the same thing from David Essig. He talked about how different the culture was down in the States. He came up here and discovered this community.

KW: Sure. Dave is one of the Americans who comes up because of the political situation and he goes way up to Emsdale, Ontario, but he's willing to drive down to Toronto for gigs. My brother and I actually started playing with Dave, as well as doing Sloth Band gigs. We played on his records and are still friends, after all these years. Dave started a record label and he recorded the second Sloth Band album that we did along with Willie P. Bennett, who I played with. So, there's all these kinds of connections. All of these things in the 1970s are kind of bubbling up out of this folk community.

KN: And in the mid 1970s, Mitch has this idea of doing this festival in Winnipeg, as an extension? Like the wave is spreading west?

KW: There were things already happening out west. I'm pretty sure that the Regina Folk Festival started in 1971. There were folk clubs. Don Whalen, who was involved in eventually doing the Edmonton Folk Fest, but at that point he was running a club in Edmonton. There was a folk scene happening all over the place. I think Mitch was inspired in many ways by Estelle Klein and what she had done and, at the same time, thought he had some ideas for how we wanted to do things differently.

I mentioned how in 1971 there was this big clamour of people trying to get in free to the evening concerts, so in 1972 Estelle has this idea: no more evening concerts. It's just going to be daytime until the sun goes down. We don't have to get into lights. It would be a multi-stage event, people will do concerts but it will all be daytime. It gives it a whole different emphasis, because then the workshops are potentially as important, in some cases more important, than the concerts. That's where incredible things happen. This is one of Estelle's brilliant, intuitive understandings. Of how to create magic on stage with the way she would combine people, talking to them beforehand to percolate a collective process.

In the early years of Winnipeg, Mitch would go through old Mariposa programs and literally take the titles. If he had some of the same people, he'd put them on. "The Seven Deadly Sins"? Okay! Do the same workshop in Winnipeg. But he also missed the old evening concerts. He missed that kind of big show element and so he wanted to bring back the big show and also have these really vital workshops where exciting things were happening in the day as well. And through both of those things, make a really exciting event.

KN: Were there other ways that Mitch borrowed something or made things his own?

KW: For a long time, Mitch was very doctrinaire about acoustic only. As the 1970s went on, that became less and less viable. You can't have a Chicago blues act because the traditional Chicago blues is plugged in since the 1940s, as they begin building pickups in acoustic guitars. If you can run your acoustic guitar through a pedal board, is that an acoustic guitar, or is that an electric guitar? The distinctions became meaningless. So eventually he let that go. But when he started for the first few years, he was very doctrinaire. Now with the Sloth Band, we played both acoustic and electric instruments. We'd mix it up. We had horns. We played with drums. Drums of course are the original acoustic instrument—they go back many tens of thousands of years.

THE IMPACT OF THE WINNIPEG FOLK FESTIVAL

I think that one of the other special things about what Winnipeg created in those early years, that has continued to the present day, is it really created a special event for Winnipeg, for Manitoba, for the prairies. I think that really also has had a big impact. And it had a big impact on the scene in Winnipeg, and people carrying it forward. The musicians that were encouraged, and inspired, and so on, from that. It really nourished and nurtured a very vibrant scene.

KN: One of the questions I like asking— and it helps to ask it far from Winnipeg—was what happened in Winnipeg at all unique? They say it matters where the grapes grow because there is something in the soil.

Or not. Maybe it's just another festival, and that is okay. Is it different, what Mitch created?

KW: It's interesting that you talk about the soil because one of the things that was unique from a performer's perspective was that you are out there on the prairie. You weren't in Winnipeg, you were in Birds Hill Park. We were forty-five minutes from the hotel and this whole rigamarole with buses. But hanging out on the bus with Stéphane Grappelli, or Roosevelt Sykes, or whatever, that becomes part of the experience. You get out there and you're out there for the day. You're not like, "I will go back to the hotel, have a nap, and come back for my concert tonight." You're out there for the day. You're out there on the prairie. If it's hot, if it's raining, whatever, you're in the elements, as the audience is. That kind of creates this *in this together* sensation. I think that that is kind of unique: the dust, the mosquitoes, heat in the day, cold at night, depending on the year. All of those kinds of things are something that was very much of that place, of the prairies. You know, because you weren't in Winnipeg per se, you were at Birds Hill Park.

But you know, the things that were so incredible for me, and others like me as young musicians, were the chances to play for 12,000 people. It was incredible, and to play with and meet with these people like Bernice Reagon and Sweet Honey in the Rock, or Roosevelt Sykes. Through a few festivals I became very good friends with a great piano player named Blind John Davis who was the house piano player for Bluebird Records in the 1930s and 1940s and had recorded with many blues legends. So, with the Original Sloth Band, we actually began touring and recording with John Davis after the festivals. We became very close. I've had so many incredible workshop experiences over the years.

KN: Tell me about that. Any awkward moments?

KW: I was never freaked out. One of the funniest ones was when Rosalie Goldstein, who succeeded Mitch as the artistic director, had hired Ladysmith Black Mambazo—who had just come off a world tour with Paul Simon and were quite well-known and popular—and this great African-American gospel group from Wilmington, Delaware, The Gospel Ambassadors. They were really fire and brimstone singers, great players. She said, "Ken, can you just host this with these two

FIGURE 62. AUDIENCE AT WINNIPEG FOLK FESTIVAL, 1980. PHOTOGRAPH BY DAVID LANDY. ARCHIVES OF MANITOBA, WINNIPEG FOLK FESTIVAL 1980 NEGATIVES, P5266/3, 80/659.

groups, because neither of them have ever been at the Festival before, it'd be great if somebody who's kind of more familiar with the scene could kind of help set the stage for them."

I said, "Yeah, I would be honoured. I'd love to do that."

So, I get there and then you know the guy from the Gospel Ambassadors said, "Well, you're going to sing too, aren't you?" So, we go out, it's essentially the two acts, as Rosalie had envisaged it. But then we go out and we're doing "Amazing Grace" as the finale. I've been listening to all of this and introducing people through this whole thing. These sixteen incredible singers on the stage and I'm the lone white guy. I get up. The energy I felt in that moment when I broke into my verse of "Amazing Grace," and the look on their face—they're like, "Okay! He can do this." That was an early time where I had this really affirming experience, at a very profound and deep level that I was doing the right thing. And getting the approval of people like that meant so much to me and encouraged me.

Another incredible, life-changing experience has been what happens in the evening after the Festival. Back at the hotel with the parties. I remember from the very first festivals, they used the Fort Garry Hotel downtown, the big, old, railroad hotel. Staying up till dawn, singing with Mimi Fariña. All these people singing songs, trading songs, and things like that. That continues to be part of the amazing thing about folk festivals.

That's what's unique about a folk festival, as opposed to so many other kinds of festivals, because it's not just that artists all fly in, do their show, and leave. There is this interaction, and that interaction and the energy that's generated between the performers carries over out into the audience. The audience feels that. They're not just seeing someone doing their show.

KN: I wonder if there is anything else we can say to summarize the essence of the Winnipeg Folk Festival?

KW: I am trying to think right now, going through my mind, and picturing the Festival as it exists in the last decade, where I have had the privilege of going, through the different decades that it has existed. I think that it's always aspired to do and to be as good as it could possibly be. I think that is certainly one of the hallmarks of the Festival, that it's always trying to see, "How can we do this better? How can we be better?" And really, it's taking the idea, "We want to make a better world." Well, maybe we can make a little better world for three-four days on Birds Hill Park. That is something which you see. That changes. It's by no means static. And how the site evolved. Yet it's coming from that same impetus to make things better.

THE
WINNIPEG
FOLK
FESTIVAL
75
PRESS

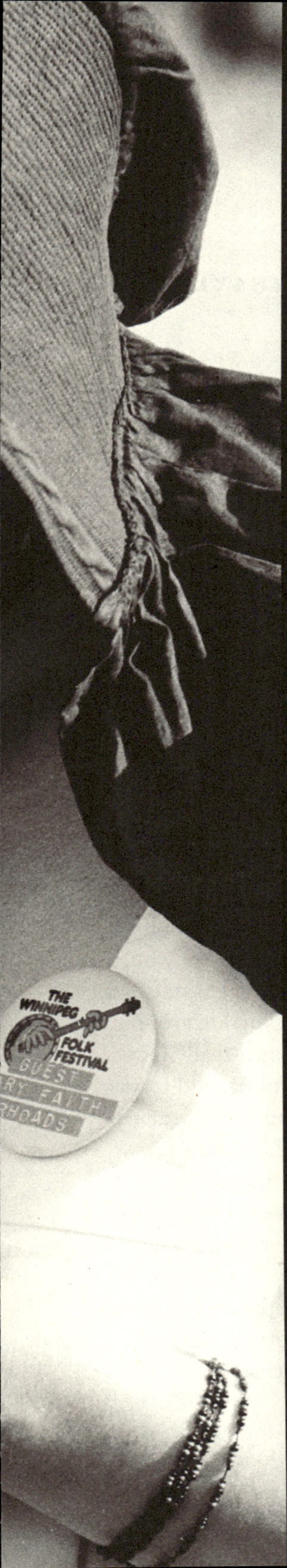

Mary FAITH RHOADS

Mary Faith Rhoads is a singer-songwriter from Allentown, Pennsylvania. Her first instrument was the violin at the age of eight, but she later found her passion for the dulcimer and playing folk music. She spent her time playing coffeehouses and festivals in Europe before returning to establish her name as a performer at North American festivals. At Mariposa, she met Mitch Podolak, who invited her to the Winnipeg Folk Festival after hearing her play. Mary Faith played the Festival twice solo, then with The Dobbs Brothers, and also returned to play twice with John Pearse. She is most known for her skill at both the mountain dulcimer and hammer dulcimer. In 1980 in Pennsylvania, she and John Pearse established Breezy Ridge Instruments—making hammer dulcimers and later instrument strings and accessories—to which she still devotes her time.

FIGURE 63. MARY FAITH RHOADS, 1975. PHOTOGRAPH BY DAVID LANDY. ARCHIVES OF MANITOBA, WINNIPEG FOLK FESTIVAL 1975 NEGATIVES, P5266/1, 75-4523. 11.

MARY FAITH RHOADS

30 MARCH 2022: CENTER VALLEY, PENNSYLVANIA

KEVIN NIKKEL: How did you get started in music? Eventually, we'll bring that story to the Winnipeg Folk Festival.

MARY FAITH RHOADS: My father played violin as a child. There was always music around. My mother sang and my older sister played piano. I sang all my life. My mother had a wonderful voice but she couldn't stay on key. I learned early on that if I sang harmony with her, she didn't jump keys in between phrases and so I think I was singing in harmony very early. She had the songs that she grew up with as a child up in Northeastern Pennsylvania. People forget that those are just as much the Appalachians as Kentucky and Virginia. As I got older, we had the *Fireside Book of Folksongs* and my sister would sit at the piano and we'd sing through them, page by page by page. That was a wonderful compendium of what was considered folk music at the time.

When I was in high school, my mom found an old Gibson flat-back guitar at a church jumble sale. I started about learning how to play that. A friend of mine knew guitar better than I did, so she showed me some chords and things. I found that suited me in a lot of ways. Then when did I get my first mountain dulcimer? I got an autoharp first because that was more easy to find. Then, as luck would have it, I met a woman who had met Frank Warner and as a result had met Frank Proffitt who was a traditional singer from North Carolina, and he made mountain dulcimers. She said, "I think you'd really like one of those." So, I wrote a letter to him in South Carolina, and it was returned. About a year later I found this letter that had been returned and realized it should've been North Carolina by the ZIP Code. So, I sent it and I got a dulcimer from him. Which I truly identified with. I mean, it just spoke to what makes me run, I guess. I was going to meet him in 1965 at Pinewoods, that was one of the reasons why I wanted to go Pinewoods, and as it turned out he was ill, so he never came. In fact, he died later that year. But I met Jean Ritchie because of being turned onto the dulcimer. It was wonderful meeting Jean and she and the Pinewoods folks certainly showed me a lot.

There was another proponent of the dulcimer at that point. His name was Richard Fariña. Mom and I got to see him. I would say it would've been February 1966. He was down at the Main Point, Philadelphia with his wife Mimi Fariña, who was Joan Baez's younger sister. He was killed a month later, so I was incredibly lucky to actually see him perform. Mom and I were in the seats right in front of them and he kept looking at my mother, trying to figure out why was she here? It was a wonderful experience to me because I already knew his recorded music, but it let me know you could do anything with a dulcimer. Anything you wanted.

Eventually, my mother bought an old hammer dulcimer at an auction, or it might have been an antique show somewhere. We had it downstairs for years and one time a friend came to visit. He said, "Let's see it." So, I got it out and it never got put away because in the meantime I got in the wire I needed to put on it. I learned how it should be tuned. So, it never got put away. I started learning that about 1975 and so that's what I've been doing ever since.

STARTING OUT AS A PERFORMER

KN: You eventually began to perform. Tell me about that.

MFR: My first professional concert was in 1963, the year I graduated from high school. There was a local DJ, Bill Ayres, and he was holding talent shows during the summer at the car wash at 17th and Tilghman in Allentown. The people that he then picked became part of a group he called The Minstrels Ayers. We did some concerts around, so that felt good. He tried to make us like the Christy Minstrels. We'd sing some songs alone but then we'd sing some songs all together. That was how it actually started. Then when I got in the college there were occasions and opportunities to play there.

By the time I graduated college, I was performing. That was 1967, and in fall of 1967, I went to Europe and started travelling with my instruments. I played a lot of the coffeehouses in those days, where they have the candles to burn up the smoke. You open your guitar case the next day, the smoke comes out. Drive you crazy. But it was an extraordinary time to be travelling. Then I lived in Boston for about a year and half. So, I got into a whole different bunch of stuff there.

At that point in time, you were either a singer-songwriter or you were a traditional performer. There certainly were people going across, but it's like you were known to be one or the other. I always did both. It just kind of gathered steam from there. I lived on and off in France. I went back in 1970 and I travelled around a bit and ended up coming back to France in January 1971 and from then until 1976 maybe, I'd spend the winters there and would come home in the summer.

It was a totally different feeling for a performer. For instance, anybody can play a mountain dulcimer, but not everybody can do extraordinary things with the traditional fingerboard. Nowadays, and even in those days, people were making extra frets, so they could get away from the modes that the traditional fingerboard constricted you to, but for me that was not a restriction. It made it easier because I knew exactly where I was and if I wanted another note, I had to find another way to play it. And I did. I had to fool around a bit to get that, but at the same time I could still play all the traditional things and I didn't have the trouble of trying to remember which fret not to hit. I was always happy with that.

In France there is an instrument called épinette, and it has the same roots as a mountain dulcimer. [It is] even earlier actually because at that point it still divided between strings on a keyboard, or on a fretboard, and then [had] open strings like the zither. That's really the thing that made the mountain dulcimer different. There are frets under all the strings and the traditional way of playing would have been to play just on the top string, as if you didn't have the frets underneath the others. But you do, so you can use them. But at the same time, the whole idea of droning, that's why I liked open tunings on the guitar too. It was just that I was not a great guitarist. And you could do interesting things with open tunings. But there's something about the drones that's just fundamental to my feeling about music. There is an ancient response in me to that.

MEETING MITCH PODOLAK

KN: How did you eventually end up coming to Winnipeg for the Folk Festival? You would have met Mitch Podolak?

MFR: I had been in Europe. I was getting ready to come home, but I had gone to the Isle of Wight and came home. One of the first festivals after that was Mariposa. I knew some people up there, so I went up. I think David Amram was there that year and David Amram was a friend from Pinewoods, I think that's where I met him, and he allowed me sleeping room on his floor, because that's just what people did with one another. He let me sleep on his floor. Later, I was in a room with people like Stan Rogers and the McGarrigles because we weren't the big fancy known ones at that point.

What happened at festivals in those days, people would go off to their rooms with groups of their friends at night and just sit and sing or whatever they would do. There was a bunch of us that kinda didn't have any specific places to go and we kinda kept company. We were in the more public room and so that's where we would play. I think that's probably the first time I met Stan. We're in there playing, I'm playing a song on the dulcimer that I wrote. I didn't know who Mitch was at that point but he must've been in the room listening. He basically said to me, "If I give you fifty dollars, will you come to Winnipeg? It's all booked, but I'll find you a place to stay." I said, "Sure. I'd be delighted." At that point, quite honestly, fifty dollars paid my gas to Winnipeg and back. Hard to imagine that. I got to Winnipeg and Mitch put me in the hotel for the railroad?

KN: The Fort Garry Hotel?

MFR: Yes. Big, fancy, luxurious, red velvet, and here's this bunch of crazy folkies. It was completely nuts. I had the bedroom in the hospitality suite and I ended up kinda being den mother of the hospitality suite, which was very dear. I used to try to make sure people got to bed okay. If they had had too much to drink, I'd walk them back to their room. Just what you did. It also was neat because it really helped me get to know people up there. That was wonderful. I had a wonderful time up there.

Playing at Winnipeg was something special. I remember I met a gal from Philadelphia Folk Festival. She said, "How did you get so good and we didn't know about you?" It was kind of like, well I lived in Europe. That's where I did my apprenticeship. Got my chops. I was very lucky. I arrived there at the perfect time.

Coming to Winnipeg was good for me. It kind of put me in the big pond. In a way, it's easy to be a big fish in a little pond, but that was what Winnipeg was for me, it was like a big pond. I just had such a wonderful time there. I went in 1975 and I think maybe I wasn't playing hammer dulcimer at that point in time, I was just plain guitar and mountain dulcimer.

Then, I remember when Mitch asked me back for the next year, I remember that I stood outside—because I have a hammer dulcimer—I can remember standing outside in a wooded area, kind of away from everybody else and just played and played. Because I was just trying to make sure I would do it right. Trying to get my chops up on the hammer dulcimer because you can play for six months and barely be able to hit what you want. I wanted to hit what I wanted. Winnipeg was wonderful.

KN: Any memories of playing there?

MFR: I think that I felt I was totally accepted and received with my own songs. I did a workshop called "My Home is in the Country" and I was the only woman in the workshop. I was standing there playing. Steve Goodman was in the workshop and he just walked up beside me and started playing guitar with me. It was so funny because I was getting to a bridge and I'm trying to let him know that there's a bridge coming while I'm singing this song, which is really awkward and stupid because he was playing like he knew the song better than I did. That was just extraordinary. I wrote a song about it because he was just an extraordinary musician. I never got to talk to him at that festival. I never got to talk to him again, which was kind of bizarre. I would've loved to.

One of the things that was really wonderful was everybody's together in this park. They're all walking around there. There was a performers area, where the food was. It was Harry who ran the food area, and he was great. God, it was like a home away from home. He made me feel incredibly comfortable. I'm not sure if he did that for everybody. But I was a little nervous. Here I am, in the big pond, not like I was worried about what I had to offer, but I'm a shy person. Get me in the music and it's fine. I'll talk about the music, it's fine, but I'm basically a shy person.

The second year I went, I took my mom and I guess the third year as well, which was 1977. I think I played on Main Stage with Dave Fry. My mom—I loved it—her badge, they made it "Mom Rhoads," and everybody treated her like their mother. Everybody was looking after her. Harry took really good care of her. She had such a good time. It was just wonderful and there were lots of workshops. Lots of instrumental workshops.

PLAYING THE DULCIMER

KN: Tell me about the teaching and learning that happened.

MFR: One of the things I did a lot in France was teaching dulcimer because there weren't a lot of dulcimer players at that point. There were épinette players, but it was like a different animal and people seem drawn to a dulcimer, by comparison. The épinette is an earlier member of the family. It has knife frets on one side, and then there are strings that are only drones. So, it can have two melody strings, three sometimes, up to maybe four or five or so in the drones. You played on the knife frets like a zither. Because of the fact the drones are there, a lot of the time you had to play with the emphasis away from you. . . . You'd be playing the melody and then you'd go "zoon" and bring in all the other strings because they're out there. So, you had to play in that direction and, personally, I play in this direction. It's more comfortable for me. It was always awkward for me to play épinette.

The difference about the mountain dulcimer across the board was it had frets under all strings so that you didn't just have drone strings and melody strings, they actually could all be played on. If they're tuned differently, then you have different scales, and that's the trick of what I learned with the mountain dulcimer. The one thing you really learn when you're starting to teach an instrument is there's two kinds of musicians: either the music is important, or the musician is important. If you teach an instrument, you find out very quickly that it's the music that's important.

The hammer dulcimer was just like a breath of fresh air for me. You couldn't stay unhappy. Five minutes. I tried one time. How long could I stay miserable. It was about five minutes. There is such joy and such . . . I want to say ecstasy, but it's close to it. Like when you play fiddle tunes, you talk to any old-time musician, when you've played a tune for half an hour with a whole bunch of people, and you're all into it. It's like a meditation. It's a mantra. You go somewhere else. And with hammer dulcimer, it was always that. I mean, you're just going to this wonderful place and it just feels so good to be there. It's just a joy, by comparison to the stuff I would write. You know, it's hard to write happy songs. It just is. If I was happy, I was out doing something, I wasn't sitting alone with my guitar trying to get the feelings out, or trying to express myself. So, the hammer dulcimer was a really good thing for me.

I mean, a lot of my songs were very deeply introspective. John made the comment one time, bless his heart, "Yeah, the people in the last row were slitting their wrists in time."

My mother worried about my songs and my saying that I wrote them. She'd always say, "Don't tell them you wrote that. You don't want people to know you went through that."

And I said, "That's the only thing that's worth anything. That they know the experiences that they have are not unique and they're not alone in it."

THE IMPORTANCE OF THE WINNIPEG FOLK FESTIVAL

KN: You said people will either have the music as important or the musician as important. When you came up to Winnipeg and saw the world that Mitch had created at the Winnipeg Folk Festival, what did you see as important to Mitch?

MFR: The music was important.

KN: Tell me more about that.

MFR: For me, I perhaps had a weird perspective because of where I was in my career, and that this was really the first time I was accepted at a big festival in North America. The fact that he heard one song of mine and that made him have me come. He was always really good to me. I loved the workshops I was part of because they were a real conglomeration of things. I didn't realize it at the time, what a gift he had for putting people together. I mean, I think about that "My Heart is in the Country" workshop that I got put in, that Steve played along with me.

There was such a respect for everyone. Everyone was glad to be there, everyone was so happy to share, I mean, even now, I suppose, even someone like Steve, who at that point, certainly was a headliner.

I think because of the nature of the grounds, in a way it's almost like the old Newport used to be. If you were there, the performers were walking around, they were accessible. At some point in all of this stuff, people changed and the festivals became different. It became, "who's going to draw the most people" because they had the bottom line to pay attention to. But I honestly think that this was probably never a question with Mitch. I'm sure there are some people who may have thought that he was rather high-handed, perhaps, in his handling of things. Down inside, I think he had a really good handle on how to create a space.

People just came to share and to just be in the energy of that music. Obviously, there was every kind of music at Winnipeg, everything from bluegrass, to bijou, to straight traditional, you know, everything. It was one of the festivals where there was maybe not a lot of playing with people there. Playing and jamming on the grounds, with people bringing instruments. If there was that, I don't so much remember that. But there was just a, "we're all in this, this is for us, this is great." It was wonderful.

KN: What was happening in folk music in the 1970s? Where was it trending?

MFR: In the 1970s, oh my God. In France, it was exploding. In North America, it certainly existed. But it was getting bigger. Now at that point, there still were the traditional things like Glenville, Galax Fiddler's convention, and I think Clifftop was going on at that point, but festivals certainly had started and I think more and more people were playing. You think about the people like Stan, people like Archie Fisher, who came over from Scotland, the Balfas who came up from Louisiana. This might've been the first time most people heard people like that. It was kind of like, whatever your own voice, you could find a place within this music that spoke to you and made you valued and made you a member of humanity, if you like. In that way, I think it was incredible.

One of the things that was important for me, as an American if you like, Canada, and especially Winnipeg had a very strong Native

American presence there. And that kind of awareness didn't hit down here. We're still far behind. For me that's why meeting people like Winston Wuttunee and having Buffy Sainte-Marie come, the entire crowd of Indigenous performers who were there—one who wanted to offer five horses for Mimi Fariña—God bless them both. It was like a different world. And not only that, one thing that happened out of the Festival—I'm sure you're probably aware of this—Mitch always had some of the performers stay over and go play at the prisons. That's how I got to be really good friends with Stan because through the night that we stayed over, he and I ended up in the room together with my mom and we were just having the time. I met Archie at Winnipeg, it must've been the next year. I taught Stan how Archie played a tune. They ended up being really a good connection. Garnet [Rogers] has an extraordinary connection to Archie, which has been wonderful.

It was just wonderful to be there. I don't know how it happened. I mean, if that one song I wrote is what got me involved, lucky me. But it was an extraordinary experience. I mean, as a performer, it was different than Philly. In a way, to me it was like the early Newports because everybody was there and the performers walking to the workshop stages, which were usually just a raised little platform on the ground, and you were sitting on the ground and they were sitting ten feet in front of you. The nights, we were dancing. We all got dancing. I've never known that to happen at another American festival.

FIGURE 64. MARY FAITH RHOADS PLAYS DULCIMER, 1976. PHOTOGRAPH BY DAVID LANDY. ARCHIVES OF MANITOBA, WINNIPEG FOLK FESTIVAL 1976 NEGATIVES, P5266/3, 76/4. 12.

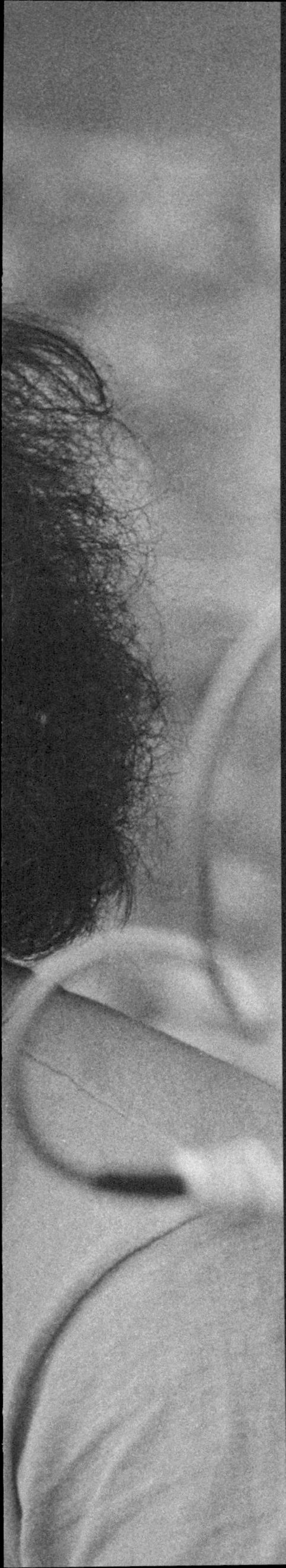

Grit LASKIN

William "Grit" Laskin is a musician, singer-songwriter, and luthier based in Toronto. While apprenticing as a guitar maker in the 1970s, he began playing guitar, banjo, and dulcimer at coffeehouses—particularly the Fiddler's Green coffeehouse in Toronto. It was there that he was invited to join the band The Friends of Fiddler's Green, which provided occasions for him to begin touring, playing coffeehouses, venues, and folk festivals. He performed at the Winnipeg Folk Festival three times with Friends of Fiddler's Green, and once as a solo act. Grit has also had his own success as a solo artist, with four albums to his credit. His songs have been recorded by other artists, such as Pete Seeger and The Tannahill Weavers. He was one of the co-founders of Borealis Records, Canada's first national folk music label. Grit makes beautiful guitars, instruments treasured by the best musicians and housed in museums.

FIGURE 65. GRIT LASKIN, 1976. PHOTOGRAPH B DAVID LANDY. ARCHIVES OF MANITOBA, WINNIP FOLK FESTIVAL 1976 NEGATIVES, P5266/3, 76/4.27.

GRIT LASKIN

27 NOVEMBER 2021, TORONTO, ONTARIO

KEVIN NIKKEL: How did find your way into the folk scene?

GRIT LASKIN: I hitchhiked to Toronto and got a job at Eastern Sound recording studio. They were big enough at the time to hire a gopher. After six months, I left that. I started just playing music. I ran into Jean Larrivée at Mariposa Folk Festival and he was willing to take me on as an apprentice.

I heard about Fiddler's Green, that anybody could go and do a guest set there and play three songs, if you just called and booked. Sure enough, Tam Kearney's model at the time was two guest sets, then the feature. So, he let me do that. Then Tam really liked me because I was doing more than playing guitars; I was playing banjo and dulcimer and, at the time, was getting into American traditional stuff. I was writing some funny songs. He really liked it and said, "Hey Grit, why don't you play guitar with this little group we're starting to form?" which was The Friends of Fiddler's Green.

I had actually seen them play at this one Mariposa, just a bunch of singers and they'd rotate. But when I came along, they said, "Hey, why don't we try a fiddle tune." I was playing guitar, I had no idea of the structure of British fiddle tunes. I had to give them nicknames in my head so I could remember what I was supposed to do. That was how Friends of Fiddler's Green began. So, with Fiddler's Green I became part of the house band.

It's important to know that Fiddler's Green was a hub for the entire folk scene at that time. It ran two nights a week. It ran concerts and they were almost always sellouts, with lineups waiting to get in. In between, on the other evenings, the Irish traditional music society would meet there for their sessions. The bluegrass people would meet for their sessions. The Shape Note Singers would meet for their sessions. The Morris dancers would meet for their sessions. All this was happening in this little condemned house that belonged to the YMCA. Eventually it was torn down and Fiddler's Green had to move after about eighteen years.

That's the world I fell into, at the very same time that I met Jean and was becoming an apprentice with him. It was he and I for the bulk of two years. All this was happening just after my eighteenth birthday. I was high for two years nonstop. That's almost unhealthy. I was just so excited by everything I was doing. I was learning to play other instruments. I started learning the British instruments, concertina, Northumbrian pipes, tin whistle, and I even had a harp made, which I never pursued.

MITCH PODOLAK

KN: How did you become associated with Mitch?

GL: We all knew about Mitch. We were aware of him as somebody on the scene and he had been in Toronto, doing various things. He invited us out to the Festival. The Friends [of Fiddler's Green] played the Festival, I think two times. Then I also did it one other time as a trio, with Ian Robb and Margaret Christl. For a short time, we had this trio thing happening. But with The Friends, we were out there, it was the early days. I still remember the old hotel where they used to house us, in the city. It was an old one that hadn't yet been reconditioned.

KN: Or demolished.

GL: Or demolished, yeah. It was in pretty rough shape. Kind of funky, and we were all into that. At least it didn't have fleas, which they did in some of the places where we stayed, at other festivals. So, we got to know Mitch that way. Coming out to the Festival, we loved his programming and we went because of him. I had a great time. I remember the great food. You ate well at Mitch's festival because he knew, you make the artist happy and satisfied, you're going to get greater performances out of them. On top of that, he learned programming from Estelle Klein, who was the first person to come up with the concept at music festivals of putting disparate artists on the same stage under a theme with a host and see what happens. Put people you wouldn't think would go together but see how they react to each other's music. Even as an audience member, I still have memories of brilliant moments because of that kind of programming.

Lessons that he learned from Estelle, at Mariposa in the early days—she brought artists from all over the planet, before world music was coined as a marketing term. I first heard African music there. I first heard South American music. I heard old blues guys from the Southern United States. I remember her programming women's songs workshops and putting guys in the workshop. And getting a lot of heat for it from the women, but she said you have to be talking to them. They are the people whose minds you want to change. Let them hear your issues, in your music, and respond. She was so far ahead of her time and Mitch was probably the best exponent of her approach. He learned that lesson intuitively. But he brought with it his own sensibilities of being aware of the little guy in the world and how folk music played a role. Whether it was protest, whether it was social issues, whether it was humour, whether it was the music of the lower classes that travelled and came to us in our modern times through the folk process. He understood intuitively, so his programming was as creative as anything Estelle ever did.

KN: Let's take a step back and get some context for what was happening at the time. What was happening with folk music in the sixties and how did it change during these years?

GL: The folk revival, so-called, which we're basically talking about the couple years when it was the pop music of its day, would've been the late fifties very early sixties, just before The Beatles hit. When it was the popular form, first in the UK, and then it spread to the United States, and then eventually up to Canada, it attracted all kinds of us, including me, who got hooked by Pete Seeger and The Weavers, things like that.

It was the relevant music of its time, and there was a lot of it because it was the anti-racial stuff in the U.S., or anti-war stuff. That was the music that spoke to the people. Phil Ochs, even early Dylan. Those kinds of people. Often, the songs would be more socially relevant, even though they were heading up to the pop charts. They still had a social relevancy that was so critical to that time. The hippie era was happening at the same time and everybody's brain was thinking about different lifestyles. But then it swung the other way, and everything went very right wing, very conservative. I think the folk boom was, in part, a response to that. Eventually rock 'n' roll came out of that, too.

Mitch grew up with those sensibilities—left-wing and believing in the little guy and unions and all that stuff. That was his driving philosophy—from who he would book at the Festival, what themes the workshops would take, who he would put together with whom. To try and get that artist's mind a little shifted towards how that one thinks. We just ate it up.

KN: I love that. Other people have called Mitch a trickster.

GL: The disruptor. He understood that so well. We're just talking about the Festival here, but in his life, look what he's done for the scene in Canada: Home Routes. Stuff that was happening sporadically by people, "Oh, you're coming through town? I've got a big living room. We could do something." Then he formalized it, and what a gift to the artists in this country. Then classical people twenty years later happened to notice. I remember reading articles in the paper of the classical scene, they discovered little concerts in people's homes. I'm going, excuse me, we've only been doing this for decades. I once even wrote to the newspapers and said, "Please do your homework. Look up Home Routes. They have been doing this for a long time and they made it a viable, functioning way to perform and tour." That's yet another gift. Never mind all the other festivals he helped start in this country. It's unbelievable.

UNIQUENESS OF THE WINNIPEG FOLK FESTIVAL?

KN: How did the Winnipeg Folk Festival compare to others across Canada?

GL: Winnipeg was one of the first big ones, and, by big, I mean the number of the audience. Now Edmonton is probably the biggest, but at the time Winnipeg was there before. It was one of the early Festivals and it was bigger, even, than Mariposa. Mariposa was as big as it could be, but Winnipeg had the physical space and drew a bigger audience. Its location was kinda funky. The only negative was that the site was so big, it took so long to get from one stage to the next. As an audience member, if you didn't plan ahead, it would take you the length of a workshop to get from that stage to that stage, and you would miss some things if you didn't plan carefully. Performers ran around on golf carts, but when we weren't performing, we wanted to just listen to music, and we were traipsing around like any other audience member. That's one thing I remember. That and the mosquitoes. The advantage, though, of the site being so big and the stages so far apart, is you had none of the sound leakage, which often was a bugaboo for many other festivals. That's often what happens, but not at Winnipeg. That was Mitch just using the site that they had.

KN: From a Torontonian's perspective, what was it like looking over at Winnipeg? Was there something in it that was different?

GL: Technically, any festival could be set up anywhere. Wherever there's infrastructure, space, and some funding-willingness from agencies—government, whatever, because it's not cheap to do it. You can't always count on ticket sales. So, you want to have some funding as well. I think for us, going west, before we went far west—and The Friends did play Vancouver once or twice—there were different artists there than you would see at an East Coast festival or even a central Ontario festival. Partially because of the budget, they always looked nearby to people who you didn't have to pay for flights, or had border issues of bringing them up from the States or from the UK. You'd see a different roster and we always enjoyed that because you're seeing some artists you wouldn't get a chance to. They may not tour where you are, or you didn't see them. So, there is that difference.

Other than that, once you're on the site it wouldn't be dissimilar from other festivals, from the artist point of view. Except the variation on how well you were taken care of and thought about. Some festivals did a better job than others. Winnipeg was masterful at it. And I think a lot of festivals learned lessons from that.

KN: And the audiences at these festivals? They're smart, they know what they're seeing, and know the songs.

FOLK, ROOTS, AND WORLD MUSIC

GL: Sure. We're all like that. Stuff you listen to and go see live. There is something appealing about that. As a performer, I'm excited about my newest repertoire because it's the newest, but if I don't do some of my old favourites that the audience likes, they're not going to be happy. Their eyes light up when it's the one they know and they can sing along to the chorus. That's part of being a performer.

When it's a music form that is a niche in the music world, it's not only in pop where you know there's a degree of shallowness. You do get more connected to the music and get more excited about seeing the real thing being performed. It plays a stronger role in your life.

You would always get people who go, "you did that wrong" or "you shouldn't ever do that on guitar, that was written on banjo and that's the way it should be."

KN: Or react to plugging in?

GL: Or, God forbid, plugging in. But tell me an artist that doesn't plug in nowadays. Even just a pickup in their acoustic instruments. It's the world we're in. On a folk music record, none of us care anymore if there's drums, electric bass, and backup electric guitar. Yes, if it's all acoustic, that's a strong signal that they are coming out of the folk/roots world. More, we're listening to the songs themselves and the structure of the music they compose. It tells us what they've been listening to and what they've been influenced by.

If you have two acoustic singer-songwriters on their acoustic guitars, you can tell which one is a wannabe pop star by their song structures. The other one has been listening to folk music, and learning lessons from how to tell a story, how to engage the audience, how to make them feel something. Then a chorus to sing along and participate in the music, to keep their attention span at 100 percent, because when you sing, you wake up. You feel connected to the rest of the people in the audience. Pete Seeger understood that, more than anybody else on the planet. He'd get everybody singing together. He knew why it was important.

That is still happening in music, even as the interpretation of the songs change, and the way you accompany them. I mean, one good example of that is a group out of Québec nowadays, Mélisande (électrotrad). They do research, search for the original sources of the songs, like a folklorist would. They travel around Québec. They even go down to the Library of Congress and dig through stuff. They find traditional songs and versions that are known and then they put them with electronic beats and percussion and everything behind it. But the way they perform the songs still evidences an immense respect for the tradition. Their accompaniments aren't arbitrary, which happens sometimes—I'm going to take this old ballad and blend it with jazz chords. Okay, it may work, it may not, but you can tell they're just trying to do something to get noticed. As opposed to feeling the music deeply and then saying, "How can we interpret it in our modern

FIGURE 66. GRIT LASKIN ON RIGHT, WITH THE FRIENDS OF FIDDLER'S GREEN ON THE WORKSHOP STAGE, 1975. PHOTOGRAPH BY DAVID LANDY. ARCHIVES OF MANITOBA, WINNIPEG FOLK FESTIVAL 1975 NEGATIVES, P5266/1, 75-4617. 17A.

times? In some forms that might attract some people who don't normally listen to this genre?"

That brings me back to how I got hooked on traditional music. It was the first album I bought with my own money as a kid, and it was The Byrds' *Fifth Dimension*. I bought it because of a song that was on it, I think it was Dylan's "Mr. Tambourine Man." Then I heard two songs on that record that were traditional ballads that they did with electric guitars, electric drawstring drums, the whole thing. But they sang the song straight. I remember as this kid thinking, *I've never heard stories like that. Holy mackerel. What is this? Where did it come from?* On the record, it said public domain. I didn't know what that meant. Now they might say "trad," but these stories were incredible. One was a broken token ballad about this couple separating, he's going off to war, or fortune hunting. He comes back seven years later and his wife doesn't recognize him but they have the coin they broke between them and it matches, and it's him. And he's back and everybody's happy. That is after he tested her loyalty to see that she wasn't having affairs while he was away. "John Riley" was one of the songs, I think. That hooked me, traditional songs.

The power of the storytelling and the conciseness of the lyrics because they've gone through a couple centuries of going from one person, to the next, of fine tuning. There is a better word we can put here. That first didn't scan very well. What if I put it this way? Then you get this thing that's just a thing of beauty, that's been polished. Anyway, that hooked me on traditional music. So, in modern times, trad stuff is still happening, but people are giving it different settings, different beds, different ways of interpreting the song, or blending it with other music. I just love that it's still alive and vibrant.

KN: I like what you're saying about this passion. This music that has a message, something inside it. Maybe of story, maybe of protest. Do the audiences at these festivals coming out of the 1960s and 1970s have this earnestness? What do you think, about where we've come since then? What is the legacy of that idealism?

GL: There's still that passion. It is still out there. Maybe with younger people. With newer generations, and there's been a few, I have to admit some of the most relevant music is coming out of rap and hip-hop. That's speaking to their community, not necessary to me personally, but I see where it came from and the honesty of it, coming up from the street. I'll grudgingly admit, there are parallels there to early folk music. You gotta give them credit for that. It may not speak to me, that's fine, but it speaks to its generation and the people who grew up with those experiences. It's speaking to their frustrations. I understand the power of music and how it can effect change.

To the people who think, "it's just music," then why was Víctor Jara[18] murdered in a stadium, in front of people who were forced to watch his hands being chopped off and then killed because of his music? Because the leaders there were afraid of his songs. They had to set an example. That's happened around the world. You cannot deny the power of music. Because when it's well done, it goes right to your emotional centre.

People like Mitch, boy could he tell talent. He had the experience to even see the seeds of it in a young artist and know what's coming and would support them. Just thinking about somebody like Mitch, somebody who was selfless and never cared much about himself and his own living or income. He probably just lived slightly above poverty levels his whole life and was just content because he was doing important things. People like Estelle. We don't have people like them anymore. The mould's been broken. I'm not saying there aren't good and talented people out there, but they were special. They had bigger global vision and they found ways to enhance that through these local events.

WHERE IS FOLK MUSIC GOING?

KN: It's not lost on me, here in your workshop where there are all these moulds and patterns hanging on the wall to make instruments and you're talking about these moulds for good people. I can't help but think about where we are today, with the problems of today, and maybe there might be some solutions to our contemporary problems in the folk music and festival experiences. Where is the music going?

GL: Where might folk music be headed and how does it connect to what's happening in the world? And all the issues. And of course, there are great people on the scene writing terrific songs about environmental issues, to withstanding the pandemic, to political issues, they're certainly there. Just like they were with the civil rights issues, and all that stuff. And now Indigenous, my God, yes. We are in the middle a golden age of Indigenous artists. They're not where they should be yet, but they're heading there and there's so much brilliant music coming out of the Indigenous scene nowadays. They are coming out of their culture, and speaking to it, and writing about it in ways that are universal, that anybody can appeal to anybody.

KN: What is the difference between the Canadian and American folk scenes?

GL: I mean, it's just a different flavour, really. They have their own traditions, whether it's the mountain regions of the central United States, or in New England, or in the South. Different genres emerged, different forms. Where up here, a lot of the traditional stuff comes from the East Coast, mostly because a lot of British immigrants were settling there and bringing Irish and other British forms. Then they morphed and evolved. That's where the fiddle tune tradition came in Québec, but now it's totally its own thing. My God, the Québecois stuff is totally different than anywhere else. Whereas the Irish really influenced Newfoundland and the Scots really influenced Nova Scotia. You can't get in a cab where the cabby isn't also a step dancer and a fiddle player in Halifax. It's incredible. Out West, it was more of a songwriting and new composition approach, even though they would take the traditional forms—banjos, mandolins, acoustic guitars, and standup bass—but they would do different things with them. So, we have our own flavours, because of the geography and immigration history. But similar trajectory in the wax and wane of the root forms.

The difference down there, I think they have an advantage. Some people down there came up with this term: Americana. They just invented it and started to push it as a marketing form and Americana now brings in all the roots forms; folk music, rootsy country stuff, all of it is there. It's giving some *oomph* to the folkier forms. God love that they've created it as its own marketing form. We don't have that here. There's been a push to allowing an Americana category at the Junos, but it's mostly rejected as, "Excuse me? That's an American term." They use it, we have to do our own thing here. But that's how strong it's become. That's where more of the rooted music is happening.

Folk festival audiences more often come expecting to participate in the music. Singing along, dancing along, hearing music that they could, in some form, make for themselves. Whereas if you go to a rock festival or a hip-hop festival, you are just the audience. You're just absorbing the music and the performers are up there. Big stars in the light and the costumes and everything. Folk music, you're closer to the artist and the artists like it that way. That's a big difference that carries on to this day. Folk music is a genre that you could make for yourself.

KN: I would throw in the terms "spectator" and "spectacle."

GL: Consume it. You're a consumer of music. But in folk music, more often you can be a participant in the music. That has not changed. That's another side to the folk community, welcoming all artists of all different types. Even though many of them then head on to different areas in the pop world.

KN: One question I have to ask, because of your background. What do you notice about the instruments people are playing at these folk festivals? You would see these stages and players differently than most others because of your background as a maker. Mitch really made an effort to structure his workshops around the instruments.

GL: Mitch was very good at that, for sure. You're making me recall going to Mariposa as a teenager and seeing, because of Estelle's

programming, an Egyptian guy playing a kanun. He had metal on his fingers and played it like this. There was a religious man from Africa who played this thing with a gourd and all the strings up here. He was royalty in his country. Estelle brought him. Or the pan pipes from South America. I heard them first at folk festivals. I saw them played live. You name it, from whatever culture, and Mitch did that as well. It's another way he absorbed Estelle's approach. Even with Mitch, this was long before world music was even coined as a marketing term, he had the goal of introducing all these things. So, if you are on a stage with these other instruments, it was a treat as a performer. I could see what I could do. So as an instrument maker, backstage I'd say, "Can I take a look at that? How do you even attach the strings on that? How is it tuned? Oh, really? How do you play it? Your thumb is always doing that? Like that!" You were excited, like a kid, seeing all this stuff. But you're right, as an instrument maker I would especially look at all the other guitars. The flip side, though, is so many of my early orders were from performers who would see me at festivals. Backstage performers would say, "Hey Grit, your guitar sounded great, can I have a look?"

KN: Anything else we should mention about your memories of the Winnipeg Folk Festival?

GL: I do remember on the bus from the motel. One time I was sitting next to Peter Gzowski, who was there doing some emceeing. I remember he recognized me because I'd been on the show a few times. He was really a supporter of rootsy, folky music. He asked me, "My son, he's playing bass. He wants to be a full-time musician. Do you think he has a chance of making a real living?" [Laughs] He asked me this question. I don't even do music full-time and he's asking me!

I said, "Absolutely. Of course. The world needs music. If he's got some skill, he'll get there."

FIGURE 67. WORKSHOP STAGE WITH WORLD MUSICIANS AT WINNIPEG FOLK FESTIVAL, 1979. PHOTOGRAPH BY DAVID LANDY. ARCHIVES OF MANITOBA, WINNIPEG FOLK FESTIVAL 1979 NEGATIVES, P5266/9, 79/12.

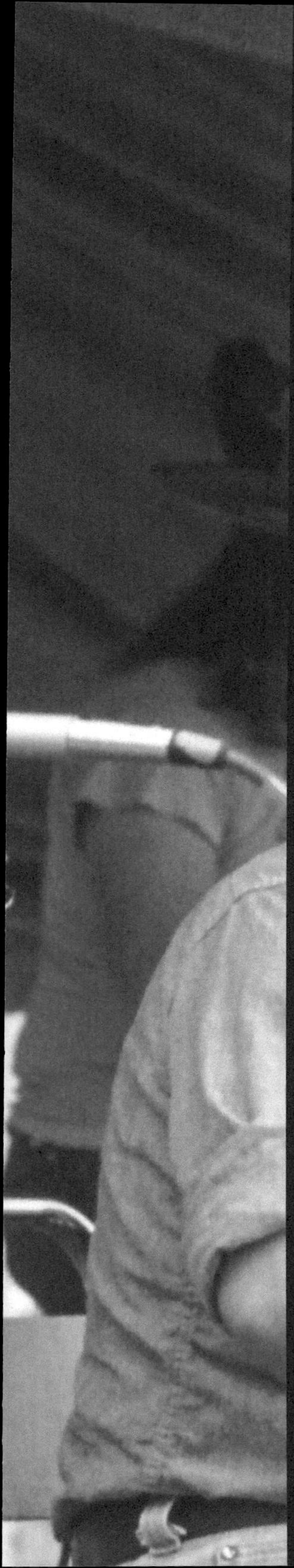

David ESSIG

David Essig was born in Maryland, United States, but emigrated to Canada in 1971 where he made his home, settling in Emsdale, Ontario. He has had an extensive career as a touring singer-songwriter, playing coffeehouses, venues, and folk festivals in North America and in Europe. David's playing at the Mariposa Folk Festival was the occasion for his introduction to Mitch Podolak, who invited him to play the Winnipeg Folk Festival—David would return to play at Birds Hill Park thirteen times over the years. Besides his confident track record as a touring performer, David also started Canada's first folk music record label, Woodshed Records, a label that was artist-owned and -operated. He was also the host of the CBC Radio show Six Days on the Road.

FIGURE 68. DAVID ESSIG ON A WORKSHOP STAGE, 1974. PHOTOGRAPH BY JOHN BACHMANN. COURTESY OF WINNIPEG FOLK FESTIVAL.

DAVID ESSIG

9 NOVEMBER 2019, WINNIPEG

KEVIN NIKKEL: What is your background, and how did you find your way to playing the Winnipeg Folk Festival?

DAVID ESSIG: I grew up playing bluegrass and country blues in the United States. In March of 1971, I came to Canada and decided to devote myself to a musical career. I felt there was a scene going on. I really was a war protester. For me, Vietnam—Nixon bombed Cambodia, I said, "I'm out of here." I came to Canada and lived in central Ontario, up near Algonquin Park. I started getting involved in the music scene in southern Ontario and Toronto. It was actually Estelle Klein, who founded the Mariposa Festival and was the artistic director for years, she heard me and invited me to Mariposa. I played at Mariposa a couple times. I think the second time I played there, I met Mitch. He said, "I'm starting this new festival out in Manitoba." I didn't even know where Manitoba was, at that point. I was fresh off the boat, so to speak. But he invited me to come out and play at the second Winnipeg Folk Festival. I played six subsequent ones under Mitch's tutelage and guidance in those early years. I was involved when he helped start the one in Vancouver, and then we did stuff in the Yukon together. I was, kind of, one of the early guys in. Then it was wonderful.

I had never experienced anything like this in my musical life, growing up. The States was very territorial and competitive and tight. I was in the scene that was not welcoming and friendly. Here I was in Canada, in a scene that was incredible— it was my home. These guys that are here are like my family. It was Mitch who stirred that pot, to mix a lot of metaphors at once, stirred the pot and got us all together. It was the Winnipeg Folk Festivals, along with the ones in Mariposa, that really put me on the map. I started playing all over Canada and I wanted to make CDs. I realized the commercial record companies weren't interested in the records, LPs in those days. I started Canada's first folk music record label, that was artist-owned and -operated, which was Woodshed Records. I went and got a bunch of my friends to make records with me. Kind of similar to what Scott Nolan is doing now here in Winnipeg.

This was a long time ago, back in the early 1970s. I produced and recorded the first three albums for Willie P. Bennett, Jackie Washington, Margaret Christl, Cathy Fink and Duck Donald. I had about ten acts on Woodshed. People like Mitch were very instrumental in making sure that we were able to succeed. It worked. It was the thing that really got my career going. Then I was able to travel all over the country and perform. That's what I've done now for forty-some years.

PLAYING THE WINNIPEG FOLK FESTIVAL

KN: Coming to the Winnipeg Folk Festival, what was going on back then?

DE: It was loose. Mitch was a great organizer but he also understood: don't organize too much. He made a lot of important protocols and set up systems that worked really well. But you never felt him hemmed in or tightened in by them. I'd never played a gig where I showed up at the airport and there was somebody waiting for me saying, "I'll take it. I'll take you. You're okay." And give you the badge and away you go. He knew how to take care of all the details, without the details becoming an oppressive envelope that we had to live in. There was a lot of freedom and he encouraged a kind of looseness at the same time. He was the biggest fan. He was there for the music, himself. This was another difference, it was the first time I'd ever played gigs, big gigs, and big audiences, where the artistic director was right there watching. He came to hear you play. Usually, they'd be off there in the trailer, but he was right there. That was the big difference. Mitch was the biggest fan that the music ever had. And here he was, hearing us, right with us.

It was out in the early days at Birds Hill Park, had no amenities and that was just camping, basically. Then we'd get in the school buses and go back to some cheap motel that he had rented. One place, and it's still there, out by the airport, it used to be called the Viscount Gort. I recognize that ugly building. That was our festival headquarters a few years. But you would get on these crazy school buses then go back to that crazy hotel and party the night away. Some people did. But that was the familial quality that Mitch brought to it.

The beauty for me was the relationships that he nurtured and engendered among us. Encouraging us to be cooperative and collaborative,

rather than competitive and territorial. That cooperative sense enabled us to become friends forever. There are people here that are like my brothers. Like Peter Paul Van Camp, we've known each other for over forty years, doing this. We're still in touch, still friends. Mitch encouraged that. And with Home Routes, more of that kind of encouragement. Gary Cristall, he founded the Vancouver Festival—couldn't have done it without Mitch. That was what he did. He was always encouraging you to be part of this larger fraternity, sorority of performers.

KN: Can you remember that first show you did in Winnipeg? How were you feeling?

DE: I was a new guy on the block. Mitch had no qualms about putting a relative newcomer, guys just starting out, up there with seasoned veterans. I can remember being on stage with Ramblin' Jack Elliott. Holy good Lord, what am I doing up here? That was it. The story that comes to mind is actually about that very thing. Mitch encouraged us to bring our best game to the Festival and he'd make sure that you got some challenges out of it. This was about the sixth or seventh year in, maybe the tenth? The Festival is well-established at this point and, of course, there were the parties in the hotel every night that went on most of the night. Some of the performers partook of those parties—were more involved than some others. I never was. I don't like to stay up late, as I've always been an early riser. I like to go to bed early. Except if I don't have to do a gig, I'll stay up. Mitch knew this, because we'd been up in Yukon together. He knew that if you put me in a workshop to start at ten o'clock in the morning, I'd be there. I'd show up and I'd be able to play. This one year, he scheduled this guitar workshop for Sunday morning at ten o'clock with four guitar players. There were three British guys and me. Mitch knew what was going to happen. They all showed up on time for the bus but one of them puked on the way out to the Festival. They were all so hungover, they could hardly play. I remember one of them played like half of an instrumental piece and then he said, "I'm turning it over to Dave." And he got up and left. By the end of it, the other two were still sitting there, holding it in. They were really sick. I'm just

FIGURE 69. DAVID ESSIG WITH OTHERS ON A WORKSHOP STAGE, 1974. PHOTOGRAPH BY JOHN BACHMANN. COURTESY OF WINNIPEG FOLK FESTIVAL.

FIGURE 70. WORKSHOP CROWD, 1978. PHOTOGRAPH BY DAVID LANDY. ARCHIVES OF MANITOBA, WINNIPEG FOLK FESTIVAL 1978 NEGATIVES, P5266/7, 16/78. BETWEEN 2–3.

HARRY'S
EATS

STRATHCONA
OUTDOOR

playing away. It was fine, we completely covered it. But if I hadn't been there, I don't know how they would've done, because I was the only one who didn't have a vicious hangover on the stage. Mitch was right there, watching this. Afterwards, a big hug, "You handled it great."

Those were the kinds of magical moments that Mitch was capable of. He also had me emcee one year, which was a really interesting thing. I'd never done anything like that. But I was working at CBC Radio in Toronto. I had a country music radio show on CBC Radio One. He thought, well I guess you got some announcer chops in you, why don't you emcee the Main Stage concerts? So, he got four of us, all performers, to go in and emcee the concerts. It scared the hell out of me. It was much more frightening than any musical work I'd ever done, because there I was, having to fill time. Along with a lost child announcement, you gotta keep things going. But again, he challenged you to bring your best, and that's what he's done with all of us. He made us feel that we were worthy of his encouragement.

The last time I saw him was just a few years ago, coming through Winnipeg on a Home Routes tour. I happened to be on the southern Manitoba swing and I was able to stop in the office and have a chat with him, and lunch. It was the same thing, total encouragement, and commitment to what you are doing and that's the legacy to me.

GROWTH OF THE FOLK FESTIVAL

KN: Any comments about how the Winnipeg Folk Festival was unique?

DE: The Winnipeg Folk Festival was unique when it started because he took Estelle Klein's model, which she took from the Philadelphia and Newport Folk Festivals in the States, and each successive iteration changed. Estelle changed it somewhat, she had it out on the islands off of Toronto. It was daytime and there weren't any evening concerts, just during the day, so it was like a picnic. Mitch took that idea and turned it into a camping thing. It was the first festival in Canada that I knew of where the audience came and stayed in tents and campers, right on the site and was way the heck gone from town. The Toronto

FIGURE 71. VALDY AT WINNIPEG FOLK FESTIVAL, 1979. PHOTOGRAPH BY DAVID LANDY. ARCHIVES OF MANITOBA, WINNIPEG FOLK FESTIVAL 1979 NEGATIVES, P5266/9, 79/24.

Islands are 200 metres from the CN Tower, it's not a long way. So, this was a really different thing.

The other thing was, Mitch had the daytime programming running on multiple stages, all the time, all day long. And then had the evening concerts. Mariposa started having concerts as well, but their daytime programming was their centrepiece. Mitch kind of turned that a little bit into the evening. Concerts became very much a focus for a lot of audiences, but the daytime was where the magic happened because it wasn't scripted. There was a chance for spontaneity. That model that Mitch developed kind of became the model for folk festivals all across Canada. But his was the first, and the best one.

And, one thing Mitch did that I've never encountered at other festivals, is he built the crews of volunteers and encouraged them to become a social group throughout the rest of the year. Those people stayed on those crews year after year after year and it became their social coterie; they were really like clubs. I can remember playing at the Festival twenty years after it started and the guys running the parking lot were the same guys who had been running it the first year and they all had kids and they hung out together, they did stuff all winter as a group. That enabled him [Mitch] to depend on his volunteers to do a really good job and it became this incredibly well-oiled machine that worked perfectly. There was never a glitch.

KN: Can you put a finger on when the Folk Festival got big?

DE: I'm terrible with dates. About halfway. After the Festival had been running for maybe ten or fifteen years, around in there. I think when they built the permanent stage out there. That was a big deal and they've started to turn up the production values and then the evening concerts became really big productions. There was a move towards larger ensembles performing. Those early years, most performers were either solos or duos, three people at the most. But then it became bands, and larger groups, and it became more of a show and a production in the evening.

But the beauty of it, the genius that Mitch brought to it, was he never lost sight of the importance of the daytime programming. That was so important for people like me, who'd never been a Main Stage kind of guy. He always relied on me to do the workshops during the day and always gave me a chance to do a concert. It was a few times on the Main Stage, but it was between the bands and that was fine.

The whole festival scene in Canada started shifting and became more oriented towards the evening concerts. That was a big change. Also, Mitch did some marketing research back then which indicated that people came to the Festival for the event, not for the headliners. He said they would come and they trusted him to put on a good concert. That was great for people like me, who don't have the enormous followings, because we were able to still come and play. I value the opportunities immensely. They changed my life.

JOHN PRENTICE: Mitch understood the interface and that doesn't happen now, even with small festivals. There is the magic of your openness on a workshop to the audience, as well as the other performers on the stage. Do you agree with that?

DE: Oh, yeah. I think for me, personally, the key to my career, that I've been able to maintain in Canada, is a personal relationship with the audience. Any gig I do now in Canada, I will know probably one-third to half the people in the audience. Other guys in my generation say the same thing. Valdy is a really good friend of mine; he says the same thing. He knows everybody in the audience. It's those workshops, those daytime events at these festivals, and particularly Winnipeg, where that kind of relationship started. There are people who would come to the workshops and afterwards, you're right there. They'd come up and talk to you. Now they come up and ask you to do a house concert at their house and it's just wonderful. It's the house concerts and the small venue opportunities around Canada that are keeping that spirit alive. That's what's keeping me going as a performer because the commercial music business in Canada and in North America generally has become very difficult for people like me. I was just listening to my friend Scott Nolan's concert; the backstory was how difficult it is for a solo singer-songwriter to develop and hold an audience. The way I've been able to do it is by keeping a personal relationship with them and they feel that they know me and they'll come to the gigs and they still buy CDs. Every time I think about that, I see Mitch up there in the background, making this happen.

FIGURE 72. BIKES AND MAIN STAGE, 1975. PHOTOGRAPH BY DAVID LANDY. ARCHIVES OF MANITOBA, WINNIPEG FOLK FESTIVAL 1975 NEGATIVES, P5266/1, 75-4547. 17A.

Centurion
Soun

PART FOUR

THE LURE OF LOCAL:

Home-Grown Talent Takes the Stage

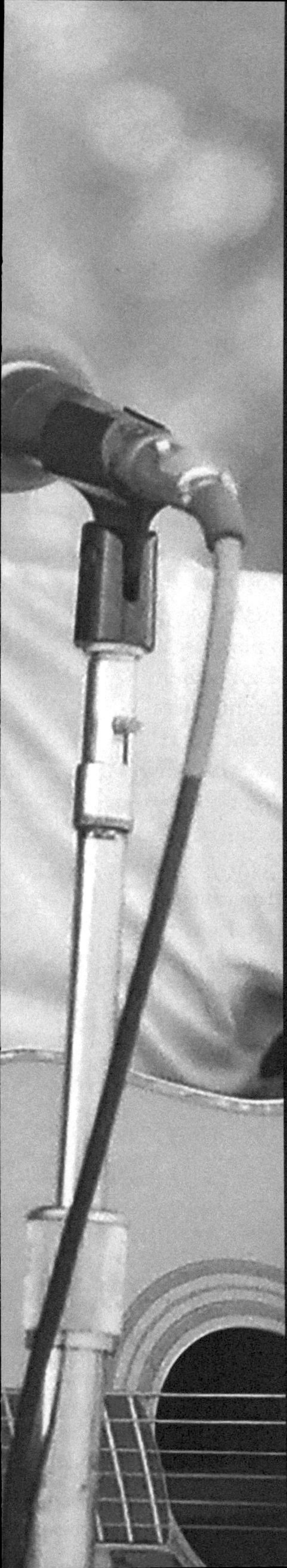

Rick NEUFELD

Rick Neufeld grew up on a farm near Boissevain, Manitoba. He studied architecture at the University of Manitoba, but quit to pursue a career as a singer-songwriter—he is most remembered for his hit "Moody Manitoba Morning." His touring took him across the continent, playing coffeehouses and festivals, including the Mariposa Folk Festival—and later to a performance at the Grand Ole Opry in 1971. Rick was a friend of Mitch Podolak, and a frequent performer during the early years of the Winnipeg Folk Festival. In 1976, Rick hosted The Road Show *and* Songsingers, *television shows for CBC. When he grew tired of touring, he transitioned to tour bus driving—he bought a tour bus and began an era behind the wheel—driving Bruce Cockburn, Sarah McLachlan, Norah Jones, and others. He lives on Salt Spring Island, BC.*

FIGURE 73. RICK NEUFELD, 1980. PHOTOGRAPH BY DAVID LANDY. ARCHIVES OF MANITOBA, WINNIPEG FOLK FESTIVAL 1980 NEGATIVES, P5266/11, 80/602.

RICK NEUFELD

5 AUGUST 2021, WINNIPEG

KEVIN NIKKEL: How did you get started in folk music?

RICK NEUFELD: Well, it's a good question about how I got started because it was certainly not family tradition, by any means. The music was pretty much in the church. Every once in a while, my Uncle Henry would play his guitar and my Aunt Lena would sing. I was a bit of a rebel child and somehow guitar was the symbol. My parents didn't really object to it, although they certainly were not under the impression that someone made a living that way, and they're very close to being right, in most cases. So, I learned how to play just by myself. I got some basic lessons, I guess, from my uncle. And then I just worked it out. I spent a lot of time with the guitar and it really helped me because I was a reluctant labourer as a kid on the farm. So, this was an escape for me. I almost immediately began writing songs. When I got to Europe, I got a guitar there, too. When I got back from Europe, I'd met the man who would ultimately be my publisher and producer, Bob Hahn, who is quite well-known as a jingle writer. He liked my songs because of the basic Manitoba roots of the music. As soon as I got back to Fort Garry, 79 Marshall Crescent, I wrote "Moody Manitoba Morning," virtually the day after I got back. I don't even remember how we did things in those days because now we just email or text or whatever. But I got the song to him and he was about to produce a band called The Bells. So, it all happened rather quickly. Radio stations liked that one.

KN: A quick diversion. You mentioned living on the farm. Before you moved to Fort Garry.

RN: No. Fort Garry was first. I moved from Fort Garry and I met the woman who would become my bride, she was going to the Canadian [Mennonite] Bible College on Shaftesbury. Our first date was to see Paul Simon and Art Garfunkel at UMSU. I was studying architecture. Those were the days. I quit university the next Monday. We ended up getting married. My wife, Diana, was renamed Rosie by Humphrey and the Dumptrucks during a crackling rose-infested night, shortly after our nuptials. Her grandkids call her Granberry because we have four grandkids. We're long apart, but we're still good friends. What was the question?

KN: When I do these interviews, I like to ask, how did you get to be who you are? Maybe someone wants to know the route of another Mennonite because I'm Mennonite, too.

RN: The farm came after living in Winnipeg, after we got married. It was amazing, this place we ended up getting. It became a haven for musicians. Especially Bruce Cockburn and Valdy would camp out in the yard, whenever they were on a tour. Come on by. It was a great place. Got a railroad track where you could jump cars over. And a creek out back for canoeing. So many parties. So many parties. The farm itself lent itself to writing the kind of music I was writing, which was my first album.

Rosie and I were both living out there at the farm and Mitch Podolak would come out and we'd have great cookouts. He loved to cook, of course. We'd been friends for quite a while. A lot happened at that farm. I mean, guys like Tom Jackson, Paul Hahn, and Shingoose would come for extended stays and it was a great environment.

KN: From what I've heard, I think Lorna Hiebert mentioned it, there is an interesting story there.

RN: She lived there, too.

KN: I'm interested in the Mennonite artistic renaissance of the last few decades and it seems your farm could be a chapter of the story.

RN: It was always open season there. We were both open. We had a huge garden. I actually got a farm tractor and the garden kept getting bigger because I loved playing with the tractor. Now, that was by choice and not by orders of growing up on the farm near Boissevain.[19]

KN: So, in terms of music, were you playing shows before the Folk Festival?

RN: Just coffeehouses. In terms of trying to remember exactly when the Festival came along, and me doing CBC television here in Winnipeg, it took a guy named Marv Terhoch to create interest and showcase singer-songwriters, especially. There was always a folk scene here, of course, going back to The Fourth Dimension, when even Neil Young was a folksinger and beginning [his career]. There was always a rich tradition here. Jim Donahue, especially. We forget more than we remember. It seems so long ago, yet when the memories flood, it's just like it was yesterday.

THE FIRST WINNIPEG FOLK FESTIVAL

KN: Were some of those clubs, and the CBC, too, important infrastructure of what would come later with the Folk Festival?

RN: Yeah. Mitch did like to do things on a grand scale. Whether it was a meal he was cooking or a folk festival. We talked about the Folk Festival forever, before it actually came to fruition with the centennial. I'd already performed at a couple of festivals like that in Toronto and he'd been there at the Mariposa. He'd gone to those festivals. I got involved, to some extent, with it just because we were around each other. Either watching hockey or eating, usually, or both. We talked about it a lot. Then when it came down to actually planning the workshops, which really was a great strength of his, I got to chip in there a little bit. He valued that. It was so exciting. Rosie, my wife at the time, started the Handmade Village—the crafts area. So, it was a family affair, his family and my family got together a lot.

KN: I want to talk about the conversations that were happening with Mitch in the lead-up to the first Folk Festivals. What were you thinking?

RN: Well, we had models to base the concept of a folk festival on. But he always wanted to figure out a way for it to stand apart. And it did. Because so much of our being together involved food, he was determined to have great food, and that the entertainers would all be treated royally. That was a distinction that the Winnipeg Folk Festival had. Of course, when he started Edmonton—with others, too—he had Winnipeg to draw on the experience there. I remember us talking from the very beginning, the thought that he should be a little more open about electric instruments, for instance. It took him a while, but eventually it happened. But boy, he stuck to his guns on that.

He just wanted to make sure that every artist that ever came to the Winnipeg Folk Festival would remember the festival and want to come again. Even if they got to be well beyond the Folk Festival budget,

FIGURE 74. RICK NEUFELD (MIDDLE) SHARES A WORKSHOP STAGE, 1975. PHOTOGRAPH BY DAVID LANDY. ARCHIVES OF MANITOBA, WINNIPEG FOLK FESTIVAL 1975 NEGATIVES, P5266/1, 75-4794.

and it happened quite often. The Festival got entertainers that would travel all that way for what the Festival could afford to pay them, which would in most cases be the same as Jim Donahue.

KN: If we tried to distill the essence of the core members at the time, what was the spirit in the air back then?

RN: I mean, Mitch obviously loved Pete Seeger, and the whole New York Greenwich Village scene, and wanted to bring that here. Because he'd seen it and wanted other Manitobans to see it. This was actually early in the singer-songwriter craze, which is what it became—that folk scene that New York had, and that Toronto was starting to have. Mitch didn't want to have to travel to New York or Toronto, he wanted it to take place here. He was going to make it happen. He was so determined. The singer-songwriter craze hadn't yet taken hold, but it was starting, and he helped a lot. He introduced so many amazing individuals, like Fred Eaglesmith. It was really important to him to have an Indigenous aspect to the Festival, and to really chronicle folk music in its wide bandwidth at the time. He was inspiring to all of us. He made us work.

KN: I love that angle, of bringing New York here. What was the first festival like?

RN: The very first festival was free, basically sponsored by the government. It happened at quite a different part of Birds Hill Park than the site that became its annual site. It was juvenile, that first one. None of us really knew what to expect. It was probably easier, that first one, for Colin and Mitch to put together because expectations were not all that high and you weren't charging people money. So, we didn't have to worry about that part of it. It was later on with the second, third, and fourth Festivals, it became really hard work to keep it afloat because people hadn't come for free.

Once you are a Folk-Festival-goer, you would usually go every year. You'd see the same people every year and it grew every year. The lineup of talent would grow every year. It was awesome. It became the highlight of every year. It took the place of Christmas every year, it was Christmas and New Year's, everything all rolled into one. It was amazing. We were so proud to be from where the Winnipeg Folk Festival was held.

KN: You played the first year?

RN: Absolutely.

KN: Tell me about that.

RN: It was all quite rudimentary, the sound systems and all that. And I don't remember it as being huge, as what the Festival ultimately became. Mitch didn't really get to work in his workshop angle that first year. He got, really, an expert on that, and he got very tricky with it, too. Especially for people who he knew well, like me, or Stan Rogers. He was a trickster. He tried to put us in situations and combinations. If there was animosity between two musicians, he'd make sure he put them in a workshop. That was the kind of thing he got a kick out of.

KN: Examples?

RN: Oh, well. Let's just say, Stan and I didn't exactly get along. Somehow, [Mitch] did the workshops for the Sudbury Festival one year, also. He made sure Stan and I were on the same workshop, where we had to write a song. Yikes. I think he actually gave me a hint. I think he actually wanted me to win. I wrote a crazy, pun baseball song.

I remember Mitch also putting me on early Sunday morning workshops, partially because he knew that if I was on a Sunday morning workshop in lieu of church, that I'd probably do "Hundred Miles of Hard On," for instance. In fact, he probably even told me that I had to do it. Graham Shaw had a similar song, and I used to do that one, too. I think he did it with me once. But it was mortifying, when you looked out in the crowd, knowing that you were stuck in the situation, thanks to trickster Mitch, and you'd see the minister from your home church in Boissevain, Manitoba sitting there all excited about seeing you play, and you realize that you recognize him there about halfway through that song. He had to pretend, after, that he didn't hear. It was nuts. But it was fun. Sunday morning workshops, they were hard work because we stayed up all night.

KN: What was the atmosphere in the crowd, back then in the 1970s?

RN: At the first few Festivals, most people had no experience of how a festival works, but they were fast learners. And people like being in big crowds. You actually have a lot of responsibility or power. I mean, the Main Stage was the hierarchy, whoever got to play the Main Stage. But the real fun was the workshops. I think that the crowds loved them both equally. The biggest problem would be, which workshop to go to when there are four you want to see at same time. The weather was always a factor, too. It really affected attendance and decorum. But it was always amazing.

KN: Talk about the weather.

RN: I mentioned that I also played a little festival here in Kelwood with the Harvest Sun Festival that Nadia and Delano put on.[20] It got rained out one year and it reminded me so much of that first big rainout in Winnipeg. Washout. It was a disaster for the attendance. But people got creative and a lot of people just got wet. And that's how it was. Most of them had seen Woodstock so they're not going to wipe out over a little bit of rain. For the sound company and the lighting companies, it was just so hard on them when it got windy or wet. And yet it wouldn't affect the spirit of the crowd. If anything, it would probably enhance it because that's what happens when you endure

FIGURE 75. RICK NEUFELD, 1975. PHOTOGRAPH BY DAVID LANDY. ARCHIVES OF MANITOBA, WINNIPEG FOLK FESTIVAL 1975 NEGATIVES, P5266/1, 75-4795. 2A.

a trial and tribulation and you get through it. It's like when Prince played the Super Bowl in the rain. It's just amazing how it can bring that out in you.

KN: But this can also bring the Festival to the brink. With all the expenses.

RN: I know that that got dire, there. All of us were asked to contribute to the fund, to keep it alive. Some could and some couldn't, and some did and some didn't. The volunteer contingent was probably the most determined to keep the Festival going. The volunteers were right up there with all the performers, in terms of keeping the Festival happening. I think a lot of the volunteers kicked in money, too, so that they'd have a place to volunteer next year.

KN: You played on the Main Stage?

RN: A number of times.

KN: Describe that. Was there pressure on you to bring your A game?

MITCH AND "MOODY MANITOBA MORNING"

RN: I'd always have a good band. Playing by myself, to me, was not the same as playing with Don Zueff, the fiddle player, and banjo, who is now with the D. Rangers. He and I started out playing as a duo. Then eventually we had a band. I'm the one who had Bill Merritt as a bass player, playing on the Main Stage. He became the business manager at the Folk Festival for a long time. And Gord Osland of Prairie Dog, of course. I remember one year when we were on stage for the prime time of the Main Stage, and CBC Radio [broadcast] it live across the nation. I think they did more than one year. So, it was especially fun to sing "Moody Manitoba Morning" there after being specifically instructed that I was only getting to play the Main Stage based on the fact that I wasn't going to do that song. But I think I relented on "Hundred Miles . . ." and I don't think I did that one on the CBC. I wouldn't be surprised if I did. I can't remember.

KN: What was the significance of the song "Moody Manitoba Morning?"

RN: Well, Mitch liked to tease me as being a bit of a one-hit wonder and he said, "You know you can just go out there and do that 'Moody Manitoba Morning' song. First of all, I can't stand it." I don't know if he really felt that way or if it was just a game. Again, like I said, Mitch is a trickster and there wasn't a time when he told me not to sing it that I did. So, he must've figured out that I was going to do it anyway. It was a memorable thing for me because I had no choice but to do it. It was better to do it because he didn't want me to. He said, if he ever walked up to a stage, whether the workshop or the Main Stage, and I was doing that song, I'd never get to play it again. That's just how he was. I had nothing but appreciation for him. We had absolutely no disputes whatsoever and this was just a running thing with us.

KN: I think it's great that you trickstered him right back. In fact, I heard a recording from the 1976 Folk Festival stage with you saying, "this song goes out to Mitch and Colin." And you played that song.

RN: Yeah, that sounds like something that happened.

KN: What parts of the Festival did you take on as a tradition or rituals?

RN: The scariest time for every Festival was when you finally got the program in your hands and you had to see exactly where Mitch had plugged you in, to which workshops. You asked earlier about not getting along. I must say I got along with most everybody, but Murray McLauchlan was another person [that I didn't]. For some reason, I can't remember why. Of course, Mitch knew that. I think Murray might've asked if there was a special request and this guy I knew said, "Why don't you sing 'Souris River Valley Ups and Downs.'" It was one of my songs. And Murray was just fumed. I said, "I've got farmer songs, too."

STEVE GOODMAN AND DAVID AMRAM

JOHN PRENTICE: Do you remember the workshop that Steve Goodman and David Amram did?

RN: Oh, jeez. Steve Goodman became such a good friend of mine. I went to Cubs games with him in Chicago. Incredible.

KN: What was the significance of people like David Amram and Steve?

RN: David Amram, he was the conductor of us all. We all knew to be on standby for him because he did things on a grand scale. And you better be ready to go when he'd call on you. David Amram was amazing. Then songwriters that I absolutely treasured were people like John Hiatt, John Prine, and Steve Goodman, especially Steve Goodman because he was such a sweetheart. I remember years and years later, when my band was playing at the Norwood, I had a bus always backstage in the early days, and when John Prine and Steve Goodman came to Winnipeg to play, I picked them up at the airport. They knew that we were playing. They must have said something on stage because they came right after the show and the lineup was out the door, down the street, all the way to the hospital. So, everybody from the show must've come. Bill Merritt was in the middle of singing "Spanish Pipe Dream," they didn't break stride, they came right up on stage. I gave John my guitar and Bob White gave Steve a guitar and they finished "Spanish Pipe Dream" and then they did an hour and half straight, no break. Then upstairs to the band room. I love those guys. John Prine—what a force.

JP: David told the story about, what would happen at workshop was, they'd ask the audience for a word and they had to write a song. Then workshops eventually became artists only doing their best stuff. Now into the 1990s, you follow people around the Festival and they're only doing the same three songs. Or the latest stuff on their album because they want to sell records. But that is different than Mitch's idea, and what you were intimating, of what you did with Stan Rogers. Where Mitch actually said, "We want you to come up with a new song or make up a song during the workshop."

RN: Amram didn't have to be prompted, he was so creative and so multifaceted. He made things happen. He knew exactly how to wind up the crowd and also to draw the special gifts out of the people he was on a workshop stage with. I don't think Mitch ever had to plan a Dave Amram workshop. David was always amazing. He surprised us all the time. It was such an honour to be in workshops with him.

KN: How did you prepare for the workshop?

RN: I think you never knew how a workshop was going to turn out and that, again, is part of the brilliance of blending different facets together to come up with something that would be interesting and entertaining. That's why the workshops, I think, were for some people more interesting than the Main Stage performances. I knew people that would go home after the workshop. How we prepared for an early morning workshop is by staying up partying all night. That's basically how we did it. And we all did it that way, pretty much.

KN: The closing wrap-up. How did the Festival wrap up?

RN: I remember one. When David Landy's picture of the "Good Night Irene," or whatever it was we were doing, and my daughter was quite young because I'm sitting in a chair in the middle, front and centre, completely passed out holding onto her. I gave it all. You gave it all, all weekend, and then a lot of people would leave early the next morning. And you'd still manage the Sunday night parties.

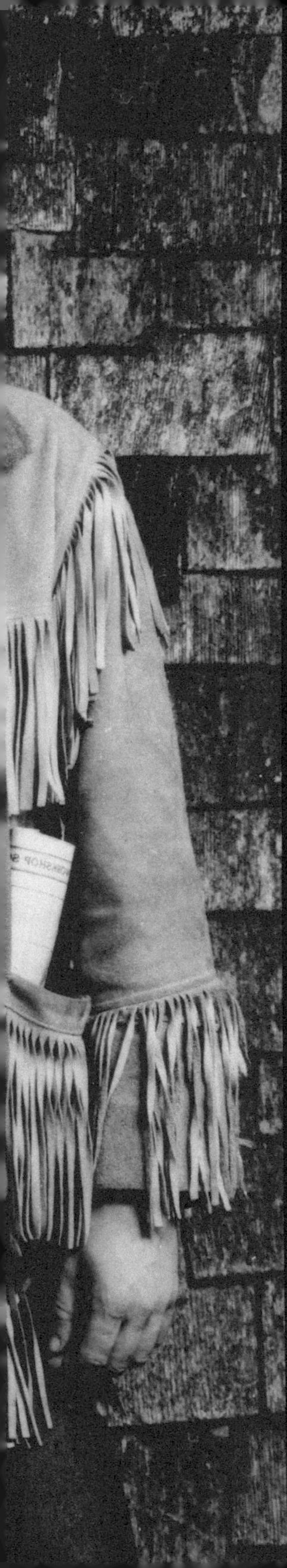

Big Dave MCLEAN

Big Dave McLean is a renowned blues guitarist and singer-songwriter from Winnipeg, born in Yorkton, Saskatchewan to a concert pianist mother and minister father. The family eventually moved to Winnipeg when Dave was eight. He and his brother made their way to Mariposa in 1972, which provided a burst of inspiration to pursue not just harmonica, but the blues guitar—as well as the life of the singer-songwriter. Dave is a veteran of the blues in Canada—with an extensive resumé, touring clubs and festivals to support his many albums. Dave has performed a total of thirteen Winnipeg Folk Festivals and has a long list of awards for his music—including several Maple Blues Awards, Western Canadian Music Awards, a Juno, and multiple nominations. He has been the regular host of the Sunday night blues jam at Times Change(d) club in Winnipeg for thirty-five years, mentoring the likes of Colin James and Shaun Verreault of Wide Mouth Mason. He received the Order of Canada in 2022.

FIGURE 76. BIG DAVE MCLEAN (ON RIGHT) AND GORD KIDDER, 1977. PHOTOGRAPH BY GERRY KOPELOW. COURTESY OF WINNIPEG FOLK FESTIVAL.

BIG DAVE MCLEAN

8 DECEMBER 2021, WINNIPEG

KEVIN NIKKEL: Start things off with introducing yourself. What was your entry point into music?

BIG DAVE MCLEAN: My name is Dave McLean. I've been playing in the music scene for almost fifty years. I was happy to be at the 1974 Festival, was that the centennial festival? And then in 1975 it became the Folk Festival.

My brother Grant used to play folk music. Music by guys like Pete Seeger, Woody Guthrie, and sometimes ragtime players like Fats Waller, Scott Joplin, and his favourite Blind Blake, and that kind of stuff. I was always interested. I love listening to my brother, he was a wonderful player, and he had a folk album collection and he'd play songs by Lead Belly. I was like, "Who's that, I like this guy." I liked all the folk stuff. Dylan was really heavy back then. I loved his stuff and quite a few others. But there were local guys playing, too: Jim Donahue, Glen McCabe, Cast Iron Potty Band, and Bobby Purvis (later Bobby Stahr) here in Winnipeg. I really enjoyed listening to these guys, but it's the early days. I didn't play an instrument at all, but I loved listening to the music of Robert Johnson, Johnny Shines, and a host of country blues artists.

The blues was what really moved me more than any other style of music. That's how I got involved in playing it. I just loved the sound. I have such respect and admiration for the men and women from Mississippi, Chicago, Texas, Louisiana, that created this style of music. I can sympathize with their hardships that they suffered to create the music through not just racism, but working for the man and barely scraping by. The songs that they wrote, they just touched me so deep.

KN: So, your discovery of records was an inspiration. You were also starting to look at the scene and what was happening?

JOHN HAMMOND'S GUITAR

BDM: Actually, before that, go to 1972. I was already playing harmonica. My brother and I had saved up money and went to Mariposa together on the train. I got to see Leon Redbone and Roosevelt Sykes and John Hammond for the first time. That's when I had my socks blown right off my feet. I was getting up to go to the washroom and John Hammond just started into Robert Johnson's "Preachin' Blues" and he just starts chugging on his National Steel guitar. I stopped dead. I turned and said, "Who's this guy? What is he doing to that guitar?" It was earth-moving for me. I'd never seen or heard anything like that. And he presented it so well, and he was such a gentleman. Later that day I saw him under a tree and I went over and I got my very first guitar lesson. I didn't pester him; I didn't want to be one of those kind of fans. I just went over and said, "I've been listening to this style of music, it's still fairly new to me, but I sure have never heard anything like what you are playing." I almost didn't make it to the washroom. He showed me how to play "I'm a Man" by Bo Diddley in open tuning slide guitar. I had a five-dollar guitar back then that I took to the Festival, but I didn't know a single chord, I just thought, *Maybe the girls will come over and say hi if I'm carrying a guitar.* But that didn't happen. I said, "Can you just show me how, I noticed you are playing with that thing on your finger." He had an 11/16 socket that he used, a Craftsman deep socket.

The slide guitar blew my mind. I thought, *what sound.* It is so beautiful, you get so deep. You can get everything. Open tuning and the chords were much easier to play because it's already tuned to a chord. If you have the guitar tuned to an open D, and you strum it, that is the D. So that was the spark that ignited everything for me. I really focused on it.

WINNIPEG MUSIC SCENE

KN: What was the music scene in Winnipeg like?

BDM: The Winnipeg scene was basically coffeehouses which were wonderful. There was a whole series of coffeehouses: the Wing'd Ox, The Wise I, the Latin Quarter, Fourth Dimension. There was a handful and they had live music, but my most frequently attended was the

Ting Tea Room on Broadway—where most of my friends were. We would congregate there all the time. Late 1970s early 1980s. In those days you'd sit down and there'd be a candle on your table, maybe soft lighting, it was really cool. I wish they'd recreate that sort of thing. I don't think any of us thought that stuff that we grew up with was going to go the way it did. I mean, I try playing music of that era, a lot of it is still popular today. The blues is the basis for everything today, but I think back in the 1940s, 1950s, and 1960s it was just hitting the heights in Chicago, Detroit, and Texas. And then the Piedmont guys down farther, to Alabama in the south—everybody had their own sound. You could hear the first few lines of a guitar and you'd know what kind of style and where he's coming from. It's like a stamp. This guy played a Piedmont style song by Blind Boy Fuller.

KN: So, there is this local scene, coffeehouses, at some point we need to introduce the character of Mitch Podolak.

BDM: Absolutely. In 1974, I was at the Festival and I loved it. I met Bukka White because that was the year I got my National Steel guitar, but I still didn't really know how to play much slide. I did know how to play "I'm a Man" by Bo Diddley. He was playing his National Steel and I was so thrilled. He was the main reason I wanted to get one. I'd been listening to his music and I thought, *That guitar is unbelievable. I've got to get one of those*, and it took a long time to find that sort of instrument because I was looking around Winnipeg. I got it off a big-band guy named Al Sprints. I think he had bought it in New Orleans and it was in somebody's closet for thirty years before that. So here's a 1932 guitar. When I got the guitar, it was totally warped. I took it to Long and McQuade and they had a heat bar that they attached to it. They would clamp and then heat it, then clamp it harder until it straightened out. I only had to have that process done twice. I still have the guitar and it still plays perfectly. It was totally unplayable when I bought it, but I wanted one, I didn't care. I had to get my father to co-sign a loan for me for $300 because I didn't have that much money. When I got it, I was just doing backflips and howling down the street. It was unbelievable. I couldn't believe I had a National Steel guitar. Then I started learning about the slide. All these years later, I know a few more steps.

GOING TO THE WINNIPEG FOLK FESTIVAL

KN: What was the Folk Festival like when you went?

BDM: It was wonderful. Like a big yard party, but a really big yard party. It really knocked me out. There were a lot of folks that inspired me, but the blues guys, I was at all their workshops and all their concerts because that's what really moved me the most. I was so thrilled that Winnipeg was putting on this sort of an event. When people ask me how I learned how to play music I'd say, "I went to blues school every summer at the Winnipeg Folk Festival. I owe so much to the Winnipeg Folk Festival and my friend Mitch Podolak." I was so grateful to Mitch. He's the only communist I know that knows how to work the capitalist system so well. He's the king of grants. I remember marching into his offices and saying, "I want to play your festival." He was quite taken by my forwardness with him. We struck up a friendship pretty much right off the bat.

KN: What year would that have been?

BDM: I believe it was 1975 or 1976. I have a failing memory, the years all flow together for me.

KN: You asked to play?

BDM: Yeah. I was playing harmonica in the late 1960s and early 1970s. I'd only started playing, I didn't really play guitar and perform yet. But later I wanted to get my brother Grant and I in there. We worked up a duo and we'd stayed at the Calgary Father Lacombe Centre for a Calgary Festival a few years later, they had this festival and that was a lot of fun. That was with Duck Donald and Cathy Fink and a lot of these folks were around. They were at the early festivals, too. Later I teamed up with Gord Kidder, one of the best harmonica players in Canada, and he was a major influence on me—he mentored me. He taught me about the guys at the Winnipeg Folk Festival and who was coming every year—and what records to be listening to.

KN: I find it interesting that you were growing and emerging as a player and the Folk Festival was, too. There is a parallel.

BDM: Absolutely. I watched it grow from this little nut into this tree. It's amazing. I'm so proud of it. I tell people about it all the time. You got any music in Winnipeg? Well, let me tell you. Sit down. We've got one of the biggest festivals in the world and it was created by the king of creating festivals, Mitch. He was brilliant. A lot of people don't know: Edmonton—Mitch was behind it. Vancouver—Mitch was behind [it]. The old children's festival, this festival, that festival. It was always a thrill for us because it'd be like walking into a candy shop. I'd be like, "I was just listening to your records this morning. And now I'm smelling the sweat under your armpits. Now you're sitting beside me." Wow. To me, that's amazing. I loved it.

KN: That's such a potent image.

BDM: I remember telling that to Johnny Shines; he used to tour with Robert Johnson. I go, "This is probably the closest I'm ever going to get to somebody knowing Robert Johnson." But I got to know Johnny at a few festivals and he was just an amazing man, he kept the history straight. He knew how important the music was. Same with Willie Dixon, playing the electric Chicago stuff. He knew this was going to be the basis of it all. So, he kept it all straight. Who's who, and what they played, and how they played. And styles. There were a few guys who knew that this was history. It was an important history to music, so you know somebody's got to get it straight. And keep it. He [Willie Dixon] was one, Johnny Shines was another.

KN: Did you feel pressure to bring your own material?

BDM: Original songs? No, not at all. I didn't do any back then. I only did covers. But I did the covers the way I could do them because I wasn't as developed a musician as these guys. That's the point I was going to make; getting up on stage with Johnny Shines to play guitar, it felt like a dream. I kind of played a simple style, but I always tried to put as much heart, and stand behind the licks, and stand behind the songs. I find that a lot of the people here playing today, they sing the lyrics, but they're not selling it. You've got to sell it. Even songs that you write. Why did you write that song? You're not making it believable if you just "la la la," so you got to sell it.

KN: Let's go back to the early years of the Festival. What were you seeing on the stage and in the crowd?

BDM: Most of the time, in the early years, I wasn't a Main Stage artist. I was a workshop guy and became workshop host many times. I was thrilled to be asked to play and I loved the workshops. It was more selfish, because I got to hear the people that I liked, that were sitting right beside me. I'd be like, "Oh, that's what you're doing! [Laughs] That's very clever." Having that kind of connection with the people sitting down on the field, I mean it was really just simple back then. There's a stage they're sitting on and we're sitting in the dirt and if it had been raining out there, sitting in the mud. Many times, that's exactly it, for all of us, we all got soaked. It just drew us all together even more because we were on even ground. You made $200,000 last year? Hey and I made $1,800 shovelling snow or something. But I think I'm just as wet as you are! We have a common bond here.

I thought the workshops were a brilliant idea and they were smaller back then. It was more intimate. There'd be four or five rows of people sitting down there, and people were explaining what they were doing, more than just putting on mini-concerts. However, that has its place, too. You have to feel it out while you're on stage. If you have fifteen minutes, do you want to spend half of that talking about it, or do you try to fit in an extra song? It's your call, but you have to give it some thought. I always took it very seriously, what I was going to do. If I was going to talk, I would try and minimize it, and write out what I wanted to say, and then I'd try and chop it down and see if I could say it in fewer words. I even got to the point where I would use a stopwatch to time myself. This song is three minutes long and the introduction is four minutes, well, scratch that. I'll just do the song by so-and-so. If you like it, go hear his version. Go buy the original.

JOHN PRENTICE: And music came out of being together, too.

BDM: Oh, that too. Of course. Just the mini-jams with all the other players, that was the most brilliant. Those mini-concerts were some of best of them all, some of the workshops. Everybody took turns singing a song and everybody else added to it. But most were professionals, they knew not to stomp all over everybody else. The more people, the less you play. If you get the nod, then do a solo. But whoever is driving the boat, or singing the song, is in charge, and it's up to you to play something that complements that song and complements that artist. It's not up to you to play every lick you know to show off your talent on their song. Do that on your song, or next time where there's more time for people to perform. You don't pick a fifteen-minute slow song.

That's just rude because then you're just making it all about you, and there's like seven other people on the stage. Most of the time, people would be very courteous and very aware of how much time they're taking to perform.

DIVERSITY OF MUSIC AT FOLK FESTIVALS

KN: Did people know what they were in for, coming to the Folk Festival?

BDM: I think most people that came to the Festival kind of had an idea or had heard already about how things worked. The very first one, everybody was surprised—even the promoters and everybody putting it on—to see how well it ran, with the ideas that they had for running a festival. Some of them became golden rules and, some of it, not so much. *Well, we won't do that next year.*

I didn't hear a bad word about the Festival. I only heard compliments, about how Mitch and his crew ran the Festival because he had a wonderful group of people working with him. To me, Mitch was definitely pulling the strings. He was the Wizard of Oz. But he always had good people working with him. All through the years, and then that passed on, too. There have always been good people working at the Festival.

KN: Why does blues music fit in at a folk festival?

BDM: It's a crossover. The festivals, though, some of it I think doesn't fit in with it. Not necessarily the Winnipeg one. I was at a festival in Ottawa where Snoop Dogg was the headliner at the Blues Festival, and they'd had James Brown, and I mean, hey, I got nothing against either of those guys. I actually like Snoop Dogg and I love James Brown. But I wonder why they were headlining at the Festival. But it's because they have to draw the younger crowd. If the younger crowd has been more exposed to James Brown than they have to James Cotton or John Hammond or any of the blue stars, they'll probably go with that because it draws more folks in. And of course, [Mitch] would have great blues artists, too. I'm actually a big fan of the Ottawa festival and the Edmonton festival. They do a great blues festival and they do a great folk festival, too. And Vancouver. They all kind of picked up Mitch's vibe because he was the root behind them, too. I remember being at the 1982 Folk Festival in Vancouver, it was either the second or first, I'm not sure. Mitch had spearheaded that and it was brilliant. It was run just like the Winnipeg Folk Festival, of course, and Mitch just took his formula on the road. And boy, it hit on every note. I think Mitch was quite the genius, but boy, he had another side, too. I rubbed noses with him a couple of times.

KN: Tell me about that.

BDM: No. [Laughs] We had a few little run-ins, but nothing that couldn't be handled, and we were friends already. Barking at your friend is a lot easier than barking at somebody you're just mad at and you don't know. Whether I was playing or not, I'd have coffee with him, and we went and ate lunch a few times. But yeah, he had a side to him that, it wasn't mean or anything, it was conniving. He knew how to manipulate, and you didn't see that side of him very often. I guess everybody probably has that side to them. The many sides of Mitch Podolak. Most of them were just right on, perfect. I loved Mitch very much. We were very close friends.

KN: What was your first impression of arriving at the Folk Festival site?

BDM: It was like opening a door. Like going to Disney World. Which ride do you want to go on first? I usually went with my wife, and our kids, they've been there more times than I have. They've worked for the Festival, every summer they go. The first thing we do is look at the schedule, who's playing where. What do you want to take in? Look at the stages. Okay, well, if we go to this stage and it's all the way over there, if you want to hear this guy, then we're going to have to leave that stage by this time so we can make it back over here to catch the full show. There is always a little bit of figuring it out.

I saw stuff that I'd never seen before. One year they had a didgeridoo and I went, "Whoa! A guy blowing into a big pencil over there." But a hurdy-gurdy, things like that. What is that other thing? [Makes high droning musical sound]

KN: A theremin?

BDM: Theremin. Actually, I played a Tom Waits thing last night at The Times and there was a girl who had one of those. And I thought it was Jaxon Haldane playing the saw. There is a great instrument. You get the D. Rangers, you get Jaxon Haldane playing the saw, wow, what a sound. What a beautiful sound, what a beautiful instrument. He can play it, and not have to tune it.

KN: It seems like that is a big part of folk music: you use what you have. You don't need the expensive guitar.

BDM: Yes. Diddley bow, when it started out, guys would put nails in the side of their house, run wires to them of different lengths, and stick a bottle under it to get the tuning. You pluck it and slide it with glass, metal, whatever. It's like, wow. You'll have to come over to jam at my house, though. If you want me to come to your house, I'm coming with four nails and some wire and a bottle.

KN: I think that gets to something about the Folk Festival, too. If we distilled it down.

BDM: Absolutely. I have been reading about Buddy Guy, who took part of a screen door and made strings out of it for his homemade guitar. And then his dad finally saw how dedicated he was trying to play, that he actually bought him [a guitar]. The rest is history. He became one of the world's greatest guitar slingers. The inventiveness of people. Most of the people I've been following were like really dirt-poor farmers in Mississippi, Louisiana, various parts of the South. That's the style I like so much.

KN: How would you summarize the raw essence of the Folk Festival?

BDM: The Winnipeg Folk Festival, in particular, because that's what I grew up with, I knew I was going to have a good time and I knew I was going to come away with more knowledge about music. More happiness from being around the people that shared the same music, that I liked being around. The thing I love about Winnipeg is that we have such a diverse music community, every kind of music. If you want Lithuanian folk dancers, there are probably two troops to choose from. I don't know. We've got jazz, we've got folk, we got classical, our orchestra is top-notch, and then some of the other styles of music, too. Winnipeg is a melting pot of music. Man, you have any style you want. At the Folk Festival, that's where they get them all to come for a weekend and everybody's together and you get to see everything.

KN: Why do we have such a diverse festival?

BDM: Mitch Podolak. Mitch had a vision and Birds Hill Park; brilliant spot. And now the Festival site has become a permanent fixture. But, yeah. Winnipeg? Why not? We're in the centre. Come on to the middle, folks. We'll show you a good time. In the summertime, that's where people want to be. It's going to rain, so what? Bring rain clothes. The mosquitoes are bad? Bring a can of Off. We've been up against everything and we're a hardy group. The locals know how to take care of it. I've been to some pretty horrible rain showers out there, but so what? They know how to handle it. As soon as the first drop hits, the speakers are covered. All the crews look after that. Technical guys are on it. We've even had power failures where, okay we'll just get the loudest performers to just walk out the front of the stage and play a few tunes until we get back up rocking. You adapt and overcome whatever the problems are.

Like playing last night. I broke a string but I had to finish the song because I was only two verses in. I'm not going to stop playing, so I had to play with five strings. But that's okay, there are ways to do that. Plus, I had other artists playing, so if I'm having trouble, I can throw a solo to that guy. It worked out fine. They know how to handle anything to do with the weather. We got this thing. It's something I've always admired about how they run festivals. They are prepared for anything. I mean, if it's going to snow, they probably would have that covered.

KN: Yeah, the Festival crew is dialled in and ready for everything. That comes back to you saying you've got to stand by what you're playing.

JP: The audience is important. You can play for six people or you can play for 2,000 people.

BDM: You better put on the same show. Damn straight.

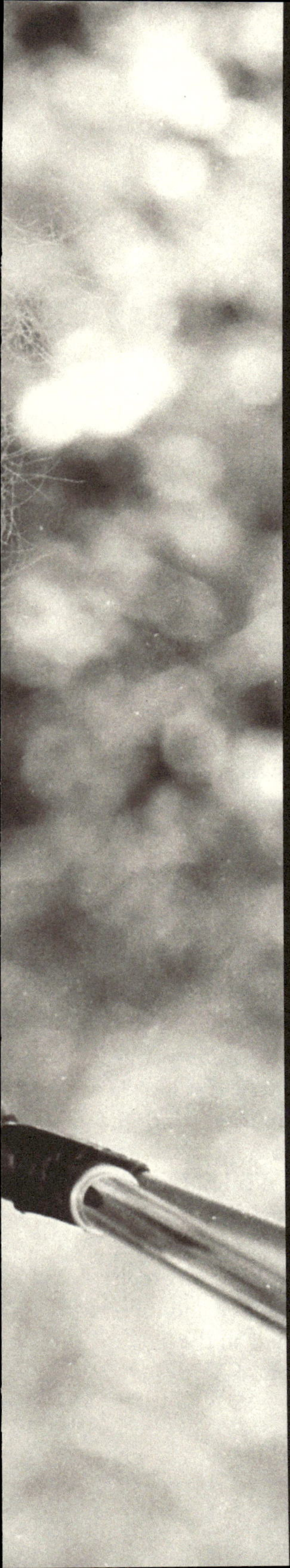

Dan DONAHUE

Dan Donahue is an acclaimed musician and record producer based in Winnipeg. He grew up in Winnipeg, looking over the shoulder of his musician brother Jim Donahue. It wasn't long before Dan had picked up the guitar himself and charted his own course to being a singer-songwriter. Dan began playing coffeehouses in Winnipeg and eventually found his way to the stages of folk festivals across the country—he played the Winnipeg Folk Festival on four occasions in the first decade of the event. Dan made a shift in his career in the 1980s towards record producing—a fruitful decision, keeping him busy for the last forty years, with twenty Juno nominations.

FIGURE 77. DAN DONAHUE, 1975. PHOTOGRAPH BY DAVID LANDY. ARCHIVES OF MANITOBA, WINNIPEG FOLK FESTIVAL 1975 NEGATIVES, P5266/1, 75-4633. 11.

DAN DONAHUE

8 SEPTEMBER 2021, WINNIPEG

KEVIN NIKKEL: Where does music begin for you?

DAN DONAHUE: I think the story begins for me in late 1950s, early 1960s. I was around seven years of age; my brother was six years older than me and he became totally ensconced in folk music. A neighbour who lived down the street, a very eccentric fellow originally from Minnesota, had taught himself how to play guitar. We were very close friends of the family and this fellow is somewhat of a surrogate father. He piqued my brother Jim's interest. Jim wanted to learn to play guitar, George helped him along. My mother never forgave him. From that point on, he was really involved in folk clubs and glee club. It was The Kingston Trio, Pete Seeger, The Weavers—the house was full of this music. He had this great bedroom downstairs that he would sit down for hours, playing guitar and inviting his buddies over, who were in much the same headspace. I was intrigued, as he was my big brother. When he would be at school or whatever, I would sneak down there and strum away, try to teach myself. I can remember the day I picked up the banjo and taught myself the first two chords. I think it was in grade one. I got the first two chords for "Michael, Row the Boat Ashore" and damned if I couldn't figure out the third one. So, I'd run home after school, knowing he'd be home at four o'clock and I got in at 3:30 pm. I managed to figure out the third one. Then I started to monkey with a guitar. I would sneak into the cloakroom and I would sit amongst the coats so that nobody could hear me. One day he did, and he just looked at me and said, "That's great! Play something else." From that point on, I literally came out of the closet and I'd just play for fun.

In 1964—February 7, I believe—Ed Sullivan and The Beatles. I walked into my mom's bedroom [and the program was] on the little black and white TV in the corner, my sister and her friends were screaming at the top of their lungs. [Before then] I had no interest whatsoever. I just took one look at the television, I was abducted by aliens. It was then and there. That's what I want to do. Next morning, I go to school and all the kids were in Beatles haircuts. The radios, everyone is tuning in to Beatles songs. They were the talk of the town. So, I gathered up a few friends at school who were kind of into playing guitar, we were trying to figure it all out. We monkeyed around for the longest period of time as a trio, being told by our teachers that, it's a nice hobby, but you'll never make a living.

One summer I was playing my electric guitar, I'd graduated to my electric, and my mom suggested I go and maybe set up in the garage. I was sitting there in the garage strumming away, and in walk three or four guys. I was terrified. They just walked in the side door. They looked at me and said, "Hey, wanna join a band?" We did the proverbial community clubs, church basements, and rural gigs because they were plentiful, if you knew where to look. The local scene was really vibrant because the drinking age was twenty-one, so if you wanted to hear music, most certainly original music, you didn't go to bars because you couldn't get in. So, what was happening in the community clubs, sock hops, school dances, and church basements was such a vibrant scene. There was a ton of work. You didn't need a paper route.

But then they lowered the drinking age. And a lot of the pubs, in an effort to appeal to the younger generation, started booking bands. Well, what happened then is that the control of content went to the owners of the bars who said, "We don't want any original material, we want to hear covers." We weren't interested in that. They want us to dress up in little outfits. And if you didn't have a girl in the band, you had to get a girl in the band. There was this formula, and I eventually got fed up with it.

I said, "To hell with this, I need to find something better."

THE WINNIPEG MUSIC SCENE

It so happens, at Vincent Massey, there were two fellows that were actually starting up a coffeehouse at the YWCA downtown. It was called The Wise I. It was a mainstay. It was one of the nicer places to play, and it paid well. I was really ticked off because my band had been booked to play on CJAY television [later CKY], I forget the name of the show.

JOHN PRENTICE: *Teen Dance Party*?

DD: *Teen Dance Party* with Bob Burns, thank you. I was so ticked off. I missed my golden opportunity. So, I took my guitar and I went down to The Wise I, after being invited by these fellows. I was too terrified to do a solo gig before then. I thought, *I'm going to show them.* I walked in and did a gig and people really liked it. That was the beginning of my association with the folk scene.

KN: What year was that?

DD: I would've been seventeen, so that would have been 1968–1969.

KN: Tell me more about the local folk scene that was happening from the late 1960s until the first Folk Festival in 1974, because it takes off quite quickly.

DD: Oh no, the seeds had been sown. The folk scene itself was really vibrant. There were a lot of kids that didn't want to go to the bars and weren't the least bit interested in what was happening. The universities and colleges played a huge part in that. Mind you, even within the context of the high schools, there would always be a group who would show up for coffeehouses. There was hardly a church or community centre that didn't have someone who took up the initiative to actually start a coffeehouse. They were everywhere. I mean I would be playing sometimes three or four places a week. You could be in Transcona, Charleswood, River Heights, out in St. Norbert. This scene was already there. And performers were coming to town who were popular. It wasn't people like Pete Seeger; those folks weren't coming to town prior to the Folk Festival. There was an awful lot going on.

MITCH PODOLAK AND THE IDEA OF A FESTIVAL

My feeling was, when Mitch arrived into town, the timing was absolutely impeccable. Mitch had been an old friend of my brother Jim's, back in the days when they hung out in Yorkville. Mitch had his ideology and folk music was really somewhat representative of that conviction and was very much a tool of respect to spreading the gospel of communism and socialism and what he believed to be the right approach to a civil society.

I think when Mitch arrived in Winnipeg, he was already well-connected to people who had a fairly good understanding of what sort of lay on the ground that just needed to be nurtured. I think that coupled with the fact that it was the city's centennial. When word got out, most of us didn't know what a folk festival was. We had no idea. I had seen the Mariposa Folk Festival on the CBC, they had produced some television specials, which is where I became enamoured with Bruce Cockburn.

I think the scene here was thirsty. You had a young generation who are already enamoured with this music and now they're going to get a chance to really experience some of the greats, first-hand. It was like a sea of mentorship and learning. At least, that's the way I think many of us perceived it. I think, as a prelude to the Festival, it was as if to say, "The tree is in full blossom, all you gotta do is pick the fruit."

JP: If Mitch hadn't existed, what might have happened?

DD: As much as I've referenced it as having been a perfect storm that I think really helped with the initial success of the Festival timing, I do think that it most likely wouldn't have occurred without Mitch. I think you needed someone like him, with his determination. It was born of the belief of a great many things. Not unlike Woodstock. There was a handful of guys that made that happen, and probably wouldn't have happened, and almost didn't happen. I think if you look at the history of music, as we've known, certain individuals are pivotal. Mitch was one of those characters. There are the Brian Epsteins—without which there probably wouldn't have been The Beatles. It's Elliot Roberts, the tough-nosed manager of everybody from Neil Young, Joni Mitchell, to The Eagles. I do think that leadership is everything.

We had scattered rock festivals that occurred through that point in time, but they were just kind of thrown together, willy-nilly. There was no regularity to them and no organization. It was a bit of a free-for-all. I think Mitch really set a template that served as a tremendous example. I still believe his greatest accomplishment was those early festivals because I think that really set the tone. Without those, I think the city would look very different.

THE EARLY YEARS OF THE FOLK FESTIVAL

KN: I want to get a sense of the growth and evolution of the Festival. Eventually, you would work with so many musicians—your ear is quite tuned. How would you track the development of the Festival, sonically?

DD: I think we were all learning. I think that applied as much to the folks who were in control of the technical aspect of delivery, sound people, what have you. Acoustic music was not the strong point of a lot of sound folks. We were a rock 'n' roll city. I think it was a fair bit to learn there. I actually felt that the Festival reached a really lovely point three or four years in. I thought there was a point when it began to get far too big. Just personally, I knew that it attracted people that virtually had no interest in the music, but it was a scene. Booze was unregulated, there could be a bit of debauchery that I felt was certainly not my style. That was around, I would say 1980. But then society in general was exemplifying a lot of that anyways.

I think it got to a point where it got so large that I remember one year there was a CBC special and they had a complete production crew coming from Toronto. They had the largest television cameras on the stage, they had helicopters flying overhead, it was like a war zone. The show itself was interesting, of course, and that was because Mitch had a great relationship with Peter Gzowski, and some really lovable folks who had a lot of influence and who themselves could draw an audience. I think it got to become a little bit of a spectacle and I think that got realized over time.

I don't fully understand the mechanics or the politics of what's going on behind the scenes, or the economics of the Festival, but I think you reach a point where you can get so large that you can get a couple of bad years and you're in deep trouble. We all know how weather-dependent the Festival is. I really relished playing the smaller festivals. Just because there is a greater sense of camaraderie and less of a sense of competition. Yes, size matters, there is no question. In my thinking, folk festivals have to be really cautious as to how far you take it. The size of it just doesn't appeal to me. I don't necessarily adhere to the presentation of what gets placed on Main Stage. The volumes, I think, are out of whack, and I think we can do better with respect to the choice of performance, actually. I know I'll make enemies saying that.

KN: Is that informed by the old days, or first principles of the Festival?

DD: I think it's a bit of both. I think there's an assumption that we need to appeal to a new generation, that's a valid concern. But I also know that you have an older generation that doesn't attend any longer.

So that's been lost. I don't know why things are always viewed as an either-or. I think there is a way to encompass many ways of attracting people while respecting their own personal tastes. I don't think the Festival needs to be four or five days. I don't think that's essential. The Festival could also present itself in many different ways throughout the course of the year. I just feel that it's really good to sit down and think about what is it we can do in addition to what we already know works because eventually everything needs a sense of renewal. Don't hang onto tradition for the sake of tradition. I wouldn't be at all surprised if you staged the Festival much like the first few, that you would have a tremendously successful festival. That would be an interesting experiment, just to see, because much of what seems conventional to us, as boomers, is completely novel to a younger generation. They might actually find some real interest in that. I'd say that adding more technology and size to things isn't necessarily going to attract audiences. In fact, it may be the exact opposite.

One of the things that always drives me crazy about Winnipeg is, you can look at the calendar and you know exactly what festival is on at any point in time. It's all so predictable. Shake it up. After a while it's just more of the same because it's always been that way. I think we like our traditions here, but, you know, foundations need to be rattled. Especially when they're already starting to crumble, and the irony of it is, Mitch would be laughing at this point in time. He would be saying, "I told you so." I think that if you actually took a Mitch model of the first two or three Folk Festivals and you applied it to today, it would work incredibly well.

JP: Can you remember any workshops you were part of? Because they were smaller venues.

KN: And more intimate.

DD: I stopped doing festivals around 1980. There was a reason why I decided to; they became far too large for my own liking. That and in a sense my own music was kind of growing or evolving to where it didn't seem to fit that particular point in time. Festivals were still fairly traditional. I was starting to play with larger ensembles. My music was being infused with jazz and world, and stuff like that, just because that's where my interest was. I think that needs to be performed in relatively small environments where the crowds are intimate.

I do recall doing my first gig on the Main Stage. It was a hot night, staring into the setting sun. My strings were dead by the end of the first tune. I think I was put on for sound check. I said, "No, this isn't the way I will approach it." From that point on I always requested I be put on a concert during the afternoon at one of the small workshop stages. Then the people who were your audience showed up, and those were some of the best gigs. You might have a thousand people in the crowd. But it was just like playing at a local coffeehouse, except you could see everybody. I love the sound of music outside and hearing it bouncing off the escarpment or wherever. Those are some of the great moments for me, when I think in terms of the environments in which I was most relaxed and I think most in touch with my audience. And I certainly played to the best of my abilities.

At one point in time, I'd finished an album, had an obligation to tour it. I did it and that's when one day I was doing a festival in Thunder Bay and said, "That's it. I'm not doing this anymore. I want to work in the studio."

BEING FROM WINNIPEG

KN: I want to go back to an idea of Winnipeg as the location for this event, and more broadly, Winnipeg as an underdog. I'm endlessly fascinated by the idea and how we negotiate it.

DD: It's funny, I think sometimes our inferiority complex creates a sense of collectivity. It binds us together. It's like inverse snobbery. We're inferior and we're proud of it. But I also think that we're just very humble. I think that's just born of the character of the city that's evolved over a long, long period of time. When I don't like it is when we're put down, and that's when Winnipeg will fight to the death. I do think we are prone to somewhat of the lobster-pot-syndrome—where one is trying to climb out of the pot and others are trying to pull it back in. I think we can be our own worst enemies and sometimes that's because the decision-making is being made by people who really don't know what they're talking about. I think it's really important to base decisions upon the experience of the people actually living the lives, with respect to the work that you are making decisions about. I think it has been a bit of a top-down mentality, that if you have an MBA, or a law degree, you know everything you need to know about running a festival. No, you don't. In fact, you haven't a clue. You know when maybe the balance sheet ain't working, but there's more to it.

I do think there are so many wasted opportunities because we do function in silos. That's one of the greatest things I think that holds us back. We can be very territorial unto ourselves, with respect to organizations and festivals, community arts groups in general.

I think that's a dynamic that really needs to change here. None of us got into this business to get filthy rich, but it's a damn good life, and it shouldn't be predicated upon a simple "who knows who" and, "where do you exist in the social hierarchy." I think opportunities have to be afforded to everybody. I do feel that when I apply that to my experiences in music, and folk music in particular, I do think that there is a tendency of thinking, "Well, we're good for Winnipeg." Without thinking that this could resonate or reverberate far beyond the Perimeter Highway. We have to be there for each other, and applaud the successes because those successes will, in turn, draw in others. It's like the old saying, "I'll hop the fence and once I'm over I'll help you over."

I think, in truth, when you look at the music scene in the early 1970s in a place like Laurel Canyon, all those great songwriters, I mean they were all aiding and abetting each other. In many cases, refusing to sign with labels unless they sign their buddies. A lot of that stuff, we would never have heard had it not been for that sense of community, so it's making the community, the smallest of what you are, work for you. And see it as a strength.

I'm glad you asked that question because Randy Bachman said, "There's so much music coming out of Winnipeg, it's the long cold winters. You hear the furnace going thump thump thump, creating a rhythm. . . ." There are a lot of places that have cold winters that don't have that same creative magic that seems to persist here and has for a long time. I think it's because Winnipeg was settled by people whose cultures were very musical in the first place. They were working-class folks who didn't have a lot of money and music was a form of, not just entertainment, but it was a means of retaining that connection

FIGURE 78. AUDIENCE AT WINNIPEG FOLK FESTIVAL, 1979. PHOTOGRAPH BY DAVID LANDY. ARCHIVES OF MANITOBA, WINNIPEG FOLK FESTIVAL 1979 NEGATIVES, P5266/9, 79/7.

to the homeland and to their ancestors. In some cases, I also think it was a way of defining themselves to others. I mean, whether it be the Jews, or Irish, Ukrainians, Mennonites, it goes on and on. With every passing year, it shifts. Now we've got a tremendous African component to that. I think that's what made this place great, musically. It is so deeply rooted in our DNA.

I'm actually working on a project that's talking about community choirs, and how community choirs reflected the hopes and aspirations of the Diaspora and if you want to understand Winnipeg, just delve into the choirs that existed throughout the various communities. Even going back as far as the 1919 Strike. It was somewhat organized and staged out of the old Ukrainian Labour Temple.[21] There were choirs and all sorts of arts groups. It was all part and parcel with this sense of a fair and just society, which came to alter the political and social landscape of the city and the province. I mean, when you think of the origins of CCF and the NDP and how deeply rooted those are in this very city, you can see how it played out.[22] And I think the music is somewhat representative of that tremendous diversity.

KN: And it's not a stretch to connect that to Mitch and his ideology.

DD: Absolutely not. It's alive and well here. And it continues on. I don't know if it's something that existed in a lot of other cities. You know, I don't think so. Not even in places like Toronto. I think in Winnipeg, it was very different. I think we were also a series of many different towns and cities that now represent the greater Winnipeg. So, all parts of town had distinct characters. They had their musical heroes and that encouraged more individuality.

JP: The other thing is the audience. Audience is a key component. Winnipeg audiences brought, right from the beginning, a sophistication, or is that going too far? That they would be a good audience to play for instead of a Wild West audience. And Mitch may have known that, too.

DD: I would bet ten-to-one that a lot of the performers who came here, for that first Folk Festival, were somewhat taken aback by how knowledgeable the audience was, not just about the artform itself, the history of such, but of their own work. They probably had no idea that this existed here. Even for my own experience, travelling to different places that would seem somewhat remote, I was always astonished to show up and have people calling out requests for songs that I had no concept that they'd have ever heard. So, you never know. But I think Mitch knew that. I think he was well aware of the fact that these performers were going to really dig it here.

Curtis JONNIE (SHINGOOSE)

Curtis Jonnie, performing under the name Shingoose, was a singer-songwriter based in Winnipeg. Originally from the Roseau River Anishinaabe First Nation, he was adopted into a Mennonite family in Steinbach, Manitoba. At the age of eighteen he moved to the United States to begin playing in bands. He eventually returned to Canada, living in Toronto, where he began to play as a singer-songwriter. When he played the Mariposa Folk Festival, he made the acquaintance of Mitch Podolak—resulting in an invitation to play the Winnipeg Folk Festival. Curtis then called Winnipeg home as he continued to perform and collaborate with other musicians—including Duke Redbird, Bruce Cockburn, and Tom Jackson. He founded the Native Country record label, wrote for theatre, and as a film producer created a program for CKND-TV called First Nations Magazine, *and* Indian Time *for CTV. Curtis joined Buffy Sainte-Marie and Elaine Bomberry to petition the Junos to create a category celebrating Indigenous musicians. He passed away in January 2021.*

FIGURE 79. SHINGOOSE, 1975. COURTESY OF WINNIPEG FILM GROUP.

CURTIS JONNIE (SHINGOOSE)

30 SEPTEMBER 2019, WINNIPEG

KEVIN NIKKEL: How did you get your start in music?

CURTIS JONNIE (SHINGOOSE): I've always been involved in music, ever since I was a child. When I got to my teens, I got into a rock band and played blues and stuff. I grew up for a couple years in Fargo, North Dakota. So, I was hanging out with all the musicians in that town, like Bobby Vee and his brother Bill. When Bobby made famous, he left town and I got to join the band for a while. That's where I got my band experience, for a short time. I was only about eighteen then. After that I ended up in Washington, DC and I played there in bands for about four years. I wasn't writing then at all, but I got a kind of a lucky break. My band won the battle of the bands in Washington and the producer ended up being Eddie Kramer, Jimi Hendrix's engineer and producer. He also built a recording studio called Record Plant in New York City. I got to do my first album there with a band I formed called Puzzle, and that was a good experience for me. Then in 1969 I ended up going out to California and stayed there for a couple years. Then I went back and forth from East to West. But I guess slowly I got out of playing with bands. I started thinking about doing my own stuff.

I came back to Toronto. I had a friend of mine named Johnny Esna. Johnny liked the songs I was singing, about what was going on socially. I'd written a song called "Reservation Blues" and that just talked about the situation that happened in South Dakota, a hundred years ago or more. I guess that kind of sparked my interest in speaking up for Native people. And also singing songs about what it was like to be part of that movement. But I noticed that a lot of songs at that time were just songs about railing against the system. I wanted to write some things that showed us as more, like just regular human beings. So that's where Johnny got interested and he introduced me to the director of the Mariposa Folk Festival. So, in 1973 I got hired to play the Festival and that's basically where it started for me. Then I did a lot of the other festivals and that's where I met Mitch at that time, too.

MITCH PODOLAK

KN: How did that friendship with Mitch develop?

CJ: When I played Mariposa, I was being looked at by other artistic directors and I guess Mitch took a liking to me, mainly because of what was going on in the industry. At one time I was questioning what I should be doing. He told me, "Well, you're the expert, so you tell us." I took that as a way of saying that I should just go ahead and say what I want to say. After we met each other, we instantly had a good strong relationship. He was also from the streets of Toronto, so we had some places we knew, and the same people, and so on. Over the years I almost became part of his family. That was always a source of the comfort and inspiration to me. When I finally moved back to Winnipeg, I got back into the Festival. I wasn't there every year but I was there probably there every two or three years.

Of course, later on in his life we [Mitch and I] became particularly close. Every Sunday morning, we'd get the boys together and go have breakfast. Through Mitch, I got to know a lot of restaurants around Manitoba. That became our socializing thing, where we got together and traded stories. Talked about what we would do next. I was very sad to see him go and I have nothing but good memories and a lot of appreciation. We never got to finish the last project I wanted to do, which was my upcoming album. I'm glad to see that Leonard is now going to produce. I'm still part of the family. Keep making good music.

KN: Let's go back. I'm curious to hear about the response at the Folk Fest. What was the feeling then?

CJ: From what I experienced, I was accepted. People wanted to know more, and so I felt this was going to be my calling. People were looking at me as a way to carry on the tradition of storytelling and so on. I kinda resisted in some ways, because I didn't want to be known as an Indian singer-songwriter. I just wanted to be a songwriter. While I was in LA, I took courses with some of the great songwriters who had written music for Elvis Presley and a whole bunch of others. I learned about the craft of writing songs and how you put things together and present them.

KN: Do you remember the first year you played the Winnipeg Folk Fest?

CJ: Yes, I believe it was 1975.

KN: Tell me about that.

CJ: The audience was huge, 10,000 people. So, all of a sudden you can go from a small little folk club like Egerton's in Toronto, where we might have forty people crammed into the place, and suddenly here, you're in front 10,000 people. It was quite a difference and quite exciting. It was enjoyable. I'd done some of that kind of work back in Washington, DC, when I was with the band. We played for large festivals. Once you start to get involved in that music industry, it stays with you. You keep working. Even today, I will release another album, it'll probably be my swan song. I've had a good career, in the sense that I had a lot of great experiences. I never made any money at it. Other than that, I really enjoyed it. I like to say that I arose from minor obscurity to a relative unknown, overnight.

KN: I love that. I like to call myself an internationally unknown filmmaker, so I sympathize with you totally. I want to know about the 1970s you lived through. In the 1960s too, with the protest movements, and then into the 1970s, there was something in the air. What was your impression of what you were seeing at the Festival?

CJ: I certainly noticed the willingness to listen to my material was something I hadn't experienced up until that point. But I felt, generally, the folk music audiences were fairly well-educated and were really interested in what was going on. And everybody knows how America was really inhabited. I look at it now, I turn on CNN, and they talk about the terrorists and all this, well, 500 years ago. If we'd had television operations, that's what we'd be saying at that time. So, now I look at it with different eyes, but the story does not change. I mean, America will never lose that black mark on its soul, from having invaded another continent and taking over without asking. And putting a lot of people at risk, killing a lot of people.

INDIGENOUS MUSICIANS AND THE WINNIPEG FOLK FESTIVAL

KN: How would you summarize what you were doing with your songs, in those albums from the early 1970s?

CJ: Well, the summary was—to show that I understood what was going on and I didn't like it. But I also wanted to leave it a little bit on the humorous side. I wrote several songs like "I Got a Natural Tan," things like that, which broke the ice a bit with most audiences. Then I would carry on from there. So, I was aware of the way things were shaping up in the industry. The kind of music that was coming out of the folk industry, all the way from Dylan to the recent ones. I made friends along the way, with John Prine, other people. I learned from them. It was always a great experience.

KN: Do you remember which album came out in the early 1970s?

CJ: Actually, my first album as a solo artist was called *Natural Tan* and I had about ten songs on there that spoke to my experience as a Native man in this particular era.

KN: Some of the photos and film footage from the early 1970s seem to show a number of Indigenous artists playing and pow wow drum groups and hoop dancers from those early years. Was Mitch really conscious of doing something there?

CJ: Mitch was a folklore critic, I guess. He loved to find out the roots of the music that he was listening to. All the way from the civil rights movement all the way up. I guess he identified with the Indian Movement, more so because it was very current and there was a lot of content that could be explored, in the folklore sense. So, he supported that. When others hadn't quite got there yet, he was ahead of it. But he especially took notice after Mariposa, and the way the audience there took to it. He thought Buffy Sainte-Marie was one of the best songwriters of the era and he just used that as an incentive to explore what else was going on in the Native community.

KN: What was the reaction from audiences at Folk Fest, those years when you were doing your thing?

CJ: It was awesome. It was like a great response. People really supported it and they applauded a lot and just supported the artists. And the way people took to me, personally, by coming backstage, and talking, and taking pictures, and all that. They felt like they finally found someone they could identify with or could at least learn something about the culture through me. So, that was stimulating and I enjoyed that.

FIGURE 80. SHINGOOSE, 1975. COURTESY OF WINNIPEG FILM GROUP.

KN: When I saw the footage, I was just amazed because I know, with what has happened recently, with the truth and reconciliation efforts, it just seems like there's this huge renaissance that has happened in our era. But looking back to the early 1970s, I was thinking, *Wow.* On one hand, there's something starting then, but then part of me was thinking, *Shouldn't we be further along now?*

CJ: I think that a lot of people felt the guilt and shame that Canada and the U.S. had caused because they weren't willing to accept that just 100 years ago, they were still killing us and now that the big corporations jumped in and [they] were taking all of the resources. If you think about it, in the last 200 years, it's like trillions and trillions of dollars taken from Mother Earth to build this country, from oil, to lumber, to all the things that come out of the earth. There was a sense that, maybe we could, through the truthfulness and . . . reconciliation, address some of those issues and maybe smoothen things out a little bit and allow the Indigenous people a chance to grow on their own. That sure helped. And, as you know, in the last fifty years or so we've produced a number of lawyers and doctors and other people in the arts. We're starting to take our place in modern society. We're still there, reminding everybody to take care of the earth and that this is our mother. So, it's still relevant to go out and sing those songs about our relationship with the planet.

KN: Yeah, absolutely. Is that something that was a part of the Winnipeg Folk Festival spirit and a message in the other acts playing there?

CJ: Yeah, I think it was. Like, it was all-inclusive. They had more experience here in Manitoba with the Aboriginal communities—First Nations—than they did in Ontario and BC, or other places. But the most active, politically orientated Native people, as soon as they ended up integrating into society, they were the ones that were pushing for political change. I was always being asked to come and perform at those kinds of events. So that's kinda how I became known more as a social activist. I wasn't just going out playing gigs just to promote Native people because there would only be a few people that would respond to that. I would get folk people coming to my concerts but, other than that, the general public didn't know about me. I had to take it one day at a time.

KN: Did that change for you after the Folk Fest?

CJ: Somewhat, yeah. Definitely more people had an idea of who I was and what they would be listening to. I've been singing since I was five years old. The family that took me in were missionaries, so my first music was gospel hymns. Gospel hymns are a great source of folk music. I enjoyed the harmonies and the emotional content of them, and I try to apply that to some of my music. It seemed to work. I guess the stuff I've written in the last two or three years has a little bit of that. But I'm accepting a whole lot more of the culture today than I ever did before.

KN: Why is that?

CJ: I guess because I'm getting older. I don't really want to live a life of confrontation. I'm trying to reconcile that within myself and remain positive and have positive relations with other people. It seems to be a lot better than just being angry all the time and ranting and raving against the system.

KN: What about in the 1970s? There was a lot of anger in those years. Did you see that at festivals?

CJ: Yes, there were a number of artists that'd probably take that line. But then I'd come on to do something a little bit lighter and more trying to . . . let's talk about this. Let's open up a dialogue between our nations and see what we can come up with. I was always trying to balance things out.

KN: After you'd been to the Folk Fest a few times, was there anything that became a tradition for you when you got there?

CJ: I loved the crafts area a lot because they brought together a great many different types of Native artists that really made some beautiful work out of leather, beads, and so on. I always had a $100 bill set aside for the festivals so I could buy some of these beautiful pieces of art. That's what I thought they were. I enjoyed that a lot. The other thing I liked about the Festival is I got to meet all these other wonderful artists from all over the world, from the U.S. particularly. That was exciting, too. We'd end up in the green performers' tent and talk about our last year since we saw each other. The Festival is always something I really loved being a part of.

DAVE BARBER: Did you meet Steve Goodman?

CJ: I did. I didn't hang out with him much, but I definitely loved to hear him play. He was a great guitar player. He was such a neat guy.

DB: He was friends with John Prine.

CJ: Yes, right. That's kinda how I met him, too, was through John. There are so many others at the Festival that I enjoyed meeting and speaking with.

KN: You knew Tom Jackson.

CJ: Tom was from this [folk] community, and had a radio show, so we both recognized that we were both in the same kind of industry together. When we found that we were each singer-songwriters like that, we got together. We teamed up with another fellow named David Cramer, and the three of us had really good harmonies. Probably a lot like some of the other acts that were current at the time. As a result, we became good friends. He was a great pool player and I loved to play pool, too. He'd always beat me, but I loved to play with that calibre of pool player. We played for three years at this little place called the Tipi Restaurant and Lounge. That's where we met most of the Native community that were involved in development—politically, economically, all those things.

THE NAME SHINGOOSE

KN: Where did the name Shingoose come from? Tell me the story.

CJ: As I dug into my own past, as to where I came from, I found out that my great-grandfather was named John Shingoose. In order to keep the culture alive, I adopted his name as a start and then it just stuck with me. Actually, Shingoose itself, the literal interpretation would be a small white furry animal, particularly addressed as the white weasel. If you look at any of the wardrobe of some of the Medicine Men and Chiefs, they always had like, eight or nine weasel skins hanging from their clothes. It was supposed to be a spirit animal because it can change colours with the seasons. That's where it came from. I was always trying to fight with how to define myself. The one artist that I took a lesson from was Liberace. It was just one word, Liberace, but you knew he was a pianist and into classical music. So then, I can just be Shingoose. I don't have to have two or three names. Then I found out I also had an Indian name that was given to me by a Medicine Man, [Says his Anishinaabe name],[23] that means the two voices that move along the ground like thunder. So that really appealed, too. Most of my close friends know that name, but Shingoose was my performer name.

KN: When did you feel like this was something you had to do as a career? Like a calling in life?

CJ: Mariposa. That was the big start for me. It just focused it a lot for me. This is something that I can do, and here's my audience. So, it stuck. I was trying other things, too. I did a number of TV shows, *Due South* and other kinds of shows, but I never did like the movie industry that much. But Mariposa would focus the whole thing for me. Now I realized that here was something I could plug into and that I was capable of doing. I was being accepted, even though I wasn't a great guitar player or even a great singer. I had a way of communicating with people because that's what I was doing. I was communicating with non-Native people all time. I knew how to be, how to become part of the scene. I always wanted to have a smash album and all that stuff, and really become a big player in the scene, but it never happened. Part of the reason is because the record people didn't see me as having that quality for the masses. But it didn't stop me from trying. I guess it will remain to be seen—maybe my last album will sell more than my first two.

DB: What does music give you that other careers didn't give you?

CJ: Music, I've always felt, was just from the tensions of the string, or vibrations, like all the strings of the guitar are all different, it's the vibration and you put them all together. It's a collaboration of all those vibrations that create a chord structure and a sound. As I grew older, I was interested in the spirituality of things. I came from a very spiritual family. The family that I was adopted into, they were Christian Mennonites, they had a very strong view of the world and how to act in it. They dwelt more on the spiritual than the physical and I started on that, too, through yoga and doing meditation, things like that. As I grew older, I came to find out that all life is vibration. It just all seemed to fit. So, the music in me, which I hear constantly in my head, soothes me and helps me get through my day. And also, when I lay down and rest, I can pick from a bunch of great artists that I've met, and those I haven't met, but I just like their music, and I play that back in my head. That just calms me down. Music is really the essence of my soul and being. So that's why I keep coming back to it.

KN: I like that a lot.

DB: Any memories about Mitch working at the Festival?

CJ: Mitch's view of folk music—he was always interested in where it came from and why. He was always searching. If a song came up that he hadn't heard before, we'd dissect that. His heroes were people like Pete Seeger, the granddaddy of folk music, basically. He also tried his hand at playing banjo. We'd sit around his house and just play. He was really hitting it good and we enjoyed practising together. As far as his own vision of folk music, he just had an overwhelming curiosity of all of the music and the people involved with it. He just wanted to immerse himself in the whole picture, which he always did. He became almost like a great historian. He would know so many things about so many people and so many styles of folk music that it was amazing. It was never a dull conversation with him, he was always bringing something new to the table. Or a new awareness of something. It made him a very unique person.

Winston WUTTUNEE

Winston Wuttunee is a singer-songwriter and Knowledge Keeper, originally from the Red Pheasant Cree Nation in Saskatchewan. Winston picked up the guitar at age ten and quickly found it his favourite means of expression. He joined the Canadian Army in 1960 and became a clarinetist in the Canadian Guards Band. Winston completed a music degree from the University of Saskatchewan. He began playing coffeehouses and festivals with a band and also as a solo act. His musical career found its focus when he started playing for kids, and later incorporated music into his work as an inspiration speaker and traditional storyteller. Winston has released seventeen albums.

FIGURE 81. WINSTON WUTTUNEE, 1975. COURTESY OF WINNIPEG FILM GROUP.

WINSTON WUTTUNEE

21 JULY 2021, WINNIPEG

KEVIN NIKKEL: Tell me how you got your start in music.

WINSTON WUTTUNEE: We moved off the reserve because Dad wanted us all to get an education. Mom knew that I was interested in music. She knew my sister was musical and so she bought a big Emerson grand piano and my sister went up to grade ten on that, and she taught me how to play the piano. Six years later, I was ten years old, a guitar salesman came to all the neighbourhoods, selling guitars. A neighbour, Gordy Sayers, bought a new guitar. I bought a two-and-a-half-dollar used guitar that another neighbour, Archie Dennison, had. I just happened to have two and a half bucks because I'd sold all my bottles that I picked up all the time. It had a big crack in the back, so I fixed whatever cracks were in there and glued them all up. And that's how I started.

The first song I ever learned was a song that my next-door neighbour taught me. It's a silly song about milk, but it was the start of my musical career. I went to music lessons and I went to about grade six with an old lady. And that was the worst thing I ever did because I had to pass by this mean dog every Saturday morning. Every Saturday morning, I had my slingshot full of stones and a stick but that dog still chased me. I don't know how many times I shot him and hit him right on the head, but he still came after me every Saturday morning. I was so glad when I finally quit going to the music lessons.

But then after that, people could see that I was naturally a musician. In school, whenever we had anything, they would always get me to go to the front of the school to be the emcee because I wasn't nervous to talk. My sister before me, she was not nervous, so she was always the emcee. Our uncle before us, he was always able to talk and that—he became a doctor. [Another] uncle, he became a lawyer, so he was talking all the time. My sister was in university to become a doctor, but she got married. I just went on my merry way, not worrying about anything and doing jam sessions wherever I found one.

My neighbour Gordy Sayers bought a new guitar and then I got that used guitar. Then he and I were the two guys that were the most popular in the town of Battleford. We went to all the parties. We didn't have to buy anything. We sang all the time. He's still singing in Saskatoon, him and a guitar and an accordion.

KN: Where was home? You said you moved from the reserve.

WW: For me it was Battleford, because when we moved out of the reserve, I was only two years old.

KN: Which reserve?

WW: Red Pheasant, in Saskatchewan. Where we get our white blood is from Cuthbert Grant, and you know about him. He had Grant's Mill down here, that was him.[24] What happened is they had their North West Trading Company in Battleford and they had trading companies all over. Anybody that wanted to make a fast buck, the best thing to do was set up a trading company to get a whole bunch of stuff there. The Indians would come in and the trading company could steal off them as much as they wanted. And that's what they did.

I wrote a song about Gabriel Dumont[25] and with my group there, we sang that song on many shows and talked about Gabriel Dumont and also talked about the land, sang many Native songs. *Nêhiyaw* which is Cree. *Nêhiyaw*, the four-spirited people—the water, air, fire (to keep you warm) and *aski*, the land. So *nêhiyaw* means four-spirited people.

So, we lived in Battleford when we moved off the reserve. Dad was an older man and he was a very wise businessman. The courthouse would always get him to interpret as he understood Saulteaux, Cree, and Ojibwe. He was kept quite busy.

EARLY YEARS OF PLAYING MUSIC

KN: Tell me more about the band you were in. How did you transition from solo to a band? It's like trying to get a kite in the air, I imagine.

WW: That's a really good analogy. Well. I started out with just my buddy and I, Gordy Sayers, he lived next door and he had that nice guitar and I had a two-dollar guitar, but that didn't matter. We both played and we were playing all over the place and sang at country dances for seventy-five cents a night. Then we hired an accordion player. There, that was the third one. So, then that went, and then we eventually hired a bass guitar. Because we found that what really works in a band is a bass, an accordion player—so you've got the chords, and a guitar and a singer and a lead. So that worked. And then from that time on, I always had people singing with me. I barely sang alone anymore except in schools and when I'd sing for children.

I came to Winnipeg to record and this guy said to me, "Are you recording with anybody or are you all by yourself?"

I said, "Yeah. I'm all by myself."

He said, "Why don't you get [Ilena] Zaramba. You know who that is? The Kozub family."[26] So, I got her and, wow.

Then she said, "Winston, I know another singer, Honey [Hill]. Why don't you get her?"

I said, "Okay." So, Honey came there, and I was singing "Musee Cho," which is a beautiful song. I didn't know that Honey was there to listen. Apparently, she was really worried about singing with anybody because she was so pure in singing and her mind and heart are so good and she was getting screwed around with bands that had no scruples. So, she listened to me sing. Then I met her afterwards and she started crying. I said, "What's the matter?"

And she said, "I was going to quit singing forever and you have given me back the desire to sing."

"Good," I said.

And they were so good. . . . They had made their own dresses, bands, moccasins, everything. If I forgot my songs, they could sing all my Indian songs with words and everything. This one time I had a sore throat and I couldn't sing and I would just start the song, I'd say, "These are the prairies" and they'd come in right in after that. All the way through. They were just super. And the harmonies were so good and they were so beautiful on stage. Richard Denesiuk was there too, bass guitar player. He and Honey were a couple. It was just a beautiful band.

KN: When did you first hear about the Winnipeg Folk Festival?

WW: I was singing for kids all the time. By that time, I'd already written that song that got me a lot of work, "Daddy's Not My Friend," and that became a big hit. I was getting invited all over Canada. Then of course, when the Winnipeg Folk Festival was on, I knew Duke Redbird and so they invited me right away. So that's when I first I heard about and did a big show over here. I did other shows back

FIGURE 82. WINSTON WUTTUNEE, 1975. PHOTOGRAPH BY DAVID LANDY. ARCHIVES OF MANITOBA, WINNIPEG FOLK FESTIVAL 1975 NEGATIVES, P5266/1, 75-4713. 2.

in Saskatchewan and then from that show came festivals all across Canada. Children's festivals and also for adults, too. I could do both.

Then another time, I don't know if you know Edward Peekeekoot, he was nominated for best guitar player in British Columbia for ten years in a row. He and I were doing a show in Regina for the

Children's Festival and so we did that in the morning and then in the afternoon Edward said, "Winston, there are these Native entertainers happening, let's get a cup a tea and sit and watch." So, we went there and we're there at one o'clock and they weren't there. It was after one o'clock. I thought, *Oh God, this band. They're going to give us all a bad name. Why don't they smarten up?* Ten after one o'clock and they're still not on, and me and Ed we're just shaking our heads, so embarrassed. And the lady was looking at us. I was thinking maybe she thought that we knew them and would go get them. So, we waited for fifteen more minutes. Then finally that lady sent over someone and she said to us, "Winston, are you ready to go on yet?" And I looked at Ed. "Ed! That's us, those Native entertainers on stage—It's us, we're waiting for us to go on. We're mad at us." We got on there and we just started singing immediately and got the crowd going. But it was so funny. Thankfully, I've never done that too many times, to be totally unaware. I am usually very aware of my audience, my stage, and everybody like that.

MEETING PEOPLE AT THE WINNIPEG FOLK FESTIVAL

KN: Talk more about the Folk Festival stages.

WW: Well, that's when the Irish Rovers were very popular. They were playing fast-paced music, and I went there and I just jumped on stage and started jigging. Afterwards, they said, "Wherever we are, you're welcome on stage as soon as we play any jigs. You just come on up and start jigging." So, I did that. Wherever I went, if they were there for the fest, I would get up on stage and jig.

There was this one time, there was that guy, he said that he had just arrived from Brandon and he had walked all the way. He was that guy that did those poems about that very queer monkey. He did poems about a monkey's tail. All the different poems. And he looked like a really simple guy and I fell for it—hook, line, and sinker. He said he walked up from Brandon and I thought, *Well, he didn't walk on the highway.* I said, "Well, did you walk up along the fence?"

And he said, "Yes." Because he could see that he had me.

And I said, "Well. On the inside where the cows walk on the path, all the way?"

"All the way," he said.

And I said, "Can I buy you a meal? What can I get you?" I went and got him a meal. Then afterwards he got on stage and did his show. I can't remember his name, do you remember?

JOHN PRENTICE: Peter Paul Van Camp.

WW: Exactly right. Peter Paul Van Camp. He just had me hook, line, and sinker. And then him and I became very good friends. Al Simmons. He and I, and also Fred Penner. I began meeting these great musicians and great storytellers, everything like that. It was one of discovery, all the time. I was always on there and I was always with my hand drum and I was always singing. And Shingoose, a dear friend of mine, he couldn't sing, but he wanted to be up there with me, singing. What happened was, he thought he couldn't sing, he could but he couldn't sing right off the bat. He had all the blood memories to sing that kind of music. And so, when he'd come and they'd set up a mic for him and then I'd start to sing and he would just be singing away. So, we kinda became the heroes of the Native people that were in the audience. Consequently, I got to be so well known by all the Native people all across Canada.

KN: What was going on in the early years of the Folk Fest and what were the attitudes in the 1970s towards folk music, and Indigenous folk musicians, in particular?

WW: You know what, everybody was just one big gang. There was no fighting. They were wearing shirts with different things on them. Like, whatever was happening in North America at that time, they would wear it. There was a lot of happiness. It was a great time. You would meet other people and you'd be friends right away. There'd be no prejudice. We were honest performers—good songs, did our best, and loved our crowds.

There was Floyd Westerman, who was just the most beautiful singer and had this beautiful, deep voice. Everybody loved his voice. And then there was also that guy from down east that died in an airplane crash? He died in an airplane down south in the States, after he was helping everybody else get off. And he succumbed to the smoke.

JP: Stan Rogers.

WW: Exactly right. And Stan was there, he was there all the time. So, I heard a lot of Eastern music—and I liked it, music that wasn't me, but neither was I them, you know? So, we were different and we knew that. Wherever we went, you had your friends that came and stuck by you, and all the Native people were so proud of me. Finally, they had someone there that was singing. Me, Floyd Westerman, Shingoose, a couple other guys. Willie Dunn. Duke Redbird. When Duke Redbird would do his poetry, the press would be there. Television would be there. The big shots would be there. The Governor General, Ed Schreyer, he invited us to his office one day, just so we could recite some poetry for him. A magical time.

We went to New York and New York was something else. We had to get out of there because it was so weird. We were trying to become superstars by that time and everyone was making us into superstars and I was no longer Winston Wuttunee, I was Winston Talltree and Duke was no longer Duke Redbird, he was some fictitious name. We got out, got back to Canada, and we bent down and kissed the ground. We were so happy to get out of New York.

KN: What are your memories of Mitch?

WW: He was a very, very friendly person. There is never a negative thing in his stuff. He was always happy with what you did. He was always willing to let you do more. He was organizing everything. He always had some funny words to say. He was always a perfect host for musicians. We all could understand him and he could understand us, and he would give you the breaks. He would hire people that were good. I think that's why he could give everybody a break because he knew that we were good.

KN: Do you have any memories of the Festival site at Birds Hill Park?

WW: Festival site. When you go about the place, yeah, I liked that outfit there because it was wide open and that's the thing I miss most of being older and living in the city, is we just don't have those wide-open places. When we came from Red Pheasant, it was all wide open. You'd go on horseback and ride horses in town. The hitching rail is all ripped off the Main Street. And so, when I saw that Birds Hill Park and you came in, there is an area where it was sacred for Sundances. I was so happy to see that, too. I had never seen that before, like in a public place, where there were Sundances.

KN: What was it like backstage?

WW: Like I said before, we were honest performers—good songs, did our best, and loved our crowds. You'd make sure you were tuned up. You made sure you were looking decent. You made sure that you didn't make any noise right there, like tuning your guitar. You just really took care. It was very professional. They really took care of us. As far as I know, we never worried about or complained about what we were getting paid. It was all good enough for me and I think a lot of us sold many CDs at those festivals. I remember one time I sold $800 worth of CDs in one night. I remember this one French family and they had CDs, and I had mine wide open like this, and so that anybody could come and would buy a CD. This French family, I said, "Where are your CDs?"

They said, "We have them in the car."

"What do you mean? You're never going to sell them in the car. Go get your CDs and put them on the table!" I said.

"But we're all too scared to," they said.

I said, "That's what you're here for! Do it!" So, I bullied them into selling their CDs. Boy did they ever sell. They just sold right out.

KN: Was Winnipeg unique in inviting Indigenous performers to play?

WW: Yeah, it was. Plus, they were bigger, too, than a lot of other festivals.

KN: Why?

WW: I think because you have Native, French, Métis, Ukrainian and those are four nationalities that go big on entertainment. I remember going to a ball here for the Festival du Voyageur, and, boy, something made my heart just go warm. It was these women and they were dancing. With their dancing, they looked so beautiful, and then when they turned fast, you'd see the high-top moccasins on, instead of slippers, and it just warmed my heart when I saw that. Because I grew up that way, with moccasins. We all wore them. When I saw that memory, in such a modern setting, it just took me back to my youth. I always played the Festival du Voyageur, too. I can say that Winnipeg was big. It was very big. You know, there was always good music on there. And of course, there was Mitch. He and I got along very well together. And Mitch was a show all by himself.

Peter Paul VAN CAMP

Peter Paul Van Camp is a rhymester, some-time poet, and general gadabout. He is originally from Coshocton, Ohio but moved to Canada in the early 1970s, where he began performing poetry at coffeehouses and folk festivals across the country. Drafted by Mitch Podolak for the Main Stage after he'd been busking at the 1975 Winnipeg Folk Festival, he would go on to play the Festival thirty times. He has had a long career of performing, publishing poetry, and entertaining audiences. In 2002, he was awarded the Winnipeg Folk Festival's Glass Banjo award for outstanding contributions to the Festival.

FIGURE 83. PETER PAUL VAN CAMP, 1976. PHOTOGRAPH BY DAVID LANDY. COURTESY WINNIPEG FOLK FESTIVAL.

PETER PAUL VAN CAMP

9 NOVEMBER 2019, WINNIPEG

KEVIN NIKKEL: What is your connection to the Folk Festival?

PETER PAUL VAN CAMP: People may remember me as "that poet" who used to show up at the Winnipeg Folk Festival year after year for about the first thirty of them. I'd like to tell you a little story, if I may, about what happened in 1975. Here I was, just twenty-two years of age. I'd been busking around the grounds all weekend. I actually bought a ticket to the Festival, for the pittance it cost at that time. I was making the most of it by doing a few random shows around the site. Sunday afternoon I heard from someone, "Mitch Podolak is looking for you." I thought, *Uh oh. What have I done?* I knew Mitch more by reputation than as an intimate pal, at this stage. But I knew him for his bluster and his cantankerous nature and I thought, *If he's looking for me this could only mean that he's heard that I'm busking. Interfering with the workings of his festival, and he's going to have me thrown over the fence as soon as he can locate me.* Well, it turned out, when I timorously approached him, he said, "Van Camp! You're going on the Main Stage tonight."

Gosh! I thought. *Is* that *all?*

POETRY ON MAIN STAGE

I went up there and it was far and away the largest crowd I'd ever played for. I don't quite remember what I did or said, but I guess I was up there for ten or twelve minutes and for some reason the audience, to my surprise . . . they just went for it. By the time I finished and was walking back to safe land, coming up the steps backstage was a legend: Ramblin' Jack Elliott. He puts out a big paw and says, "Young man, that's some fine po'try. Mighty fine po'try." I thought, *Well! My reputation is made here, this minute.*

So, I'd like to just give you one of the poems that I think I might've delivered on that occasion. It's just a short little item. So many things in 1975 that I hadn't written yet, but I know I had this one in my kit bag. It goes like this. It's called "The Finer Sights":

Give me more inspiring sight
Than flight of pigeons. Am I right?
See them swarm up from the ground
Flapping wings and wheeling around in the loose formation
Hither, thither. Unseen force directs them whither
They will circle in a dither
Leaving shower of soot and feather. . . .
Now I ask you,
When we've sights as these
What need have we,
Pornography?

I'm pretty sure I would've delivered that one on that night. It was, up to that point, my crowning achievement. I have Mitch to thank for that opportunity.

KN: Let's go back. What did you know about the Festival? Did you hitchhike there?

PPVC: Well, I also had gone in 1974, the first one. I took a city bus out to Birds Hill, I believe. And it was free that year. And again, I did a little bit of busking that time, as I recall. I was newly arrived in the city. I'd only come to Winnipeg in February of that year. So, the Winnipeg Folk Festival starting up had an awful lot to do with my staying for the next forty years as a resident of the city.

No one knew anything about the Festival the first year. I think we heard that Bruce Cockburn was going to be headlining. So, people went, had such a time. The volunteer organization was beginning to develop. It became more streamlined and efficient over time, of course. But the foundation was there.

It was my first folk festival. I have been to many others since, but the Winnipeg one was my first and it was a revelation. The people who were coming to play at this thing were people we could only dream of. Roosevelt Sykes, for instance, coming up from New Orleans. He'd been playing since the 1920s and here he *was*. I think the audience just fell back and said, "*What* are we getting to *see* here? We never thought this would happen." Again, that was Mitch and

Ava and the others who had this vision and realized that these people were still alive. Sam Chatmon, people who were on scratchy 78s in people's collections, on stage in front of you. It was a great place to learn how to be on stage and to surreptitiously steal the notion of how to present yourself. I was soaking it all up. It was a vast school for all of us.

KN: I'm curious how it was to cross over from the audience to suddenly be on the stage and seeing behind the scenes?

PPVC: Well, I could never go back. It was very hard to go back to just sitting in the audience. This first time, in 1975 when I was up there, it was Don Cullen, may he rest in peace, a friend from Toronto, who introduced me because he knew me already. I got in the habit, because I became a Main Stage host as well a couple years later, of watching shows from the seating backstage where you could see performers coming and going, "Howdy! Great set," and all that kind of thing. So, I was completely spoiled as an audience member. I never wanted to sit in the crowd again. I always prefer that access. Can't be helped, I guess.

KN: Was there any difference for you as a poet at a Folk Festival?

PPVC: Sure.

KN: Were you second class on the bus?

PPVC: I felt like I had to prove myself. People were saying, "Okay, a *poet*, you say? Let's see what you've got." So again, because I was watching everybody, seeing how *they* did it, and everybody was more experienced than I was, I had to find my way in. I found there was always a niche to occupy. That was what I was trying to do . . . to justify my presence. I had to appease not only the audiences with my own notion of the way things should be done, but also the other performers, especially in a workshop setting. Otherwise, I'm taking up their time if I don't do it well. I worked hard at making it serviceable for everybody.

FIGURE 84. PETER PAUL VAN CAMP, 1978. PHOTOGRAPH TAKEN BY DAVID LANDY. ARCHIVES OF MANITOBA, WINNIPEG FOLK FESTIVAL 1978 NEGATIVES, P2566/7, 4/78. 26A.

FIGURE 85. PETER PAUL VAN CAMP ON MAIN STAGE, 1978. PHOTOGRAPH BY DAVID LANDY. ARCHIVES OF MANITOBA, WINNIPEG FOLK FESTIVAL 1978 NEGATIVES, P5266/7, 4/78. 23A.

KN: I was thinking, too, that there's a precedent with Ginsberg's involvement with some shows in the States, right? It's not too far out.

PPVC: I guess. We all have to start *somewhere.*

KN: What was your approach in the years following? Were you becoming more of a presence at the Festival stage? Did you have a strategy of how to approach it? A shtick?

DAIRY PRODUCTS

PPVC: Well, 1 January of every year I'd wake up and think "Oh, no. Here it comes again." I had to have new material. I had to top myself, because with a large audience if you don't seize them and hold them—boy, you're in a pickle. So, I began planning things and by about March or May, I'd think, *I've got it now.* I'd have a new piece written, then realize, *Oh, that's not going to work.* After a few years, I found out all people wanted to hear was "A Milkman at Heart." They want to yell, "Dairy products!" and no matter what else I'd want to offer, they'd yell "Shut up, do 'Dairy Products'!" That became a kind of a bone of contention between the audience and myself, I must say. But there was a time there before that started happening where I had some nice pieces that I worked on, especially after dark. If you are keyed into the audience and the situation and who was coming on after, who just played, and all that. Strategizing, we called it. If you knew the setup of the night, and if you did the right piece, the audience might just buy it wholesale and the response could be huge. A few times, there was so much vocal chorus response that I felt that I could walk out on top of the audience, just on the sound they were making. It was a palpable thing. I could step on that. I'll never get over it.

KN: Can you do some "Dairy Products" here?

PPVC: It begins like this. You have to be that the audience of 8,000 people.

Dairy land, dairy days

FIGURE 86. AUDIENCE AT WINNIPEG FOLK FESTIVAL, 1976. PHOTOGRAPH BY DAVID LANDY. ARCHIVES OF MANITOBA, WINNIPEG FOLK FESTIVAL 1976 NEGATIVES, P5266/3, 76/9. 35.

Dairy man, dairy maid
Dairy farm. . . .
Morning mist hangs low in the valley
Bulging sun burns red in the east
Rooster crows but the cows are up already
They can't sleep for the zeal of making
Dairy products
DAIRY PRODUCTS!

You can imagine—8,000 people on cue. I had a few others, after a while. "I Want a Pancake." And a rouser about John Wockenfuss, a ballplayer whose name was difficult to abbreviate in the box scores. . . . It was such a time. I can't imagine my life without all this having happened.

KN: How is the Winnipeg Folk Festival unique?

PPVC: It was the organization. And it was the way that Mitch decided to treat performers because he'd been to other festivals. I don't want to mention any cities in Pennsylvania, but Philadelphia, where the performers are fed lavishly on baloney sandwiches and that's about it. Mitch's theory was, if you want to get the best out of performers, treat them like kings, queens, and princes. Make us feel good and we'll do our best. [The volunteers would] meet you at the airport, the train station, or the bus depot. You were an honoured guest.

Then, of course, the other festivals he helped establish in Vancouver, in Owen Sound, in Edmonton. They're all built on the same model. Everybody is treated equally and everybody gets fed like they may not get fed for the rest of the year because these are folk singers. We're talking about poor, scrawny little poets. That was the thing. You wanted to be there, not only because of the food, of course, but the parties, and also the company you would keep. These were the top people. Some of them, like myself, just starting out their careers. And here were the real writers, the real performers, people who could walk out on that stage and hold thousands of people in the palm of one hand. And everybody felt terrific! The performers, at that time, used to stand off at the side of the Main Stage during the evening concerts. They were not in the audience, they were backstage in an area off to the side. You could sort of play to them as well. I know *I* did because I was really thinking, *I want to give* them *my best.* I wanted to be in that club.

MITCH PODOLAK

KN: Tell me about the significance of Mitch to this apparatus.

PPVC: No Mitch, no Festival. Don Cullen used to run a coffeehouse in Toronto called the Bohemian Embassy. He hired Mitch when Mitch was about fifteen as a busboy, just rattling around in there. Within a couple of years, Mitch was booking the place as a sixteen-, seventeen-year-old. So that's Mitch. He saw an opening and he was in there. Let me *at* it. I know how to do this. He saw it was to be done in a certain way.

When he got to the point where it was the Manitoba centennial year in 1974, there was money to be granted, and the people with the money said, "Folk Festival? I guess we can let him do it once. See how that goes." But again, Mitch and Ava and the others, had these ideas. Visions. We'll call them visionaries and there's nothing wrong with saying that. Because it all meant a lot to them, to pull a community out of the disparate neighbourhoods of Winnipeg and around the province. People always coming up from the Dakotas and Minnesota. They wanted to be here because it was great. It was *great!* I'm so happy that I was part of that. My presence was due to Mr. Podolak. He tapped me on the shoulder and said, "You're up."

KN: What about the significance of this happening in Winnipeg and not other places?

PPVC: Mitch was living here and the centennial money was here, so I suppose that's why that happened in Winnipeg. He made his life here. He and Ava were living in Manitoba, but it could have been any number of other places. Just our luck, you'd have to say.

You've probably flown into Winnipeg from somewhere, at some time, and you realize after you've been flying for hours from either direction, suddenly for some reason there's this *city* down there. How did that *get* there? It's always seemed like an unusual location, to me. I'm not from here. I'm from Ohio. But when I first came here, I thought, *My gosh, this is a long way to go to be wherever this is.* But I made it my home. And Winnipeg is as likely a place as any, because people are the same pretty much everywhere. If you give them something real, they're going to like it. And they're going to thank you for it and support it. There it is.

Al SIMMONS

Al Simmons is a Manitoba-based entertainer. He began his career in 1970 in a band called Out To Lunch, and then Kornstock, but soon struck out on his own. His stage antics of using strange gadgets, quirky costumes, and hilarious songs have pleased children of all ages—as well as adults who wished they were still kids. He has performed at the Winnipeg Folk Festival thirteen times and is often recruited to emcee both the Main Stage and workshops. Al has won a Juno and a Western Canada Music Award for his recordings. He has released four albums.

FIGURE 87. AL SIMMONS, 1980. PHOTOGRAPH BY DAVID LANDY. ARCHIVES OF MANITOBA, WINNIPEG FOLK FESTIVAL–[AL SIMMONS], [C. 1980], P5267/12, V13.

AL SIMMONS

24 NOVEMBER 2021, WINNIPEG

KEVIN NIKKEL: How did you first become associated with the Winnipeg Folk Fest?

AL SIMMONS: What happened was, in 1977 Mitch Podolak saw me perform my act "The Human Jukebox" at Old Market Square[27]—long before there was a stage there. The Jukebox was made of plywood and about the size of a porta-potty. There were three sets of doors; one for my head, another for my hands and one for my feet. I would stand inside and wiggle a little sign that said "Deposit 25¢." It was up to an audience member to start the show. Eventually someone walking past would stop and put money in. The quarter would roll down a tube: ding ding ding ding. At the last minute my hand would pop out and grab it. They'd push a button with titles like "Dig this one man," "Wow," or "A Scottish Air." The doors would open and I would do a music and comedy routine. I had bells, whistles, and sirens, an ahooga horn, a banjo, and a rubber chicken. For "A Scottish Air," I played a bagpipe made out of a balloon and a harmonica.

Mitch invited me to be at the Folk Festival. He said, "I don't know where I'll put you. This stage? That stage?"

And I said, "To be honest, I don't think it's a stage act,"

He said, "Well, you decide. You come on the day of the Festival and set up wherever you want." When I arrived and saw where the stages were, I found a place that wouldn't be bothered by the sound of any of them—it was way out in the middle of the field. I don't know what I was thinking.

We put the box on a 4 x 8-foot sheet of plywood. I'm standing inside the box wiggling the sign and . . . there's nobody there. It was so foolish. I went outside for a bit, and I guess I yelled out, "Showtime! It's almost time for a show!" Some folks came and I went back inside and wiggled the sign. Somebody put a quarter in, then I whispered, "Push a button! Push a button!" So, they pushed the "So-so Calypso" button. I opened the doors and yelled "Number nine!" I played banjo and sang "Yellow Bird" while shaking six maracas that

FIGURE 88. AL SIMMONS WITH THE HUMAN JUKEBOX, 1970S. COURTESY OF MARSHA WINEMAN.

were strapped to my head, then closed the doors, and wiggled the sign. Someone else put another quarter in and I did another bit. I did the whole show, twelve tunes, for maybe six people. Then I put a sign out saying: "Next show at 2:15pm." There were sixty people there and a lineup to put in quarters, and the crowds multiplied over the weekend. Word spread. I was invited to the Vancouver Children's Festival, the Edmonton Folk Festival, and the Vancouver Folk Festival. The plywood Jukebox was so big and heavy that I had to drive everywhere, so I made another one out of corrugated plastic and I built an aluminum case to transport it in. I was able to do the act at the Kerrville Texas Festival, Mariposa Folk Fest, Festival of Friends in Hamilton, the New York State Bear Mountain Festival, and eventually Pete Seeger's Hudson River Revival. It's all because Mitch took a chance on me.

ALTERNATIVE PERFORMERS AT THE WINNIPEG FOLK FESTIVAL

KN: Some people at the Folk Festival might think that there's this high tradition of folk music and yet, here you are, with this zany approach. Was it an easy fit?

AS: It's a curious thing; I felt like I fit right in. After a couple of years in the Jukebox, I felt like a change, and I asked Mitch if I could be in a workshop or two. Mitch was always supportive and willing to take a chance, so he said yes. Mitch was so brilliant at putting diverse acts on the same stage.

He put me in a blues workshop. It was delightful because John Hammond, Big Dave McLean, and other blues greats backed me up while I sang my ludicrous takes on blues tunes. I sang an anthropological version of "Mannish Boy"; "I'm a man . . . I can touch each finger with my thumb." I would gradually de-evolve and become "gorilla-AL-simian." It was so much fun. The workshop would go from serious blues tunes to my eccentric songs. I remember being in a harmonica workshop with Howard Levy, Carlos del Junco, and Gord Kidder, and all of those serious harmonica players, and I'm there because I can play harmonica with my nose. That's my talent. I also play harmonica and accompany myself on springy-door-stopper piano—and Mitch made me the host! But that was Mitch. He said, "Do what you do and it'll work." I got the musicians to show everyone how they travelled with their harmonicas. Some had padded cases while others just threw them into a bag.

From my first performance as the Jukebox, and then on a workshop stage, I felt that I had finally found my audience. They understood my wacky sense of humour.

KN: You had been playing for ten years before starting out like this. What was your background? Your education?

AS: I had a feeling in my heart that I could be an entertainer. My dad was a closet vaudevillian. He knew all of the vaudeville routines and did them at home in our living room. My sister and brother and I grew up thinking that all kids had a dad that could make one arm longer than the

FIGURE 89. AL SIMMONS, WITH OL' SPOKE AND KARL, 1984. COURTESY OF AL SIMMONS.

FIGURE 90. CHILDREN AT WINNIPEG FOLK FESTIVAL,1978. PHOTOGRAPH BY DAVID LANDY. ARCHIVES OF MANITOBA, WINNIPEG FOLK FESTIVAL 1978 NEGATIVES, P5266/7, 23/78. 8.

other or make his face look like he was a gorilla. We thought that was just the norm. My mom was playful, too. She was the kindest person you could ever meet, and she was quite a wordsmith. She was a real punster.

I had a hankering to make people laugh. When I turned twenty, I decided, *That's it, I'm going to go for it.* I quit my job at Manitoba Hydro. One day I was a clerk earning minimum wage, and the next day I was an unemployed entertainer. I had nothing lined up. I just quit and never had a steady job after that. I formed a band but I had no idea what songs I wanted to sing. I just knew I wanted to entertain. I learned my craft onstage. The audience was my director. I quickly learned what people paid attention to and when they ignored me.

A friend of mine, Rick Skene, has a saying: Every now and then you have to throw your favourite hat over a fence because then you have no choice—you have to go get it. So, if there is a fence and you wonder what's on the other side, throw your hat over. Then you've gotta go. I have learned to look forward to a brand-new challenge. There is another saying; Take the leap and you'll grow wings on the way down—which is, I think, what I did. I didn't think of that at the time, but I just decided and took a leap and it took me maybe a couple months before I had an act that worked in bars with the band.

KN: I love that hat analogy. I could tell you my own stories of throwing hats farther and farther away.

AS: Still to this day, before a show, I'm usually overly concerned but as soon as I step on stage I feel at home. I always feel comfortable in front of an audience. When what I'm doing on stage gets too easy, I shake it up. I rearrange the order, or I put something new in that's going to keep me on my toes. A few times I've even created a brand-new show, where I don't allow myself to do anything that I've done before.

KN: Let's go back to the workshops. How would you prepare?

AS: At the best of times, I will talk to the other performers and find out some highlights of their career or if they have a new recording that I can mention. I try and see if they can back me up on a few of my tunes or vice-versa. Is there a song that we all know that we can do together at the end? More often than not, there is too little time to figure all of that out. We step onstage and just wing it.

During the workshop, invariably the players would not be pleased with the sound system. They would say, "Can I have a little more banjo in the monitor, please?" So, I did that on one of the workshop stages.

"Give me a little guitar in the monitor, please?" I bent down and pick up a little guitar that I had hidden in the monitor speaker and say, "Thank you!" If I had time, I would plant a few little gags here and there around the stage.

KN: Eventually the Festival starts to realize that there is an audience for children's programming. And musicians for children. Talk about that.

AS: The kids' stage, in those early days, was fun for me to do, but I said to Mitch that it felt like a kids' ghetto. I meant it seemed that parents would sit their kids down and then stand around the back talking and smoking cigarettes, or parents would drop off their kids and go and watch other stages and come back two hours later. It just wasn't fair to anybody, especially the kids. Also, there weren't as many performers who could hold children's attention. Sometimes, other performers, that Mitch thought could do it, would be successful, but it often didn't work. Mitch was always open. I told him why I thought it wasn't working and he said, "Okay, what should we do?" He ended up hiring people that I recommended.

One time, I said, "I would rather be out where families are; adults, kids, everybody. I have friends who are vaudeville performers that wouldn't enjoy working on a kid's stage but a family audience would love them."

He said, "Let's do a vaudeville tent!" I think it was three years—1983, 1984, and 1985—that he had a vaudeville tent. All day long, there were vaudeville shows and he asked me to hire performers to come to the Festival. I brought friends of mine from all over the continent. It was so much fun, especially for me to go onstage and do a full one-hour vaudeville-style show and then watch all of the other eccentric performers: Bob Berkey, Avner the Eccentric, Laughing Moon Theatre. It was glorious.

KN: It seems like very early on Mitch was really thinking outside the box. Any other things you helped lead?

AS: I certainly wouldn't claim that I led the way on any of these things. Mitch was a true collaborator. I don't know if I suggested it, but there was a parade. "Let's have a parade to the Main Stage." The last show at the kids' stage would end half an hour before the Main Stage would start. We organized a parade; all the kids dressed up. They made themselves hats and costumes at the Festival. They had homemade flags and musical instruments and I spoke with the musicians and invited all woodwind and brass players to join us. "Lead the parade to the Main Stage," were my instructions. Okay, that was all I was told. We marched through the Handmade Village—talk about a bull in a china shop. It was craziness. We wormed our way through the food area, then to the Main Stage. Where do I stop? I don't know. So, I led them through the security gate, up the stairs, onto the stage, across the stage, and around the back, down and out again. Parents were probably wondering: "Where is he taking my kids?"

The crew told me years later, "You screwed us up for that whole night. All of the cables, patch cords, effects pedals, everything was trampled over." It was chaos. It took them about ten minutes to get everything back in order for the first performer. I was told: lead the parade to the Main Stage! Whoops.

KN: Do you have any stories of other misadventures?

EMCEE ON MAIN STAGE

AS: Mitch asked me to emcee. People don't realize what goes on backstage. We are told it's a three-minute turnover to get the next band up. So, I would go out and do a two-minute bit and begin to introduce the act; the stage manager would shout, "Keep going. Another ten minutes." You really have to think on your feet. Other emcees told me that they would make up names to meet at the Whale's Tail. They'd say, "Lisa and Craig meet Liz and John at the Whale's Tail." Or they'd announce fake licence plates to "move your car please." Stuff like that.

I found it to be more like fun! I'd say, "You need more time? Yes! Excellent." I would go off on a tangent. I would encourage the audience to shout at me and I would ad-lib until the act was ready. I once told the audience that, last year the Regina Folk Festival won an award for the cleanest site after an evening concert. "Tonight, if everyone picks up all their belongings and garbage, plus someone else's trash on the way out, we could take the prize." The volunteer clean-up crew was quite pleased with the result.

Bruce Steele and I were co-hosting one night and, all of a sudden, in the middle of an act, the sound died. Of course, backstage they're checking the plugs, the breaker, everything. They said, "Get out there, tell them the sound system is not working and we are working on it."

Well, there's how many thousand people out there? So, Bruce and I went out and were muttering to each other and Bruce says, "What do we do?"

I said to the first few rows, "The sound system is out, but we're repairing it as fast as we can. Pass it on."

So, they turned around and said to the people behind them, "The sound system is out, pass it on." And we heard it go all the way back, till we could hardly hear it.

And then Bruce said something else, "We think it's the breaker, but we're not sure. They're following the cables now." And out it went all the way to the back again. The next thing you knew, questions started coming from the back forward to us. We would answer the question, and it would travel back to the distant horizon. It was amazing. I can't remember what the questions were—of course some of them were ludicrous. You know, "Can we still buy a Whale's Tail?"

The worst part of being an emcee is dealing with encores. After a performer is finished and the crowd is going wild, I'll ask the stage manager if they can do an encore. "Definitely not, we are behind schedule as it is." If the band is performing at a workshop the next day, I simply tell the folks that the band will be on the stage tomorrow at three and that's it. Buddy Guy closed Saturday night one year. He finished his last song, walked off the stage, handed his guitar to his guitar tech and got into a limo. Buddy's band was still wailing away as the limo drove off. I'm sure the limo was at the perimeter highway by the time the band ended the hard-hitting tune. The entire audience was on their feet yelling for more. "Bud-dy! Bud-dy! Bud-dy!" The stage manager gave me a nod.

I stepped out and said "Buddy Guy has left the building. Thanks for being such a great audience. Good night and drive safely." The audience shouted even louder. "There will be lots more music tomorrow, folks." The stage lights turned off and the house lights shone on the audience. It seemed obvious that the show was over. "Pick up your garbage on the way out. Don't forget anything. Take a look around and make sure you've got all your family members." The band started packing up their gear. The stage crew were wrapping up cords.

Yet, a bunch of diehard fans were still shouting at me: "Bud-dy! Bud-dy! Bud-dy!" "Bring him back, we want more, we want more!"

"You are a wonderful audience, Buddy loves you but he is long gone now, see you tomorrow." Finally, everything quieted down and everyone was heading out. I'm sure the sound crew was wishing I would get off the stage so they could shut the system down. But I persisted: "When you wish upon a star, remember where you parked your car." The stage was pretty much cleared. I am not sure what possessed me but I shouted . . . "Well, alright . . . LETS BRING BUDDY GUY OUT HERE FOR ONE MORE SONG! What do you say? Come on out here Buddy!"

The handful of diehard fans came running back and went berserk. "YA! ALRIGHT! Bud-dy BUD-DY."

I said, "You know what? Buddy Guy is probably in his hotel room in Winnipeg by now. I was just kidding. Good night, folks." For years I encountered people who were furious at me for not giving Buddy an encore. They would yell at me from across the street or out of car windows. "You're the jerk who wouldn't give Buddy Guy an encore!"

KN: Any other personalities you met that stand out to you?

AS: I loved watching solo performers that could have the audience listen to every word they sang. Valdy and Connie Kaldor's songs taught us how to be better people. Stan and Garnet Rogers and their band always had the audience spellbound. It was somehow exciting, simply watching them tune up.

David Amram is a composer and multi-instrumentalist who was a regular at lots of festivals in the 1980s and 1990s. He had a banquet-size table onstage, filled with an assortment of woodwind, percussion, and stringed instruments. All by himself, he captivated the crowd. If you put him into a workshop, he could accompany anyone, in any style of music, without overshadowing them. My wife and I stayed at David's place when I was performing in New York. I spoke with him on the phone the other day, he is in his nineties and still going strong.

Ken Whiteley is another musician who can back anyone up and blend right in. I was in awe of his Gospel Workshops. I got to know him and he produced three of my albums. We won a Juno for one of them. Ken appeared on my local CTV television show, *All for Fun.* Stan Rogers, too. Stan was a great guest. We worked up some comedy schtick. Sadly, CTV destroyed all the tapes. So, the episode is lost.

k.d. lang was at the 1985 Festival with The Reclines. I introduced them on the Main Stage. We went on to the Edmonton festival and she watched my show. I was thrilled to see her laughing as I sang my cowboy song and rode off into the sunset on Ol' Spoke, my horse-cycle. Her producer and longtime collaborator, Ben Mink, played fiddle on one of my albums.

I remember a conversation in 2003 with artistic director Rick Fenton. Me backstage wearing a 1920s-style bathing suit and flippers and holding a nine-foot-tall flyswatter: "Do you think Billy Bragg has a sense of humour?"

Rick Fenton: "I guess we are going to find out, aren't we." End result . . . he does have a sense of humour.

I could, of course, go on and on. Mitch organized the Festival's backstage with the idea that everyone was equal. The performers and volunteers and staff all lined up for food together and ate at the same tables. Consequently, we got to know each other. Jam sessions would spontaneously start up backstage.

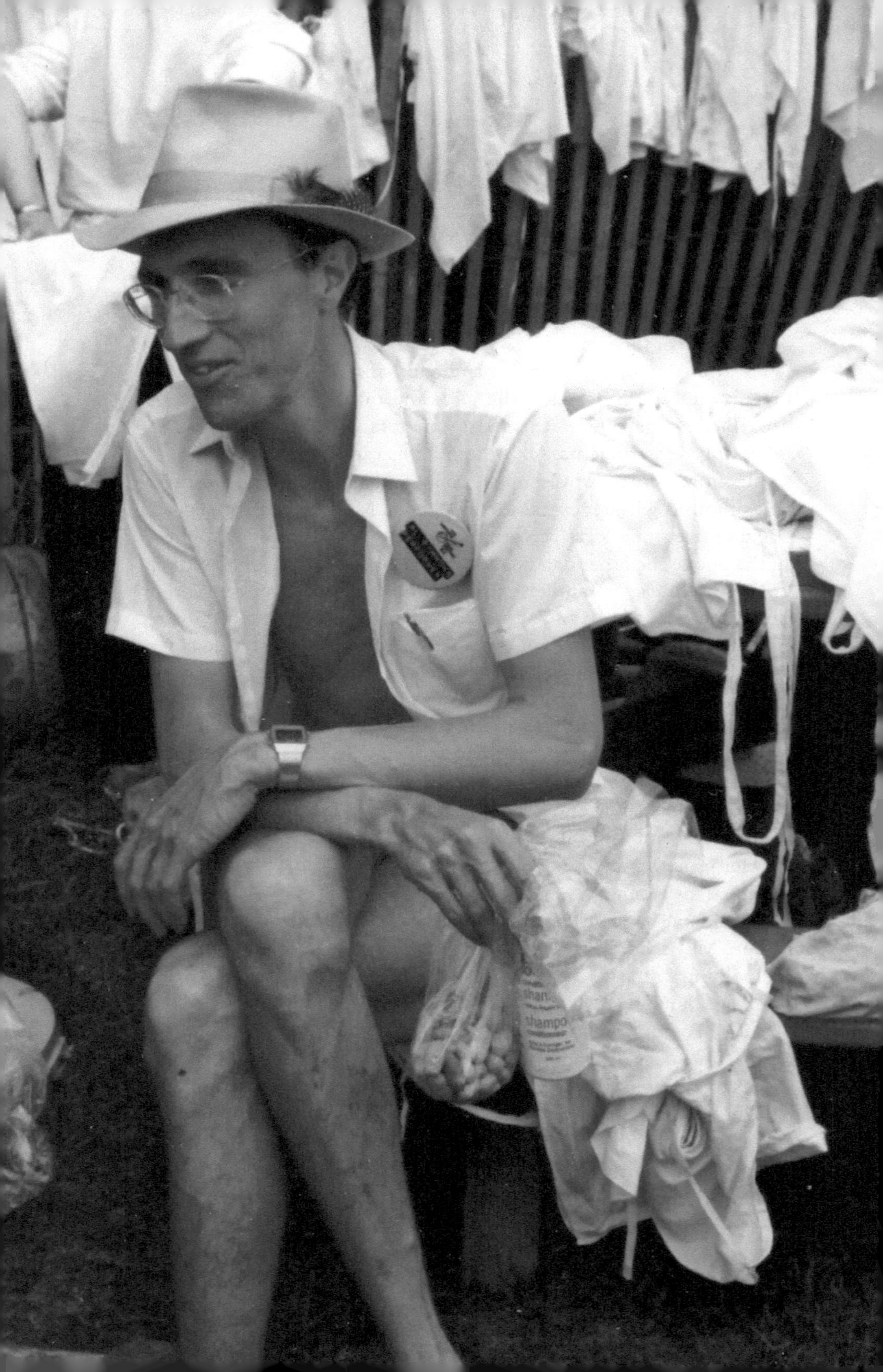

Al Simmons

Some of the folks that I'm most grateful for having known are the staff and volunteer crew members; security, schleppers, stagehands, sound technicians, etc. I am always glad to see their familiar faces again and share a laugh. Harry Paine was in charge of the kitchen in the first few years. What a great guy.

KN: I like the instrument that you've created that you play at performances with all the crazy sound makers hanging off it. Maybe that is a good metaphor for the Festival.

AS: Absolutely. The Festival certainly presents an eclectic assortment of music. My crazy horn was inspired by my friend Roldo, who gave me a baritone horn that had been run over by a truck. He said, "Make something out of this." I removed some of the piping. I had one valve channel the air to a trumpet and, through there, to another trumpet. To that I added another trumpet so the thing had twelve valves—only one of them played music. The other ones were connected to noisemakers. All the valves re-channelled the air to make the various sounds. I could play the entire 1812 overture on it, including all the church bell, firework, and cannon parts. It was so much fun to play. I thought the Folk Festival audiences would enjoy it. I said, "Mitch, put me in an unusual musical instrument workshop." So, I shared the stage with musicians and their harp, zither, bagpipe, and spoons.

KN: If we wanted to examine the essence of the Winnipeg Folk Fest, take the lid off and try to figure this thing out, what is the Winnipeg Folk Festival?

AS: I remember when Rosalie took over from Mitch—it was then that they subtitled it "People and Music." That was it, because the Folk Festival, in my mind, is all about the people. People are so open and friendly. I know it sounds like an exaggeration, but it feels like there's no negative energy. The Winnipeg Folk Festival is the way the world should be.

FIGURE 91. AL SIMMONS IN THE KITCHEN AT WINNIPEG FOLK FESTIVAL, ND. PHOTOGRAPH COURTESY OF MARSHA WINEMAN.

PART FIVE

THE STRONG AND THE MIGHTY: A Peek at the Inner Workings

FIGURE 92. VOLUNTEER CREW, 1980S. COURTESY OF WINNIPEG FOLK FESTIVAL.

PSI

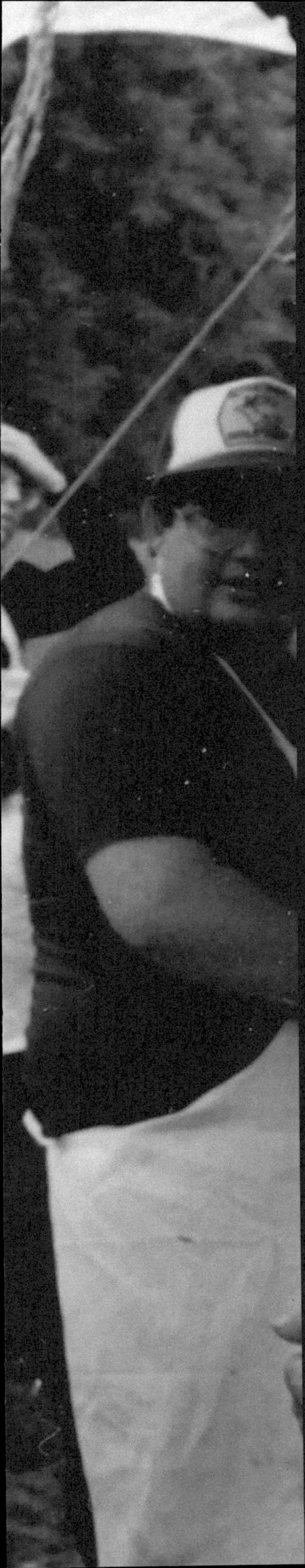

Marsha WINEMAN

Marsha Wineman is a visual artist based in Toronto. Originally from Detroit, she moved to Winnipeg in 1970 after graduating from Michigan State University. She became a volunteer for the Winnipeg Folk Festival in its second year, starting in the backstage kitchen. She spent five years on the organizational side of the kitchen crew with Harry Paine. After leaving Winnipeg, she earned her MFA in Chicago. Returning to Canada, Wineman worked in the film industry and then at Seneca College in Toronto.

FIGURE 93. MARSHA WINEMAN IN THE WINNIPEG FOLK FEST KITCHEN, 1970S. COURTESY OF MARSHA WINEMAN.

MARSHA WINEMAN

27 NOVEMBER 2021, TORONTO, ONTARIO

KEVIN NIKKEL: What was it like at the Folk Festival when you first started volunteering?

MARSHA WINEMAN: It was the second year of the Festival when I began my first year of volunteering and it rained a lot. To stay out of the rain I spent extra time in the big domed backstage tent ringed with benches and packed with staying-out-of-the-rain performers. Quite an introduction to folk music! In the tent, musicians took turns playing or were called on to take a turn. I remember Elizabeth Cotten playing her guitar upside down, as she had learned to play it. I feel lucky to have that firsthand memory.

Ah, back to the kitchen and the food. In the early days, Mitch called on his old friend Harry Paine from Toronto to make the food for the volunteers and performers. As it happened, my neighbour was coordinator for all the volunteers. She befriended Harry and, through her, I got to know him, too. During one of our many suppers together, Harry was planning his first menu. I asked him, "So how will people get plates? How are they going to cut bread?"

Harry said, "Hm-m! I don't know." So, I ended up taking on the organization of the kitchen, joined later by Maryam Decter. I did that intensely for about three or four years. When I was ready to try something different, kitchen volunteer Karen Dana took it over.

Here is a memory . . . my first year volunteering we had no running water. The water had to be carried in a golf cart from all the way across the Winnipeg Folk Fest site property. We hauled five-gallon jugs of water at a time. Water for cooking and washing dishes. It was not easy to function with so little water, for a kitchen serving hundreds, but we did it. The next year the Festival got an ATCO kitchen trailer and, thankfully, we could hook up directly to water. It was a tremendous change and truly a luxury compared to the previous year of hauling water from across the fields. That same summer I remember working in the kitchen tent when one of the performers came up and asked, “Do you have Perrier?”! Based on how difficult it had been just the year before to acquire any water, I had to laugh.

I had not been aware I possessed such organizational skills until volunteering at the Festival. It was a gratifying discovery, something that I had not been aware of previously.

KN: How old were you then?

MW: I was in my late twenties—about twenty-eight.

KN: It makes me think of what other people have said about volunteering back then. People who did not have the expertise—but they had drive. They could discover their abilities through these opportunities.

MW: In the seventies, there were government funded OFY grants (Opportunities for Youth) providing money for projects deemed worthy, like the Winnipeg Folk Festival. It is unfortunate that there isn't something like that now. It was such an incredibly good opportunity, in so many ways.

The successful reputation of the food area was attributed to Harry. The Winnipeg Folk Festival crews all wore colour-coded T-shirts labelled with their names. Initially, Mitch dubbed the kitchen crew “Harry's Eats” as a nod to names associated with little diner restaurants. The kitchen T-shirt had “Harry's Eats” on the shirt backs. With sensitivity for the largely female crew, and feminism, the name was edited to read “Eats” in the following year.

Again, the backstage food success was associated to be because of Harry. For instance, Peggy Seeger wrote a song about the Eats kitchen and Harry's meals. In the rustic kitchen area on site, it took thirty volunteers, all working hard, to prepare and deliver food. Harry designed the menu but feeding the performers and volunteers was more than planning the menu. Harry got the accolades, but it took a small army using everybody's skill, time, and effort to produce the popular meals. It really was quite impressive to pull it off.

ATTITUDES OF THE 1970S

KN: I want to hear more about the 1970s, to place this festival in context, to understand the people who are volunteering. It's not just Winnipeg, it's happening elsewhere, too. What was the spirit of the times?

MW: As it happened, the volunteers at that time were largely of the postwar baby boom who thought they could do any- and everything. Life and the economy then supported that thinking. We had opportunities to apply for grant money for project initiatives. We had the drive and we were eager to learn. On these created [OFY] jobs, we could test ourselves. I worked on several other grants where I learned other aspects about myself. It was a rich time. Now there is nothing like that and it is tough. I am grateful not to be young now, when it is hard to make money, hard to find a place to live, or to test your skills, and hard to pay for school. Then, fortunately for many, the Folk Festival provided a rich proving ground.

KN: I like that idea of finding a place where you discover yourself. Find a way to contribute to part of something bigger than yourself.

MW: I saw it as being a cog in the wheel of a major event, a giant thing. The volunteers were crucial and made all of it happen. If not for the volunteer army, it could not have happened.

KN: Were Mitch's philosophy and ideology an important part of how the Festival operated and succeeded?

MW: Mitch was a determined and magnanimous person. People collected around him. He was an ideas man, who strived to do big things, and people banded with him do it. These were big efforts that you were more than happy to support. You may have heard Mitch's expression from other people, "If you feed them, they will play their hearts out for you." That was his philosophy, and we were all behind making it be true. The Winnipeg Folk Fest was an amazing experience, especially in the early years. You sat in the dining tent, ate with performers and other volunteers, and made new friends. You could eat next to Leon Redbone and have Steve Goodman carving turkey for you. People made lifelong friends, and met, and got married, having worked together at the Folk Festival.

KN: Tell me more about the background of Mitch, and the volunteers in that era.

MW: Again, I am grateful to be part of the postwar baby boom—there were so many of us of a similar age and maturing at the same time. The economy was hugely different. Many of us were able to afford an education. The slogan of the time was, "Don't trust anybody over thirty." From our youthful vantage point, and we were many, we thought we could change society. There was a belief that the world could and should be a better place. We wanted to make it that way.

Life was easier then because everything was more affordable and easier to do. I grew up in the States, in Detroit. I decided that after university I would get a fresh start in a new location. As a teenager, I had been a babysitter for a family in Detroit, who moved to Winnipeg. During their visit stateside, they offered me the possibility to stay with them, if I chose to come to Winnipeg. I did just that. I drove to Winnipeg and stayed with them. Two months after I arrived, they ended up moving back to the States. There I was, in Winnipeg, Manitoba, Canada on my own. I was twenty-two then and continued living in the 'Peg for twenty years. With my fine arts background, I found a studio. I would freelance. There were some lean years, but everything was more affordable. One could somehow scrape it together and make things work. But not now, with everything so much more expensive. Then, I had a studio for eighty-five dollars a month that was bigger than my current Toronto apartment.

KN: That is a whole other conversation, about the benefits of Winnipeg as an affordable place for creative types. I want to come back to something you said, about how we felt like we could change things. Did you feel the previous generation messed things up? What do you think of those thoughts now? Do we need another generation of people who want to make things better again?

MW: We do. Probably Greta Thunberg is representative of the dedication of today's youth. Back in the seventies the dominant issues were with society and politics, now it is the economy and the environment. Then we chanted that anyone over thirty messed things up, we saw them being slaves to their jobs. As well, Vietnam was a disgrace, and we were going to have none of that. For me, open-minded and with blind faith, I got into my car (VW, of course), left Michigan State University in East Lansing, and drove north. Once I crossed the border into Canada, I made a left turn to drive to Winnipeg. Canada promised a better life in so many ways.

But what we, the baby boomers, did have, by our numbers, is that we were the ones then and now still, who are changing things. There were so many of us as a movement in the seventies. It seemed as if change could be in our hands. We were trying to make different things be better. With our numbered mass, we forged ahead.

VOLUNTEERING AT THE FOLK FESTIVAL

KN: How many years were you at the Folk Fest?

MW: I guess ten years in total. I also volunteered for some of the other crew areas.

KN: Every year, you went back—were there some moments of the Festival that became more of a tradition for you? Part of your weekend?

MW: The backstage was really the best. As the Festival grew, the backstage was no longer available for the volunteers. Mitch experimented for a couple of years with giving tickets to volunteers to get food from the general population food booths where we sat and ate with everyone else. Newer volunteers never had the backstage area experience, but those who could remember how it was certainly missed it. Luckily, it was reinstated and everyone eats together again.

Another ritual that other interviewees must have told you about was the finale, the closing songs of the Festival. On the last day of the Festival, the last hour in that final evening, everyone who had a hand in making the Festival happen was invited up on the Main Stage. Together we stood arm on shoulder and, with the audience, sang the last songs of the Folk Festival for that summer. Getting up on the stage and just—I have goosebumps. Hundreds of voices together, everyone singing "Irene, Good Night." It was over for another year. So incredibly special.

KN: Describe that moment in more detail.

MW: I'm thinking about how we experienced the Festival at the edge of the stage—not out in the prairie fields with the audience but at the foot of the side stage. If it was raining, we were still there in our ponchos. If it was cold, we were there with extra blankets. That was true of everyone attending. The weather just did not matter.

As the last evening ended, being up on the Main Stage was a very emotional experience for us all. We were full of big feelings, from too much sun, to mosquito bites, to good music, and new people. We were tired, but we were going to stay for the very last of the weekend experience, for the ritual of the closing songs. Once over, we would join the stream of the crowd heading to the parking lot, find our vehicle, and drive back to the city. But for us, it was not over. We would attend the wrap-up parties at the hotel. High on festival energy, we headed to the party at the hotel, not wanting to let any of that summer festival go. We hung with the performers who were jamming, and of course there was more food. A surprising number of us diehards lasted till the sun came up.

KN: What do you have on the menu there? [Looking through Folk Festival ephemera.]

MW: Before we had the ATCO kitchen trailer, eight turkeys were cooked in various volunteer Winnipeg home kitchens, then collected and driven out to the Festival site. This was how we managed, initially. When we did get the ATCO trailer, it was only equipped with domestic stoves which were not meant to be used for three days, continuously. We literally melted them. Next year, the kitchen trailer was outfitted with much-needed industrial stoves.

Here are highlights from the menu from 1982. Breakfast: eggs to order, bagels, cream cheese, fruit, coffee, tea, and juice. Friday night: turkey and stuffing, lemon beans, sweet potatoes, ham, chicken wings, and Russian vegetable casserole—food for vegetarians. For dessert, we had apple and rhubarb crisp, all made fresh on-site. Sunday night: Barbecue lamb, short ribs (Stan Rogers helped barbecue one year), this was what we fed everyone involved in making the Festival happen.

The lunches were good, too. Saturday: borscht, cold cuts, cheese, and perogies. Sunday: gazpacho, cold cuts, corn on the cob, and fish. We made home-cooked meals out on the Manitoba prairie. It was enough to make you sing for your supper!

KN: This was gourmet.

THE
WINNIPEG
FOLK
FESTIVAL

Jane GRAHAM

Jane Graham was an educator for Youth Corrections for thirty-six years and is a volunteer-at-heart. She joined the Winnipeg Folk Festival's hotel hospitality crew in 1976. She was the coordinator at the hotel for ten years. Afterwards, she moved to support the site office during the Festival. She is a past Winnipeg Folk Festival Board member and past-president of the Board for three terms. In 1996, she was awarded the Winnipeg Folk Festival's Glass Banjo award for outstanding contributions to the Festival. In 2015, Travel Manitoba awarded her the Volunteer of the Year prize.

FIGURE 94. JANE GRAHAM, N.D. COURTESY OF JANE GRAHAM.

JANE GRAHAM

1 SEPTEMBER 2021, WINNIPEG

KEVIN NIKKEL: How are you connected to the Folk Festival?

JANE GRAHAM: I have been involved with the Folk Festival from, I believe, the second year it was at Birds Hill Park. I missed the first one, I attended the second one, and I believe I started volunteering at the third. I have been there every year since. I have not missed one. I tell my friends they can't get married on that weekend. It's just become part of my life. I always book my holidays. I had to have those days off. It's part of life. It really is.

KN: Were you always interested in folk music before you got involved?

JG: I hadn't a clue. I was actually born in Scotland so the only kind of music we had in the house, if we had any, was Scottish music. That's the only music I really knew of. I'd heard country music and stuff, but I was a little farm girl and really didn't know a lot about music. A folk festival? What's that? A lovely lady named Hope Dyson, who used to be a volunteer, saw me out at university and said, "Why don't you volunteer for the Folk Festival."

So, I said, "Sure." I signed up.

VOLUNTEERING AT THE FOLK FESTIVAL

You had to show up for your crew meeting. If you didn't show up for that meeting, you were not volunteering. And I missed it. I got the wrong information. So, I called up the next day and heard, "Nope. You're off the crew."

I went, "No. I really want to volunteer."

They said, "Well, you have to come in and meet with Mitch." So, I went down and met with Mitch. I believe it was on Lilac Street, where the offices were. I sat down with Mitch and he asked me a few questions. I was quite scared, but he was wonderful. He took me in and it was history. I started off at the hotel hospitality crew. I was the coordinator there for nine or ten years, I'm not sure. Lots of good stories from there. Because you were doing so much time at the hotel, you missed a lot of the music. But once I got out there, I can remember my first year out on the field wearing a badge and just being so proud of being a volunteer. Look at me! I have a badge and no one else does. I volunteer. That's the kind of thing that was instilled in us. Pride in your work. Just get out there, and yes, you're the most important person here. Your crew is the most important. Mitch made you feel that way. And he always backed up his volunteers. And recognized if you were doing a good job, he let you know.

You may have noticed me wearing this banjo around my neck. Mitch gave these to us as recognition for a job well done. We figured there's about fifteen banjos out there and it was a huge honour to receive this, let me tell you.

KN: That makes me wonder, where is the reward for the work you're putting in? How would you respond to that? Is that even the right question?

JG: I don't know if it's really a fair question because the reward is being there and doing what you're doing. I was hotel hospitality quite a number of years and then I moved out to site office. I've been there forever now. That was back in the day before we had telephones. We got a telephone thanks to the Pope when he came here.[28] The little shack that they had for his security office was brought over—it was the site office. They brought in his telephone line that they had set up for the Pope to have an emergency line. They had brought that over and that was the first phone we had out there, which was really amazing. I've been in the site office ever since. I love it. People on my crew were pretty well-seasoned veterans, because we're problem solvers. Somebody wants something or wants an answer to something, we either know it or know where to find it. And we just have a hoot.

I just love being there every year. It's like a reunion every year, with people from across Canada, across the world actually. We see the same people every year, and that's a wonderful thing to happen. Through the years I also became a board member. . . . I was president of the board for at least three terms. That was back during lean times, too. We had some really interesting times and interesting meetings. I just remember everybody working through it and, you know, keeping up that positiveness, that we could do it.

HARD TIMES AND HOPE

KN: During those times, did you ever think, maybe this won't be able to continue?

JG: I don't recall that feeling. It's going to be hard, but we can do it.

JOHN PRENTICE: Do you want to talk about the year we were $186,000 in debt? And I think it was the only time that Mitch got up on stage and said, "We need to save this Festival."

JG: I think it was after we'd had several years of rain. I don't remember the year, but it was a dire situation. We had this big plan, we had pails, and we had volunteers. Mitch did get up and did a plea to the crowd, "If we don't get some money, this isn't going to happen. We can't do this anymore." So, people went through the crowd from one side to the other with these buckets and they came back with these buckets full of coins and bills. It was amazing. It was totally amazing. People just dumped their wallets. They brought everything back to the site office and we sat there, and honest to God, we sat there and bawled.

JP: I just remember seeing Jane with this bucket. More tears in the bucket than money. That was back when there were dollar bills. The lovely thing was, whether it was on purpose or by accident, every twentieth bill was a twenty-dollar bill. But there is a bucket full of money.

JG: There was no other way. We'd had several years of bad weather, but it saved us. We went on the next year and we are still here. So, it was a plea that was well worth doing and our audience, bless their hearts, were behind us.

KN: It sounds like a scene from *It's a Wonderful Life*.

JG: Yeah, totally. You can hear the bell ringing. We probably would have had an adult beverage while we were doing it. I have to admit. It was a magical moment.

KN: At the board meetings, was there talk about needing to change what you were doing?

FIGURE 95. SITE CREW JAMMING AT WINNIPEG FOLK FESTIVAL, ND. PHOTOGRAPH COURTESY OF MARSHA WINEMAN.

I was a on non-profit board previously—I know these conversations need to happen.

JG: I've been on several boards and of course it's always financial considerations, but I don't think any of the boards I've been on were at the mercy of Mother Nature the way that we were. That was one of our downfalls. Bill Merritt was wonderful—he kept a tight rein on the purse strings. Within the board level, we came up with some real innovative ways to raise money. In fact, some of us even put up some of our own as a loan to make it through the next year.

JP: Did we ever get that back?

JG: I believe we did. Ha.

KN: While you were on-site during the Festival, were there any traditions that are part of your festival experience?

JG: I used to go to the Sunday gospel. That used to be a routine, but not so much anymore, because it's so far away, and I'm older. But no, I don't go for the music, I go for the event. I have to admit. The music is a bonus, and there's some wonderful music out there, let me tell you. If I catch something, that's great. I do like wandering around from the stages and watching from the side and going, *Oh, that's cool.* If it's not my cup of tea, I wander over to the next one.

You just never know what's going to turn up on the stages. It could be magic and very often is. It is the event. It's knowing that I'm going to see Tom. He's going to be here again this year. I can't wait to see him, catch up. That's it for me.

WHY ARE WE DOING THIS?

KN: I'm always curious to know about the attitude in the 1970s. What were we thinking then? What were we trying to do?

JG: I think it's sort of like, we fell in love with what we were doing and we wanted to make sure it happened. We had a lot of very committed people that were out there to make sure this happened. The lean times were lean times, but there was no despair. No one gave up. No one wanted to give up. Mitch could be . . . trying to find the right word to describe it, he was a don't-give-up guy. He could be very convincing, and he came up with some really interesting ideas. We'd have to work through things and sometimes they didn't pan out, but yes.

KN: Examples?

JG: Instead of having food vendors we would run the food vendors, and we would sell hamburgers and hot dogs and stuff and we would make tons of money. It was a harebrained scheme that didn't work. We went back to having food vendors, who actually knew what they were doing. We had special bucks and we had to go and buy our lunches. We had *Goldstein Bucks.* Instead of having a kitchen, volunteers went and bought with so many dollars that we got. That was a harebrained idea that was really silly. Some of them were good, some of them were not so good.

But he could certainly pontificate—is that a good word? He could be quite convincing, but it was always fun. I [remember] leaving board meetings really exhausted, but I don't remember ever leaving one angry, or upset, or thinking, *this is the end.* They were always good meetings. Good meetings. And we were all heard.

KN: Did it matter that it was folk music? Could it have been a choral festival?

JG: Yes, I think the folk music mattered. That's because it brought a certain genre of people, a certain type of person. It wasn't loud and raucous like a rock festival. There were quiet times and then some rowdy times, too, of course. But I think it didn't matter to me. The music was a bonus to the event for me. That's the way I feel about it.

Candice MASTERS

Candice Masters began volunteering on the hotel hospitality crew, then transitioned to various positions on the Festival site, and eventually went to work as Main Stage Coordinator / Artist Liaison, which she has been doing for over twenty years. In 2014, she was awarded the Winnipeg Arts Council's Outstanding Volunteer Award, and in 2022, she was awarded the Winnipeg Folk Festival's Glass Banjo award for outstanding contributions to the Festival. She has returned to volunteer at the Folk Festival every summer since the 1970s.

FIGURE 96. CANDICE MASTERS, N.D. COURTESY OF CANDICE MASTERS.

CANDICE MASTERS

1 SEPTEMBER 2021, WINNIPEG

KEVIN NIKKEL: How are you connected to the Winnipeg Folk Festival?

CANDICE MASTERS: I am a volunteer at the Winnipeg Folk Festival. I've been doing that for lots of years, I don't remember the exact year, but I started as a teenager. I was moping around the house because my boyfriend and I split up, so my sister said, "Get off your butt and come down and volunteer for the Folk Festival. They really need volunteers and it will give you something to do." So, I did. And that was the start of forty-plus-year love affair for me and the Folk Festival.

VOLUNTEERING AT THE FOLK FESTIVAL

KN: Tell me about that first season. Do you remember where you were placed?

CM: I was on the hotel hospitality crew—we were based in the City Centre Hotel. We checked all the performers in upon arrival, answered questions, got them on the school buses that went out to the site, and set up the parties. We also did "room runs"—we would have to go put a welcome package including fruit, juice, a handwritten postcard in artist and guests' rooms. We would knock and, if no answer, let ourselves into the room, and sometimes we would encounter interesting situations. One year we knocked, no answer, so walked in and there was either Sonny Terry or Brownie McGhee (can't remember which one) soaking in the bathtub—door open. We said hello, delivered the package, said bye and carried on. It was all fun.

KN: Was it the same vibe as the Festival site?

CM: Probably. For the first couple of years, I was never at the Festival site. I stayed in the hotel and went to the parties—it was really fun. Yes, absolutely, the vibe was amazing, the performers were so happy to be there.

KN: It seems like the role you would play would almost be a dorm supervisor.

CM: Yeah, you were the first line when the performers came in and they counted on you for assistance. You registered them, gave them their keys, told them where the rooms are, showed them how to get the buses out to the site. Try to answer any questions that you can. We also put on the parties every night after the Festival ended and everyone came back to town. They were epic. Jams until the sun came up. They are still talked about. They are legendary.

For me, the first year was really hard because it was the day before the Festival that I got pulled in. I didn't know anything about anything. I was a rock and roll girl, I wasn't really a folkie in those days, but that sure changed fast.

I coordinated the Hotel Hospitality Crew and parties for a few years, prior to moving onto crews onsite. First at the Airliner Hotel, then at the International Inn.

KN: When you made the transition to the Festival site, what did they get you doing?

CM: I started out there doing the backstage bar, way before they could really sell beer in Birds Hill Park. I think everybody was allowed two tickets or three tickets per day, which was ridiculous. How do you tell your friends, "You can only have three beers." But that's what was agreed to at that particular time. We might've slipped the odd extra ticket or two to everyone, or at least I did. Then I worked in the bank counting money and doing deposits for a couple of years.

One year I had the "privilege" of getting driven down to North Dakota to pick up a Greyhound bus with our American performers and bring them back to the Festival. They'd flown everybody from the States into Grand Forks to hop on the bus to come to the Festival because they thought it would be more cost-efficient. It was a disaster. Had some of that night's performers on the bus and didn't make it to town until around midnight. A whole lot of shuffling went on. They never did that again.

Then moving up into the last twenty-plus years, I've been the Main Stage Coordinator/Artist Liaison. This was a job the artistic director created for me and I've been doing it for over twenty years. It involves problem solving, taking care of the hosts, helping with the non-performance stuff that happens on the Main Stage, assisting the Festival artistic staff, doing whatever needs to be done.

FIGURE 97. PETE SEEGER AT WINNIPEG FOLK FESTIVAL, 1980. PHOTOGRAPH BY DAVID LANDY. COURTESY OF WINNIPEG FOLK FESTIVAL. ARCHIVES OF MANITOBA, WINNIPEG FOLK FESTIVAL 1980 NEGATIVES, P5266/12, 80/678. 36A.

Volunteers basically run the Festival over the weekend and, especially in those early days, we did everything before, during, and after—from cleaning toilets to creating contracts. It was a family. No difference between volunteers and artists, in those days. It was just a big old family and it was just magic. Pure magic. When you look at the fact that you've done the same thing every summer of your life for forty-plus years on the same weekend, it's pretty spectacular, and speaks volumes.

KN: What were you thinking as you were meeting some of these folk musicians that you had probably never heard of before?

CM: I'll tell you a story. I was on shift, working at the Festival check-in desk at the hotel and this gentleman came down the lobby stairs and sat down beside me. He picked up the *Winnipeg Free Press* Saturday comics and he read them to me, making funny voices for the characters and, in between, we chatted and he was very charming and loads of fun. He hung around for half an hour, forty-five minutes, and then he left to get ready to go to the site. Once he left, other volunteers came over very excited and were saying, "Oh my God, what did he say?"

And I said, "Who?"

And they said, "Pete Seeger!" It was Pete Seeger reading me the Saturday morning funnies and I didn't know it was him. I was just a green rock chick. I really truly didn't know it was him. I, of course, knew who Pete Seeger was, I just didn't realize that the gentleman sitting with me was Pete Seeger.

KN: That's an awesome story.

CM: It was pretty spectacular, and probably means more to me now—a special moment in time I experienced with an amazing person.

KN: What were the attitudes towards folk music amongst your peers back then? You were hanging out with the rock and roll kids in high school—was folk music a part of your world at all?

CM: I come from a Scottish family, so it was lots of backyard parties which always included singsongs, or sitting around a campfire at the lake singing "Michael, Row Your Boat Ashore," "Four Strong Winds," etc., which I loved. So, I had a sense of it. I used to sing Scottish folk songs with my granny when I was a wee one. She used to always have the record player on and I've always loved that memory. It was just not something when you're a teenager that I thought was cool. The first concert I ever went to is Led Zeppelin when I was thirteen years old, that was cool. My sister's ex was a musician, so I was lucky, I got taken to concerts and introduced to rock music. It wasn't until I started to volunteer at the Folk Festival that I realized, "Ah—you rockers don't have anything on folkies."

MITCH PODOLAK

JOHN PRENTICE: Tell us about Mitch.

CM: When I first met Mitch, I'd had a little bit of a run-in with somebody when I was on shift at the hotel and he stuck up for me. He didn't know me from Adam, but he was a champion. I was volunteering and this person was not particularly nice to me and he [Mitch] stood up for me. I thought *wow, he really does stand behind his volunteers, it's not just a line*. He lived by his rule: we all treat each other the same. So that was a pretty good introduction to him.

Over the years we became very close friends. There were loads of times he was a big pain. I remember once having a heated argument and he pissed me off so much I ended up throwing my binder across his desk and saying, "If you're so damn smart, you do it."

He was arguing with me saying, "No we're not doing it that way." (The way I had organized it according to artist schedules.) "We're doing it this way and it wasn't possible." (Based on the same schedules.) I turned around and I walked out, I got to the door and he said, "Okay, wait. Come back, sit down. You're right."

I said, "Pardon me? Can I have that in writing, please?" But that was just Mitch. He was a gruff person, he loved to challenge you, but he had a big heart. He loved the Festival dearly. He loved the artists dearly, and he certainly loved and cherished and respected the volunteers because, without the volunteer organization he built, there wouldn't be a festival. Especially not in those days and he was well aware of that.

And he would do fun things. He, Bill, and Rosalie would instigate elastic fights in the office and that was always fun. Running round and around and around trying to dodge elastics, which hurt like hell if you got hit! But everybody was in and everyone had a sense of fun. It was more fun than serious most of the time, but most importantly, we got [the work] done.

KN: So, you get in the habit of being at the Festival year after year. What are some of the habits that you get used to doing? Something you never miss?

CM: Hug a lot of people. Friday nights, Jane Graham and I go for dinner at one of the vendors. It's become a long-time tradition.

KN: Is there a particular show you would never miss? Like the last night?

CM: You're always at the finale. In the really early years, it was always just a tear-fest. You'd just stand there and weep during the songs. Now it's part of what I do, getting everybody on the stage for the finale; volunteers, staff, and the artists all participate in the finale. It's not a tear-fest for me anymore. There have been people over the years that have said we should stop doing the finale. I've always been adamant, NO. You can't. You just can't. The finale is about the audience and the volunteers. Putting arms around the people you love and care about, singing "Amazing Grace" to close the Festival. It's a really poignant moment for people. So, the finale will always be or should always be. I think there were one or two years we couldn't do it due to severe storms. We had to close the stage down, it was really hard for people not to have the traditional close. But other than the finale, no. I mean, my traditions—I like to just wander around and stop at stages, discover new artists. Listen to what's going on. I wander out in the field and listen away from the crowds.

GROWTH OF THE FESTIVAL

KN: How has the Festival changed over the years?

CM: Electronics and water. Toilets. It's moved ahead with time. Sometimes I long for the days when we didn't have phones and computers and printers. We used to, if you needed something from the city, write a note, give it to somebody to put on the school bus. It'd take the hour to get back to the hotel, and then it would take however long it took to get whatever you needed, and then the item or answer went back on the bus and it would go back to the site, eventually get delivered to whoever needed it. The process was probably easily three hours, if not longer. It was not instant gratification, it was, *okay patience*. If someone said, "I left my guitar," the reply would have to be, "you should borrow one because it's going to be a while."

KN: Hard to imagine, because we expect everything immediately.

CM: No, it wasn't quick, and we didn't have cellphones. We didn't even have a hard-line phone at one time. So, it was all the notes on the buses. And the water trucks. It was fun. It was interesting, it was really folksy. It's become far more of a business, which isn't necessarily a bad thing, but it was really fun in the old days.

The thing about the Festival in the early days, there wasn't any manual. We winged it. We created it as we went. It was, okay, let's do this. Okay, that didn't work. Next time we'll try to do it a different way. Okay, how? How do we solve this challenge? This band wants us to go get them mice for their snakes. No. They can go to the field across from the hotel and get their own mice. Sorry, we do draw the line somewhere. We wrote the rules/processes for festivals, because there were not events like this, so none to go by.

WHY VOLUNTEER?

KN: Why do you volunteer at the Winnipeg Folk Fest?

CM: A big part of what I get out of it is joy and pride. We work so hard at the Festival to ensure people come and feel the passion and the magic. We want the artists who have just spent four days in a provincial park in this little prairie city to leave and tell the world how fabulous the Winnipeg Folk Festival is. How magical it is. In the early days, this was something that was really important; to get these folks to go and rant and rave about it so other musicians wanted to come and play the Festival, so we could grow the Festival. Happily, that's exactly what happened and what we did. We created this magical place that people from around the world, folkies from around the world, and others, too, heard about it and wanted to come to be a part of it.

We had people come in from all around the world as hired artists, as volunteers, and as audiences. This is something we take great pride in. I've made friends with people from the early days who, some forty years later, are still dear friends. It always goes back to the magic created that lives on forever.

KN: I love that. It brings me back to the topic I enjoy exploring: why Winnipeg?

CM: Why not? We're the little city that could, and did, and inspired runoffs across the country because of Mitch's vision that started here in Winnipeg.

KN: Could this have started somewhere else? Is there something special here?

CM: I think it potentially could happen anywhere. But they would still have to have had Podolak and Kobrinsky and Merritt, and key folks at the CBC. Everything just fell into place at that particular moment in time in Winnipeg; a group of people who had the vision, the desire to create this, felt the magic, had the community. Winnipeg had that special something and we did it.

LIQUOR & LOTTERIES

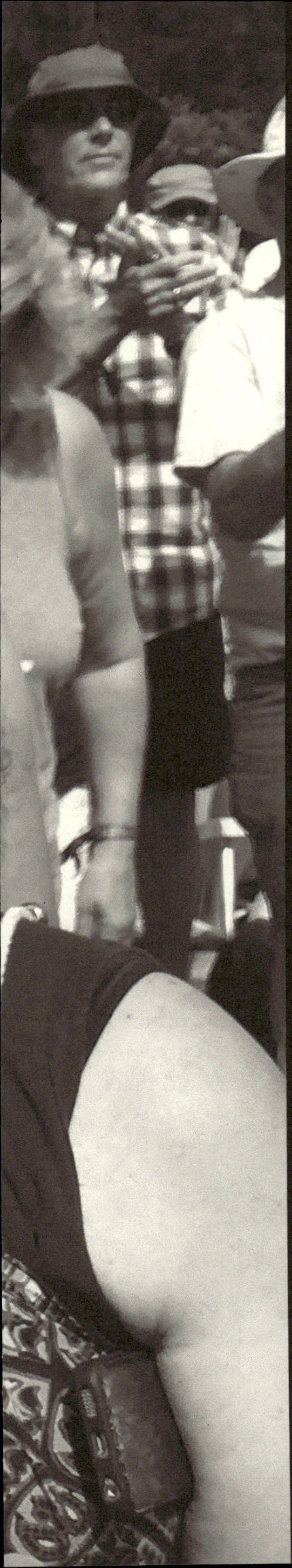

Karen DANA

Karen Dana has a social work background, but every summer she can be found at the Winnipeg Folk Festival. She began volunteering in 1978 in the backstage kitchen, advancing to the kitchen coordinator for ten years until 1994. She helped create the apprentice crew to help train young people to join various volunteer crews at the Festival. She has served on the Winnipeg Folk Festival board. In 1994, she was awarded the Winnipeg Folk Festival's Glass Banjo award for outstanding contributions to the Festival.

FIGURE 98. CANDICE MASTERS AND KAREN DANA N.D. COURTESY OF JOHN PRENTICE.

KAREN DANA

1 SEPTEMBER 2021, WINNIPEG

KEVIN NIKKEL: How are you connected to the Winnipeg Folk Festival?

KAREN DANA: I'm a long-time volunteer at the Folk Fest. I started volunteering in 1978 in the kitchen, which was then called "Harry's Eats." Run by Harry Paine, who was chef extraordinaire who happened to be a plumber that would come in every year from Toronto and run the kitchen. He was an old friend of Mitch.

When I decided to volunteer, there was room in the kitchen. I think, at that point, I probably had only cooked a Cup-a-Soup, so I was little bit nervous about going in there. I got there and I remember the first thing they did was get me to barbecue chicken. I'd never barbecued in my life. The next day, I was grilling steaks—I'd never worked with the grill before. The third day someone handed me a pot and said, "Here, go make this." And I said, "Where is the recipe?" And they said, "Just make it up." So that was kind of my introduction to the Festival. I thought, *Oh yeah, I'll do it for one year and that's it.* I stayed in the kitchen for, I think it was seventeen or eighteen years. I coordinated for my last ten years there in the kitchen. Then I retired in 1994 from the kitchen, but I'd also been on the board during different parts of it. Then, in 1995, my partner and I and Leslie Hambleton, who had been the coordinator with me in the kitchen, went and we began the apprentice crew. At the time, we placed twenty-five thirteen- to seventeen-year-olds on different crews over the course of the weekend during the Festival. It grew to 225 kids. The apprentice crew just celebrated twenty-five years and that's pretty cool.

THE APPRENTICESHIP PROGRAM AT THE FOLK FESTIVAL

KN: Can you summarize the strategy of the apprenticeship program?

KD: Well, the truth? The truth was that we were going into the backstage area and Leslie said, "There's a lot of hormones back here." Because everybody's kids had gotten older and kids that'd been really cute and little were suddenly really older and obnoxious. So, we decided we had to put them to work. That was one reason for it, but also, I remember sitting around the board table many years ago, we were like in our thirties probably at that point, and one of our dear friends, Rochelle Desroches—a long time coordinator and board member and volunteer—said, "I don't know how to say this you guys, we're not getting any younger." Who is going to take our place? Who's going to carry this on? That was one of those things that was planted. I think we'd always kind of thought we might do something like that. Then eventually the kitchen was getting bigger and bigger and my body was getting sorer and sorer. It was time to do something else. So, we retired to the apprentice crew and really built it, from kids picking up garbage, to kids working on different stages, and doing video and photography. All over the site, really. From people in the very first year saying, "Well, I don't really want a teenager."

We'd go, "Just try it. They're really enthusiastic."

Then eventually people would be saying, "About your teenagers, could I have a few more?"

And I'd say, "Oh, I'm sorry, I didn't think you wanted any!"

So, we did it very strategically. We built very, very slowly. We could easily have put 400 kids out there in jobs that people started asking for, but we really thought that 225 was manageable. In the beginning, it was just Leslie and I. Ultimately, she left when she had her daughter, who is now thirty, and started slowly taking on apprentice coordinators and training them. Ultimately, they're taking over the crew, which is great. I waited twenty-five years to pass it on.

Everybody learned the jobs that were around and I guess the other thing was that initially crews worked very much by themselves. They were entities unto themselves. People didn't really know what other crews were doing. As far as they were concerned, they were the only crews really working, and nobody else really did anything and there was a little bit of conflict. So really, what it became was an opportunity for kids to see what the different crews did.

At the beginning, we never put kids on the same crew as their parents. And, it wasn't only kids that were Festival brats—kids that only knew the Festival because they grew up at the Festival. They would bring their friends on. We would have kids from the inner city, newcomer kids, and kids from all over. Really exposing a lot of youth. Ultimately, we hoped that when they turned eighteen they'd go into a regular crew with a really good idea in terms of what they would be expected to do. Or what they didn't want to do. Some kids said, "Oh I love doing this." Or, "Please don't make me do this." We really tried to match them so that some poor little kid didn't have to go and sell raffles who couldn't open their mouth up. Kids discovered, as I did, the Cup-a-Soup maker, that I could become a really good cook, and I still love to cook. I don't think I've made Cup-a-Soup in a really long time.

JOHN PRENTICE: I think that the majority of these kids were eager. Really excelled. Did that surprise you?

KD: No. We never let any kid volunteer that we hadn't talked to. We had to interview them. We didn't want their rebellion against their parents—who would force them to be volunteers—to be that they wouldn't show up for their shift. So, we really made sure that the kids that were volunteering really wanted to volunteer and that it was their idea. Very rarely in the whole time, and I mean we interviewed hundreds of thousands of kids, maybe one or two didn't work out. Because they were really motivated, they really wanted to do it, and they were really excited. They also got to know each other from all over. They got to be really good friends, just as we did within the volunteer organization. Long-time friends for me and that was really good.

Kids came up to me from the time they were seven and would say, "Karen, only five or six more years and then I'll be on." So, it really became something that they wanted to do. We made a big hoopla, too. We always went around touring the site, and you can imagine how twenty kids grew to thirty, to fifty, to 225 kids wandering around the site was quite a sight to behold. Mitch would often just come and welcome everyone.

KN: I love the idea of that conversation of "we're not getting younger." How do we preserve what we've built? Before that conversation, what was the attitude like? Was there a fear that people weren't going to continue?

KD: I think we always thought we'd see everybody again next year. I mean, Harry Paine would always say to us, "Well this is my last year. I won't see you guys next year."

We were like, "Okay, this is your annual goodbye. Harry, we'll see you next year, and I will pick you up at the airport." Whatever. Even though we weren't sure, I think we always thought that we'd be back there. You know, there's just such a magic to the Festival that you just wanted to preserve it. You wanted to keep it going. We all did the bottle drives, the bucket brigades, the garage sales, the millions of raffle tickets, the calendars. As board members, we felt like all our friends were walking the other way whenever you'd approach because we'd constantly be fundraising. We never knew if things would continue, but we always believed that it would. Just because we couldn't imagine life without it. I think that was a very strong motivator for all of us. Whatever they asked us to do, we did. We never got asked anything that was—well—there were some outrageous things, but nonetheless, you knew that it was for the greater good.

You wanted to make the experience of everybody that was at the Festival the best that it could be. I learned that at Mitch's funeral, because the rabbi was also a coordinator of volunteers for one crew, and he said that Mitch always would come to their crew meeting and say, "This is the most important crew of the Festival."

I remember sitting there going, "He said that to you guys? That's what he said to us. We're the most important!" He needed to make sure that nobody thought theirs was a slug job. Everything that everybody did, from putting toilet paper into the outhouses, to chopping a million chickpeas, putting face paint on kids' faces, to putting up a fence post, or whatever—that every single job was for the greater good to make sure that we had the best possible festival for the performers, the audience, and the volunteers. It was something that we all wanted to do. Something we all still want to do. We just have to stretch a lot more now than we did at the beginning.

ON THE BOARD OF THE WINNIPEG FOLK FESTIVAL

KN: You're a board member?

KD: I was.

KN: I'm curious about what the conversation was like at the board level. There must have been times where you were thinking, *I wonder if we can pull this off again.*

KD: We were always concerned. We never knew for sure. And of course, as a board member—I think I was on the board for about nine or ten years and I remember being terrified every time I saw the clouds out. I remember not being on the board the first year that it rained and I went, "I'm so glad I'm not on the board right now!" Just because I didn't have to worry about it for the first time. I didn't have to find out what the numbers were at the gate. I didn't have to find out how many tickets presold, or anything like that. I could just focus on what my job was at the site.

But certainly, I met people from all walks of life. One of Mitch's big things—I think there was thirty-three people on the board—we all got a chance to talk. When Mitch was on [the board], we listened to him a lot and there would be times the board meetings would go till like one o'clock in the morning. I remember breastfeeding my son out on the balcony at one o'clock in the morning as I'm listening to what's going on because we were hearing about stuff. My son is thirty-five now, so that was a few years ago.

We believed that it was going to continue. We prayed a lot. There were times that we couldn't pay some of the bills. I remember I used to duck through a small town near the Festival because we had bought some things we couldn't pay for at the beginning, and so I was worried that they were going to come out and accost me in my car and say, "Karen, you haven't paid our bill!"

But I think seeing the Festival thrive and continue has been really exciting. There were times along the way that it was pretty scary. We were young. We didn't know. It was the first board I'd ever been on. I thought they all functioned like that.

KN: They probably do. Do you think individuals shaped the Folk Fest?

JP: My long-standing memory of Karen is seeing her holding a bucket with tears streaming down her face.

KD: Obviously Mitch shaped the Festival and all the artistic directors after, and all the different people that coordinated in different areas. It wasn't just volunteers and performers and staff. It was also people in the Handmade Village, that just became their thing. We started things but continued on from there and built on them.

One of the things I can talk specifically about is the kitchen. Mitch felt that if you fed the performers well and made them feel like kings, they would get on stage and do an amazing show. He vowed that he would never give a stale bologna sandwich—like they did at the Philadelphia Folk Fest—to the people at the Winnipeg Folk Fest. And we heard the bologna sandwich story every year at our meetings. We were committed to not having a bologna sandwich. I don't think we ever actually served bologna.

I think there was just this basic idea that we did the best we possibly could. I remember the health inspector coming and making sure that everything was okay. And they'd say, "Where is your mayonnaise?"

We said, "We don't serve things with mayonnaise because we don't want any of our performers to get sick." We couldn't guarantee that it would be stored properly, so there were certain things we just kept away from. Through the years, we built different relationships on the food end. In town, there were people who would let us use their commercial kitchens to do precooked meals. Lots of people just kind of wanted to be a part of this in some way, to be able to contribute, because the Festival really developed an amazing reputation.

When I think people initially thought that it was all a bunch of dope-smoking hippies that sat around and did nothing, and no doubt that was a part it, but there was also a million other people that were working their butts off to make sure that what came on the stage went off without a hitch, or at least it seemed that way to the audience. They didn't know we were scrambling in the background. It just looked like it was well run and it was always a really clean Festival. We had somebody to do a job for everything.

I mean, we used to have to time plugging in the coffeemaker so we wouldn't set off the Main Stage breaker because they were all together. We had one electrical pole at the beginning. So, "Okay, we'll make sure that all the coffee is made by 6:00 am because then they have to do sound check and we might blow the fuse again and we got in trouble yesterday." Okay. You did it. Half the time, we didn't even realize that we were in the middle of a field, and everything we were doing was miraculous.

STAFF

Jon SINGLETON

Jon Singleton was the past Provincial Auditor General of Manitoba, but he can be described as an accountant that really enjoys folk music. He began volunteering with the Winnipeg Folk Festival in the site office, helping coordinate ticket sales and helping Mitch sort out the budgets. He joined the Board of the Winnipeg Folk Festival and acted as treasurer from 1978 to 1987. In 1997, he was awarded the Winnipeg Folk Festival's Glass Banjo award for outstanding contributions to the Festival. He was also appointed a lifetime Honorary Board Member.

FIGURE 99. BEHIND THE SCENES FOLK FESTIVAL STAFF, 1977. PHOTOGRAPH BY DAVID LANDY. ARCHIVES OF MANITOBA, WINNIPEG FOLK FESTIVAL 1977 NEGATIVES, P2566/5, 77/5. BETWEEN 6–7.

JON SINGLETON

8 SEPTEMBER 2021, WINNIPEG

KEVIN NIKKEL: What is your connection to the Folk Festival?

JON SINGLETON: When the first festival came along, I'd just quit teaching high school and hadn't decided what to do with myself. I escaped to Europe for a year. Decided I want to be an accountant. So, I was enrolled in a chartered accountancy program, but I loved folk music, and music in general, so I was excited for the opportunity to go out with my wife and attend the first one.

After that, my sister-in-law invited me to help them in the second year keep track of the food vendors. They'd come up with what would be, today, quite a crazy arrangement with these food vendors, which was that they were supposed to keep track of their sales and pay a certain percentage to the Folk Festival. Of course, that's an accounting nightmare. Also, it relies pretty heavily on trust. The situation was hard to keep track of things. I was asked if I would visit the vendor from time to time to show that we were actually watching them and trying to make sure that they were getting everything they needed, and making sure they were keeping track of sales.

KN: What was it like when you showed up? Did they hide the money?

JS: Some of them resented it because they felt, *We're honest people. We don't want to steal here. We don't need somebody checking up on us* and they were busy and didn't want someone getting in their way. I played it pretty low-key when we recognized that we had to deal together. They had services to provide and provide money to us for being there. It's fine. I had to be delicate with them because of the situation they were in. It was a big gamble—would they make any money?

MITCH PODOLAK

KN: Do you remember what it was like when you first met Mitch?

JS: I would say he's a character different from practically anybody else I'd met up until that moment in my life. He was very gracious. He was also desperate. You could tell he was under a lot of stress because the Festival was on pretty fragile financial ground at the time. The odds of it being around for very long were low. This was a key thing for him. In the case of my own little project monitoring the food vendors, he was very gracious. He said, "I'm not an accountant." I wasn't either at that point, I was just a baby accountant, in first or second year of my program. He just said, "You figure it out. And do whatever you think needs to be done." That was as far as the guidance went. The goal was to make sure the Festival didn't get ripped off from the vendors.

KN: So, there is a sense of urgency. That this might not happen next year.

JS: Yes, that's right. This is the second Festival. Eventually I was elected to the Board of Directors as treasurer. Basically, my career for approximately ten years as treasurer was trying to help keep the Festival afloat. We were really on edge almost every year for the first decade or so. People loved the music, the crowds were reasonable, but not as good as we needed to be financially self-sufficient. So, starting from the beginning of the get-go, okay, we're on the edge here. We need to do everything we can to keep going. Deal with all the threats that were there.

KN: What were some of the conversations you were having with Mitch? Were you coming up with ideas?

JS: He came up with lots of ideas. It became up to him and a couple paid staff members, Hal Doran and Bill Merritt, who were the business managers when they got hired. I can't remember exactly when they started.

Okay, so we got rained out this year, and we don't have enough money to pay our suppliers. We can't pay the people that supplied the sound equipment. We can't pay the people that supplied the porta-potties. We can't pay anybody. But he always had one cardinal rule that we all had to live by, which was that all the performers would get paid, no matter what. That was our first responsibility, to make sure that those who were presenting the music got their money. Nobody got anything until they got paid. We were able to do that from day one. Sometimes we had to say, "Okay, dear sound and lighting people, we can't pay you. But we need you to come back again next year." We needed to negotiate what our arrangement would be. So, typically he would work out a deal. He'd pay twenty-five percent say, fifty percent of what we owed them, with the promise that they would have a contract for the next year. And if it didn't rain, we'd get caught up. So, he was very heavily involved in that kind of strategy to keep the Festival afloat.

He also organized getting a bunch of volunteers to go around and collect beer bottles. Sometimes we'd passed a pot around amongst the audience to get them to donate some extra money. Mitch's goal was always to do everything we can to get enough cash to get from one festival to the next.

OVERCOMING ADVERSITY

KN: So, it's a matter of a household on the poverty line. Sorry kids, it's bread and water again. Were there any vendors or suppliers who said, "We can't do this?" Or threats of lawsuits?

JS: I don't remember it getting ugly. They weren't always happy, but they were there for the rain, too. They could see the fact that there weren't enough people attending the Festival to pay for all its bills. So, it wasn't a surprise to them. They were certainly hesitant about, should they invest more money by doing it again, when they hadn't been paid the first time. Or, hadn't been paid the second time, and now we're going to do it a third time. Could they trust the Festival to come through? It was a bit of a gamble for them, too. So that's where I think it was primarily Mitch, but also Bill and Hal, who had a charm that could persuade them to help out. And make heartfelt promises to do our best to make them whole at the end of the day.

KN: What were your conversations like with Mitch, when you knew there was a chance of rain?

JS: One of Mitch's famous sayings was, "Man plans, God decides." Something like that. Okay, all we can do is what we can do. The weather is beyond our control. But we should put the Festival on, regardless. So, we had to plan for the rain. At least the music experience would be there. And he'd remind us that all the performers had to be paid. I can remember one year particularly—I think it was either the second or third in a row that rain had significantly hurt takings, or attendance—Pete Seeger was one of the headline performers. At that time, one of my jobs was paying the performers who wanted to be paid on-site. That could be turned into a negotiation, too, because we paid by cheque, and they were thinking, *when I get back home to Minneapolis, will the money be in the bank? Would you mind giving me cash to take back, preferably U.S. dollars?* But when it came time to pay Pete Seeger, he'd been there a couple days and he could tell we didn't have any money to speak of. He donated his fee to the Festival on the spot. That was always a very generous gesture, and every little bit helped.

KN: That's a great story. You were also on the board. What were the conversations like, around the table as treasurer? Did you have to keep Mitch on a leash? Bring him back to the ground? He dreams big.

JS: He does. I saw that as a key part of my role. It was trying to work with him to find out what a working arrangement could be, for what he could live with as the artistic director. What did I think the board could live with in terms of the level of risk we could take? I remember him telling us one board meeting, I basically said to them, "Well okay, Mitch's role is to book the Festival. It's his job to book one that he believes will be successful, both artistically and financially. If he wants to hire all left-handed guitar players for some reason, that's not a board decision, that's the artistic director [decision]." If ultimately the board doesn't like the artistic direction, they have to make a decision, if they want to stay with the artistic director or get a new person. But our job as the board is to set what is a realistic financial budget. How much do we think we can afford to spend, based on what we think is a likely attendance if it doesn't rain? Then there was tension. Should we assume it will rain? But if we did that, we wouldn't have a festival. If we did that, we'd be left not having money to hire musicians to attract people to come anyway. You'd lose either way. So, you had to trust the weather would be reasonable and set a budget on that basis. It was always a very tough conversation with Mitch and the board—what is the right number? We always sorted it out.

The next part of my job was to keep track of what was being spent. So where is that money coming from? Mitch was more of a dreamer and had a fabulous knowledge of the music and the people that produced music, but he wasn't that keen on the details. Especially financial details. That was basically my role. But he did also drag me directly in to help deal with unpaid suppliers. Not very often, but

CKAL 1070
Ed
The Perfect Union
SBN

a particular one he wanted me to deal with was Revenue Canada because we didn't have enough money. We barely had enough money to pay staff. Sometimes house staff would go for six or seven months without a paycheque. They were donating their time on the promise that one day there would be enough money to pay them back, with some interest on that. In the meantime, they understood there wasn't money. But we did pay them, and of course there were deductions for Canada Pension Plan and Employment Insurance and income taxes. We didn't have enough to pay Revenue Canada for the deductions, so we decided, well at least we'll pay the staff their net pay and try to hold out on Revenue Canada. Ultimately it took us about three years, but Revenue Canada would phone us and say, "You know you have a legal obligation to pay this. It's not your money, it's the employee's money deducted from their cheque. You should pay it to us."

I said, "Well yes, you're right. And we will do that. Eventually. But right now, what you're asking me to choose, should I pay my staff at the Festival, or should I pay you. Our staff are living on very low wages as it is. We've gone for a long while without being able to pay them, too. So, my choice is, I'm going to pay the staff. I'll make you a promise that we will pay you back eventually." So, Revenue Canada actually listened to that and were patient and eventually we did pay them all back, plus interest, and penalties. I hadn't expected to get into those conversations when I first started volunteering as treasurer, but there it was.

KN: That's a great story. Another question about Mitch. How would you describe him, in relation to you and your personality? Was he a glass half full or glass half empty kind of guy? What role did you play in conversations together?

WORKING WITH MITCH AND THE VOLUNTEERS

JS: We were able to build a lot of trust between the two of us. He really counted on me to take care of the books. There were staff hired to do the bookkeeping but he was counting on me to oversee that,

FIGURE 100. MUSICIAN AND AUDIENCE AT WINNIPEG FOLK FESTIVAL, 1979. PHOTOGRAPH BY DAVID LANDY. ARCHIVES OF MANITOBA, WINNIPEG FOLK FESTIVAL 1979 NEGATIVES, P5266/9, 79/289.

make sure what we were doing was legal and was reasonable. Where we would get into tension sometimes would be around the budget and how much should be spent on this and how much we should spend on that. He and I would present it together to the Board of Directors, to get the budget approved. He was glad to have someone, that he could rely on to take care of that part, so he could spend more time dealing with the music and technical issues and artists and putting together a show that people would want to come and see. I couldn't do that for the life of me—that was not one of my talents. But I can certainly appreciate it in him. I think he could appreciate what I could bring to the table with the financial stability. So, they [the Festival] could carry on indefinitely in the future.

KN: The Festival has obviously grown. You were there for part of the rise on the graph. Was that part of the vision back then? Any five-year plans, or was it just something that happened?

JS: I think Mitch, and the subsequent artistic directors as well, all had ideas of what it could be in an ideal world. I believe that Mitch had a vision it could become what it is today. I think it was frustrating that he couldn't get there faster or that it just didn't happen.

I think that was one of the things that I'd say was very unique. He had a great way of being able to persuade other people that this vision made sense and you should come along for the ride and be a part of building something that nobody had really seen before. The way that it's done in Winnipeg makes it one of the premier folk festivals in North America and I think that's what we all were hoping to be able to accomplish. But Mitch was a visionary, he could also express it in a way that sounds like something that would be worthwhile for me to spend time and effort helping to make happen. He found people from all over the place with different talents and different backgrounds needed to create the very complex Festival that it is now.

KN: From your role as an accountant, you have a different view because you look at spreadsheets. You read the Festival from a numbers perspective. Do you think what happened here is unique compared to elsewhere?

JS: I think Winnipeg is pretty special, in some ways. We're kind of isolated here in the middle of the prairies, hundreds of miles from another major metropolis, and it's very cold. I think it all contributes to the feeling amongst Winnipeggers that, well, we're all in this together. I think a lot of people are persuaded to give money or give of their time and expertise. They could listen to Mitch talk about it and make up in their own minds what kind of vision would make sense. I do think the personality and culture of Winnipeg made it possible. If it wasn't for 1,000 volunteers and hundreds of suppliers and hundreds of musicians that were willing to travel here that were not 100-percent sure of getting paid in the first decade of the Festival. Though they'd all heard the stories of how the Festival had never not paid anybody, so that always gave them comfort, but that had to be built up. That kind of trust. I think this is the coming together of forces. I don't think even Mitch knew that. But he found it here and was able to build on it here.

KN: Was there anything from your days with the books that you really dreaded? Having to call a particular vendor about toilet paper or something like that?

JS: I didn't have to get involved in that very much. That was Hal Doran or Bill Merritt. Or sometimes Mitch. I did have sometimes painful discussions with Mitch about what the attendance was. One of my jobs during the Festival every day was to give him updates on the attendance. Here is what we budgeted, here's where we're at. Sometimes the gap was pretty big. So, it was very unhappy news to pass on to him. But, of course, he could see the weather, too, so he knew that was not good news.

KN: Walk me through the conversation you'd have with Mitch about the numbers. Was there a routine or ritual of where you knew to find him? Did he avoid you?

JS: No. But I did have to find him. We didn't have a meeting because it was in the early days of the Festival. We hired an outside firm to run the box office for us. This was another Mitch brainwave. He got concerned they weren't giving us all the money that we were entitled to. I have no idea whether that's true or not, but he asked me, "Do you think we could run our own box office with volunteers?" So then one of the *other duties as assigned* as treasurer is designing a volunteer-run box office operation that would have good internal controls. So, the volunteers and everyone were protected and all the cash that'd come in was accounted for and balanced against ticket sales. That probably took us two or three years to get to the point where it was humming along nicely.

We did have one incident where someone had misplaced a whole box of wristbands that were tickets. One of the ways I estimated sales was to count—we have this many wristbands and we have this many left, so the rest must have been sold. With this misplaced box I then thought they'd been sold. So, I said, "Okay Mitch, a really nice number for our attendance!" And two hours later I had to go back and tell him, "Ah Mitch, I'm afraid that really nice number is a lot less than I told you." He was not very happy about that. It wasn't one of my more pleasant experiences with him. It was a fact. So, we all had to live with it. I didn't feel good about having raised his hopes and then dashing them. I would have avoided that if I possibly could have.

KN: When you were walking around the Festival, could you enjoy yourself? Or were you just counting heads the whole time? Did you enjoy it?

JS: I did. I guess the first year we ran the box office I lived at the box office for most of the time. By the second and third years [the Festival] was starting to build up a cadre of volunteers that knew what they were doing and kept coming back. So, I could let that go for a while and go enjoy the music. That was important to me, too. I wasn't doing it because I didn't love music. And there were a lot of performers that I wanted to see. Most of the time I would be able to get out and enjoy the Festival as well. We made the promise to our volunteers to work so many hours and the rest of the time you could go and enjoy the Festival.

THE "SAD STORY BOOK"

KN: Was there a problem with people sneaking into the Festival?

JS: A major problem we had at the box office was people who said they paid in advance and hadn't got their tickets. We ended up creating for the crew what we called our "Sad Story Book," which we actually saved from year to year. The crew chiefs would take down all the details of the people and write down their sad story of how they didn't get the tickets. Probably 99 percent of the time we said, "Well you're going to have to buy your tickets because we can't verify this here today. But here is our "Sad Story Book," and after the Festival, we will take it back and check the record book and we will send you a refund, if, in fact, you paid twice." Of course, some people didn't like that, or were angry, and a lot of people who came to the Festival didn't have much money themselves. The ticket price for coming to the Festival was a big deal, and if you had to travel from the States or another province, it was often a sad hit to have to come up with another fifty or hundred dollars to get in to the Festival. But we learned. None of us had experience with that. How can you deal with people under that situation? The "Sad Story Book" even became famous with people coming in line.

They'd say, "I've got a story for your 'Sad Story Book,' would you mind writing it down for me. Here is all my contact information. If there was any way you can solve this, that would be great, if not I'll buy my tickets and trust you to get back to me with a refund." It's too easy to say, I lost my ticket can I get in? You can't run a festival by giving out free tickets.

KN: Was there a problem with people sneaking in and hopping the fence?

JS: Yes, there were in the early years, but it seemed to fade off over time. I don't know if you remember the Festival Express train tour with Janis Joplin and a few other people. When it performed in Winnipeg, it was a one-day concert. There were actual crowds outside chanting that they wanted to come in because festivals should be free. There was that whole subculture out there that said, "We shouldn't have to pay for this, it should be a public good." Mitch would make a reasonable argument that performers have to eat, too, and earn a living. They created the music and they should benefit from it. Look at all these people here supplying lighting, supplying sound, providing security, all those things cost money. Somebody has to pay for it. From my perspective, it was a kind of a carryover from that feeling that these concerts should be free. A lot of people tried to get in free. It was pretty ugly sometimes, in the early days.

JOHN PRENTICE: Lorna mentioned that she'd shame people into buying a ticket. When the fence went up.

JS: I think at one point there were parts where, if you were trying to get over the fence, you wouldn't be able to walk there without walking through poison ivy. [Laughs] A little bit of discouragement there. We did have some pretty strong people. I don't remember when they started hiring these off-duty police officers to help with the security.

JP: Thinking about how an accountant estimates the value of volunteers—were they ever in the books? The 2,000 volunteers in the 1980s? Does that factor in as the monetary value of the volunteers, if you had to pay them?

JS: An economic analysis had been done in the past, to show what the Folk Festival contributes financially to the economy of Manitoba. And according to that analysis, the contribution is much bigger than the funding that comes from government. You can make a pretty good case that it's in the government's interest to keep having the Festival because it is an economic driver. As well as an artistic driver, it's good for the reputation of the province from a music and artistic point of view, but it is also good for the province, financially.

JP: Did you help determine the number they wanted to reach for fundraising every year?

JS: No. I didn't really get involved in that. Part of my job was to deal with outside auditors. Often when you ask people for funds, they often want to see the audited financial statements. That made it very important for the Festival to have good-enough accounting records that if the auditors looked at it they could say yes, these are the right numbers, and show funding partners.

This triggers another story, not really related to fundraising, but related to financial health. After two or three years of rainy festivals we had reached the end of the patience of our banker. One of the ways we got through the winter was cash flow money from the bank. Then our plan was to pay them back from proceeds of the Festival. But after two or three years of not being able to pay them back and having to say, "Can we roll that over and, by the way, can you bump it up so we can get through another winter?"

They said, "Well, no. We can't do that anymore. We think the risk to us is too high." So, we had a long, painful discussion with them and ultimately, they said, "Well, if you can get enough members of the Board to sign a promissory note, where they are personally going to promise to contribute up to $10,000 if the Festival goes bankrupt to pay off this loan, then we'll consider it." That was one of the jobs I had, to go back to the Board and say okay, we're at a cliff here. Board members are volunteers, they all have their own financial challenges, for some of them what they're being asked to do here is way beyond their means. We can't ask them to do that. For some, that's a risk they'd rather not take. Some were willing to take it. At the end of the day, we were able to get enough board members to agree. Part of it was adding to one of the promises of what we're going to do with the money we're going to get. We had a long-standing rule, performers always get paid, but I said rule number two is, this debt will get paid next. So that is something that I can do to lower the risk on this so we never have to honour this promissory note. I think that went on for about three years. It was a tough hole we were digging out of, but eventually we got that removed. The books are in good enough shape now. We'll let that go. I think that was the lowest point, financially.

F.O.H
LEVON HELM
Carpet
KEY
JAN
TYSON
MATT
BRIANNA
JESSE
LEN
EVERYONE
STRIKE NOTES
TAKE WHAT YOU
BROUGHT ON
Then STRIKE ALL
OFF THE
WINNIPEG
folk
FESTIVAL 2007
VOLUNTEER

Martin LANDY

Martin Landy has had a lengthy career in community development and seniors' advocacy—but he also has a passion for music and helping backstage. Martin's interest in sound and stages is likely because he spent so much time helping his photographer father, David Landy, carry camera bags around events like the Winnipeg Folk Festival. Martin began as a guest on-site and eventually stayed to work on volunteer crews. He helped coordinate the Main Stage crew at the Winnipeg Festival for seven years (2006 to 2013). He has also spent twenty years as Main Stage manager for the Calgary Folk Festival, assisted with the Vancouver Folk Festival stages, and held special event management roles for the Royal and Papal visits to Manitoba, Expo 86, and the 1988 Calgary Olympics.

FIGURE 101. MARTIN LANDY BACK STAGE, 2007. COURTESY OF MARTIN LANDY.

MARTIN LANDY

19 JANUARY 2020, WINNIPEG

DAVE BARBER: Can you introduce yourself and share how you are connected to the Folk Festival?

MARTIN LANDY: My name is Martin Landy, I am the son of David Usher Landy. David was the first unofficial photographer for the Winnipeg Folk Festival. He was there in the very beginning. I was his camera-bag-holder for many years, and that got me sort of into the folk festival circuit that way.

DB: How did he become involved in the Folk Festival?

ML: David was a photographer for the provincial government. His job was to photograph events, people, and activities for the province that would be used in a variety of ways. He loved photography. He volunteered his time. When the Folk Festival came up the very first year, he went out as the governmental photographer to record the event, and he just loved it. He loved the people, the musicians, the atmosphere, and for the next several years he was *the* photographer. He was the very first one on the crew and unofficially developed the whole photography crew because people were trying to keep up with him.

DB: You became his assistant?

ML: I was his son. I carried his camera bag. I really wasn't a photographer at the time, but he needed help carrying things to and from because we didn't know what the experience was going to be from year to year. I was just always hanging out with my dad.

DB: How old would you have been back then?

ML: I think I would've been probably sixteen in the beginning of it. My dad became a photographer when I was thirteen. I had about four years of carrying gear.

FIGURE 102. PHOTOGRAPHER DAVID LANDY, N.D. COURTESY OF MARTIN LANDY.

KEVIN NIKKEL: What years would that have been?

ML: 1974. It would have been 1969 when he started as a government photographer. He worked other jobs till then. I was eleven when he got that job.

DB: Do you have a sense of what made your father's photographs so good?

ML: He had a wonderful eye. The pictures are the end result. It's the vision of what he saw. My dad could see something very simple and capture it. One of his favourite Folk Fest photographs was the little kid who put his hand in the tuba. Something he saw just simply wandering around. He never looked at this like, I need a cover shot, I need this type of shot. He went with the moment. He could sense what was going on. He had just a really good eye. And they were simple [photographs]. Very simple black-and-white. One person, one element.

DB: It's interesting that he went back to the Festival every year. They must have liked what he did.

ML: He was easy. He volunteered his time. All the film went to the government. He was shooting for them. What he got out of it was the camaraderie and the experience. The pictures were his "in" to it all. If you ever see a picture of David, it's always with cameras around his neck, a big hat and a smile. He was in his element there.

DB: Are there any specific performers that he really favoured from the Folk Festival?

ML: There are so many stories I have from so many festivals it all gets mixed up. I know he and Stan Rogers got along really well. He was really affected when Stan died. Odetta, she just touched everybody. You touch her and she senses who you are, there's a connection. He really didn't have favourites, he enjoyed the whole thing. It was just hanging out, being a part of it, seeing it, listening to the music. Being a part of something bigger.

DB: Do you have any early memories of those days at the Festival? The musicians?

ML: Oh yeah. It was just so wonderful. He was a very comfortable person. He got along with people so he was always a part of whatever we were at. Whether it was backstage at the Ballet, or the Symphony, or the Folk Festival. He just enjoyed the people. I met a lot of incredible performers before I realized who they were. From David Amram, Sam Chatmon, Odetta, Leon Redbone, Buffy Sainte-Marie—these were people that we would just sit and chat with.

DB: Any memories of those performers?

ML: Sam Chatmon, Redbone, and David Amram. I mean, they were just unforgettable performers. They were so charismatic and there was no sense of ego. They were performers, they were with other performers, that was the beauty of the backstage. That's why I could never be an audience member of the Festival, or a large event, because I knew the camaraderie and the special life that was backstage.

DB: So, you saw a different side?

ML: Oh, very different. It was so much fun. My mother, who's 104 years old, still talks about how she would take her knitting and sit in the green room and listen to all the jam sessions and all the performers would come and chat with her. It was just, everybody was friendly with everybody, there was no hierarchy.

MITCH PODOLAK'S VISION

DB: Any memories of Mitch?

ML: Yeah. I have a double connection to the Festival, through my dad in the beginning, but when I came back to Winnipeg in 1982 I was at the Festival with my dad and I ran into somebody who was the production manager who eventually became my wife. I had a real tight feeling with that whole family. With Mitch, Rosalie, Bill Merritt, Valdean, Lindsay. That was when the Festival was in its infancy, for me. We were all a big family. We'd just do everything together. I ended up doing audio for the Winnipeg Folk Festival's Sunday at the Norwood. I would do all the audio for the Winnipeg Folk Festival concerts that they had at the WAG [Winnipeg Art Gallery]. We were at everybody's house, always barbecuing. I babysat Bill Merritt's kids for years. It was just a real wonderful environment.

DB: Do you have any sense of how the Folk Festival developed? I heard stories about how there was incredible rain. They were in debt. They overcame these hardships.

ML: Tenacity, really. Mitch had a vision. He had a good crew around him. Rosalie, Bill, they really believed in the vision, and Mitch was tenacious. He wouldn't let go of something. He had the contacts in the power ring, so he could get an ear in there and it made a huge difference. It was a time when Winnipeg as a city was looking for something that would make it different than all the others. This truly was a Festival that was different, unlike any folk festival in Canada. Anybody who has done the circuit knows that all the festivals are different. They all have that vibe wherever they are. Edmonton being urban in the city. Vancouver being out on the water. Toronto being on the island. They all had that whole sense of the village. But Winnipeg was known as the granddaddy of them all.

VOLUNTEERING AT THE FOLK FESTIVAL

DB: And you started to volunteer there?

ML: Yeah, I started volunteering in Winnipeg on side stage crew. I was doing side stages and it was just so much fun. I learned that from my dad. It was about the people you work with and that shared experience. I worked with such wonderful people on the side stage—Jonathan Austman, Shawn Kettner, Peter Harrison—we were all sort of that group together and started doing side stages. It was fun too, listening to the music and watching the backstage.

DB: You're talking about the workshop stages?

ML: Yeah, I started on workshop stages in the beginning. So, that was early 1980s until I left, about 1986. I was working there, just hanging out. Funny thing was, in all the years I went to the Folk Festival, it was my very last year, the first time ever when I went into the campground. I was never in the campground in twenty-some-odd years at the Folk Festivals. Once I was there, I realized why I didn't. [Laughs]

DB: [Laughs]

ML: I like the peace and quiet of the backstage.

KN: Can you describe a little bit of the setup? When you first arrive as a volunteer—you're there before everything. What does it look like, when there is nothing there and then once they start constructing a festival?

ML: Birds Hill Park is a wonderful site, but there is a lot of field and trees. You don't realize where you are until fence-day starts. Fence-day is when we start putting in the exterior fence and the Folk Festival site gains its shape. Main Stage in this area, which just looked like a huge field until the structure starts to come up. I would be involved primarily four to five days before the Festival started, setting up the Main Stage. I would be involved in the planning stage—lights, sound, where things would go. I would arrive early in the week, when they're just putting the deck up. All of a sudden, from the field comes a deck. From a deck then comes a shelter. From the shelter then comes the lighting structure and the sound and that gets put from that. Then we put in the backdrop, from there, then we're putting in ramps, stairs, and then we'd need lights. In terms of backstage lights, all of the glow tape, so performers can see their way around the back. We set up the side-stage for where all the gear goes. We built a living village in four to five days.

When the Winnipeg Folk Festival went to starting on Wednesday, the Main Stage crew was probably one of the busiest and longest-running crews because we started on the Monday building the backstage, having it up and running. It was a herculean job. That was probably the toughest year we ever had, with Elvis Costello. It was wonderful, but it takes a lot to build and run that village.

I can only tell you about the twenty to thirty people who were responsible for building the Main Stage. Putting the lights and sound in there. Then we would come in and then needle them for the final things. Like, we need washers for hanging that sliding barn door every year to get it rehung. We'd have to put in all the backstage lights and railings in. We'd have to finesse things after all the raw structure was put up. In the end, the audience never knew what was going on. It just looked so homey.

DB: How critical are those volunteers?

ML: The Folk Festival is built on volunteers. It was all built on, here's an idea, this is what we want to do. Mitch had a vision and he got people to believe. They put their heart and soul into it. It's all about camaraderie. The volunteers, the first production meetings when people get together, everybody's just so happy to see each other. They haven't seen everybody over the long, cold winter. We've been isolated. The volunteers are your family. You look forward to seeing the same people that you work with, or the interaction with the other crews. I get to see my friends on the schlep crew versus those who would be in administration. You walk around and it's like, "Hi, how are you? How is your mom? How is your brother?" It was wonderful. That's what made it a unique experience because everybody appreciated the fact that we were all volunteers. All the egos were left at the door. We're all there to do the job. A job we loved. It was never work; it was always fun.

KN: Talk about the importance of Harry Paine's food for crew.

ML: Crew runs on food! Volunteers need sustenance. Especially when you're running long hours. And the Winnipeg Folk Festival had the best cuisine ever. It started out roasting pigs and feeding people a good, hearty, earthy meal. And to this day it still manages to feed thousands of people a good amount of food. We never went hungry. We were always able to access food when we needed. And in the end, it started coming to us.

I remember the roasting of a pig. They'd have all the barbecues and the smokers out so in the backstage so you could smell it. You knew what was coming. There was always a desire of, what are you going to get today? It was never like, "My God, I got slop on a plate?" Never that. Harry set the bar so high and did it for so many years.

SETTING UP AND TEARING THINGS DOWN

DB: You must've seen the Festival grow enormously from the early days.

ML: Oh yeah. From first raw tent structures which were just the canvas canopies on poles, to actually building the stages. The permanent stages and the roof systems that went in. We went from low-tech scaffolds to all these rigging systems that would come in. Also, how technology shrank everything. I remember Christy Wigston climbing up on scaffolding to fix lights and adjust them—now they're all motorized, you just hang them and focus. It makes it so much easier technically and gives you such a great show. It's different. It was fun to watch it grow. You don't really realize it, just as we grow old. I still remember the Folk Festival as being a simple get-together. Get in my camper and sleep. Get up the next day and work. It was five days of my life that happened every year. Year after year.

KN: You did a great job of describing the setup. What happened after the last encore? Take us through the decrescendo.

ML: So, it's the finale. The last act is on. They finish and we all come on for "Kumbaya." It was always a surreal experience for me because I have to stage manage the "Kumbaya" moment where everybody comes on and sings, and all the crew members and everybody who lives at the Festival but never gets to actually stand on the Main Stage, be recognized and they get to see for the first time what I see the whole Festival. It's a very lovely moment. A lot of people are very emotional at it. Then they finish the last song and everybody leaves. Everybody's hugging and really enjoying what they just pulled off. Then we start wrapping cable.

We would have to clear the mics. We have to basically deconstruct all of that gear that went up. All the mic stands. All the cables. All the equipment. All the gear has to come off. We would clear everything so we're back to just a bare stage of walls, tables, and chairs. It looks ghostly, because an hour before all of that, we were in the midst of this beautiful moment and performers and everybody knows that a beautiful Sunday night at the Folk Festival is a sight to be seen. Then it's just the remnants. It's like a bomb had hit and everything that's breathing is gone and all you're left with are the structures. It is a very surreal thing, especially when it's like two or three in the morning. You've been there since eight in the morning. We always celebrated as a crew afterwards—a job well done. Nobody knows that we're there. The best thing about a festival is that nobody knows that any of the production is going on. They're so captivated with what's happening onstage. We always took real pride in that.

DB: When did David retire from taking pictures at the Folk Fest?

ML: His health got in the way. I would say probably late 1990s, he started to slow down. I think 2000 was probably his last Festival that he attended. He had a heart problem and diabetes, so walking became difficult. He carried two or three cameras and walked miles and miles. The Festival is everywhere in our house. The pictures on the wall, to the golden banjo in the window. It was never a start-and-stop thing. It was just a part of our lives.

DB: Did he ever have a showing of his photographs?

FIGURE 103. MUSICIAN ON STAGE AT WINNIPEG FOLK FESTIVAL, 1979. PHOTOGRAPH BY DAVID LANDY. ARCHIVES OF MANITOBA, WINNIPEG FOLK FESTIVAL 1979 NEGATIVES, P5266/9, 79/341.

ML: No, he never did that. His pride wouldn't allow it! It took Sheldon Oberman to get things started and go with *The Folk Festival Book*. That was something we had to get him to do kicking and dragging because he didn't want to have any recognition.

PART SIX

SETTING THE STAGE: An Affectionate Look Back and Look Forward

FIGURE 104. ROOSEVELT SYKES ON A WORKSHOP STAGE, 1974. PHOTOGRAPH BY JOHN BACHMANN. COURTESY OF WINNIPEG FOLK FESTIVAL.

John PRENTICE

John Prentice is a forty-year-plus volunteer at the Winnipeg Folk Festival and has attended every Folk Festival. After completing a science degree at university, he pursued a career in video production, working over twenty-five years with Winnipeg Videon as a producer/director for television. He has had a long career in media work and volunteerism—the Winnipeg Folk Festival being a highlight of his year. He served on the Folk Festival Board from 1983 to 1999 and was coordinator of the Media Crew from 1981 to 1986 and volunteer director of the Main Stage video screens from 1997 until the present. John has also been a volunteer radio host and producer for a weekly folk music radio show called Planet Mainstage *for over twenty years on CJUM (UMFM), the University of Manitoba campus radio station.*

FIGURE 105. JOHN PRENTICE AT FOLK FEST, N.D. PHOTOGRAPH COURTESY OF JOHN PRENTICE.

JOHN PRENTICE

14 OCTOBER 2022, WINNIPEG

KEVIN NIKKEL: What is your connection to the Winnipeg Folk Fest?

JOHN PRENTICE: Folk Fest has been an integral part of my life. It's been the thing-to-look-forward-to every year. I've been to every Folk Festival. The first few years I was just excited that my favourite music was being presented to me and Winnipeggers. Gradually, through various projects, I got involved and was able to meet Mitch and help him with some media work, TV commercials, for example. In 1983, I was asked to be on the board and so I was on the board of the Festival through some very interesting times, through until 1997, actually. And other than that, I volunteer at the Festival. I started off on the media crew. After doing that for a year, I became the coordinator. I did that for several years. Of course, when on the board, it was a year-round commitment with fundraisers and board and committee meetings.

For twenty years now, I've carried on as a volunteer. I've been the director for the video screens on Main Stage. It's called iMag and basically if you wanted to see—well, pick a name: Jann Arden—and you're 10,000 people in the evening audience, you get a picture of her close-up. The main objective is to just make sure that you give people a close-up of Jann and her fiddle or whatever she's playing, or whoever is playing on stage.

KN: At what point did you meet Mitch Podolak? Did you know him before the Folk Festival?

JP: I didn't know him before, but just as the Festival got going, I certainly at one point would have put myself forward and introduced myself to him and showed him how much I appreciated things. Professionally, he became aware that I had this media experience that could be useful to him. So that's where I got to know this amazing man. I saw that he was a visionary and that his dreams were starting to come true and I so wanted to be part of it.

ATTENDING MUSIC FESTIVALS

KN: Tell me more about the conditions that precipitated the flourishing of the Folk Festival. As if the soil was just ready for the seed to be planted.

JP: I think an event that was a precursor of the Festival was Niverville,[29] which was sort of a combination rock-and-folk festival. Anybody that was getting known as a performer would have played that festival. It was a total disaster in terms of the weather, but it was attended by 12,000 people.

KN: Did you go?

JP: Yes.

KN: Tell me about that.

JP: It was just a mud bath, basically. We sat a long time in line in the car to get in. I remember seeing Dianne Heatherington, who was an amazing rock singer, well-known in the early 1970s. Other than that, it was Winnipeg's version of Woodstock because of the weather. Everyone is like, "Here we are. It doesn't matter what's happening with the weather. We're going to enjoy life." And there were pockets of people playing music, wherever you were, stalled in your car. It was free.

Another one that was similar to that was Festival Express, which brought amazing performers through Winnipeg and was at the [Winnipeg] Stadium. It was the same sort of feeling of the Woodstock-kind-of-event that could happen in Winnipeg. Although there weren't any local performers, it generated the same kind of feeling that another festival might happen. You're talking about the soil . . . that now things might be ready to be planted in. Yeah, the time was ripe for the Festival to start.

KN: Niverville and Festival Express were both in 1970. Do you know if Mitch went to either? He did go to Mariposa out in Toronto.

JP: I didn't know much about Mitch, beforehand. I've heard the stories of his involvement with the coffeehouse scene in Toronto before he came here and the connections he had, and everything leading up as to why the Festival could not only happen in the first year, but subsequent years in Winnipeg, and of course, all the special Mitch tricks and skills that made the Festival come to life more and more each year.

KN: I would consider you a folk music addict. And I mean that in the most complimentary way. Were you always this strung out? When did it begin for you?

JP: I love to sing, but I never learned an instrument. I didn't get forced to play the piano, though I wish I had been now. I did actually sing in the operettas in high school and was a lead in the *Mikado* in Grade twelve. I had the benefit of one of the best music teachers in Winnipeg schools, Barry Anderson. He nurtured along the ones who had the ability to be able to go out and perform. When I was in Grade twelve, my chemistry teacher was angry at me, he threw my paper down and said that at Christmas I had got an A+ and my marks took a dive because music took over my life. I don't think it's ever let go. Ha.

KN: Let's talk about the Folk Festival. Do you remember the first one? Any memories?

JP: I thought, this is it. This is the event that I want to be at. Right at the beginning, the way festivals were set up. The fact that you had a choice, and that there were multiple stages, that was Mitch's model. You could go from one place to another and hear different aspects of folk music and, of course, I did. Mitch had some local performers, like Jim Donahue, playing on a workshop stage with—wow, isn't this neat—Murray McLauchlan. Just seeing the exchange that could happen, with several people at once taking turns singing songs. Amazing. So much potential in that format.

KN: What was the philosophy behind the Folk Festival?

JP: Mitch was a socialist. And he saw the power of bringing people together. He saw the power of music to unite people under a cause. I've seen it described more academically and have read it to him and he laughed. He said, "You know, I think that that's pretty close to what I do." He didn't like to be nailed down, exactly. It's the power that the singer on the stage has to unite the audience and not only have them vicariously living through the singer's music but participate in it as well. So, one grand kind of joint, unified experience of the joy of music and the power of music.

A DEFINITION OF A FOLK FESTIVAL

KN: What would be a working definition of a folk festival?

JP: Well, a leading word is a *celebration*, where people come from near and far to get together, with old friends and new, and listen to, and make music. But another way of looking at festivals, I've often thought, is as a musicians' convention. Get all these performers together who would always love to be together in person—they come and they get to play with each other on workshop stages or backstage, or just generally talk and find out what makes each other tick. Then as the audience, you get to be like a fly on the wall. You get to be part of this and wow, what an experience. Especially when you see, hey I don't just have to be sitting out here in the field watching this, I can volunteer! They want me to go and help carry that guy's guitar. I can be right there. Right at the hotel, while he or she is playing at the party. It's like, wow. What a gift for somebody to get right in there and experience this musicians' convention.

When I talk to performers about it, they say, definitely, the audience makes a large difference in terms of what happens with this music. It's about the joy that you create and that back-and-forth thing. It's a give-and-take between performer and the audience. And it builds during a festival. Right through the whole weekend.

KN: How important are the workshops?

JP: If you look at folk festivals, just in terms of how they are laid out, they have multiple stages. You've got 100 performers, and you're able to have this wealth of music because the funding model allows you to bring in all these people. You've only got room for sixteen or so performers to perform on the night-time Main Stage. So, multiple stages are the obvious answer. Now, what do you do with those multiple stages? A stage which is maybe smaller may attract fewer people, but maybe you only have a certain type of music on those stages. On a given stage, you might get every banjo player at the Festival that year to play. And you can expand that from just the instrumental level to different themes. The Festival became known for its cleverly created themes. The performers would perform their songs on that particular theme and, of course, there would be an exchange. The word *workshop* could be looked at as this misnomer these days. In Irish music they're called *sessions*. Some of the festivals have changed their workshop names to sessions because it's just a matter of a number of different performers of the same ilk getting together and playing music together.

KN: The workshops haven't always been like that. Mitch had some different ideas back in the day for what the workshop could be, as more of a lab and experimentation. Can you think of any examples of things being much more of an experiment to make a new song? I'm thinking of Steve Goodman and David Amram, and the goal to challenge them.

JP: Yes, that's the theme-based approach that Mitch was so good at. That's probably the most exciting thing about workshops—it's a one-off experience that you are a part of. The magic that happens that next hour never occurs again.

KN: Give me some examples.

JP: It happens when there's a lot of different instruments. One performer has written a love song, but on this stage, there's a bunch of people with congas and a bouzouki and maybe a couple of French horns or something. They're just as eager to be heard on every song. So, they all start in, all contributing, and when the time comes, the person leading the song will say, "Let's hear from the French horns," or "Let's hear from the banjo," or "Let's hear from that beautiful guitar." All the leader of the song needs to do is nod in that direction and, all of a sudden, you get something you've never heard before. And by the time that song ends, with all of these musicians participating together, it's like this totally beautiful new musical experience which has been created, [but] never heard before. Hopefully it's been recorded, but not always.

KN: What about Birds Hill Park? Would the Festival have been different if it'd been launched in Assiniboine Park?

JP: Birds Hill Provincial Park—the Festival site is such a gift in terms of how it physically presents itself. From the time you come to the site and park, you say, "I wonder where I'm going." You leave the parking lot and you go down this umbilical cord through the woods and boom! There you are, at this Festival, which comes at you piece by piece, stage by stage. It's magic in terms of the physical layout. It hasn't changed in

FIGURE 106. MEDIA CREW MEMBERS CLAUDE FOREST AND JOHN PRENTICE, 1985. PHOTOGRAPH COURTESY OF JOHN PRENTICE.

all these years. Every workshop stage has its own magic, its uniqueness and isolation.

KN: You were on the board. Do you remember what it was like to cross from being a volunteer and then see this Festival from behind the curtain? What was it like?

JP: The image that is coming to mind is the duck swimming on the pond that looks so serene, and it's battling like crazy underneath. There's so much behind the scenes, coming from the heart of all the people who were volunteering or sometimes getting paid minimally to keep this thing going, and keep it afloat. The thing that became apparent to me as I went along on the board, was that we were going to go through the growth experience as an organization. Mitch knew that, too.

There was a point there where the board said, "What we are gonna need now, is to get an Operations Manual for doing things correctly, things need to be documented." I remember there was a board member called Ted Lightly, and at one of many especially long, hard meetings, where everyone had an opinion on how they thought this and that should be done, he said, "You know, we have to think that we could be all wiped away tomorrow, and the audience will walk over our bones. There needs to be something that somebody can pick up and know how to carry this on." He had a way with words.

KN: It's interesting to think about the evolution of any organization. You have to be able to keep the thing alive for the future because people don't last forever. Does the ghost of Mitch haunt the Festival?

JP: I'd start off by saying that the memory of Mitch should always be present in the Winnipeg Folk Festival and other festivals, and the festival model, in Western Canada. Just be aware of the effort and the vision that was there for the initial impetus. It's totally appropriate for him to have a legacy within the organization.

PLANET MAINSTAGE RADIO SHOW

KN: Where did the idea for your radio show *Planet Mainstage* come from? Is it connected to the Folk Fest?

JP: I have the great fortune of doing a radio show on 101.5 UMFM, University of Manitoba campus and community radio. In the late 1990s, Rosalie Goldstein, who was the second artistic director of the Festival, was doing her own folk music show at UMFM. I offered to help her, which I did as co-host for a while, and then, all of a sudden, after a year or two of doing the show, she decided that she was going to go back to re-qualify and to end her career as a pharmacist. She said, "You know, I think you're ready, John. You can just take it over. You can have it."

KN: How does the Folk Festival inform how you prepare your show?

JP: Jeff, who was one of the other roots DJs out at the station, always said, "This is John and his show is called *Planet Mainstage*, but I think it should just be called the Folk Festival Show." I've never been asked by the Folk Festival to do it. There hasn't been that kind of relationship. I have always had a good relationship with Lynne Skromeda or anybody else since I've been involved year-round with the Festival. It is my way of keeping involved with the Festival, but it's all on my own terms.

Pierre GUÉRIN

Pierre Guérin has had a long career in the arts as a musician, artistic director, broadcaster, and amateur photographer. Pierre's musical career began with playing the accordion at the age of nine. He joined the Montréal Celtic band Barde, performing at coffeehouses, concert venues, and folk festivals across Canada and the United States for nine years—the band played the Winnipeg Folk Festival on three occasions. Pierre moved to Winnipeg, left Barde, and became the artistic director of the Folk Festival from 1991 to 2000. During this time, he also served as the Chair of Folk Alliance International. He went on to a twenty-year stint with CBC/Radio Canada, with his last position there being Regional Director for Western Canada for French services.

FIGURE 107. BARDE ON MAIN STAGE AT WINNIPEG FOLK FESTIVAL, 1978. PHOTOGRAPH BY DAVID LANDY. ARCHIVES OF MANITOBA, WINNIPEG FOLK FESTIVAL 1978 NEGATIVES, P2566/7, 4/78. 27A.

PIERRE GUÉRIN

13 OCTOBER 2021, WINNIPEG

KEVIN NIKKEL: How did you find your way into folk music and eventually the Winnipeg Folk Festival?

PIERRE GUÉRIN: I started playing music when I was nine years old. One evening, somebody showed up at our door. She was selling accordions and music lessons and my parents thought it would be a good idea. My younger brother and sister also took accordion lessons for a while, then they both dropped out and I was the only one who kept on going. In retrospect, I could have learned to play the piano, or the guitar, but it was the accordion which led me into a number of different musical directions and styles, and eventually Celtic music. Certain types of music affect you in different ways. Even though they don't necessarily have any direct connection with your roots or family history, when you first hear them, they feel as if they've been part of your life forever, or your DNA, even. It's a very interesting phenomenon. For me, that was Celtic music and, to a lesser degree, South American music. Both spoke to me, but particularly Celtic music.

Around 1970, I fell in love with the music of Alan Stivell, who is a Celtic harp player. His *Renaissance of the Celtic Harp* and *At the Olympia* albums changed my life. I started learning all these songs and playing them on the accordion because that was the only appropriate instrument. One thing led to the next. At the time I was studying photography as well and presenting a project to Canada Council. I was going to different musical events in Montréal, taking photos. One of those events was a fiddling contest, where I met a guy named Bruce Murchison who told me about this group of people who would get together on a weekly basis to play Celtic music and he invited me over. So, I ended up bringing my accordion to one of these sessions. Lo and behold, this was roughly the bunch of people who eventually became the group known as Barde.

The connection to the Winnipeg Folk Festival happened in 1978. We played our first folk festival—Mariposa, which was considered *the* folk festival at the time. There were always rumours that Bob Dylan would show up, or Joni Mitchell, or some famous musician of some kind, incognito of course. The other members of the group knew a little bit more about these events than I did. For me, it was a completely new and strange experience. It turned out to be a fairly successful event for us, and that's how we met Mitch Podolak, who came up to us after one of our performances and said, "I run the Folk Festival in Winnipeg, and I'd like to invite you guys to come and perform."

A few weeks later, we were in Winnipeg. It rained most of the weekend. One of the first images I have of the Folk Festival was sharing a workshop stage with another band called the Boys of the Lough. Six of us, four of them . . . ten people on this rickety little stage, plywood boards on milk cartons with a tarp over it. And the rain pouring and people in the field jumping up and down and dancing in puddles, some of them wearing garbage bags. My first indelible image of the Folk Festival.

Nobody knew us, we weren't part of the folk music community at this point. Mitch had decided that we would perform on the Main Stage. Saturday night rolled around and it finally stopped raining. It was a gorgeous evening and, for whatever reason, Mitch had decided to schedule our set in the sweet spot of evening programming. The sweet spot is when the sun starts setting and the lights come on and all of a sudden Main Stage becomes a little bit different, more of a focal point. It's easier to see what's on stage.

We go up on stage and started playing and, all of a sudden, people start getting up and dancing . . . more and more people getting up and dancing. We're on stage, we're playing, this is our second or third tune. We're looking at each other and we're all thinking, *What the hell is going on here?* This is the biggest crowd we've ever played for and somehow the music seems to have this incredible impact on them. At one point there was this chain of people dancing across the field as the sun was setting, their heads rimmed in this beautiful golden light. It's an image that I will never, ever forget for the rest of my life. That was the Winnipeg Folk Festival. That was Main Stage.

We finished our set. We walked offstage and the crowd was going nuts and wanted us to come back, so we came back for an encore. There weren't many encores at the Folk Festival and because there were other acts following us, we decided to play a very slow quiet piece

FIGURE 108. AUDIENCE DANCING, 1975. PHOTOGRAPH BY DAVID LANDY. ARCHIVES OF MANITOBA, WINNIPEG FOLK FESTIVAL 1975 NEGATIVES, P5266/1, 75-4562. 5.

called “The Dark Island.” It started as an instrumental piece and we gradually dropped the instrument and just sang the melody and the audience started singing along with us and it felt like the whole crowd was singing along and then we walked off the stage. Peter Gzowski, who was emcee at the time, came up to me and said, “That was a fucking classy thing to do, you guys.” And that was how I fell in love with folk festivals.

Mitch told me later that, while we were on stage, he was walking around the field with a group of politicians trying to get some funding for the Festival. I believe Lloyd Axworthy was there and a couple of other people. He said, “I was trying to explain to them what the Festival was, how important it was, and what it did to people. All of a sudden, we all stopped talking and started looking at what was happening around the field, you guys on stage, and everything. I didn't have to say anything anymore. They got the point.” He often referred to this as a seminal moment for the Folk Festival. It was one of those extraordinary moments of my life. I was a performer for close to ten years and moments like that, you can count on the fingers of one hand. The unforgettable concerts. The rest of the time you're onstage playing music trying to make all the pieces connect and they don't always. But in that particular moment, we were connected as a band and the audience was connecting to our music and it was incredible . . . a beautiful experience.

KN: Wow. What else needs to be said?

PHILOSOPHY OF AN ARTISTIC DIRECTOR

PG: For me, that experience greatly influenced what I ended up doing as an artistic director. The idea that an unknown, or relatively unknown band, could get up on Main Stage and steal the weekend. It can only happen if you have a system where all the acts are relatively equal. You can't have a situation where you have megastars and then the rest of the acts because then the event is no longer as balanced as it should be. The idea of giving everybody a chance to steal the show was really important to me and it ended up being fundamental in the way I approached programming.

KN: When did you make the transition from performer to artistic director?

PG: Barde performed at the Winnipeg Folk Festival in 1978 and we came back the following year, and then in 1983. I had moved to Winnipeg in 1981 because one of the other impacts the Folk Festival had on my life is that I met Karen, who became my wife. She was working for the Folk Festival organization at the time. We've been together ever since. For a couple of years, I worked at Home-Made Music and also volunteered at the Festival as well. Then eventually in 1984, I started working at Radio Canada or the French CBC. I worked there for six years but lost my job because of budget cuts. I freelanced for a year, and then, the artistic director position came up. Never in my life had I thought, *One day I'm going to be artistic director of a festival.* That's not the way things work. But for a number of reasons and, given the different ways the Festival had been part of my life, it sort of made sense. I applied for the position. Showed up at the interview wearing a jacket and a tie. Everybody else around the table was in jeans or shorts and sandals. Did a horrible job interview, and found out a few days later that the position had been offered to someone else. I thought, *Okay, that's that.* But that person turned down the position and I got a phone call saying, "We would like to do a second interview." So, I came back for another interview, which apparently was a little bit better and I was eventually offered the position. That was summer of 1991 and, at the time, Rosalie Goldstein was the artistic director. She left after the Festival that year and I became artistic director for close to ten years and programmed nine festivals.

KN: Tell me more about your philosophy and approach. I'm also curious about Mitch's legacy. Did you have to carve out your own space?

PG: It was an interesting set of circumstances. Mitch and I, because he had brought us to the Festival, because of the importance of the event in his mind and in my mind, and because I ended up being his boss for a couple of years when I produced *Simply Folk*—a show that he hosted at the CBC—we had this interesting relationship over the years but were always fond of one another. My relationship with Rosalie was more difficult. I found out after I got the position that she had told the Board that this was the worst decision they could possibly have made.

I remember my first day on the job, walking into a room that used to be Rosalie's office, and there was a chair, a desk, and a phone. No records, no files, no nothing, it'd all just disappeared: a blank slate. An interesting way to start a new position, but it was also incredibly liberating and more than a little bit scary. I mean, the biggest things I'd managed up to that point were some recording sessions and a couple of radio shows for CBC. All of a sudden, I find myself coming into an organization where there were more than a thousand volunteers, staff of about a dozen people, depending on the time of year, and a Board of Directors.

In many ways, that first year sort of felt like landing a jumbo jet with the user's manual in my lap. Flipping through pages and trying to figure out where the controls are, learning as I went along. Plus, the Festival was in dire straits, financially, along with most folk festivals at the time. The end of the 1980s, beginning of the 1990s, was a fulcrum point for most festivals. As a matter of fact, Mariposa shut down for a couple of years. The granddaddy of them all couldn't keep going. Winnipeg, Edmonton, Calgary, and Vancouver all had financial problems. Audiences were getting older, the genre was getting tired, the events had expanded, and some were living beyond their means, government funding was drying up—a number of really important things had to change.

We were talking about philosophy, some of those changes were really obvious because we were on the edge of the precipice, if you will. Scaling down was important. Finding ways to rejuvenate the audience was extremely important. Reducing our dependence on government funding was crucial. Making the event more accessible to a larger audience was crucial. Folk festivals, particularly Vancouver and Winnipeg, because of Mitch and Gary Cristall, who was artistic director in Vancouver for a number of years, had this left-wing political identity, which had worked for a while but eventually created a situation where a lot of people felt excluded. If you weren't at that end of the political spectrum, the event wasn't for you. And, last but not least, increase advance ticket sales. Those were all the variables we were dealing with at that particular time.

In terms of programming philosophy, the idea of not using headliners was really important to me. Because of what I described before, to me, a Festival is a situation where all performers are, more or less, on equal footing. Then what happens on any given weekend is dictated by the acts themselves, by the quality of their performance, by the contact they establish with the audience. The model for festival promotion at the time was these posters where you have acts listed and you had the top acts in 64-point font, and then you had the lesser acts in 32-point font, and you had the rest of the gang in 12-point font, which always upset me. One of the first things we changed, that first poster in 1992 used the same font size for everybody.

The other element I always thought was really important was reflected in the tag line that we created that year, "People and Music." To me, this was a social event before it was a musical event. Reason being that, it's not an urban festival. Urban festivals, people go to the show, and then take the bus or drive back home, and they come back the following day. The Winnipeg Folk Festival has a campground which creates a community where people live together for three to four, or now five to six, days. It's a completely different approach. For a lot of people, it ends up being more like a family reunion than a musical event. In a way, I was comparing my job to that of the music man at a wedding. You are an important part of what's going on, and music is one of the reasons why people come to the event, but not necessarily the most important one. "People and Music" was a way to emphasize and celebrate that idea.

The "no headliners" part was also somewhat dictated by economics. As I said, we didn't have a huge budget and if you start bringing in huge acts, then you become a slave to that particular formula. You have to bring a bigger act the following year, and then again, the year after that. And then you're stuck. If you get rained on that particular year and the money doesn't come in, you have a real problem because your audience has become accustomed to this idea that every year there's a bigger act. Bigger acts are more expensive. I didn't want to be stuck in a dynamic where you are endlessly competing with yourself.

So, the idea was, come to the Festival and you'll be hearing stuff you've never heard before. If you promote concerts, you're selling tickets for a particular act, and maybe an opening act, but essentially, you're drawing people based on the notoriety of the main act. With festivals, you have sixty to eighty different acts, and they can be anything you want. Like being a kid in a candy store. When you're programming a festival, you can literally do whatever you want.

And the last piece of the puzzle to me was world music, which at the time was becoming more and more of a factor. Up to that point, the Festival had featured mostly North American and European music, Western European music, with a few exceptions. So, there were all these opportunities to bring music that people were not familiar with, instruments they were not familiar with, and sounds that they'd never heard. Somebody a couple of years down the line summed it up best: "The best music you've never heard." So, the idea was to bring people in, create opportunities for them to see and hear some things they were familiar with, and then start throwing them some curves and taking them to places they'd never been. Building a relationship with the audience on that basis.

But it was rough. Those first couple of years were really difficult, from a financial point of view. If you can imagine, and not too many people know this, but it was a situation where we would finish a festival and most of the money that we made would go to pay bills from the previous year. Once we'd done that and paid what we could of the bills from the current year, we essentially depended on the kindness and patience of many suppliers who were also Festival supporters. One of the people who had to deal with that reality on a daily basis was Bill Merritt, the business manager of the Festival. Bill in many ways is an unsung hero in this whole story.

A number of artistic events of all kinds, including festivals, were created in the 1970s with government funding. Some of them operated on the basis that this funding was always going to be there. Artistic directors focused on programming and not so much on the business side. Business managers were responsible for the financial side and, in some cases, were largely powerless to influence artistic decisions. An artistic director has to always be conscious of the fact that they're running a business. If not, you create problems for the whole organization. And that's why these events were in such a precarious position by the end of the 1980s.

At the end of the eighties, beginning of the nineties, a second generation of artistic directors happened to arrive on the scene at the same time in all the Western Canadian festivals. We ended up working together and collaborating on programming.

CHANGING DEFINITION OF FOLK MUSIC

KN: Let's rewind for a second. You have the desire to make some changes, but there is a precedent of people reacting to change. Thinking of Dylan going electric. People don't always like change. What was the response to change?

PG: This actually goes hand-in-hand with the evolution of what was called folk music. Festivals back then were much more rooted in this traditional vision of folk music. Lots of discussions about the folk process, traditional music being transmitted orally, without the influence of commercial recordings, and passed down from one generation to the next. Trying to make a living playing folk music was a sacrilege for some. You had to have a real job, you played gigs or festivals during the weekend, and went back to your real job. There was this sort of denial that folk music was in any way part of the music industry. When we arrived on the scene in the late seventies, there was still some of that tension. I remember some people coming up to us after a workshop and complimenting us on the music but questioning the use of microphones and speakers. If you fast forward a few years to the eighties and mostly the nineties, things begin to change and evolve. There's a realization that if you want to be a professional musician, you have to tour. If you're touring, your tours have to be viable.

In 1992, my first year, we started changing a number of elements. Before, we had seven or eight daytime stages and the Main Stage, with some 1,250 volunteers. The event had been running on that model for a while. As I mentioned before, we had to scale the thing down. The plan that was presented to the Board was essentially: fewer stages, fewer volunteers, cutting expenses. It was a radical set of moves. Change is difficult, but change always comes with opportunities. Eventually, the Festival grew back to what it had been, but not before we could afford it. By that point we were living within our means and we were in control of our destiny.

The other part had to do with restructuring ticket prices. If you base your economic system on the idea that government money is plentiful, you don't want to charge too much. But if you want to reduce your dependence on outside funding, you have to confront a reality where ticket prices have to go up and be managed creatively. It was a bit of a shock within the organization, and for the audience, but it had to be done.

JOHN PRENTICE: Eventually you became president of Folk Alliance.

PG: I attended my first Folk Alliance conference in Calgary in 1992. It was in February, before I'd even programmed a festival at all. I discovered the conference was all about how folk music was becoming a part of the music industry. In some ways a distinct part, people were doing things differently, but part of the industry. Performers, agents, festival directors, publicists, radio hosts—all these people getting together once a year to share experiences—to talk about successes, common challenges, and solutions. It was a major revelation. Folk Alliance became a very important part of what I was doing and I was eventually asked to join the Board of Directors and became president for one term.

LEAVING THE WINNIPEG FOLK FESTIVAL

KN: Why did you call it quits?

PG: It was a combination of factors. I think the shelf life of an artistic director is limited, for a number of different reasons. First, there's the phase where the organization is getting used to you, and you're finding your way around and experimenting. The changes that were made initially proved successful, for the most part. We started realizing that we could control our destiny, that we could rain-proof the event by emphasizing advance ticket sales and reducing our dependence on government funding. The event was becoming more and more popular.

You go through this phase and for a while there, you can do no wrong. The board and staff loves you, volunteers love you, the audience gets used to the new style of programming. On the other hand, what happens, and I saw this happen to a number of artistic directors, is that from the point of view of programming you become less flexible or adventurous. You start going back to your old bag of tricks more often than you used to, start repeating some acts. You get a little bit more lazy in terms of the research, and more conservative with the risks that you are taking. My theory is that most artistic directors stick around for way too long. There comes a moment where you pass your prime and the organization does not benefit as much from your presence. Being an artistic director means providing a fresh, engaging vision. It can be a little bit less fresh and still engaging, but when it becomes neither, then you should go.

Also, going on ten years really starts taking a toll on you. I was feeling stretched in a number of ways. Things were beginning to change. And I had pretty much accomplished everything I wanted. And in the end, the decision was that I would do one more year and then move on. Oddly enough, I moved on to another event and I was asked to be artistic director for Festival du Voyageur. I only did it for one year, and then I had the opportunity to go back to Radio Canada, and that was the rest of my career for over twenty years. In front of a mic, in front of the camera, behind the mic as a producer, eventually in management, and my last gig there was as Regional Director for Western Canada for French services.

I programmed nine festivals and, for the first eight, I had an extraordinary run of fabulous weather. Rain was always a factor at the Festival. I talked about rain-proofing the Festival, which was a major challenge. For a while there, the situation was that most of the ticket sales happened at the gate. If it started raining that weekend, you were screwed. Rain was the enemy. You work fifty-one weeks of the year with your team, you put everything together, you control everything you can control, and then put it out in the field and pray to the gods that you don't get rained out. A very strange situation. But for me, this great run of mostly sunny weather eight years in a row. . . .

JP: So, you're saying you had some secret connections that you weren't sharing?

PG: There were rumours. . . . We were in this great cycle, until my very last year. In 2000, on opening night, we had the Winnipeg Symphony Orchestra as the house band. A crazy idea. We had six or seven different acts that had done collaborations with symphonies and so all of this happened on Main Stage, and it was an incredible evening of music. The minute people got off the stage and packed up, it started raining, and it poured all night. The following morning, there were streets in Winnipeg that were impassable. It was a Biblical event.

I remember waking up that morning thinking, *That's it.* I didn't even want to go to Birds Hill Park. It spelled disaster. And then I started getting phone calls from people. Volunteer crew leaders, mostly, and staff saying, "So, the backstage kitchen area is flooded. Here's what we're going to do to reorganize that part. We can move this thing. We can do that. It's gonna work."

Somebody else, "Stage three is flooded. We can't go there. So, you have to do this, do that, move this, reorganize that. . . ." And all of a sudden, it was like everybody at the same time realized that the playbook had to be thrown out the window and we had to reinvent this thing on the fly together.

Of all the Festivals I worked on, this ended up being one of my favourites. In spite of all the adversity and the sea of mud that we were working in, from an organizational point of view, it was textbook disaster planning on the fly. It was extraordinary to see the entire team come together in such fashion and rise to the challenge. Then the performers got into it. A lot of them hadn't seen mud on the field for years, but they let their inner child take over. There are pictures from that year of people with mud up to and over their knees, having fun. Instead of playing on a stage they ended up playing in the middle of the field. Everybody rolled with the punches. To me, it felt like, okay, we're good. Whatever happens in the future, we can deal with it. It was like the organization had evolved, grown up; matured, I guess, is the right word. It was the right time to pass the torch. It felt good. It felt like the job had been accomplished.

WHAT ABOUT WINNIPEG

KN: Do you think it matters that the Festival is a Winnipeg festival, or could this have happened anywhere else? It is one of my favourite topics, of Winnipeg as an underdog city.

PG: Well, one of the most incredible and, to a certain extent unfair, advantages I had as a programmer was that Winnipeg is mostly off-the-beaten-track when it comes to musicians touring. Maybe not so much anymore, but at that time it really was. Creating a festival in a major market where most of your artists are playing all over the city all year round must be extremely challenging. How are you going to surprise an audience with anything when they can go down the street and listen to almost any given act? I was grateful every day of my tenure to work in a market like Winnipeg. It was a fantastic opportunity.

The other remarkable thing is the wonderful support the Winnipeg community provides to its arts organizations. Financial support, but also direct involvement. We needed anywhere between 900 and 1,300 volunteers for the Festival every year and never had any problem finding them. A lot of these people also volunteered for the Fringe Festival, and the Kids Festival, and all kinds of other events. Winnipeg has a small population but the support it gives to its arts community and its arts organizations is unparalleled.

THE MUDDY

Leonard PODOLAK

Leonard Podolak is a banjo player and arts administrator. He grew up at the Winnipeg Folk Festival. The son of Mitch and Ava Podolak, the Festival is as old as he is. With all the time spent at the Festival as a child, and with musicians visiting the Podolak home, it is not surprising that he began playing the banjo—eventually founding his own bands, first with the award-winning Scrüj MacDuhk, and later The Duhks. Between the two bands, he has played the Winnipeg Folk Festival six times. Leonard has toured the world over playing his claw-hammer banjo music and is a Grammy and Juno award winner. Leonard is the executive director of Home Routes, as well as the founder of the Winnipeg Crankie Festival, both demonstrating his leadership and innovation in sustaining the folk music community—carrying on the family tradition.

FIGURE 109. LEONARD PODOLAK ON STAGE, N.D. COURTESY OF LEONARD PODOLAK.

LEONARD PODOLAK

1 SEPTEMBER 2021, WINNIPEG

KEVIN NIKKEL: What is your connection to the Folk Festival?

LEONARD PODOLAK: I grew up with the Winnipeg Folk Festival. My parents, Mitch Podolak and Ava Kobrinsky, were the founders. The main schemers behind it and, as such, I grew up in it from before I was born until the time my dad left in 1986. It was pretty much the central thing in our lives and in our house.

KN: What is your earliest memory?

LP: One of my earliest memories of the stage was a workshop with Margaret Christl, who is an amazing ballad singer. I was really into the Incredible Hulk. I interrupted her workshop so I could show her and the crowd my metamorphosis from Bruce Banner to The Hulk. Folks liked it. I would say a lot of my memories of the Folk Festival as a little kid were mostly backstage, like in Hotel California, which is the site campground. Stuff like fence-day. Stuff like hanging around the office. There is a famous picture that's in the 1983 program book of the entire staff. The families and the kids, but I'm not in the picture because I was aggravated at that moment. I was there, I was standing around the corner of the building while they took the picture because I refused to be in the photo. Now, obviously, I regret it.

I used to go to Fort Rouge Childcare, which was in the Crescentwood United Church—that was around the time when the office was at Confusion Corner there in that big building on Osborne. I would often bail out of daycare and walk down Wardlaw and up a half-block on Osborne to just go to the office. The culture in the office and the folks that worked in the office were all legendary figures in my life. That was a time for a kid.

My dad always told me when it was going to be crunch-time and it was really stressful, someone would start a rubber-band fight and they would start shooting each other with elastic bands, and it would really get out of hand. He would tell me about it. And I'd say, "I want you to invite me to one of those rubber-band fights."

FIGURE 110. MITCH, AVA, AND LEONARD PODOLAK AT THE WINNIPEG FOLK FESTIVAL, N.D. COURTESY OF LEONARD PODOLAK.

When I was a kid, none of my contemporaries had any interest that incorporated playing folk music. Except for the little bits that were around the Folk Festival, but that was a small group of people that were older. Somehow my dad managed to teach Jud Hepburn how to play a little bit, and Danny Koulack, too. When I decided I wanted to learn banjo and take it a step further, I had to go to North Carolina. There was no one here who I could learn that from. The same thing with Irish music.

I guess the earliest memories were really as much about the music as they were about the culture around. The vibe. The site.

MITCH DESIGNS THE PROGRAM

KN: Let's talk about the site because your knowledge is a different perspective than most people who just show up for Folk Fest. Tell me more about what you remember about the things on the calendar. Was there stress involved in some of that?

LP: I guess the biggest stress time around the Folk Festival when I was little would be whenever my dad would make the workshop schedule because he really tried to keep in mind the journey and the experience of every person on the site. Whether they were a volunteer, or whether they were a patron, or an artist. He still locked himself away, for sometimes three weeks, at a hotel. My mother, Rosalie Goldstein, and Bill Merritt were the only three people who knew where he was, besides Duck Donald who was there with him, to actually make sure he wasn't double-booking people, or not booking people.

I'd like to stress that this isn't a festival of a bunch of concerts in the park. He would program an hour of concerts across the schedule at one point in the day, and the concerts would be half-an-hour each, and so you would have to truly decide whose concert you were going to see. The rest of the whole program was workshops. He pretty much programmed most of the lineup with artists that the audience did not know prior to coming. This was at a time when there was no folk music on the radio.

The Festival spoke for itself. Even though my Old Man was a non-traditional kind of fellow compared to many, there is nothing anyone can say because it was an amazing event. He took the time that he did to program it, thinking about the experience of everybody. If you want to hear old-time music all day, you could have that route through the schedule to watch old-time, or traditional Scottish. If you wanted to listen to songwriters, if you wanted to have blues, you could somehow go on whatever journey you want. It was designed so that, along the way, while you were catching your agenda as a music fan, it would be expanded greatly by who else you would see in the day. One of my biggest regrets is

FIGURE 111. DUCK DONALD, 1975. PHOTOGRAPH BY DAVID LANDY, ARCHIVES OF MANITOBA, WINNIPEG FOLK FESTIVAL 1975 NEGATIVES, P5266/1, 75-4561. 18.

that I'm not ten years older, in a weird sort of way. I would have loved to have experienced those early Festivals as a slightly older person.

KN: When you look back at the first ten years of program guides, what are some things that make you think, "Holy cow! That would have been an amazing show!"?

LP: The 1983 program. To me, when I look at that, that was a very tough year. That was a month after Stan Rogers died. He was supposed to play at the festival. I think my dad obviously wrote the workshop schedule before that. Or maybe he didn't. But you see Richard Thompson on one stage and Jim Post on another. I forget who was all there, it all blurred, but I just remember reading that program and going, *Holy moly*. When you look at the artists, that generation of folk musicians, and the people that my generation all really look up to, a lot of them are getting way more accolades now. People realize how good they are, and how good they were.

LEGACY OF THE FOLK FESTIVAL

KN: What was your dad's motivation for creating the Festival, knowing his activist background?

LP: He was creating a weekend of socialism, as he saw it. It was pretty close. The artists got paid, but they all got paid the same. It didn't matter if you were Bruce Cockburn, or if you were Richard Thompson, or if you were Doc Watson. If you were Daniel Koulack, or you were Ann Latouche. Whoever you were. If you were at the Folk Festival, it was because there was a place of honour for you on the stage. That was how he saw it.

He saw that to be impossible without an organized, inspired team of volunteers, whom he thought were completely necessary to do the Festival. Since that was the case, they should be treated just the same as anybody else, except for they're volunteers and they're not paid because they're not coming from abroad and are not professional. However, they stood in the same lineups as the artists, they got the same meals as the artists. They ate at the same picnic tables behind the Main Stage.

There used to be a tent that had walls on three sides—that tent was for the artists to prepare to go on the Main Stage. You didn't go in the tent unless you were going to go on the Main Stage and everybody knew what that time was for. If you weren't going on the Main Stage then you didn't go in the tent. That's just how it worked. The whole rest of the space around the stage was this beautiful, open, green area where the volunteers and the artists could watch a show together.

KN: What has the Festival done for the Winnipeg cultural scene?

LP: Well, because of the Folk Festival there is also the West End Cultural Centre, also the Children's Festival. Not that it's directly related to what my folks did, but indirectly. . . . The Bella Vista or the Times Change(d)—those venues wouldn't have had as much context in town, if it wasn't for the Folk Festival—and inspired people like John Scoles. The folks at The Park, you know, want to have a place for this culture to exist throughout the year.[30] And to be inspired.

It's funny about the Winnipeg Folk Festival—lots of towns have folk festivals. Lots of towns have festivals, it's not just Winnipeg, except for in a weird kind of way it is. Because the Winnipeg Folk Festival painted the picture for the entire country, and for a lot of folks around the world, of just how great such an event can be. And how important they are to the community. I don't think there are that many festivals that have such a robust influence as Winnipeg.

I don't think it's because anybody rated my Old Man as a genius, it was just because of the time. The timing was right for everything and there was enough support, culturally, both on the political level and on the social level, to lift this thing up. Everyone saw how it lifted us. I guess the place where my dad needed expansion of attitude in mind was to know that you can be a folk music if there's a drummer and bass player. He got there—it took him a while.

JOHN PRENTICE: Would the Festival have happened if your dad was never here?

LP: No, I don't think so. Or, I don't know. The province put the call for ideas to celebrate the Winnipeg centennial and my dad was inspired by the Mariposa Folk Festival and so he suggested doing that. But yes, there's a chance that somebody else might have thought to do a folk festival. But I know they would have approached it much more cautiously, you know? They would have because that would've been the smart thing to do. You would get a group of people together who all agree. [Laughs] As you figure out a division of labour, and who can do this, and who can raise that money. But my Old Man, that's not how he did things.

FUNDING FOR THE ARTS

He went to the city, to get some money. They said, "This is a great idea, but we don't want to commit until we get a commitment from the province."

He went to the province, they said, "This sounds like a really great idea, but we're not going to commit the money until you get your commitment from the city." Great. So, on his way out the door, he happened to see on the receptionist desk, letterhead. He took a piece of that letterhead with him on his way out and wrote the letter from the province to the city. Made a fake signature and that was good enough for the city, so then they wrote the letter to the province and they switched. Then they both gave the money to start the Folk Festival.

If I could say anything to funders, it would be that great ideas don't always pay for themselves the first year. You have to convince people. It is a very narrow scope because if you supported an endeavour, whether or not it made the profit, if people went, then they all went for dinner, they all bought gas, some of them travelled, some of them got hotels. There are all kinds of economic benefits that are going to happen. Then it gives the opportunity for it to grow and organize in the community.

I learned that with the Crankie Festival.[31] We only had a little bit of money and a lot of goodwill from the community, and that includes the folks at Crescent Fort Rouge, and the artists. Because they all saw what the concept was—if it's a fun concept and it's worth it for us to invest into it.

You can go, "Ho ho ho, that Mitch is a crazy guy." But aren't you glad he wrote that letter? You know because that's provided millions and millions and millions of dollars for our city, and for our province, and for artists. And how many kids are born now because of it!

KN: I believe that. Funders have the potential to be as creative and bold as artists, as administrators of funding. . . .

LP: . . . yeah, they do, they really do.

KN: And they trigger amazing things if they are willing to be flexible and say, "I know what our mandate is, this is on the edge of it, or just over the line of our mandate, but let's give this a try because it could be good."

LP: And in these times with COVID, that's actually happened, quite a bit. Hey, what were we going to do? We can't do that now, what if we do this? No problem. We have an idea—working at Home Routes now—we had to shift from doing house concerts across the country to become an online disseminator of folk music. The different ways that you do that, learning as we go. And diving in headfirst with only this-much water in the pool. We're filling up the water. And we're getting help.

WHAT IS FOLK MUSIC?

KN: What is folk music?

LP: Folk music is music that comes from the heart and soul and is created for the purpose of creating it. It doesn't have to be acoustic. It can be in any genre. It can be what is known as punk-rock. You listen to punk-rock music, they mean it. My friend Jordan McConnell, who played with me and The Duhks for years and years—he plays punk-rock guitar, he plays traditional Irish guitar—he's like, "You know, Leonard, don't tell anybody; it's the same thing."

When it's created in a boardroom and is created completely digitally, for the purpose of selling millions of records, then I think it stops being folk music. I think it's a weird term because when you say folk music, it's kind of like when you say socialism or communism. People who don't know go to one place, you know what I mean? People who haven't done a lot of reading, they think of one news story. People who haven't listened to much folk music, they think of *The Mighty Wind.* They think of G, C, and D around a campfire. There are so many traditions in the world and there are so many ways of expressing yourself that, I think it's the elemental music. It's the verbal incarnation of the elements in our culture that make us who we are.

JP: I want to ask about the workshop concept that your dad started. Getting artists exchanging with the smaller audiences like the workshop setting at the Folk Festival. What's happening there? . . . The

FIGURE 112. PERFORMERS ON A WORKSHOP STAGE, 1974. PHOTOGRAPH BY JOHN BACHMANN. COURTESY OF WINNIPEG FOLK FESTIVAL.

performer is creating on the spot . . . when there is collaboration, something comes that's new. It's a once-in-a-lifetime experience and the audience understands it. That was important to your dad.

LP: The purpose of the Main Stage has shifted. It's not unique to Winnipeg. The Main Stage in Winnipeg used to be about showcasing as many people from the lineup as possible on the stage. So, people who never heard of them would see them and the sets were twenty or twenty-five minutes and it was like bang, bang, bang, bang. A different time. Those instrument mics, vocal mics—it was a lot easier to just walk up and make sure it was working. But the workshops were certainly what set the Canadian festivals apart. That was the brainchild of Estelle Klein, who was the artistic director of Mariposa in my dad's formative years. He just looked up to her so much. He just thought she was absolutely brilliant. They never really got along, but he really respected what she was trying to do.

I think that the workshops, that's how those magic moments happen. If you just put anybody with anybody, those magic moments don't happen. And that's how it is with anything in life. There is a recipe, and part of the recipe is intimacy and connection and that includes the relationship between the artistic director and the artists. Everybody involved. The stage is set.

A lot of shows now, when you go to see a show, there's a fifteen-to-twenty-foot gap, there's an eight-foot-high stage. The monitors are set back five feet on the stage for the lighting on these big lighting rigs. You're standing in the back of the crowd at some gig and the people look this big. What it was in the early years, the Festival was a two-and-a-half to three-foot stage with a little tent that wasn't dwarfing the artists. When people look back on that and say, "Look how silly that looked. We have it way better. . . ." But really, look how good it looked because look at the artist, compared to the size of the stage. You can see the artist. It's not a hard concept.

I think a lot of the folkiness of the Folk Festival in its early years really came from a real particularity about the aesthetic. And what the aesthetic meant. And the effect on the social interactions.

KN: That totally makes sense to me. I joke with my daughter when I'm composing a photograph, for a nice shot, I want to be close. I want to see people's eyes. That, to me, is a good photograph. That's the intimacy you're talking about.

LP: Here's the thing. You look at mainstream music and how they build it up and how they present these characters, these rock stars, and how it's so completely inaccessible. I'm never going to meet Bono. I'm never going to feel like I know him. I'll never feel like I know Bruce Springsteen. They're very talented musicians and they have a lot to say, but the most successful stuff for me, where it spoke to me, was when your man took off his sunglasses, and he spoke normally, and they dropped the big show and all the effects and they played like they did when they were in the garage. Because that's the part when they are connecting. They're human beings.

What's amazing about the Folk Festival, and particularly the daytime stages, is that you can get to know people because they are right there, two feet away. Then, chances are, if you really have something that you want to tell him, you can go and tell him. See that there, it's not like there's these big walls up.

I think a lot of folk musicians, rather than put up a wall between themselves and the audience, they're striving to tear that fourth wall, and the same thing is true of the most successful folk festivals. You can bring some fancy artist. You can sell lots of tickets. Anybody can do that, but the cultural impact on the community, in terms of how we behave and interact and will produce together, is by far the greatest lasting legacy.

THE ROAD TO PLAYING MAIN STAGE

KN: You eventually made the transition from being the son of the director of the Festival, to playing music. What's the story?

LP: Yeah. When I was in my early teens there were a couple of little clues that happened. My dad had a Ry Cooder tape that our friend Mort Goss gave us. It was just a blank tape and it had *Into the Purple Valley* on one side and *Borderline* on the other side. My parents liked that. I liked that. I was always a big Weird Al fan. And I liked parodies and so I'd always make up songs, too, like that. He was actually my first folk music hero, Weird Al Yankovic. And I say folk music because that guy speaks from the heart. No question. Actually, when I was a kid,

I was trying to convince my dad to hire him and he wouldn't do it and he later came to regret it big time.

Then somehow Billy Bragg came around. At the time, Mitch was hosting a show on CBC called *Simply Folk* and so I went to this Billy Bragg show where I was like, *Oh, okay.* I would see Billy Bragg at the MTC, he was playing with this group called the Beatniks, Michael Franti was in that band, and they had a chainsaw-player on stage. It was this wild pre-hip-hop band playing industrial music, and literally industrial. I was like, *Yeah!* I was twelve or something like that. Then Billy Bragg did a show and it was wonderful and he mentioned that the show's being recorded by *Simply Folk,* Canada's national folk show, and he was really proud of that.

Six months later, he came to the Folk Festival. I went up to him and said, "Billy, I was at your concert six months ago and you said that thing about being recorded." Now, I look back on it and they said, could you please mention that you are being recorded, that's what they do. I was like, "I really appreciated that because that's my dad's radio show. And guess what? This is my dad's festival. He started it. He doesn't run it anymore." It was like 1988. "But it's still his festival and I'm so glad you're here." He was really kind to me. And, a little bit, took me under his wing.

Later on, couple days into the Festival at the International Inn Hotel, I ran into him in the lobby and said, "Hey Billy, how is it going?"

He said, "Good. I'm going to see my friends The Oyster Band play."

I said, "Can I come with you?" That really changed me. That one show at the party at the hotel. It had the most dramatic effect, as a human being. Right then and there, I was like, *this is what it's all about.* I asked my dad to buy me a fiddle right after that. Started playing banjo a few years after that, but when I saw The Oyster Band then, I was like, *Wow.* There's a drummer, a bass player, and an electric guitar player, there is a fiddle, and an accordion. And they're putting it together, and they're singing songs and singing these harmonies, and it rocks. I went straight from there to my dad's record collection. I found a couple Oyster Band records he actually did have from several years before, and it just went from one thing to the other. From Irish music, to Scottish music, to Cajun, to old time. It was The Oyster Band, absolutely.

Also, I like to credit the Fiddle Puppets because that was before I really knew what it was. They were these cloggers, these amazing dancers, who played to fiddle and banjo and doing percussive dance. I loved them when I was kid. Eileen became probably my number one mentor, in terms of performance. Eileen Carson, my dad brought her many times. She was a crazy lady who had a ponytail sticking out of the top of her head and she could get 3,500 people at stage three up on their feet doing the basic. And hollering and getting the vibe of old-time music and getting the vibe of old-time dance. Just learning how to do a basic. She was always inspiring to me. I think it was more of a human kind of visceral sort of elemental kind of thing when I was a kid. But then when I became a banjo player, I looked to her a lot for support. She was also a bandleader, and could help me through that role, in mentoring me through how to deal with different personal relationships because you get no appreciation. It's the opposite of being Mitch Podolak. Being Leonard Podolak was a little different when you're running a band. No one's thanking you. But you know the combo of Eileen, and The Oysters, they really made me do what I did. And obviously because of my dad, because he brought them to town.

KN: Was it weird playing on stage at Folk Fest?

LP: No. I feel very, very comfortable playing onstage, at the Winnipeg Folk Festival especially, for whatever reason. It's not really a fair thing, because I get different treatment than anybody else does, and I feel different than most when I get up there. And it drives them crazy, too, to a certain extent—the amount of ownership that our family still possesses of the Festival. In our minds and our hearts, but also in the hearts and minds of the community. We can't help it. It's not our fault. It is what it is.

Lynne SKROMEDA

Lynne Skromeda was the executive director of the Winnipeg Folk Festival from 2012 to 2023, where she oversaw both the summer festival and its year-round initiatives. She is a graduate of the Asper School of Business at the University of Manitoba, with a specialization in Marketing and Small Business Management. Prior to her work with the Festival, she worked in the film and television industry as a producer and production executive with Frantic Films. Lynne has also been on a number of boards, including the West End Cultural Centre, On Screen Manitoba, the Plug In Institute of Contemporary Art, and Imagine Canada.

FIGURE 113. LYNNE SKROMEDA, 2018. COURTESY OF LYNNE SKROMEDA.

LYNNE SKROMEDA

27 OCTOBER 2021, WINNIPEG

KEVIN NIKKEL: Who are you and how are you connected to the story of the Winnipeg Folk Festival?

LYNNE SKROMEDA: My name is Lynne Skromeda, and I have been the executive director of the Winnipeg Folk Festival, since September 2012.[32] I also have been attending the Winnipeg Folk Festival for over forty years. I started going when I was a kid and it's always been very near and dear to my heart.

KN: Do you have any memories of attending when you were little?

LS: Yes, absolutely. We went as a family for the first time when I was six years old. That was the first year they had a kids' tent at the Festival so I was allowed to go along with my parents. It was really fun and had a lasting impression. In addition to seeing Fred Penner and Sharon, Lois, and Bram—those kinds of well-known kids' artists—they had big piles of sand to play in, and blocks to build stuff with, and I remember braiding headbands. I ran into a girl I went to school with, so that also made it fun for me. It was just really this wonderful, magical, outdoor place that I got to experience for the first time. From that year forward, we always went as a family. Before we had to worry about pre-booking a site at Birds Hill Park like we do now, my dad would go out on the Tuesday night with the trailer to set it up so that we could make sure we got the spot that we wanted in the Birds Hill Provincial Park campground. It was always a huge event, every year for my family, and something that has always been so important to us.

KN: How did the Festival begin to change for you as you were growing up?

LS: As I got a little bit older, as teenagers do, I was less interested in hanging out with my family and more interested in hanging out with my friends. Then I went through this period of time where my friends weren't going. Then one year my mom had something going on and my sister didn't really want to go, so just my dad and I went. We didn't have the best relationship when I was a teenager but when we went to the Festival, we were glued together. He would check out the artists that he thought I would like and share them with me. It was a really neat way to connect with my father. I was twenty-one when he passed away, and that year my photo made it into the program book—he would have loved that. After that, it became something that really was about friends and hanging with people I'd meet. Introducing new people to the Festival was one of my favourite things to do, as well.

KN: Who were some of the acts that you were keen on seeing?

LS: The big one I discovered while going with my dad really was Ani DiFranco. I still remember when she came for the first time in the early nineties, when I was a teenager. Dad was at a workshop and I was at a different one. We met up after and he said, "Lynne, Lynne, you've got to check her out. You're going to love her so much." I still remember my jaw dropping when I saw this little tiny woman with a bald head and this big guitar performing this incredible music that I'd never heard before. That's one of the things that really resonated with me, and I always remember that conversation that we had when I learned about her, and that feeling of seeing her, the excitement that I had—even to this day. When we've brought her back while I've been working at the Festival, I feel it all again. She'll always be an incredibly important performer to me for that very reason.

Then there are all the different discovery elements, too. There are artists I remember like Artis the Spoonman, who did a combination of the kids' tent and then some of the adult stuff—he ended up being in a Soundgarden video in the nineties. I'm like, "I remember when he was here in the eighties and he just played the spoons at the Folk Fest, now he's in this big music video!" There are things like that that are committed to my memory.

I love singer-songwriters. Back in the day—I can't remember which stage number it was, it's now the Bur Oak stage—it just used to be singer-songwriters all day. I just remember parking myself at the very front of the stage. . . . That's where I wanted to be all day, all weekend, just watching this rotating roster of different kinds of performers—Dar Williams, Ferron, The Wyrd Sisters, and more. The people that I saw over the years—some of them I have no idea whatever happened to their careers, but they touched me at a particular point in time. I remember all these individual performances and just feeling so invigorated and excited to see music like that come alive on a stage right in front of me. You can't see that kind of stuff anywhere else, really. That whole essence of being outside and watching the music and the feeling it gives you, you can't compare it.

KN: When we talked with Leonard Podolak, he talked about the importance of the stage and the intimacy, getting up-close. You can see these people. And be inspired.

FOLK MUSIC AND WINNIPEG

LS: Yeah, and there's something about folk music that's just so special. People are telling real stories. They're sharing real experiences in such an intimate and important way. To be able to experience it from the audience sitting on the ground, right there at their feet, is really remarkable. Again, one of those unique things that you just don't have much in this day and age, most certainly. But even that shifted over time.

KN: It seems to me that, with the Festival, there is an osmosis of its philosophy. You kind of just know it. Back then, when you were attending it, what was your sense of what this thing was about?

LS: The thing about the Festival is that it was the only place that you would get together with people that you felt that you would be friends with no matter what, in an environment to listen to music that you couldn't hear anywhere else. That was what it always was for me—just knowing that I would discover something new. The stranger beside me all of a sudden would become a friend because of this experience that we went through together. It was so emotional and so exciting. And if you are experiencing a weather situation—we would sit through the rain, we'd sit through the sun, we'd sit through the wind and everything. You're in it with somebody. There's that real feeling of community and camaraderie with a bunch of people you don't even know. We are so lucky in Manitoba because we have that whole *Friendly Manitoba* vibe, and there's a lot of people who know each other. We're like a big small town, here in Winnipeg, in particular.

That whole sense of connection, that sense of belonging, that no matter if you're by yourself, you're having as good a time as if you are with a big group of your family, just because the environment is so welcoming and so wonderful. I just remember being so invigorated for the rest of the year by attending the Festival that it was just like fuel for me. This is why I never volunteered my entire time as an audience member because I didn't want to miss a moment of the music and the musical experience. I'd rather pay for my ticket just so I didn't have any other obligations and I could just be there, be a part of the Festival audience.

KN: That's interesting. I was about to ask when you started volunteering. There is the answer. I like how you describe what happens here, and I wonder how is it possible that this happens here in Winnipeg?

LS: Yeah. I know. It's the reasons why I stayed here in Winnipeg. I went travelling after I finished university because I wanted nothing more than to leave Winnipeg, but then I came back and it's something like the Folk Fest that makes you realize this is a unique and beautiful place. There are people who come from everywhere to create wonderful experiences, especially when it comes to arts and culture as a whole. That is exemplified by the Festival. There are people who moved here because they love the sense of community that has been created by the Festival. I know at least half-a-dozen people I could tell you stories about who fit that bill.

Everyone talks about how we have the cold winters so we want to celebrate the summer time, but I think there's something more. We are hardscrabble people, yet we're also really modest people at the same time. To have something like this that has such a groundswell of support, of people who just want goodness for their lives and the community that they live in. These are the things that spring up and they become bigger than the sum of their parts, because of that energy that's created by all these well-meaning, but also strong, and beautiful, and magical people, who care so much about where it is that they live.

KN: Let's talk about magical people. Let's talk about personalities. Was there a point where you realized that there were staff at the Festival—and we'll eventually need to talk about you as a staff member. I want to get to Mitch Podolak, too, because he's a big part of the story. Almost like a ghost that haunts—did you see him around while attending the Festival?

LS: For me, Mitch was a legend. He'd become uninvolved with the Festival as an organizer when I first became cognizant of the staff. The first person I remember being really conscious of as an organizer,

I think it was Pierre Guérin, actually. Pierre was the first person that I remember as the presence and the person responsible for the Festival. I still remember one time, I was in university and he came into a restaurant that I was working in, and I was so excited to meet him. I treated him like he was a celebrity. He was responsible for one of the things that was most important to me in my life, and to be able to make that connection and to say "thank you" for doing what he did was a really amazing opportunity for me.

JOINING THE FOLK FESTIVAL STAFF

KN: At what point did you realize, "I could work at the Folk Fest"?

LS: Honestly, it was about a year before I got the actual position. I did start volunteering at the organization in 2011 because I was hoping to get onto the Board. I'd been volunteering on the West End Cultural Centre Board for six years and my final term was about to end. I was trying to think about what my next board experience would be like and I thought, well, considering the relationship the West End and the Festival had, this could be a nice progression. It's a bigger event, it's a bigger thing. I knew some people on the Board, so I made that connection. They had actually filled the Board by the time I made the ask, but they said they were filling committees so if I'd like to be involved with the committees, they'd love to have me. So, I became part of the strategic planning committee, which was a really interesting time because they had just finished with their previous executive director and they started looking at what the next strategic plan was going to look like, how they were going to see the Festival moving forward. I thought, *Huh, this is sort of interesting!* Because at the time I was in the film industry, had been for almost thirteen years, and I was not sure that I was quite enamoured of it anymore. I was starting to think about what I would do next. I didn't want to leave Winnipeg, but I wasn't sure what I would do if I wasn't doing film. Then all of sudden it just sort of started to coalesce. The executive director position came to light and then all of a sudden, I thought that maybe this was the opportunity for me to take on a leadership role at an organization I really loved. And I just became laser focused. I wasn't looking for another job, I was looking for *this* job. And then it just all kind of came together.

Lynne Skromeda

JOHN PRENTICE: We talked to Pierre and he reminded us that there was a point in time . . . the focus became more on Festivals as a business. What were your impressions of Mitch, and his legacy?

KN: Yeah, you arrive in this job, and see the foundation that's been constructed. What was your impression of the Festival that you were joining? Thinking here about Mitch.

LS: I have to think about how to answer that question, because when I got there, the Festival did not have a particularly good relationship with Mitch. Part of my responsibility was to try and fix that, especially as we were going into our fortieth Festival—a milestone year. We wanted to honour the history of the event. I reached out to Mitch. I was intimidated because I'd heard that there had been an acrimonious relationship for a period of time with the organization. He was guarded, most certainly, at first, but then also agreed to get together with me. We had a specific idea around what we wanted to do. We wanted to get all the people together who'd been involved in the Festival, from an organizational standpoint, over the past forty years to do a panel onstage and talk about the history of the event. That meant bringing together people who didn't always have the best relationships. So that was my entry into talking with Mitch and seeing him as a person, rather than this mythic character. I had no history with him, personally. I realized that this was a starting point for me, something [a relationship] that I would be able to start from scratch. I was quite honoured to have that opportunity. I think that comes from having as much experience as a patron and not so much as somebody involved on an organizational level at that time.

And so, Mitch and I started developing a relationship of our own. It became a really special thing. He told me that the concept for the Festival itself was actually started on the street that I live on right now. I picked him up and we went for Chinese food, we drove past my house, and I pointed it out to him, and he said, "Actually right across the street from where you live is where the Festival actually began. It was a conversation that we had right there in that kitchen." So, there is a nice connection over a common street in Osborne Village.

I think we both realized at that time that we had an opportunity to start fresh. It was really great, because then he did agree to do the panel and it was awesome. He had his first good conversation in a

FIGURE 114. TARPS AT MAIN STAGE, 1993. COURTESY OF WINNIPEG FOLK FESTIVAL.

KY-58

long time with Trudy, another one of the previous executive directors, with whom he'd had some challenges over the years. It was really nice. And as a result, he participated in a number of things as time went on. I think everything that he wanted the Festival to be is still there today. It was good that I did get to develop that relationship because I understood what was important to him. The music—that was important to him. The community. We talked a lot about volunteers and how the people that started it all really gave of themselves and made it what it was. I had a really amazing opportunity to connect with him on that level, and to get that understanding, and to ensure that legacy continued. It is something I still think about to this day and I want to continue to honour no matter what. It's because that's what brings everybody together over time—that initial vision. And that's the reality that needs to stay, if we're going to continue to survive.

KN: I really like how you're describing your arrival into the position. What was the state of the Festival when you arrived? Was it healthy or was it time for a reboot?

LS: At the time that I came to the Festival, they'd had an executive director for the organization in place for a decade, and then that person left to join another arts organization and they brought in somebody new. Then that person left after only two years and there'd been a big change in the leadership. I think there was a bit of a concern as to how it was going to work, moving forward with me, as there'd been a bit of changeover over a short period of time. What was going to happen next?

I know that the other thing that everybody had been focusing on for the couple of years leading up to my arrival was the site redevelopment project. The first major changes to the site in decades were being arranged and implemented. A lot of construction was happening, things that were taking people's eyes off the proverbial prize, thinking about how we make all these operational and logistical things work while we continue to have a strong artistic direction. There were too many people being pulled in too many different directions. There was a need to coalesce. One of the first things I did was put a new strategic plan in place to help guide the organization in a new direction. I helped to finish off the fundraising and finalize the decisions around the construction for the new site that was being revealed for the fortieth anniversary. There was a lot going on that needed to be re-synthesized.

I think the other thing that happened over time is that, because the volunteer base had grown so much, there had been a lot of fragmentation, just because of the sheer volume of people. I wanted to find a way to bring people back together again. People were showing up for the volunteer meeting at the Centennial Concert Hall because that was the only way we thought we could process 2,000 people, to get them their T-shirts and passes. But there was no connection to the people on their crews in advance, no connection to the people that they were going to be working with, but we still had to create a working team environment. So, we took away that big meeting and started creating a whole lot of little meetings, which is really a lot more work, but my goal was to bring people together more, and to connect people together more. And I think it worked.

We all talked about *People and Music.* It's not just a case of sitting in the audience and watching what happens on the stage, and then there's something that somehow happens behind the scenes. The people that are behind the scenes are as much of the community as the people that are on the stage and in the audience. How can we continue to make sure that people feel that they're part of that?

WHERE THE FESTIVAL IS HEADED

KN: Did that coincide with a change in the artistic approach? Because there have been changes over the years.

LS: Absolutely, there have been changes over the years, and there's been some experimentation—that's part of the Festival experience. Sometimes things work and sometimes they don't. But when something does work, you stick with that. You realize what's important to people and that's what you continue with. That's the right thing to do. I think one of the things we focused on over that period was looking at the changing audience because one of the things we need to be able to do, to last for another fifty years, is ensure that we have a younger generation coming out again—the me at six years old.

What we found over the years is that older people listen to younger people's music, but not always the other way around. So, if we catered *too* much to the "old style" then it wasn't enough of an evolution to bring in the new audience. So, we really work at a balance of all different kinds of music. We want to make sure that we are catering to the audience that we know and love, that have been with us for fifty years, but we also want to be presenting new ideas and bringing new people in. What does "folk" mean at that moment? It's not just about something that was done in the sixties, which a lot of people associate [this term] with. Folk music is the music of the people and continues to evolve over time.

KN: Inevitably, someone is going to say, "That's not folk music! You're not honouring the first principles of the Festival." How do you respond to something like that?

LS: Well, it's an evolving thing. We like to push the boundaries of what the genre means and what that evolution means. We had an artist that calls himself a "sci-fi folk" artist. How do you even define that? But it is something new and it's creative and it comes from the same value system that you are able to bring to the way you communicate, the way you perform, the way you participate. Death metal is never going to be our thing because that's not what the underpinning of that genre of music actually is, let alone how it sounds. When you have people that have the same value system, who care about that sense of goodness and inclusiveness and belonging, and the honour of creativity, then you know that you really can be quite diverse in your presentation of the style of music.

KN: Yeah. That's good. Sci-fi?

LS: Yeah. Patrick Watson.

JP: The older version of that is *filk* music[33] that Dave Clement plays. It's like renaissance music combined with folk music, or with their Trekkie thing. Maybe sci-fi is something different?

KN: Thinking back to the 1970s. Is it even possible to imagine what it would take to start the Festival from scratch? You're the captain of the ship, can you imagine building this boat?

LS: I don't know how we would build something like the Winnipeg Folk Festival from scratch now. I think that part of the beauty of what it is now is the evolution that it's gone through, through the different kinds of leaders, through the different kinds of volunteers, through the different kinds of artists, to be what it is today. I could never create something the way that we've evolved. There are a lot of small festivals that people start. People have tried to start bigger festivals and they don't last very long because I think it's just hard to create the experience that our Festival was like in the beginning. There were people who mortgaged their houses in the early days of the Winnipeg Folk Festival to make it happen.

Then next thing you know, it's turned into this juggernaut. It's a pillar of the arts and culture community in this province and it's one of the biggest festivals on the continent. It speaks to what prairie people are. I know that Mitch wasn't originally from here but he had the prairie mentality, that hardscrabble, *I'm going to do whatever it takes to build it from scratch. I am going to be there through thick and thin. I don't care what the weather is like. I don't care what challenges I go through to make it happen because it's something I believe in.* That's how we continue to be here.

KN: Has it gotten easier to have sustained funding, besides the tickets at the gate?

LS: We rely heavily on ticket sales. We really do. On a given year, between 72 percent and 78 percent of our funding comes in ticket sales. We've been getting the same amount from the provincial government for twenty-three years—the exact same amount. And now that, of course, has changed this year because (with COVID) there have been some extra concessions and we were able to advocate for the sector as a whole to the government saying "we need your help for survival." The City of Winnipeg has actually cut our funding—they cut everybody across the board by 10 percent because they were more worried about roads. At least it feels that way, so it's challenging. We can't rely on government funding, which is one of the reasons why we've really invested in a development department. Fundraising and sponsorship have become important sources of revenue for us and working with partners who share the same values is very important.

KN: Do you feel like there is pressure on you to be bold?

LS: From a creative standpoint?

KN: Well, what you're doing is creative, I'd say.

LS: I get to split the risk management with an artistic director. We talk a lot about what's going on. I guess I do have to take the risk because he's got to pitch me what he's booking in order to create the budget. We need to have acts that are going to actually draw the audience. We need to budget for that. And I have to make operational decisions which can be risky sometimes, too.

JP: So, a bold action on your part, Lynne, might be to make a sponsorship that might work because they fit the values. Is that what you're talking about?

KN: Well, the West End Cultural Centre and Home Routes, they are organizations that are not directly connected to what we're doing, but their health is integral to . . . I'm looking for a metaphor . . . the ecosystem. There is a lot of cool research about trees right now and how trees feed each other.

LS: Yeah. Absolutely.

KN: Maybe that's the right metaphor. There are ways that the Folk Festival can help sustain other trees on the prairie here. I'm not sure I am asking a question yet. . . .

LS: I think one of the great things about Winnipeg and Manitoba as a whole is how collaborative the arts and culture environment actually is here. We don't book artists on the same weekend that other festivals are happening. It's Jazz Fest, then it's Folk Fest, then Fringe, and then it's Folklorama. There's a common understanding that we are there to support each other. Then around the rest of the year, even though we started doing some of our own shows, we're still working with local venues and we're hiring local artists to open shows. We have to play a role as an arts and culture organization here. It's our duty to support what we've created, but I think we have it easy because we have that collaborative environment as a whole in this city and province.

KN: Where's the Festival going in the next ten years?

LS: That's what we're talking about right now—what the Festival is going to look like over the next ten years. We are going into a new strategic planning process right away. At the next board meeting we're picking the organization we are going to be working with. Then it's full-steam ahead. I feel like we are as big as we want to be right now.

I don't think we want to get much bigger because then we're going to start losing some of that intimacy that we worked so hard to get back again. We don't want to create an experience that makes people feel distanced from the music and the experience they love.

What does that mean going forward? How do we look at that from a more qualitative level? What does that look like? What does that mean? We obviously have lots of stakeholders that we need to talk to as well—our volunteers that have been there, our audience is a huge source of information and inspiration for us—in addition to watching trends as a whole with the music industry and how the world is changing. We're just really embarking on what it looks like coming out of COVID. Coming into this new world, what does the evolution look like from here? I don't have an answer for you quite yet. But it's something that's really rolling around in my mind right now. I think that we're going to land somewhere good because we want to continue to be the organization that came from 1974. That grew up through all of that change in the seventies and eighties, into the nineties. We have blossomed into this really important part of our greater community in this province. We want to continue to be that, but we also know that means you can't stay where you were. You have to look at somewhere else to go. I feel like there's a whole bunch of different paths in front of us and different journeys we can take. We may end up at the same destination, but we really want to explore how that could look and do justice to the legacy of this organization.

FIGURE 115. FOLK FESTIVAL VILLAGE AREA, 2022. COURTESY OF WINNIPEG FOLK FESTIVAL.

FIGURE 116. MAIN STAGE, 2022. COURTESY OF WINNIPEG FOLK FESTIVAL.

FIGURE 117. SOUND CREW ON MAIN STAGE SCAFFOLDING, 1975. PHOTOGRAPH BY DAVID LANDY. ARCHIVES OF MANITOBA, WINNIPEG FOLK FESTIVAL 1975 NEGATIVES, P5266/1, 75-4446. 6.

Acknowledgements

This project has certainly needed considerable time and effort to reach completion. I am grateful to so many for contributing to *Founding Folks* and the accompanying documentary *When We Became Folk Fest.* The grandest acknowledgements are to those interviewed that appear in this book—thank you so much for your contributions to this project. The initial idea to work on this material came from Dave Barber, I miss his collaboration so much, he was such an important part of this from the start. It was his saving of the Super 8 film footage and audio reels that really got this project started. The Winnipeg Film Group was a vital part of this project too—not only by initiating their documentary in 1975—but by allowing the project to continue in its current forms. Thanks to various Winnipeg Film Group staff that supported the project in a variety of ways over the years: Monica Lowe, David Knipe, Leslie Supnet, and Dylan Baillie. I am very grateful to John Prentice for his wisdom as a first editor of the Winnipeg Film Group's 1975 materials—but also as an essential collaborator with the contemporary interviews and on so many production details. A big thanks to the Winnipeg Folk Festival for their support of the project. Thank you in particular to Festival staffers Valerie Shantz, Lynne Skromeda, Irina Bissonnette, and Lee-Anne Van Buekenhout. Additional thanks to the staff at University of Manitoba Press: Jill McConkey, Barbara Romanik, Sarah Ens, Glenn Bergen, Stephanie Paddey, Allyn Lyons, Kyla Neufeld, and copy editor Keith Cadieux, and designer Jess Koroscil. This project would certainly not look as great as it does without this great team.

I am also thankful to those who contributed photographs for the project. Grandest credit goes to David Landy, photographer with the Manitoba Government, and his collection at the Provincial Archives of Manitoba. Thanks to the archivists and staff there for assisting my requests, especially Jason Martin for his help in locating Landy photographs. Additional images courtesy of the *Winnipeg Tribune* / University of Manitoba Archives and Special Collections. Thanks also to Martin Landy, John Bachmann, Betsy Thorsteinson, Lynne Skromeda, Marsha Wineman, and Leonard Podolak for images used. Winnipeg Folk Festival was also very helpful in supplying photos from their archives.

Thanks to Corey Whitford at Red River College and the Manitoba Indigenous Cultural Education Centre; Dawnis Kennedy, Dené Sinclair, Sharissa Neault, and Belinda Johnson for assisting with Indigenous language advice.

Assistance with contemporary interviews and finding archival recordings of past interviews was important for this project. Thanks to John Prentice for the *Planet Mainstage* interview with Bruce Cockburn—with permission from Bernie Finkelstein, and thanks to Jeff McKay and Dodi Graham McKay for interviews with Harry Paine and the additional interview with Mitch. Thanks also to my brother Chris Nikkel for the UK interview with Colin Gorrie and Caden Nikkel for help with recordings here in Winnipeg.

Additional support during the project came from Leslie Supnet, Leslie Stafford, Vonnie Von Helmolt, and Aaron Zeghers. A big thanks to John Einarson for reading the manuscript and offering comment.

I would like to acknowledge the support of my dear family; they provide such inspiration and motivation for me to find projects like this one. I love them dearly.

Notes

PREFACE

1 Kevin Nikkel, *Establishing Shots: An Oral History of the Winnipeg Film Group* (Winnipeg: University of Manitoba Press, 2023).

2 Robert Coles, *Doing Documentary Work* (New York: Oxford University Press, 1997), 74–75.

3 See Barbara Sommer and Mary Kay Quinlan, *The Oral History Manual*, 3rd Ed. (Lanham, Maryland: Rowman and Littlefield, 2018); Donald Ritchie, *Doing Oral History: A Practical Guide*, 2nd Ed. (New York: Oxford, 2014); Robert Perks and Alistair Thomson, *The Oral History Reader*, 3rd Ed. (London: Routledge, 2016); Valerie Yow, *Recording Oral History*, 3rd Ed. (Lanham, Maryland: Rowman and Littlefield, 2015); Michael Frisch, *A Shared Authority: Essays on the Craft and Meaning of Oral and Public History* (Albany: State University Press, 1990). See also the TCPS 2 (2022) guidelines as outlined by the Tri-Council Policy Statement: Ethical Conduct for Research Involving Humans: https://ethics.gc.ca/eng/policy-politique_tcps2-eptc2_2022.html.

4 Michael Frisch, "Oral History in the Digital Age: Beyond the Raw and the Cooked," *Australian Historical Studies* 47, no. 1 (2016): 96.

5 Frisch's discussion of the "raw and the cooked" is very interesting, but he also talks about the "deep dark secret" of oral histories, that being what waits for researchers in the extended audio reels that are sent to archives after a transcript has been negotiated for publication. What stories would we find if we had the time to go listening through the boxes of tapes? Frisch, "Oral History in the Digital Age," 95.

6 Yow, *Recording Oral History*, 18.

7 Studs Terkel in *Hans Ulrich Obrist: Interviews*, Volume 2, ed. Charles Arsène-Henry, Shumon Basar, and Karen Marta (Milano: Charta, 2010), 57.

8 Michael Diers in *Hans Ulrich Obrist: Interviews*, Volume 1, by Hans-Ulrich Obrist (Milano: Charta, 2003), 22.

9 See Macdonald for his interesting discussion of the two festivals, one inside the fence, the other outside carnival, at the campground and gathering at places like Pope's Hill. Michael B. Macdonald, "Back to the Garden: Territory and Exchange in Western Canadian Folk Music Festivals" (PhD dissertation, University of Alberta, 2010), 218.

10 Neil Rosenberg, ed., *Transforming Tradition: Folk Music Revivals Examined* (Champaign, Illinois: University of Illinois Press, 1993).

A SHORT INTRODUCTION TO THE START OF THE WINNIPEG FOLK FESTIVAL

1 Land Acknowledgement, https://www.winnipegfolkfestival.ca.

2 "About Us," Winnipeg Folk Festival, https://www.winnipegfolkfestival.ca/about-us/.

3 John Einarson, *Heart of Gold: A History of Winnipeg Music* (Winnipeg: A Shakin' All Over Publication, 2021), xix.

4 Jon Bartlett and Rika Ruebsaat, "State of the Art: The Folk Revival in Canada," *The Canadian Folk Music Bulletin* 3 (September–December 1980): 7.

5 Bartlett and Ruebsaat, "State of the Art," 6.

6 Steven Johnson and Sheldon Oberman, *The Folk Festival Book* (Winnipeg: Turnstone Press, 1984), 10.

7 Bartlett and Ruebsaat, "State of the Art," 10.

8 Winnipeg Film Group, *Audio reels A47-B11.*

9 Johnson and Oberman, *The Folk Festival Book,* 12.

10 This recording is from the 1976 Winnipeg Folk Festival's audio recordings as initiated by Mitch Podolak. The reels are not labelled by stages and identifying performers is tricky if there are minimal hints in the dialogue or music they're singing. John Prentice and I debated this bit of recording—is it Mike and Peggy Seeger, or is it Martha and Eric Nagler? After this exchange with the dog, the woman sings a song "My old hen's a good old hen," which Peggy Seeger has recorded, thus the conclusion that it is Mike and Peggy Seeger.

11 The first generation of Canadian folk festivals were held as a travelling event with the CPR in 1928 coordinated by John Murray

Gibbon. Michael B. MacDonald, "THIS IS IMPORTANT!: Mitch Podolak, the Revolutionary Establishment, and the Founding of the Winnipeg Folk Festival" (Master's thesis, Carleton University, 2006), 2.

12 MacDonald, "THIS IS IMPORTANT!," 11.

13 See John Street, "This is your Woodstock; Popular Memories and Political Myths" in *Remembering Woodstock* (New York: Routledge, 2004); and Sija Tsai, "Public Policy and the Mariposa Folk Festival: Shared Ideals in the 1960s and 1970s," *MUSIcultures* 38/1 (2011), 2013.

14 Andrew Burke, *Hinterland Remixed: Media, Memory, and the Canadian 1970s* (Montreal: McGill-Queen's University Press, 2019), 11.

15 MacDonald, "Back to the Garden," 116.

16 Tsai, "Public Policy and the Mariposa Folk Festival," 126.

17 "About Us," Winnipeg Folk Festival, https://www.winnipegfolkfestival.ca/about-us/.

18 Chuck Grieve, "Folk Festival, Once Was Fine; Yearly Is Folly," *Winnipeg Tribune* (17 August 1974): 21.

19 Bill Usher and Linda Page-Harpa, "For what time I am in this world" in *Stories from Mariposa* (Mariposa Folk Foundation, 1977), 196.

20 Winnipeg Film Group, Super 8 footage and audio reels, 1975.

21 MacDonald, "THIS IS IMPORTANT!," 96 and 98.

22 MacDonald, "THIS IS IMPORTANT!," 110.

23 Usher and Page-Harpa, "For what time I am in this world," 197.

24 Paul Sullivan, "Harmony sung at Bird's Hill," *Winnipeg Free Press*, 9 July 1979, 25.

25 Eric Fillion and Ajay Heble, "Summer music festivals do more than entertain, they help us imagine possible futures," *The Conversation*, 13 July 2023, accessed 23 October 2023, https://theconversation.com/summer-music-festivals-do-more-than-entertain-they-help-us-imagine-possible-futures-207587.

26 MacDonald, "Back to the Garden," 273.

27 Joseph Wasylycia-Leis, "Celebrating Community: Local Music Festivals and Sustainable Relocalization in Southern Manitoba" (Master's thesis, University of Waterloo, 2016), 178.

28 Johnson and Oberman, *The Folk Festival Book,* 52.

29 Harry Paine was a longtime social activist who moved from Toronto to Winnipeg to collaborate with Mitch on the Festival and other local initiatives. See the interview with Harry in the volume.

30 Mitch Podolak, interviewed by the author for the documentary *When We Became Folk Fest,* 2025.

31 John C. Lehr, "As Canadian as Possible . . . Under the Circumstances," *Border/lines* (Spring 1985).

32 Lucy R. Lippard, *Lure of the Local: Sense of Place in a Multicentered Society* (New York: New Press, 1997), 7.

33 Egle Procuta, "Mariposa: Does Life Begin at 40?" *The Globe and Mail,* 22 June 2000.

34 Wasylycia-Leis, "Celebrating Community," 48.

35 Sarah Moore, "Re-articulating Canadian Popular Music through a Local Lens: Examining 'Great Big Sea' and Issues of Locality, Regionalism and Nationalism" (Master's thesis, Carleton University, 2002), 22.

36 Macdonald, "Back to the Garden," 7.

37 Festival attendee interview by Five Door Films, Winnipeg Folk Festival, 13 July 2019.

38 Wasylycia-Leis, "Celebrating Community," 92.

39 Macdonald, "Back to the Garden," 267–68.

40 Lippard, *Lure of the Local,* 37.

41 Macdonald, "Back to the Garden," 24.

42 Dale Bell, *Woodstock: An Inside Look at the Movie that Shook up the World and Defined a Generation* (Studio City, CA: Michael Wiese Productions, 1999), 107.

43 Doris Sommer, *The Work of Art in the World: Civic Agency and Public Humanities* (Duke University Press, Durham: 2014), 3.

44 The Winnipeg Crankie Festival, run by Mitch's son Leonard Podolak, is an annual three-day cultural event that merges live music, visual art, theatre, and the written word—accompanied most memorably by homemade crankies, http://crankiefestival.com.

45 Tsai, "Public Policy and the Mariposa Folk Festival," 173.

46 Morley Walker, "Biggest Isn't Best to Enjoy Folk Fest," *Winnipeg Free Press*, 2 June 1996, 29.

47 Bartlett and Ruebsaat, "State of the Art," 10.

48 Wasylycia-Leis, "Celebrating Community," 46.

49 Michael B. Macdonald, "'The Best Laid Plans of Marx and Men': Mitch Podolak, Revolution, and the Winnipeg Folk Festival," *Ethnologies* 30, no. 2 (2008): 261.

50 I only wish other sources of material on the Festival were more accessible—it is worth noting that Paul Mills' CBC Radio program *Touch the Earth* recorded stages at the Festival for several years—these recordings were too expensive to access from the CBC for this project. I can only imagine the voices we'd hear setting up songs and singing tunes from the past. It's the banter of the emcee and the musicians before and after songs that reveals so much about the event, the people, and the times.

51 Michael Frisch, "Three Dimensions and More: Oral History Beyond the Paradoxes of Method" in *Handbook of Emergent Methods*, ed. Sharlene Nagy Hesse-Biber and Patricia Leavy (New York: The Guilford Press, 2008), 223.

INTERVIEWS

1 The National Mobilization Committee to End the War in Vietnam, commonly known as the "Vietnam mobe."

2 Bristol International Jazz and Blues Festival, http://bristoljazzandbluesfest.com/.

3 The Folk Festival store opened the Homemade Music store on Osborne Street in 1982. It moved to Tache Avenue in 1987 following a fire. It moved to Bannatyne at Albert in the Exchange District in 2001. It finally closed in 2015.

4 Grieve, "Once Was Fine; Yearly Is Folly," 21.

5 Mitch Podolak was instrumental in the founding of Winnipeg's West End Cultural Centre.

6 Judy Wasylycia-Leis was a Manitoba cabinet minister in the government of Howard Pawley from 1986 to 1988 and a member of the House of Commons of Canada from 1997 to 2010.

7 The World Next Door festival was a poorly attended weekend music festival that Mitch Podolak and Gord Osland organized at the Forks in Winnipeg in 1998. It ran only one year.

8 The Occupy Wall Street protests began in the United States in 2011, protesting the excesses of capitalism to benefit a wealthy minority at the expense of the majority struggling to make a living.

9 A local sound company logo that is visible in the 1975 images and footage is Centurion Sound.

10 Peter Gzowski was a prominent national CBC Radio host for shows such as *This Country in the Morning* and *Morningside*.

11 Woodshed Records. See David Essig's interview and also https://davidessig.com.

12 Fogarty's Cove Music. For more info see https://stanrogers.net.

13 *Canadian Spaces* is Canada's longest running folk radio show, broadcasting on CKCU FM in Ottawa, Ontario founded by Chopper McKinnon in 1980 and continued after his passing away in 2013. Details here: https://cod.ckcufm.com/programs/129/info.html.

14 Île-des-Chênes is a small farming community thirteen kilometres southeast of Winnipeg.

15 Osborne Village is a popular neighbourhood in Winnipeg, known for its restaurants, shops, and venues for music, which included a bar named The Zoo. The Royal Albert bar was a venue that hosted live music located in Winnipeg's downtown Exchange District.

16 Now called Sandy Bay Ojibway First Nation, located on the western shore of Lake Manitoba.

17 In October 2023, CBC published the story "Who Is the Real Buffy Sainte-Marie?," questioning Sainte-Marie's Indigenous ancestry, https://www.cbc.ca/newsinteractives/features/buffy-sainte-marie.

18 Víctor Jara was a Chilean activist and folk musician murdered by General Augusto Pinochet's forces during the coup of September 1973.

19 Boissevain, Manitoba is a small farming community 263 km southwest of Winnipeg on the border of North Dakota.

20 The Harvest Sun Festival takes place annually in Kelwood, Manitoba, 232 km northwest of Winnipeg.

21 The Ukrainian Labour Temple is a hall and cultural centre in Winnipeg's North End. It was a hub of activity for the working class during the Winnipeg General Strike of 1919.

22 The Co-Operative Commonwealth Federation (CCF) was a federal democratic socialist political party that evolved into the New Democratic Party (NDP) in 1961.

23 Knowing that some traditional Indigenous names are of great interest, a bit more detail here. As Curtis had passed away by the time we were preparing this transcript, it wasn't possible to confirm the spelling of his traditional name—this was further complicated by the fact that Curtis wasn't fluent in Ojibwe, having been raised off the reserve. After consultation with Indigenous language experts at Red River College and the Manitoba Indigenous Cultural Education Centre, it was suggested to state in the text of the transcript "Says his Anishinaabe name." The possible spelling of his traditional name phonetically would be "Nee sho ah dong" using folk phonetics when spelt in English. This is another example of the importance of saving audio recordings of oral histories.

24 Grant's Old Mill, originally built in 1829 by Métis leader Cuthbert Grant on Sturgeon Creek in Winnipeg, is now a museum and park.

25 Gabriel Dumont was a Métis leader and contemporary of Louis Riel. He participated in the North-West Resistance in Saskatchewan in 1885.

26 Ilena (Kozub) Zaramba came from the musical Kozub family of Winnipeg. Her parents, Peter Kozub and Anna Sklepowich, led Ukraininian family singers. "Trophies—Kozub Trophy," Winnipeg Music Festival website, https://www.winnipegmusicfestival.org/kozub-trophy.

27 Old Market Square is a park in Winnipeg's downtown Exchange District, popular for summer urban musical events.

28 Pope John Paul II's visit to Winnipeg included a large open-air mass held at Birds Hill Park in September 1984. The gathering was centred on a hill that has since been named "Pope's Hill" which has become an annual all-night gathering spot for Folk Festival attendees to continue their revelries, many staying to catch the view of the sun rise from the top of the hill. For an interesting discussion of the late-night parties on Pope's Hill, see

Michael MacDonald's 2010 thesis, "Back to the Garden: Territory and Exchange in Western Canadian Music Festivals."

29 Niverville Pop Festival, 24 May 1970.

30 The Bella Vista was a restaurant venue on Maryland that featured a regular stage for musicians—it closed in 2019. The Times Change(d) High & Lonesome Club operates at 234 Main Street, featuring nightly shows—Big Dave McLean's Sunday Night Jam being a regular weekly event. The renovated Park Theatre at 698 Osborne opened in 2005 as a music venue.

31 The Winnipeg Crankie Festival was founded in 2018 by Home Routes and features a cross-media collaboration between musicians, storytellers, and artists of a variety of disciplines to make and perform with a Crankie—a moving visual panorama that depicts a story, first popularized in the mid-nineteenth century, https://crankiefestival.com/.

32 In 2023 Lynne Skromeda left the Winnipeg Folk Festival to become the Film Commissioner and Executive Director of Manitoba Film and Music.

33 Filk music is a musical culture, genre, and community tied to the science fiction and fantasy genre which first emerged in the early 1950s and developed further since the mid-1970s.

Bibliography

Bartlett, Jon and Rika Ruebsaat. "State of the Art: The Folk Revival in Canada." *The Canadian Folk Music Bulletin* 3 (September–December 1980): 9–15.

Bell, Dale (ed). *Woodstock: An Inside Look at the Movie that Shook up the World and Defined a Generation*. Studio City, CA: Michael Wiese Productions, 1999.

Brown, Laurie. "Songs from the Bush Garden." *Cultural Studies* 5 (1991): 347–57.

Brunskill, Greg. "Winnipeg Folk Festival 1986." *Canadian Folk Music Bulletin de musique folklorique canadienne* 20, no. 3–4 (September–December 1986): 20–23.

Burke, Andrew. *Hinterland Remixed: Media, Memory, and the Canadian 1970s*. Montreal: McGill-Queen's University Press, 2019.

Campbell, Rod. *Playing the Field: The Story of the Edmonton Folk Music Festival*. Edmonton: B. Evan White Publishing, 1994.

Coles, Robert. *Doing Documentary Work*. New York: Oxford University Press, 1997.

Cristall, Gary. "The Function of Folk Festivals," *Canadian folk music/bulletin de musique folklorique canadienne* 26, no. 1 (Summer 1992): 38–40.

———. "A History of Folk Music in English Canada." 2008–2022. Accessed 23 October 2023: https://www.folkmusichistory.com/about.shtml.

———. "The Vancouver Folk Song and Dance Festival with Arts and Crafts Exhibition: The First Ongoing Multicultural Festival in Canada." *Canadian Folk Music Bulletin* 46, no. 2 (2012): 19–27.

Cudny, Waldemar. "The Phenomenon of Festivals: Their Origins, Evolution, and Classifications." *Anthropos* 109, no. 2 (2014): 640–56. *JSTOR*, http://www.jstor.org/stable/43861801.

Derrett, Ros. "Making Sense of How Festivals Demonstrate a Community's Sense of Place," *Event Management* 8 (2003): 49–58.

Diers, Michael. Interview. In *Interviews* by Hans Ulrich Obrist, Volume 1. Milano: Charta, 2003.

Duffett, Mark. "Music Industry and Canadian National Identity." Master's thesis, University of British Columbia, 1993.

Edwardson, Ryan. *Canadian Content: Culture and the Quest for Nationhood*. Toronto: University of Toronto Press, 2008.

———. *Canuck Rock: A History of Canadian Popular Music*. Toronto: University of Toronto Press, 2009.

Einarson, John. *Heart of Gold: A History of Winnipeg Music.* Winnipeg: A Shakin' All Over Publication, 2021.

Fillion, Eric. "Forging Solidarities at Mariposa '75: Forward into a New Decade." *Between Postwar and Present Day: Canada, 1970–2000, Local, National, Global* Conference University of Toronto. Virtual conference; 8 May 2021.

Fillion, Eric, and Ajay Heble. "Summer music festivals do more than entertain, they help us imagine possible futures." *The Conversation*, 13 July 2023. Accessed 23 October 2023. https://theconversation.com/summer-music-festivals-do-more-than-entertain-they-help-us-imagine-possible-futures-207587.

Freund, Alexander, and Alistair Thomson, eds. *Oral History and Photography.* New York: Palgrave Macmillan, 2011.

Frisch, Michael. "Oral History in the Digital Age: Beyond the Raw and the Cooked." *Australian Historical Studies* 47, no. 1 (2016): 92–107.

———. *A Shared Authority: Essays on the Craft and Meaning of Oral and Public History.* Albany: State University Press, 1990.

———. "Three Dimensions and More: Oral History Beyond the Paradoxes of Method." In *Handbook of Emergent Methods*, edited by Sharlene Nagy Hesse-Biber and Patricia Leavy, 221–38. New York: The Guilford Press, 2008.

Getz, Donald. "The Nature and Scope of Festival Studies." *International Journal of Event Management Research* 5 (2010): 1–47.

Getz, Donald, Tommy D. Andersson, John Armbrecht, and Erik Lundberg. "The Value of Festivals." In *The Routledge Handbook of Festivals,* edited by Judith Mair, 22–30. New York: Routledge, 2018.

Gillespie, Angus. "Folk Festival and Festival Folk in Twentieth-Century America." In *Time Out of Time: Essays on the Festival,* edited by Alessandro Falassi, 152–61. Albuquerque: University of New Mexico Press, 1987.

Government of Manitoba. *Birds Hill Park Management Plan*, 2013: 8.

Greenhill, Pauline. "Finding a Place for Research at the Winnipeg Folk Festival." *The Canadian Folk Music Bulletin* 29, no. 3 (1995): 14–16.

Grele, Ronald. *Envelopes of Sound*, 2nd ed. New York: Praeger, 1982.

Grieve, Chuck. "Folk Festival, Once was Fine; Yearly is Folly." *Winnipeg Tribune*, 17 August 1974, 21.

Hagen-Smith, Lisa. "On your Mark . . . the Audience's Place at the Winnipeg Folk Festival." *The Canadian Folk Music Bulletin* 29, no. 3 (1995): 16–19.

Hill, Michael. *The Mariposa Folk Festival: A History*. Toronto: Dundurn Press, 2017.

Johnson, Steven, and Sheldon Oberman. *The Folk Festival Book*. Winnipeg: Turnstone Press, 1984.

Kitching, Heather. "Gary Cristall Remembers Mitch Podolak." Roots Music Canada, 27 August 2019. Accessed 23 October 2023. https://www.rootsmusic.ca/2019/08/27/gary-cristall-remembers-mitch-podolak/.

Lehr, John C. "As Canadian as Possible . . . Under the Circumstances." *Border/lines* (Spring 1985): 16–19.

Lippard, Lucy R. *Lure of the Local: Sense of Place in a Multicentered Society*. New York: New Press, 1997.

Llewellyn, Kristina, Alexander Freund, and Nolan Reilly. *The Canadian Oral History Reader*. Montreal: McGill-Queen's University Press, 2015.

Luckey-Smith, Keegan. "The Folk Festival of the Smokies and the Role of Music Festivals in Preserving Old-Time Music in Appalachia." Master's thesis, East Tennessee State University, 2022.

Macaulay, Janet. "Stop the Folkin' Music! How I (Kinda) Found my Place at Winnipeg Folk Festival Camping." *The Canadian Folk Music Bulletin* 29, no. 3 (1995): 21–23.

MacDonald, Michael B. "Back to the Garden: Territory and Exchange in Western Canadian Folk Music Festivals." PhD diss., University of Alberta, 2010.

———. "'The Best Laid Plans of Marx and Men': Mitch Podolak, Revolution, and the Winnipeg Folk Festival." *Ethnologies* 30, no. 2 (2008): 73–91.

———. "THIS IS IMPORTANT!: Mitch Podolak, The Revolutionary Establishment, and the Founding of the Winnipeg Folk Festival." Master's thesis, Carleton University, 2006.

Marquis, Greg. "Country Music: The Folk Music of Canada." *Queen's Quarterly* 95 (Summer 1988): 291–309.

———. "The Folk Music of Anglophone New Brunswick: Old-time and Country Music in the 20th-Century." *Journal of New Brunswick Studies* 3 (2012): 57–68.

McKay, Dodie Graham. *Harry Paine: Cooking the Revolution*. Winnipeg: Moongazey Films, 2013.

McKay, Ian. *The Quest of the Folk*. Montreal: McGill-Queen's University Press, 1994.

Mitchell, Gillian. *The North American Folk Music Revival: Nation and Identity in the United States and Canada, 1945–1980*. New York: Routledge, 2007.

Moore, Sarah Janette. "Re-articulating Canadian Popular Music through a Local Lens: Examining 'Great Big Sea' and Issues of Locality, Regionalism and Nationalism." Master's thesis, Carleton University, 2002.

Moranz, Gillian. "Canadian Folk and Roots Music Festivals: An Anthropological Analysis of Value, Capital, and Exchange in Canadian Festival Spaces." Thesis, University of Lethbridge, 2014.

Nikkel, Kevin. *Establishing Shots: An Oral History of the Winnipeg Film Group*. Winnipeg: University of Manitoba Press, 2023.

Nikkel, Kevin, and David Barber, dir. *When We Became Folk Fest*. Winnipeg, Five Door Films, 2025.

Obrist, Hans Ulrich. *Interviews*, Volume 1, Milano: Charta, 2003.

———. *Interviews*, Volume 2, Milano: Charta, 2010.

Perks, Robert, and Alistair Thomson. *The Oral History Reader*, 3rd Ed. London: Routledge, 2016.

Podolak, Mitch. "Commentary: The Truth About Folk Festivals." *Canadian Folk Music Bulletin* 25, no. 2 (1991): 36.

Portelli, Alessandro. *The Battle of Valle Giulia: Oral History and the Art of Dialogue*. Madison, University of Wisconsin Press: 1997.

Procuta, Egle. "Mariposa: Does Life Begin at 40?" *The Globe and Mail*, 22 June 2000.

Ritchie, Donald. *Doing Oral History: A Practical Guide*, 2nd Ed. New York: Oxford, 2014.

Rosenberg, Neil, ed. *Transforming Tradition: Folk Music Revivals Examined*. Urbana: University of Illinois Press, 1993.

Seeger, Charles. "The Folkness of the Nonfolk and the Nonfolkness of the Folk." In *The Folk Studies in Musicology: 1935–1975*. Berkeley: University of California Press, 1977.

Sommer, Barbara, and Mary Kay Quinlan. *The Oral History Manual*, 3rd Ed. Lanham, MD: Rowman and Littlefield, 2018.

Sommer, Doris. *The Work of Art in the World: Civic Agency and Public Humanities*. Durham: Duke University Press, 2014.

Street, John. "This is your Woodstock; Popular Memories and Political Myths." In *Remembering Woodstock*. New York: Routledge, 2004.

Sullivan, Paul. "Harmony sung at Birds Hill." *Winnipeg Free Press*, 9 July 1979, 25.

Svenne, Danielle Carignan. "La Cuisine/Art: Knowing my Place as a Volunteer at the Winnipeg Folk Festival." *The Canadian Folk Music Bulletin* 29, no. 3 (1995): 19–21.

Terkel, Studs. Interview. In *Hans Ulrich Obrist: Interviews*, Volume 2, edited by Charles Arsène-Henry, Shumon Basar, and Karen Marta, 52–67. Milano: Charta, 2010.

Tri-Council Policy Statement: Ethical Conduct for Research Involving Humans. Canadian Institutes of Health Research / Natural Sciences and Engineering Research Council of Canada / Social Sciences and Humanities Research Council of Canada. 2022. https://ethics.gc.ca/eng/policy-politique_tcps2-eptc2_2022.html.

Tsai, Sija. "Electric Picking, Ethnic Spinning: (Re)defining the "Folk" at the Winnipeg Folk Festival." *MUSICultures* 34/35 (2008): 71–94.

———. "Mariposa Folk Festival: The Sounds, Sights, and Costs of a Fifty-Year Road Trip." PhD diss., York University, 2013.

———. "Public Policy and the Mariposa Folk Festival: Shared Ideals in the 1960s and 1970s." *MUSIcultures* 38/1 (2011): 147–58.

Usher, Bill, and Linda Page-Harpa. "For what time I am in this world." In *Stories from Mariposa*. Mariposa Folk Foundation, 1977.

Yow, Valerie. *Recording Oral History*, 3rd Ed. Lanham, Maryland: Rowman and Littlefield, 2015.

Walker, Morley. "Biggest Isn't Best to Enjoy Folk Fest." *Winnipeg Free Press*, 2 June 1996, 29.

Wasylycia-Leis, Joseph. "Celebrating Community: Local Music Festivals and Sustainable Relocalization in Southern Manitoba." Master's thesis, University of Waterloo, 2016.

Weissman, Dick. *A New History of American & Canadian Folk Music*. Bloomsbury: Bloomsbury Academic, 2019.

Winnipeg Folk Festival. "About Us." https://www.winnipegfolkfestival.ca/about-us/.

Index

C

Index

Index

Y

Z